R. H. Tawney and His Times

R. H. Tawney and His Times

SOCIALISM AS FELLOWSHIP

ROSS TERRILL

Harvard University Press, Cambridge, Massachusetts 1973

ACKNOWLEDGMENTS

Chief among the scholars and keepers of the public conscience who helped with this book are Samuel Beer, a superb mentor whose wise and critical eye disciplined my research, and Richard Titmuss, who encouraged me from London in a number of ways, not least by his own admirable work which finely expresses Tawney's spirit today.

Jack Fisher of the London School of Economics and the late Richard Rees were stimulating and generous with their great knowledge of Tawney at the early stages when it was most needed. John Nef, long associated with Tawney, shared his broad vision and spurred me on. Madge Slavin has helped and buoyed me over a long period in many ways.

A number of scholars and friends in various continents sent useful leads and information: Mr. Ian Angus, Dr. John C. Bennett, Mr. B. N. Bhattacherjee, Mr. Thomas S. Derr, Professor R. M. Crawford, Lord Morris of Grasmere, Professor William L. Holland, Mr. N. C. Kittermaster, Mr. Michel H. Ridgeway, Mrs. William Temple, Dr. James C. Thomson, Jr., Miss Margaret Bearlin, Mr. Bernard Jennings, Mr. John Papworth.

Workers in diverse vineyards made the research easier: Miss Trudy Jackson at the Workers Educational Association was tireless as well as charming. Professor Gladys Boone of Sweetbriar College, Virginia, willingly shared talk and materials with me. Mr. E. V. Quinn lit my path at Balliol College library, as did Mr. Walter Birmingham at Toynbee Hall. Frank Pickstock and Frank Jessup of Rewley House, Oxford, were unstinting with their time, and Mrs. Joan Dean was helpful with Rewley House materials. Professors Jack Fisher, Donald Coleman, W. Ashworth, and T. Mathias eased access to Tawney's diary; Professor Maurice Cranston helped with suggestions both at Harvard and in London; the late Dr. Rita Hinden of *Socialist Commentary* was a shrewd critic; Dr. Ernest Green went out of his way to help with many points of detail.

Those who kindly opened the door to papers included Mr. Louis Frewer, Superintendent of Rhodes House Library, Oxford; Mr. J. Richard Phillips, Archivist at Amherst College Library; Mr. P. M. Williams, biographer of Hugh Gaitskell, Nuffield College, Oxford; Mr. B. Cheeseman, Library and Records Department, Foreign and Commonwealth Office; Miss Marie Jordan, Librarian, *Glasgow Herald;* Miss Margaret McFadden of the Special Collections section of the Joseph Regenstein Library, University of Chicago; the late Lady Shena Simon, who led me to many of Tawney's writings in the *Manchester Guardian;* Professor George Yule of Ormond College, Melbourne, who kindly showed me letters of Tawney, and Professor H. L. Beales and Professor S. G. Raybould, who also made available letters and memoranda.

The following busy and distinguished people shared their knowledge of Tawney in conversations:

Professor James L. Adams, Mr. David Ayerst, Lord Noel Annan, Professor H. L. Beales, Miss Pearl Buck, Lord Ritchie Calder, Professor E. Carus-Wilson, Mrs. Margaret Cole, Mr. Arthur Crook, Rt. Hon. C. A. R. Crosland, Rt. Hon. R. H. S. Crossman, Professor G. R. Elton, Mr. Lionel Elvin, Lord Fenner Brockway, Professor F. J. Fisher, Professor Joseph Fletcher, Professor J. K. Galbraith, Rt. Hon. Patrick Gordon Walker, Dr. Ernest Green, Professor William L. Holland, Dr. Gordon Huelin, the late Dr. Rita Hinden, Dr. and Mrs. Christopher Hill, Mr. Frank Jessup, the late Professor David Joslin, Professor A. V. Judges, Sir Walter Moberley, Professor John U. Nef, Mr. Harry Nutt, Professor Talcott Parsons, Mr. Frank Pickstock, Professor M. M. Postan, Canon Ronald Preston, Professor S. G. Raybould, Mr. Scott Rankine, Mr. Maurice Reckitt, the late Sir Richard Rees, the late Lady Shena Simon, Lord Donald Soper, Baroness Mary Stocks, Professor Lawrence Stone, Professor Richard Titmuss, Mr. Michael Vyvyan, Miss Janet Wadsworth, Baroness Eirene White, Rt. Hon. Harold Wilson, Mr. Raymond Williams, Baroness Barbara Wootton, Professor George Yule.

For permission to quote published works of Tawney I am grateful to: Barnes & Noble Books for *Equality;* Harcourt Brace Jovanovich and G. Bell and Sons Ltd. for *The*

Acquisitive Society; Harcourt Brace Jovanovich and John Murray (Publishers) Ltd. for *Religion and the Rise of Capitalism;* Pantheon Books, a division of Random House, for *The Radical Tradition;* George Allen and Unwin Ltd. and Books for Libraries, 1971 reprint edition, for *The Attack and Other Papers.*

For permission to quote from unpublished materials I am indebted to the following: Mr. Michael Vyvyan, Trinity College, Cambridge, for Tawney's diary (or Commonplace Book); Professor F. J. Fisher, London School of Economics, for Tawney's historical and political papers held at the British Library of Political and Economic Science; Mrs. Violet Creech Jones, for the Creech Jones Papers; Balliol College, for letters of Tawney to A. L. Smith; Professor John U. Nef, for the Nef Papers at the Joseph Regenstein Library, University of Chicago; Librarian of the British Library of Political and Economic Science, for the Passfield Papers; Mr. Frank Pickstock on behalf of the Department for External Studies, University of Oxford, for the Rewley House Collection; Professor George Yule, for letters from Tawney; Lord Beveridge's Executors, for the Beveridge Collection at the LSE; the Manchester Guardian and Evening News Limited, for Editorial Correspondence from the Guardian Archives in the Manchester University Library; Miss Trudy Jackson on behalf of the Workers' Educational Association, for letters and papers at the library of Temple House; Miss Janet Wadsworth, for papers relating to Tawney in her possession; Professor Gladys Boone, for papers relating to Tawney in her possession.

For the loan of photographs and drawings I am indebted to the WEA Library, Temple House, London; the London School of Economics and Political Science; Miss Janet Wadsworth; Professor William L. Holland; *The Observer;* Mr. John Papworth; Professor M. M. Postan; and Mr. Frank Pickstock of Rewley House, Oxford.

During the research for this book at Harvard, the Frank Knox Memorial and the West European Studies Center helped financially.

Ross Terrill
13 November 1972

CONTENTS

ILLUSTRATIONS

Introduction

AN APPROACH TO TAWNEY

In 1960, when a dinner was arranged at the House of Commons to mark Tawney's eightieth birthday, the guest of honor remarked to a visitor: "It is very kind of them, but I don't know why they are doing it. I have had no influence."[1] It was typical of Tawney's modesty. Few were surprised when the *Times* of London spoke rather differently in an editorial next day (November 28): "No man alive has put more people into his spiritual and intellectual debt than has Richard Henry Tawney."

As an historian, Tawney was among the few most seminal of twentieth-century Britain. In workers' education, he established excellence in tutorial classes, and was the Workers Educational Association's greatest figure (even more influential, over the whole span of the WEA's life, than Albert Mansbridge, its pioneer, or William Temple, its first president). As a social philosopher, he won a position which justifies the assessment of Talcott Parsons: "His name will long be remembered among the founders of twentieth century social thought."[2] Politically, he has proved the most catholic of all the British Labour party's prophets of socialism. All wings of the party have saluted him: the right (e.g. Gaitskell), the center (e.g. Crossman), the left (e.g. *Tribune* weekly).[3]

In addition, Tawney throws light on British thought and institutions from the Victorian apogee to what S. H. Beer has called the "Collectivist Age." When Tawney was born at Calcutta in 1880, Newman, Tennyson, and Gladstone still flourished, less than three million Englishmen voted, and *Das Kapital* had not yet appeared in English. The queen was declaring, "I cannot and will not be queen of a *democratic monarchy*," and Engels observing that the British working class was but "the tail of the great Liberal Party." When Tawney left Rugby in 1899 and went up to Oxford, the typewriter, telephone, gramophone, and movie were beginning to be known; but the Labour party did not exist, B. Seebohm Rowntree had not yet written his study of poverty in York, nor J. A. Hobson his *Imperialism*. Imperial grandeur was at its height. The Sudan had just been won back and the French flag pulled down at Fashoda; Joseph Chamberlain was crying, "I would annex the planets if I could," and Lord Rosebery styling the British Empire "the greatest secular agency for good the world has ever seen." War yet seemed a glorious thing. New organizations of moral uplift like the Salvation Army and the Boys Brigades had put a military touch into their names; General Wolseley frothed about the "maddening delight of leading men into the midst of an enemy . . . [which] rapturous enjoyment takes man out of himself to the forgetfulness of all earthly considerations."[4]

By the time of Tawney's death in 1962, the empire had shrunk to a few tourist islands; the Liberal party was little more than a debating society; the clubs, universities, civil service, and House of Lords were well stocked with leftists; and socialism, which Lord Rosebery had called in 1909 "the end of all, the negation of faith, of family, of property, of the monarchy, of the Empire," was less shocking than boring.[5] By this time, an antiwar movement—the Campaign for Nuclear Disarmament—had become the largest extraparliamentary cause since Chartism; and instead of watching Labour politicians trying to look dignified at garden parties, Englishmen watched Tory politicians trying to look casual on TV.

Tawney was a scholar, yet also a teacher, soldier, writer, and public figure, and the rhythms of his life rose and fell with the history of his times. As Whitehead points out, there is a "personal identity" to each man which binds into a kind of unity all the diversities of his thought and experience.[6] So in studying changes in British political culture through one man's work, variable factors are kept within reasonable limits, and perspectives emerge which a study of general trends might be too diffuse to bring out. I have tried to be aware of the interaction between Tawney's socialism and the changing components of British political culture. Of course, a study of the Britain of Tawney's lifetime throws light upon Tawney; but the converse is also true. The context is not just the setting that shaped Tawney, but a moving jumble of forces, capable of arrangement in an infinite variety of patterns and subject to constant influences, of which Tawney's own ideas and actions were one. Focusing on a core of values and questions that are given coherence by his "personal unity," we have a window onto the changing landscape of the society in which Tawney tried to incarnate his socialist vision.

Beyond the question of Tawney's past influence, and that of his work as a key to his times, lies the question of his continuing validity. Tawney retained a fairly consistent social philosophy during enormous changes in Britain. If he had influence in Edwardian times, and still in the 1950s, is there not a presumption that the foundations of his position may be sound enough for him to retain validity even today? The years Tawney spanned were notable for distinguished intellectual casualties. Angell's rationalism was rendered futile in the face of the Third Reich and other ideologies-in-power; Lansbury's pacifism led to his timid pilgrimage to Berchtesgaden; Strachey's Marxism was born in one decade then renounced in the next. Collingwood confessed in his *Autobiography* that the coming of fascism had burst in and "broke up my pose of a detached professional thinker"; Mosley veered into fascism when the Labour party failed to meet the crisis of 1931.[7] Chesterton's medievalism had come by the early 1930s to seem a quaint irrelevance; the Webbs filled an odd void in their generally admirable philosophy with an enthusiasm for Stalinism; and Laski, too, wobbled for a while on democratic values.

Before such a parade of brittle zeal, false objectivity, irrationalism, recantation, institutional naivety, and disillusion, Tawney seems for all his faults a granite monument. Anyone who studies the 1930s might well take seriously the quip that it is wise to avoid being a radical when young, for fear one will be conservative when old. A man who was just as radical (in the British sense) in 1960 at the age of eighty as he had been forty years before, and who could republish his analyses of capitalism and socialism despite all that had happened over those four decades, is perhaps worth a second look in a broken and discontinuous epoch.

A SAINT BUT NOT A THINKER?

If Tawney was influential, the nature of his influence nevertheless poses problems of approach. How to write about a moralist when you did not know him and feel his glow? That is the task. "Looking back quite objectively," said Hugh Gait-skell when Tawney died, "I think he was the best man I have ever known. The quality of his goodness was such that it never embarrassed you. You just accepted it as you accept genius." Albert Mansbridge, the unsentimental pioneer of the Workers Educational Association, wrote to Tawney in the tough early years: "You are to me an inspiration—and a sure guide from the land of cowardice to the land where one fronts the morn." Beatrice Webb, in a 1935 diary entry, called him "a saint" and said he was "loved and respected by all who know him."[8]

So Tawney was not only a writer but a prophet; a mentor as well as a teacher. Working men went into his WEA classes to learn about trade statistics, and left them, as their letters show, with a sense of their dignity as citizens and the socio-logical imagination and reforming zeal to work not just for better wages but a better society.[9] His academic field was economic history, especially the sixteenth and seventeenth centuries, but his impact on students was that of a social philosopher. He turned many of them around (in the Old Testament sense of the idea) by teaching them not to take their mind and conscience out of history. Do not make a darkness and call it research, he would say, appealing for research that took as its starting point problems which mattered, rather than gaps which could be construed to exist.

When in 1933 Ramsay MacDonald, then prime minister, offered Tawney a peerage, the crusty sea-lion replied: "Thank you for your letter. What harm have I ever done to the Labour Party? Yours sincerely, R. H. Tawney." Ernest Green, longtime general secretary of the WEA, who saw Tawney's reply to MacDonald, was himself offered a peerage years later by Attlee. He turned it down, and when he told Tawney this, Tawney said he was foolish to have done so. Green came back: "But you did the same thing yourself"; to which Tawney rejoined: "That was different. You were offered it by an honest man. I wasn't."[10] How to deal with the *thought* of a saint who acquired the moral authority to tell committees, universities, and prime ministers what was right and wrong, yet was never called arrogant or opinion-ated? Is Tawney's thought not incidental to the moral force of his example?

There is no reason to doubt Tawney's saintly reputation, but a new generation has to look at him freshly; even to make its own Tawney. It is not able to feel directly the moral quality of the man. I think Tawney has pertinent lines of thought to offer the late twentieth century. To get at these, we have to take Tawney off his pedestal and look at him from ground level. He can be read for inspiration, as some Americans read Lincoln ("I myself belong to the 1920s," Crossman has testified, "and Tawney's *The Acquisitive Society* is my socialist bible"), but this book does not assume that Tawney's works have a scriptural status.[11]

If Tawney is to speak afresh, he must be addressed with questions which arise in late twentieth-century societies. Paradoxically, this means first of all examining Tawney in the context of his own times, the first half of the twentieth century in Britain. Aware of his context, we may see what was evanescent in Tawney and what endures. To get at what endures is partly a matter of understanding Tawney's times (to see which links in his thought were provided by inarticulate assumptions of his age, now gone; and which transcend his age).

At a meeting of the Economic History Society in the 1930s, after a paper had been read on "The Open Field," Tawney rose and uttered reverberating words: "What historians need is not more documents but stronger boots."[12] No one as erudite as Tawney disparaged documents. He meant to convey that contemporary social awareness is the door to historical understanding. History, he said on another occasion, "is the study not of a series of past events, but of the life of societies, and of the records of the past as a means to that end. Time, and the order of events in time is a clue, but no more; part of the historian's business is to substitute more significant connections for those of chronology."[13]

I take a first guiding principle from these ideas of Tawney. The present work is based upon a study of Tawney's "documents," some of them unpublished, others obscure. I have been interested not only in Tawney's "bibles," such as *The Acquisitive Society* and *Equality*, but in speech notes, letters, and diaries, lecture notes, and essays and articles *de circonstance*.[14] At the same time I have used my "boots" to march through Tawney's times and see how they have issued into our own. This study deals with the present position of democratic socialism, but only after the context of Tawney's life and thought has first been grasped, and connections more meaningful than mere chronology between past and present have been suggested. The first way to demystify Tawney, then, is to ponder the context of his work, and its differences from our own context in the late twentieth century.

RECONSTRUCTING TAWNEY

The second way of demystifying Tawney is to try and make a systematic construction out of Tawney's assorted writings about socialism. Saints may be read for the occasional inspirational text. My alternative is to set out the implicit framework of Tawney's socialism, the better to clarify the issues, sift the soft parts from the solid, and make comparisons with other men.

Richard Rees recalled that Tawney used to deny that he was a "Christian socialist"; he would say that *everyone* should be a socialist.[15] We can appreciate this attitude as a sincere (also tactically sound) rejection of sectarianism. In his own historical moment, Tawney made a socialist appeal by a subtle, and morally powerful (since he practiced what he preached) summoning of men to fulfill values they already knew something about. The remark Rees recalled has a further meaning. Tawney did not like to label himself a Christian socialist (preferring to think of the case for socialism as a universal one) because, out of a hope that everyone would accept Christian values, he often failed to distinguish Christian values from values held by those not Christian.

Tawney's attempt to win hegemony for socialist principles in Britain, like all attempts at persuasion, was existential in character. His own moral force, and the political and ethical culture of the age, were hidden, yet crucial ingredients in his advocacy. The cold fact is that it is not obvious or natural that everyone should be a socialist. It becomes important today, if it was not for Tawney, to understand how much of his socialism was derived from Christianity. The moral and circumstantial power of the saint have in a sense to be discounted for they soon become just beautiful bits of history. This is why I choose to draw out the implicit framework of Tawney's socialist thought, despite the dangers which come from using categories Tawney himself did not use.

If Tawney's socialism is still to stand, its intellectual and moral foundations must be made explicit. This consideration has prompted a basically analytic treatment, which assumes a certain constant core in Tawney, rather than a basically chronological treatment, which maps in detail the changes in his position over the years. To lessen the pitfalls of this approach, the biographical chapters (Part One) attend to the development of Tawney's thought through the various stages of his life.

Most methods have their faults. Not treating Tawney reverentially as an inspiring symbol of socialism, I fail to convey what it was like to know or be taught by Tawney. Something is thereby missed, but it is missed because two other things seem even more important: Tawney's historical significance, and Tawney's continuing validity. Tawney's own view of himself and history would seem to justify me. Being no "respector of persons," he expected no awe toward himself and was pained when it was shown.[16]

As well as being unconcerned with the furniture of biography, Tawney thought that the *questions* and *methods* of historians were as important as their conclusions.[17] "Fashions in historical interpretation change," he observed in a lecture on Tudor historiography. "Each generation has to write its own history for itself. At new points on the road new landscapes are seen. Different answers are given because different questions are asked."[18] Tawney was amused at certain historians who, earnest and indignant, dismantled some details of his conclusions about the sixteenth and seventeenth centuries, imagining that in doing so they negated his contribution to historical enquiry, or proved his methods wrong (or themselves made a substantial contribution to historical understanding). So it seems to me that an interpretation of Tawney's socialism is more apt, for all its risks, than a mere account of his life and achievements.

But does a saint not practice a manner, rather than offer a body of thought? Only the chapters which follow can prove or disprove my view that Tawney did both. Tawney's manner, to which his view that socialism was a way of life is the key, was not the expression of a mere ethical or aesthetic impulse. His life and thought were peculiarly one. He often said he "found the world surprising," and his thought, including his history, was an attempt to cope with what he found.[19] The manner he practiced was rooted in serious, acute, learned perceptions of history and society. The manner and the body of thought blend as one when "fellowship" is seen as the primordial principle of both. Because Tawney's manner has an intellectual meaning, it does not seem an undue distortion of Tawney's total significance to make a systematic construction of his thought, differentiate Tawney's context from our own, and then ask if "socialism as a way of life" in the Tawney manner contains anything of interest to late twentieth-century societies.

This book lies between biography and contemporary history on one hand and the study of political ideas on the other. Tawney's life was not a ready subject for biography. He was a man of the written page rather than a physical activist; no elaborate letter writer, no intriguer; sedate in his patterns of social intercourse. The tracing of a genealogy of ideas, relating Tawney's ideas to other people's ideas before and since, also seems a less than ideal way to treat Tawney. He was not an abstract thinker of high quality. Nor was his socialism the fruit of debate with the ideas of previous thinkers; he denied that socialist ideas move forward as a "literary succession of a chain of writers."[20] Rather it was the response he made to a variety of forces, some intellectual, but some political, military, moral, personal (he wrote a classic on Chinese agriculture because he happened to visit China). This book, then, weighs the conscious response Tawney made to his situation in all its aspects.[21] It blends history and biography with a study of his ideas, for these seem to make up the triangular reality of Tawney's response to situations.

To the question, is the work about Tawney or about socialism, the answer is "both." In the case of Tawney it is impossible to separate these two. His educational work and opinions, and his historical work and opinions seem as much a part of his socialism as his books of socialist doctrine like *The Acquisitive Society* and *Equality* and *The British Labour Movement*. Tawney was influential because he made responses to challenges widely felt. To explain his influence, and also to determine what remains valid in Tawney today, it is necessary to pay heed to these challenges in their varied forms. I make frequent comparisons with other political thinkers; either men who precede Tawney within a tradition (Arnold, Green, Gladstone) or contemporaries who faced similar problems but went different paths (John Strachey, Leonard Woolf, Harold Laski). The subject of China arises occasionally because Tawney's observations on (still agricultural) China are a revealing counterpoint to his views of industrial Europe, suggestive alike of important limitations in his thought and of characteristic strengths.

THE SIGNIFICANCE OF STYLE

It may seem that with Tawney the style is the man. Strip away the stately prose, some may say, and what remains is disappointing. Is such a style as Tawney's, in political writing, even the enemy of rigorous thought? It is true that Tawney sometimes blurred a point rather than revealed it by a stylistic device. In the simplest sense—worth mentioning because Tawney was writing in part for working people—he frequently makes citations in foreign tongues, normally Latin, Greek, French, or German, sometimes at crucial points in his argument.[22] That habit, as well as the use of irony, is mainly significant as a reminder that Tawney's style did not exactly have the common touch. But his rhetoric is sometimes facile ("To kick over an idol, you must first get off your knees").[23] And his style can grow not only portentous, but so eccentrically laced that the meaning is elusive, and the truth of the point in any case doubtful ("But rashness is a more agreeable failing than cowardice, and, when to speak is unpopular, it is less pardonable to be silent than to say too much").[24]

Yet the significance of Tawney's style lies deeper than its lapses. Tawney used language not as symbolism but as imaginative expression. Words were not only counters, of rigid definition, but also colors on the palate of his mind. Orwell made the distinction in "Politics and the English Language": "What is above all needed is to let the meaning choose the word, and not the other way about." Orwell's preference is clear, but is he right? Should writing about politics be imaginative expression, rather than symbolism, or as Orwell puts it, "phrases tacked together like sections of a prefabricated henhouse"?[25]

There are several things to say about this in Tawney's case. Persuasion was for Tawney not just a tactic but an intrinsic, permanent part of socialist political method. His socialist writings were not announcements of historical laws, nor practical manuals for a Babeufist elite, but efforts to make socialist values appealing. It was part of Tawney's socialist faith that he wrote as he did, just as it may be part of a positivist's view of politics to use words as counters, or part of Samuel Beckett's despair to pile words into mounds of paradox. There was no distinction between Tawney's public style and his private style. Letters, speech notes, his diary no less than his books, all are full of maxims, ironic doubts, biblical and classical allusions, self-mockery, and a freshness of image that suggests the writer sees and feels the things he talks about. There is in Tawney's style a feeling for the dignity of man, the moral unity of things, the seriousness of man's condition and his relationships, the hollowness of privilege and pomposity.

But the real issue is whether writing and thinking are entirely separate processes, and whether political writing and "literature" are entirely separate genres. I follow Orwell in saying thinking and writing are so entangled that bad writing—mixed metaphors, too many words concocted from Latin roots—indicates that the writer is not thinking acutely. At least in Tawney, when the style is questionable, the thought is also questionable. The style is the thought revealing itself; it cannot be "stripped away." "He was not inventing things," Gaitskell concluded of Tawney, "but simply showing them to us."[26] The comment is misleading, and contains an unwitting tribute to the power of Tawney's mind. What Gaitskell says could be said of most (not all) of the finest political writing. To show something is often a mark of superlative invention; a point is made so convincing that it seems almost self-evident. Imagination is the handmaiden not only of style but of thought. Allusion (style) is the twin brother of comparative method (research).

Tawney's pioneering works in Tudor and Stuart history, especially the questions raised, were triggered by the same imagination and moral sense that informs his style. The historical books are written in the same prose as the "socialist" books. Tawney's irony, to take one feature of his style, is an expression of his awareness of the gap between intention and performance, a way of tickling the inarticulate premises of history's actors, a debunking device for a man who sometimes suspected history was a fable on which respectable men had decided to agree.[27] If justification for economic history as literature is needed—beyond its readability—Tawney offers it in denying that economics is an autonomous realm ("Agriculture is not merely an economic enterprise, but . . . a manner of life and the basis of a social system").[28] Economic history (as distinct from economic geography), he reasoned, is about people, and imaginative expression is a proper door to such subject matter.

POLITICAL THOUGHT AND BRITISH POLITICS

Why weigh Tawney as a socialist thinker when he was an historian? Tawney's interest in the origins of capitalism and in modern capitalist society (and in China) are really aspects of one enterprise: to understand the conditions and consequences of industrialization and the relation of both to social values. Just as Tawney's interest in history arose from his will to understand and change the present, so did his interest in political science. It began, he tells us: "when I stayed in a remote village in Dorsetshire, which was ruled by a dragon in the shape of an old lady who was a kind of female squire and parson rolled into one. Fearing, I suppose, that the church catechism might upset the childrens' minds, she issued an improvement on it of her own, one of the questions in which was 'What are laws?' The answer which infant lips were required to lisp was 'Laws are wise institutions to preserve the rich in their possessions and restrain the vicious poor.' I felt that there must be a catch in this somewhere. I decided that I should like to know more about the sciences which dealt with such matters."[29] Tawney the historian, political analyst, and socialist, were all one; a persistent, smouldering idealist, consciously responding to situations presented by the vices and virtues of Victorian industrialism.

Because it was a single motor that propelled Tawney into economic history and socialist theory, I feel justified in touching on his historiography but not offering a full treatment of it; in dealing with its motives, yet not assessing its achievements and failures. (From the practical standpoint, I lack the learning for the latter task, and find enough for one book in Tawney's socialism).

But even if there is a case for dealing only tangentially with Tawney's history, is there one for treating an amateur political thinker as if he were a professional? The difference between amateur and professional does not in the twentieth century have much meaning. Indeed it was never stark. What of Burke, or Paine, or Bagehot? Political thought which is later judged important and canonized has not always come from professional political philosophers, and quite often from politicians, economists, bishops, farmers, and other amateurs. In recent decades, many political philosophers have implicitly acknowledged that political thought issues often from amateurs by concentrating their own talents on analysis and criticism of psychologists (such as Freud), novelists (such as Camus), imprisoned activists (such as Debray). Other philosophers have spurned the major problems of politics, which may explain in part why amateurs have occupied much of the territory of political philosophy.

Tawney was a learned man, but not in the history of political philosophy. His own political thought arose from his encounter with the problems of his age, and he cast it in a form dictated by his learning in history, the classics, and Christianity. "Tawney avoided being a bore," an admirer remarked, "he kept certain things in the background."[30] To a degree, we must ourselves put the system into Tawney's political thought, by bringing into the foreground things he left in the background, and putting alongside his *principles* his *methods* as historian, adult educator, and Labour publicist. But I do not dismiss Tawney as a political thinker—any more than Burke—on the ground that he did not give his thought systematic form.

From a different point of view, others may object that political thought itself is dead; or that Britain has declined so much that British political thought and institutions have lost their interest. I cannot squarely confront these two issues, yet must have them in mind because Tawney is relevant to both. A starting point on them ought to be declared.

Tawney was at his best in the vigorous years of political debate after World War I (this period I call an "interlude," between the certainties of the Victorian liberal order and the onrush of ideologies). Focusing on this interlude, I find political thought not dying, but being transformed and also to some extent starting to be transferred, in its cutting edge, from Europe to other places. The situation of Tawney illumines the process.

Liberal political thought collapsed. Then democratic socialist thought, of which Tawney's ideas were one variety, was squeezed in a polarization between fascism and Stalinism, and often discounted by the general loss of faith in reason and democracy. It did seem, from the 1930s on through the Cold War, that there was practically no viable path between the unedifying techniques of reformed capitalism, and total-itarianism. Whether that unhappy constriction is permanent, however, I doubt; perhaps Tawney's democratic socialism can face the 1970s with more confidence than any decade since the 1920s.

Isaiah Berlin aptly says that political thought flourishes only when "ends collide."[31] Looking back to the interlude, and following from there the dissolution of the British Empire, it seems possible that the "great tradition of political theory" (Berlin's phrase) has passed from Europe to the Third World, because it is in the latter much more than in the former that "ends collide." Judith Shklar proclaims the great tradition "extinct" without a single glance beyond Europe.[32] Berlin says there no longer exists "oppression or suppression of entire classes of society"; surely he can be speaking only of Europe?[33]

Tawney, like most of his generation, failed to see the full significance for political thought of the shift of the center of political struggle from Europe to the Third World. But his failure is interesting, because his work on China provides a ready test case of it. Studying Tawney may yield hypotheses on whether political thought is dead, or whether it is more accurate to say it is transferred and transformed.

The fate of political thought is a double issue; a matter of a shift of power, and a matter of changes in ideas. Tawney is a poor guide to understanding the shift of power away from Europe, for he never ceased thinking of London as the center of the world. But he is a good guide to the intellectual changes which brought an end to the interlude of fundamental debate about political ends.

We see in Tawney and his associates how a religious impulse echoes in a political commitment, yet only for a transitional generation which knew religion first hand. How the death of political thought is really the death of liberal political thought, whose faith in the harmony between individualistic enterprise and the public interest could not survive 1914. How the promise of democratic socialism was undercut by a wrenching polarization in international politics, which turned every discussion of socialist ideas into a discussion of communist power. How the technical, specialized disciplines aspired to slice into value-free portions the search for general political light which occupied the thinkers of the interlude.

But in Tawney we also see that political thought is not

dead. Rather, on the one hand, the context of political thought is now global; its crucial issues lie in relations between the West and the Third World (and in relations between man and nature). And, on the other hand, the context of political thought in the West is transformed by the moral vision of a new generation which feels no allegiance to liberal capitalism. It is impossible to weigh Tawney's humanistic socialism and still conclude that the great issues of politics have passed away. These fundamental issues can never be successfully subsumed into economic science, or into the administrative managerialism which flattens issues into problems. Political thought may miss its opportunities, or yield its territory by default to intellectual predators. But its challenge does not die; that much Tawney reminds us.

Tawney offers, too, a window on the development of British political culture. The "decline" of Britain in the mid-twentieth century can be instructive of the character of Britain's greatness in the nineteenth century. What endures, what fades quickly? Which of the great aspirations of the Victorian zenith proved capable of fulfillment, which not, and why? These questions seem worth attention, because British institutions have shown notable resilience, and have been more influential in the world than those of any other modern polity.

This book discusses politics by choosing one national laboratory of thought and institutions (Britain) to illumine a general issue (democratic socialism). Beer has observed of Britain: "consensus and conflict are ordered in a dialectic that makes of the political arena at once a market of interests and a forum for debate of fundamental moral concerns."[34] In such a political culture ideas continue to matter and merit consideration. Tawney's socialism contains some of the more estimable ideas of twentieth-century British politics, eloquent alike of what has made Britain a great laboratory of politics, of certain weaknesses, and of the nature and significance of her twentieth century "decline".

Through Tawney, we watch Britain's attempt to descend the mountain of imperial grandeur and build a juster society for all her citizens. We watch, too, the struggle of socialist ideals against the tough hide of class habits and class pretensions, that strange encounter unique to Britain of progressive ideas with elitest modes and feelings. We see the deep scar of war on the body and mind of Britain in the twentieth century. Before us parade the successive orthodoxies of British political life over the span of Tawney's life, from Edwardian liberal "consensus" to mid-century collectivist "consensus." We discern the institutional watershed which Britain has now reached, as the vessels of British political life, from parliament to the parties, crack from the strains placed against them by plebiscitary democracy. In all these ways Tawney reflects a British epoch.

Beyond the condition of Britain, Tawney reflects the rise, diffusion, and apparent paralysis of democratic socialism. "There are times which are not ordinary," Tawney wrote characteristically in 1920, "and in such times it is not enough to follow the road. It is necessary to know where it leads, and, if it leads nowhere, to follow another."[35] The democratic socialist way is committed to this constant test of the social order by the best light available. It also clings to a hope that justice can be wedded with liberty; treading the slow path of achieving social purposes without trampling on the opinions of ordinary people. These two aspects of a tradition we find spun out in Tawney.

Added to them is a third and the main one: a view of socialism not as efficiency, or order, or the symmetry of a perfect social machine, or even of abundance, but of a right order of social relationships, the unending and unmeasurable goal of which is human fellowship. "As long as men are men," Tawney began his case for socialism, "a poor society cannot be too poor to find a right order of life, nor a rich society too rich to have need to seek it."[36]

Part One. Tawney's Life

1 MORAL QUEST, 1880-1914

Tawney's life is notable as much for attitudes as activities. The range of his activities was not as wide, say, as Laski's—a bustling activist, sparkling with new projects, the ink seldom dry on the latest manifesto. Tawney was like a star shining steadily from a fixed position, rather than a meteor—Laski was the meteor—traversing vast reaches. At the same time, his life, as he himself confessed, was "that terrible thing, an unplanned economy."[1] As he pushed ahead with his few fundamental concerns—teaching, writing, advising the labor movement—the forces of demand swelled his career with additional pursuits. My purpose in this Part is to map the geography of Tawney's life and to indicate changes in his thought over time (later chapters are analytic and do not take full account of the development of his thought).

INDIA, RUGBY, BALLIOL: IN A WORLD
HE NEVER MADE

Harry Tawney was a quiet boy who stored things up inside himself. The world he encountered, at Rugby, then at Balliol College, Oxford, was not always congenial to him. He did not stride readily into a family tradition and play out its next chapter, like his Rugby, Balliol, and lifelong friend, Billy Temple. Temple, whom Tawney met at the railway station on his first day at Rugby, was arriving at a school of which his father had been headmaster. Confident, articulate, a boy stepping on stones whose feel he seemed to know, Billy became archbishop of Canterbury as his father had done. In early photos—of the literary society Eranos at Rugby in 1898, in hockey gear at Balliol—Harry is thin, with sharp nose and big ears. He is tight-lipped; his eye meets the camera equably, correctly, giving nothing away. Temple looks in surer possession of the ground he stands on and the atmosphere he breathes.[2]

In fact Tawney, as he later tells us, found surprising the world he met as a youth. In preparing to cope with it, he departed from several traditions. During the industrial revolution his ancestors had done quite well from beer and banking in Oxford and nearby.[3] Engineering, timber business, and, back in the eighteenth century, watchmaking, also occupied the family. No radicalism stirs among these Tawneys; in the year of Queen Victoria's accession one stands for parliament as a Tory. Harry Tawney seldom talked about any of his family, but he was particularly uninterested in the Tawneys of the industrial revolution. T. S. Ashton recalls that when, by chance, the records of the Tawney banking company were given to the London School of Economics and Political Science (LSE), "it proved impossible to kindle in the great-grandson even a flicker of interest."[4] Selecting another, less acquisitive, if more distant tradition, Tawney liked to say he was descended from men who fought at Naseby and Marston Moor.

These preferences are hardly surprising. But Tawney was also reticent about the Tawneys of the Victorian era, who turned in part from business to "service." His father, C. H. Tawney, was a Sanskrit scholar, principal of Presidency College, Calcutta, and a longtime member of the Indian Educational Service. In no way did Tawney choose to see himself as part of this lineage of Church and Empire. Indeed, he criticized both institutions. Born in Calcutta in 1880, he never followed up, either by example or inquiry, his father's involvement with the burden and glory of ruling and enlightening Indians. William Beveridge, one of Tawney's close friends at Balliol and later his brother-in-law, was born in India just one year before Tawney, and took much interest in, and drew a sense of identity from his Indian origins. The Beveridge family, who knew Tawney's family, was the subject of William's indulgent memoir, *India Called Them*. But Tawney cast no glances back. Few pages did he write on India (though hundreds on China). Nor did he use the occasion of his two trips to China or his trip to Australia to acquaint himself closely with the land of his birth and his father's career.[5]

Tawney's nearest link with his father's India was that he happened to marry into another India family—the industrious, family-conscious, progressive, slightly eccentric Beveridges. His impulsive and extravagant wife, Jeannette (Annette Jeanie), young sister of Harry's mate, William

Beveridge, was like Harry himself born in India in 1880. Otherwise, in matters Indian, as in numerous areas Tawney turned, without fanfare, against his classic upper-middle-class, Victorian, imperial, upbringing.

He set his sails toward social, rather than imperial tasks. Toward education as a path to emancipation for every man, not as the preparation of an elite for the task of ruling lesser breeds (Strachan Davidson's view at Balliol). Toward structural economic and political change which might enable the masses to shape their own lives, not toward religious indoctrination and philanthropy designed to make the masses more virtuous in their allotted station (which was the emphasis of the Victorian church). Toward scholarship as a way to general wisdom and a better society, rather than toward the minute, exotic scholasticism of his father (who translated the *Katha-Sarit Sagar*, the *Malavikagnimitra*, and other works, from the Sanskrit).

The Tawney family, including Harry's sister to whom he was close, and his retarded brother left India when Harry was a small boy. Harry was sent in 1894 to Rugby, a good, austere, pious school, which pounded him with the classics and the Scriptures. Frederick Temple, when headmaster of Rugby, had been known as "a just beast"—the label pleased him—and under J. Percival and H. A. James, headmasters in Harry's years, there was, Tawney's teacher says, "not enough spontaneity about the Rugby virtue."[6]

As in the case of other institutions from Tawney's Victorian upbringing, his later fierce rebellion against the public schools did not mean that Rugby had not put its mark upon him. He disliked the social conventions of Rugby, the formalism of its religious teaching—as if the events of the Gospels "had all happened on a Sunday."[7] But there are echoes in Tawney of Percival's obsession with moral "tone"; of the great Robert Whitelaw's stress on the fundamental texts of antiquity (Tawney was in Whitelaw's house); of Frank Fletcher's saturation in English verse, and penchant for oblique allusions in Latin, Greek, and other available tongues.

And there was, already when Tawney went up to Balliol as a Scholar in 1899, a slight lack of spontaneity about the young man's (own interpretation of) virtue. True, he later wrote, when defining the goals of socialism, that virtue should not be too austere, and ought to have her occasional fling.[8] Yet there was a battle in Tawney's breast about this;

austerity and gaiety danced at times a strange duet. If one is surprised to find him, in his sixties, when writing a note to Lionel Elvin in Paris to announce a brief visit (which happened to be on Bastille Day) to consult documents in the Bibliotheque Nationale, asking Elvin to dine with him, then "join the people dancing in the streets," it is because there often seemed something caged about Tawney's gaiety.[9] It was seldom given free rein, except before children, and when Tawney felt himself in an intimate circle of shared assumptions and common style. To people who did not interest him, or whom he did not like, Tawney never unbuttoned, and could seem narrowly Rugby and Balliol.

At Balliol, the social idealism of Edward Caird and the socially oriented religious liberalism of Charles Gore edged him toward the social moralism out of which his socialism later grew. Perhaps the organization that meant most to him at this time was the Christian Social Union (created by Scott Holland and other theologically liberal social reformers), whose Oxford branch he joined. Tawney as a youth found England in the grip of limited self-doubts. His was a Victorian boyhood, but of a generation late enough that he and his friends quickly sniffed faults in the piety and complacency of a fine age now past its peak. The revelations of Charles Booth on poverty and Salvationist William Booth on various urban miseries influenced many university men, including Caird. The title of William Booth's *In Darkest England and the Way Out* (1890) symbolized a growing impulse to care not only for Kipling's "lesser breeds" across the seas, but for the uplifting of England's own degraded masses. The Boer War, which burst out the year Tawney went up to Oxford, was a key event in deflating Britain's imperial swagger; it was "Britain's Vietnam" in that it led to a sudden wave of self-doubt and self-criticism. At the same time, new social issues were raised, some in a paternalist, philanthropic way, as in the Charity Organisation Society, some as a result of reassessments of the structural problems of imperialistic capitalism, guided by J. A. Hobson's *Imperialism* (1902) and L. T. Hobhouse's *Democracy and Reaction* (1904).*

*Tawney in 1903 thought of working for the COS, but later abhorred it and its methods; both Hobson and Hobhouse influenced him and won his vigorous admiration.

The "social problem" was in the air at Oxford. So was a vigorous, but not destructive questioning of religion. In the "Little Republic" which its master, Caird, declared it to be, Tawney, at Balliol, encountered these currents in an atmosphere of circumscribed radicalism.[10] Dissent was transmuted by the sense Balliol gave its students that they were being trained to run the show. Benjamin Jowett, who reigned over the college like a sovereign, and made it distinguished, said he wanted to "inoculate England" with his Balliol graduates.[11] Caird, a patriarchal figure with domed head and flowing beard, perhaps the most influential man at Tawney's Oxford, was equally oriented to what he called "public ends" and "the responsibilities of empire." When he left the Chair of Moral Philosophy at Glasgow to replace Jowett in 1893, he cheered himself against the wrench of leaving Scotland with the remark: "In Balliol I shall have my hand on the heart of England."[12] Tawney was unmoved by Caird's special stress on the Call of India—by this time, one sixth of the Indian civil service had come from Balliol, and three successive governors-general—but his decision to go into various kinds of social work owed most to Caird's explicit challenge to go and find out why England had poverty alongside riches, and do something about it.[13]

Tawney, who took "Mods" and "Greats," learned professionalism in scholarly investigation from his tutors, J. A. Smith and H. W. C. Davis, and a feeling for words and a taste for fancy, discursive scholarship from Francis de Paravicini, his learned, aloof classics tutor. He did not get into economic history because none existed; that came later, and at first more from experience than books. Tawney recalled of Oxford: "The only person there who gave me any help or encouragement with research in economic history was a Russian, Professor Paul Vinogradoff" (professor of jurisprudence.).[14] Tawney then added a remark of Vinogradoff's which had stuck in his mind over fifty years, and gives a clue to Tawney's view of Oxford. "He used to say that Oxford was not a University at all, but a high school of young gentlemen." Yet Tawney was not immune to influences from the gentleman's world in which he grew up. He did not fail to imbibe a bit of the "effortless superiority" which H. H. Asquith said marked Balliol.

Tawney was not a student leader, unlike Billy Temple who

was president of the Oxford Union. He played rugby, hockey, and tennis in the Balliol teams, but was just an average sportsman. He did not write for student papers, get into trouble, or become famous or infamous in any way. Important, rebellious things were germinating in his mind, but in externals he played to the score, and in form, if not in content, he must have been a rather conventional college man. It was a conventionality that never entirely left him, and it made his socialism a paradox to those—unfamiliar with "effortless superiority"—who were puzzled to find the strong red wine of socialism in a Balliol bottle.

This Oxford generation, to whom the mud and blood of the Somme and the Marne fifteen years later was then not conceivable even as a nightmare, had about them the glow of moral and intellectual inquirers. Few yet doubted that, as Darwin wrote to Marx in 1873 when thanking him for sending volume one of *Das Kapital*, the "extension of knowledge . . . is sure to add to the happiness of mankind"; or thought extravagent Acton's giddy words to the Cambridge University Press apropros the modern history he was editing: "now that all information is within reach, and every problem has become capable of solution."[15]

Tawney and Beveridge and Temple, and other student acquaintances, including Walter Moberley, F. M. Powicke, and R. C. K. Ensor, assumed that their education would adequately fit them to solve England's problems. Returning once to speak to the Dervoiguilla Society at Balliol, Tawney recounted his usual story of having turned to the study of history because he found the world surprising. Then he added: "particularly since I had belonged to the generation of illusion."[16] It was as if these young men were on an escalator, which bore them up from underneath in the direction they set out to go, and a few years later, in 1914, the escalator stopped.

The ambience was leisured, not urgent, and the topics were esoteric. Reading parties in the countryside could still focus on a point of religious doctrine, with interludes of bridge and wine. The social problems which Tawney and his friends debated were (to them) external to their own sense of security as men who, tempered by Balliol, would naturally lead an assault on the problems. They possessed social self-confidence, and so they could eye England's problems with noblesse oblige, without feeling uprooted or alienated by the

Tawney early in the twentieth century.

challenge. They possessed intellectual self-confidence; they would chide, reason with, or abuse each other with clever alternate verses in random tongues. They used initials (R. H.), never first names (Harry), to express their assured seriousness. In letters, they never mentioned the name of a girl, even when writing several sentences about her, to maintain reasonable distinctions. They adorned their letters with Greek, to make it clear that their concern for the contemporary and the practical stopped short of crude fanaticism. Their style had an earnest note, but eased by refinement and an unfailing sense of moderation.

J. A. Smith, Tawney's tutor, caught the slightly narrow tone of Balliol self-confidence, when he said at a dinner of men who had just gone through the golden archway of the Greats examination: "Someday, when you have listened to someone talking unmitigated nonsense, you will say to yourselves, 'If that man had read the *Republic* and the *Ethics*, he could not have talked such unmitigated nonsense.' "[17] As for the cautious, finessed radicalism of Balliol, we glimpse it in A. L. Smith, later master of the college, whose view on history—that "the significance of the past lay in great moral truths"—influenced Tawney deeply. Under the apple trees of the King's Mound, Smith was dispensing knowledge to a miner at the Balliol summer school for workers which Tawney helped instigate. Said the miner: "This is the sort of place my mates and I are going to smash." Replied Smith: "Look, let me show you round and tell you its history. You'll be able to smash it so much better, once you know."[18] Once you know, however, is your zeal to smash not a bit diminished? Be that as it may, Tawney "knew," and he knew from within.

CHARITY AND SLUMS

Tawney left Oxford in 1903, the year the Workers Educational Association was founded, Shaw's *Man and Superman* appeared, and Keir Hardie asked Lloyd George to lead the Labour party. Tawney's head was a caldron of ideas and aspirations. He had missed a First in Greats, which did not much depress him. "My Second," he wrote to Beveridge, "will be a grand weapon with which to convince them ('my people') that it's no use my trying to get into the English Civil." His father, hearing of the Second, enquired: "How do you propose to wipe out this disgrace?" But Caird said to Tawney's former teacher at Rugby: "I grant you his mind was chaotic: but his examiners ought to have seen that it was the chaos of a great mind." His intellect was as yet ungelled by the discipline of later immersion in economic history. He also wrote too slowly for exams; "I'm on the floor chewing the doormat," he later said of his agonies of composition.[19]

Fifteen years afterward the dons of Balliol adjusted matters by electing him a Fellow of the college. In the interim, the *Times* noted, "He has done a large amount of educational, economic, and journalistic work."[20] But the *Times* was wrong to describe him as "Mr. Richard Henry Tawney, M.A." Objecting to paying the fee which is the way an Oxford B.A. becomes an Oxford M.A.—on the ground that degrees should not be bought and sold—he remained, and always did, "R. H. Tawney B.A."

He went to live at Toynbee Hall, a university settlement house in the East End of London, founded and run with vision and a touch of paternalism by Canon Samuel Barnett. Booth, in his *Life and Labour in London*, called it a place designed "to bring University culture into direct contact with the poorest of the people."[21] Barnett also saw it thus; but Tawney, and Beveridge who also went into residence there in 1903, did not and outlooks diverged over the decade of Tawney's intermittent residence. Residents at Toynbee Hall paid their own way, while plunging into social work—for Tawney and Beveridge, social investigation also—around Whitechapel; so they needed a job. In letters to Beveridge during the late summer and fall of 1903 Tawney wondered what job would best carry out Caird's injunction.

Not yet aware that writing and teaching were his vocation, he looked for some kind of social work, narrowing the choice in the end to either the Charity Organisation Society or the Children's Country Holiday Fund. Both organizations, as Mary Stocks observes, were on the "Octavia Hill track" (philanthropy), rather than the "Beatrice Webb track" (structural change).[22] Tawney's family advice had been against such jobs; for where did they lead?* T. S. Ashton said Tawney decided against the COS because he found its methods

---

*Tawney, recalling once that as a young man he had been (unsuccessfully) urged not to overlook what provision there would be, with any given job, for his widow after his own death, began his next sentence: Throwing my prospective widow firmly overboard . . ." ("Speech to Temple Society," Speeches Given On Various Occasions; LSE).

"inquisitorial". But that may be reading later views too far back into the past. Writing to Beveridge in September, 1903, Tawney gave two other reasons: "I like the idea of being Secretary to the C.C.H.F. better than that of joining C.O.S. for a few years, firstly because the pay is double, secondly because I think to get anything worth learning out of the C.O.S. I should have to stick to it longer than I am prepared for."[23]

So Tawney declined C. S. Loch's offer at the COS and went to the Children's Country Holiday Fund, which the Barnetts had started in 1877 by sending nine ailing children to get fresh air in the country. Tawney got a taste of the dynamics of the world of charity. He ran the Holiday Fund efficiently, though there were complaints that, in sending children off to experience rural sights and sounds, he allowed them to rampage without adequate supervision, shattering the tranquility of the benefactors who received them.[24] One little irony sprang from his three years at the CCHF. At a Fund receiving center in Haslemere he met and took a liking to Jeannette Beveridge, William's sister. In 1909 he married her. So the CCHF work led him to the girl whom, as "prospective widow," he had "thrown overboard" by his decision to enter such precarious employment.

Tawney at twenty-three was a taut, eager, self-conscious idealist. Physically, he was a big, loose-built man; a regal head capped a clumsy body. His untidiness did not rob him of poise, nor his shabbiness hide a patrician dignity. Quiet of speech, his manner was shy, even stern. But his equable gaze could quickly melt into an attractive fleeting smile.

He had been influenced by Ruskin, Slade Professor at Oxford when Tawney went there, and by another man who saw capitalist industrialism as a threat to art and life—William Morris, whose books he liked and urged his sister to read.[25] Beyond these men, and others Tawney knew personally— Caird, Scott Holland, Gore—it is hard to trace the source of Tawney's ideas. It is interesting that Tawney said of the Webbs: "Historians of political thought are apt to be obsessed with origins and pedigrees, as though ideas were transmitted in the same manner as property . . . In reality, original people are not links in a chain; more often they are breaks in one."[26] Tawney may well have thought this true of himself.

He devoured theology, but with an impatience that anticipates his later dislike of it. "Harnack has convinced me that the most acceptable offering to the almighty would be a holocaust of theologians." From Germany, where he went walking and learning the language with Billy Temple, in November 1903, he reports on a book by Edenheim, on the Bible. A month later he confesses to Beveridge: "I began *die Glocke* but it was too much for me, and indeed Schiller in general is. His sentiments are so damnably irreproachable." He puts at the end of another letter two quotations about man and God: "Some people always sigh in thanking God"; "It is perhaps better for men like us to be ruled than to be free, since our appetites if let loose on our neighbours like beasts from a cage would set the world on fire with deeds of evil." Not yet is Tawney himself the author of such words, but twenty years later these are his characteristic views—dislike of religiosity, sobriety about human nature.[27]

His letters of the early years of the century have a religious strand, yet lightness breaks in when earnestness threatens. In Balliol style, he makes a drastic assertion, then after a semi-colon draws back with an ironic or quizzical addition. Picking his way across many topics, his tone is square and jolly. Here and there he is opinionated, as befits a youth not yet recovered from his education. He announces of an Oxford friend who used to canoe with Beveridge and Tawney on the Wye: "Dick is engaged to be married—confound him." Still six years away from his own marriage, Tawney is able to add: "What infernal rot it is. It's no fun talking to married people. One never knows when one is treading on their corns." Already he is asking, as he kept doing all his life, how scholarship can keep in touch with the weird and random events of the real world of men and women. He describes an appalling murder at Oxford, "of five gentlemen by infuriated female, of the name of Smith," then abruptly asks Beveridge: "What is sociology?" Reading these sentiments, tossed around in a jumble-sale way in the fluid months after he came down from Oxford, we are reminded of Caird's remark about why he did not get a First.[28]

But three years in the East End (he lived at Toynbee Hall from October 1903 until November 1906; then again for much of 1908, and for the spring of 1913) gave him categories of experience which clarified his mind. He gave a weekly class at the Hall on "Some Nineteenth Century Writers," and lectures on "Belief and Criticism" and other religious topics. But his characteristic meetings were on politics and economics, and he, along with Beveridge, pushed the program further in the direction of these topics than Canon Barnett wished to go. Tawney wanted increasingly not to bring culture to the workers, but to help equip them to bid for power. He lectured on "Trade Unions (Principles)" and "Co-operative Trading" and offered a course on "Social and Industrial Questions". Together with Beveridge and H. R. Maynard, he introduced a solid series on politics and industry. The concluding lecture of the politics sequence was "The Real Governors of England." Which of the three should do that one? Beveridge recalls: "Maynard and I decided by a majority of two to one that Tawney must give this lecture."[29]

In the *Toynbee Record* he wrote about the church's loss of touch with workers, which was starting to bother him and helped spark his later celebrated studies of the historical relation between Christianity and capitalism. The *Record* contains several rather sprawling "literary" pieces, which, though unsigned, look like Tawney's: "The Call of the Wild," a slightly arrogant spoof of an American's account of the East End; "Gulliver in Hampshire," a turgid fantasy. On industrial, political, and educational matters he was much better. Taking up the cause of university reform, he spurred Barnett and others on, wrote remarkable memoranda full of facts and figures on the elitism of Oxford and Cambridge, and published, in the *Westminister Gazette* during the spring of 1906, excellent articles on the subject under the pen-name "Lambda."[30]

Other lifelong interests sprouted at Toynbee Hall. He threw himself into the Toynbee Hall Trades Boards Committee; a decade later he had written two books on matters related to trades boards. He agitated against blind-alley employment of juveniles who should still be at school; a dozen pamphlets and essays eventually came from his pen on this issue. He worked on the Mansion House Committee, which secured work for unemployed men in the country—at the Salvation Army Colony at Hadleigh and on Osea Island in Essex. But, with Beveridge, he went beyond Barnett's "relief" approach, followed through with the men after they were off relief, and studied the structural problems of underemployment, poverty, and the reserve of labor.[31] Out of this came his "Poverty as an Industrial Problem" which insisted on looking beyond the special case (poverty) to the usual case (economic insecurity on the margin of poverty).

Meanwhile, he found another social world from that of Rugby and Balliol. With Beveridge, he joined a Workman's Club in Bethnal Green, learning how to play shovehalfpenny, and order a "pony" to avoid too long a drink among men who drank like fish. But he did not fit in very well, for he could not yet avoid the impression that workers were the object of his improving attentions. A note of naivety comes out in a letter from Germany of this period: "I never came across a real wood-cutter before, but I recognize the genuine article from the fact that all the heroes in Grimm's fairy-tales are sons and daughters of wood-cutters." At the Bethnal Green Club Tawney and Beveridge found that it is easier for men of different upbringings to work together than to play together.[32]

Tawney learned important things at Toynbee Hall, and by the time he left he had developed sharp criticisms of Barnett's brand of piety and philanthropy. What the patriarchal canon hoped of residents at the Hall was expressed in one of his annual reports:

> The problem of society seems to be at root a religious problem. Nothing lasting can be done to raise the poor above the cares of this world and the rich above the deceitfulness of riches till all alike live to do the will of God ... My hope is that the residents of Toynbee Hall, men often of strong and diverse opinions, hearing together the call of human needs, and discovering in every human being something divine, may at last enforce the truth of the old faith which worships as God the father of Jesus Christ.[33]

This is still the devout, paternalistic voice of Gladstonism, which Tawney wrestled with but turned away from. Tawney could not neglect the facts of religious decline: "one of the great social forces of history," he wrote in Toynbee Hall's *Record*, "is gradually and reluctantly drifting out of the lives of no inconsiderable part of society." Barnett did not seem to Tawney to grasp the import of this. Nor the gravity of a further fact which Tawney frequently commented upon: "we shall not go far wrong in stating that all over London Church attendance varies roughly in proportion to the poverty of the district under consideration." In such circumstances a mere escalation of evangelism did not seem to Tawney a path of light. He quarried two "questionable assumptions" lying beneath "wholesale evangelisation": "that the means are worth the end, even if the means be cajolery, and the end a spasmodic and parasitic attendance, and second that ethical aspirations developed amid the stress of a struggle which is in no merely metaphysical sense a struggle for existence can be interpreted and strengthened without wider experience, and arduous intellectual effort."[34]

Barnett must have understood that Tawney and some of his contemporaries were poised to depart from his own Victorian tradition of religious social work. One of the canon's reports gives an acute portrait of Tawney's mood as he struggled toward a social expression of Christianity: "The generation which is coming into occupation is unlike its predecessors. Its youth has more of the characteristics of age. It is prudent and convinced of the necessity of knowledge before action. It does not wear its convictions on its sleeve, but is in earnest and ready for sacrifice when the occasion comes . . . It is wary of enthusiasm, but is expectant of a call which will take it out of itself. It is on the watch."[35] Tawney found the call to "take him out of himself" in directions different from Barnett's. Wary of enthusiasm, possessed of doubts about Christianity, he believed the church must either find fresh approaches to politics or become a mere relic amid the chimneys of industry. A note on his experiences at Toynbee Hall observes: "Discontent is common. It cooks nobody's dinner. Enlightened discontent is very rare."[36] His own experience and investigation suggested to him that social systems "largely determine the quality of the individual characters to whom the appeal of Christianity must be addressed."[37] Hence even the evangelistic task lay along the path of systemic social and political change. The entire social system, not just spectacular abuses or obviously "moral" issues, would have to be considered the proper object of Christian action if Christianity was to retain credibility.

His idea of the Christian task began to outstrip the notion of individualistic evangelism altogether, and to center on a structural social fellowship of right relationships. In this way, people might really be able to practice the care for each other which was at present just a hopeful exhortation on the lips of a sinking church. Among the working class of the East End he discerned at least the impulse toward fellowship: a "feeling of solidarity [which] throws into more startling relief the utter incapacity of the suburbs to grasp the existence of any social ideal whatsoever." He became too "political" to fit the pattern of Barnett, who said "The sense of sin has been the starting-point of progress." In a note on his experiences at the Hall Tawney wrote: "Real friends are only made by accident. A locality is not sanctified by a club of the cultured." Though he saluted the practical value of Toynbee Hall, he had departed from its philosophy.[38]

By 1906 he was ready to leave social work for teaching, and eager to replace Barnett's approach to social problems by an approach that combined education for socialism with organizing workers and marshaling knowledge for the pursuit of state power. Considering several university jobs, he went to see Barnett, then wrote to Beveridge: "teaching economics in an industrial town is just what I want ultimately to do . . . Again the Canon approves, but his approbation is much more damping than his opposition could be. After saying several things about my character he remarked, 'If you were satisfied with your life in Toynbee Hall and the C.C.H.F. I should say "stay on." But as you are not, I am inclined to advise you to try for Cardiff.' "[39]

Tawney decided to go not to Cardiff but to Glasgow University. As assistant in economics from late 1906 until January 1908, he worked alongside Tom Jones, and under Professor William Smart, a conventional economist who was then on the Poor Laws Royal Commission and in 1909 signed its majority report (Tawney's friend Beatrice Webb signed its minority report). Jones became an intimate friend of Tawney's, from these early years in Glasgow (when Jones's mother kept an eye on the careless Tawney, even literally stripping his feet of shoes full of holes, whose decline Tawney had not bothered to arrest) through Jones's career as secretary to several prime ministers.[40] They had in common a morally based socialism. Jones was not as close to the church as Tawney. Being already a member of the Independent Labour party and the Fabian Society when the two of them met, Jones quickened the evolution of Tawney's social thought from an abstractly moral approach to the problems of society (which tended to draw liberal conclusions), to a morally rooted political approach (which was socialist). Tawney joined the Fabian Society in 1906 and the Independent Labour party in 1909.

In particular, Jones persuaded Tawney to leave the CCHF work, which Jones considered a waste of Tawney's talents, and he facilitated Tawney's first university job at Glasgow. Tawney supplemented the £50 for five months work, which Glasgow paid him, by writing rather sharp editorials for the *Glasgow Herald*.[41] But the paper was not pleased with the deflating irony that crept into his reports of social functions. In April 1907, five months after going to Glasgow, Tawney wrote to Beveridge: "You will be amused to hear that the *Glasgow Herald* has found me out, and held up its hands in horror at my depravity. We have arranged to part next October, except for such signed contributions as I care to send."[42] By November he is in controversy in the *Herald's* pages, on "Labour Exchanges and Casual Labour."[43]

The topic was one on which he and Professor Smart disagreed. Tawney described his boss as "bitten with the Exchange idea," but he himself felt hopeless about such ambulance work that reached out to men far too late in their unhappy career as victims of capitalism to do much good.[44] In Smart's department, Tawney acquired his lifelong disesteem for theoretical economics. Looking back on his time there, "as a kind of sub-assistant on economic theory," he recalled having "exchanged apples for nuts in the best manner of Marshall."[45] He quoted the words of the governess to her pupil in *The Importance of Being Earnest:* "Do not read Mill's chapter on the fall of the rupee, my dear; it is too exciting for a young girl"; then observed: "I found that my attitude to economics was much the same, and that these austere heights were not my spiritual home."* Tawney soon left Smart's department and took the first important step in his career.

HE "FINDS HIMSELF" IN WORKERS' EDUCATION

Since 1905 Tawney had been on the executive of the Workers Educational Association (WEA). Albert Mansbridge, an intense visionary with a pioneer's courage, had started a movement to promote the "higher Education of Working People," which led to the founding in 1903 of the WEA. He

*Tawney confided to his diary (December 11, 1913) an attitude to economics which he continued to hold but did not later express so boldly: "There is no such thing as a science of economics, nor ever will be. It is just cant and Marshall's talk as to the need for social problems to be studied by 'the same order of mind which tests the stability of a battleship in bad weather' is twaddle."

recalled that one day, "R. H. Tawney, of Balliol, came to the office. He had been sent by Canon Barnett. He proved to be a most important acquisition to the Association. He counted not cost of time or energy too great for his service. It was due to him that in 1906 William Temple, then a young Fellow of Queen's College, Oxford, joined us and became our first President."[46] Thus the Balliol-Toynbee Hall grapevine brought to the WEA two of its three greatest figures. For Tawney it began half a century of institutional connection (he was on the WEA executive for forty-two years, and president, 1928-1945) that for many years meant more to him than even his connection to the Labour party, the London School of Economics, or the church. He had come to think that education, not charity, was what workers needed. And he chose the WEA, rather than academia, as the arena for his first sustained phase (seven years) of teaching and research. Life in the WEA made him a socialist; work in the WEA made him an economic historian. In turn, he gave tutorial classes in England the "spirit of comradeship in study" which was their genius.[47]

He also did much to plan the establishment of the classes. Four university extension departments already existed. But the new ferment in adult education raised demands for more regular and directed study for workers, and for a more class-conscious approach, which would link classes with the spirit of the mushrooming labor movement. In August 1907, at Oxford, a National Conference of Working-Class and Educational Organisations was held to map plans. Bishop Gore, Tawney's mentor, was chairman, and two key papers were read: "What Workpeople Want Oxford To Do," by Walter Nield, and "What Oxford Can Do for Workpeople," by Sidney Ball. Consensus has it that the views of Nield and Ball shaped the conference, but this is not the full picture. Five months earlier, Ball had written to Barnett, asking the canon for ideas and materials for his paper. Without Ball's knowledge, Barnett sent the letter on to Tawney in Glasgow. The rest of the story comes in words Tawney later penned at the bottom of Ball's letter:

S.A.B. sent me this to Glasgow. I wrote (I) suggestions for Ball (II) suggestions for Nield. Both used them at the Conference from which the Tutl. Classes started. Ball, not knowing the source of his and Nield's papers, commented with surprise and gratification on the similarity of their tone.[48]

The important conference report, *Oxford and Working-Class Education*, 1908, was in large part written by Tawney, though, as with half what he wrote, he did not put his name to it. Meanwhile, the Oxford Extension Delegacy went ahead in the spirit of the report, formed a joint committee of workers representatives and university men, and planned the first tutorial classes. Mansbridge promised the locals at Rochdale, an industrial cesspool with the glorious tradition behind it of the "Rochdale Pioneers" of the 1840s, that if thirty workers were ready for regular study, the necessary money and "the best tutor in England" would be found. He chose Tawney.[49]

Tawney was hesitating between journalism and teaching. Like others at Balliol in his time—Beveridge, R. C. K. Ensor, and Ivor Brown all went to write for papers—Tawney felt the urge the college gave men to write, to address a public on the issues of the day. Spenser Wilkinson, chief leader-writer on the *Morning Post*, had gone up to Oxford for his editor, Fabian Ware, to look for recruits. The master of Balliol put Beveridge and Tawney first on his suggested list of writers on social questions. But with a thought for the Tory views of the *Morning Post*, he added: "I am not sure that either Beveridge or Tawney are [sic] Conservatives."[50] It was a piece of Balliol understatement. Beveridge was nonetheless appointed leader-writer, and, soon after, Tawney became a contributor of educational criticism. It was the first step of Tawney's long march of fifty years across the pages of the English press, as (anonymous) watchdog of educational policy from the workers' point of view.

The *Manchester Guardian* was his main forum. Already in January 1908, at the end of Tawney's Glasgow period, C. P. Scott moved to get Tawney on its staff. Tawney confessed to Scott that the job would have "many attractions"; but he decided that "educational work had a prior claim." That very month he started his encounters with potters and weavers. Not commenting on events and reviewing history in a city newspaper office, but making events, indeed making educational history in grimy local halls; and making of himself a unique kind of scholar; in every way it seemed a wise choice.

He told Scott, however, that he would send occasional articles. It was four years before he found time for the first, on school clinics. By then, Scott was approaching him again, this time to be a leader-writer on labor subjects. Launched on his tutorial classes, and the research that the classes stimulated, Tawney again declined. He had too many "ties and obligations" in the field of "the higher education of working people."[51]

Tawney did take another newspaper job, but briefly. In July 1908, when he was back in residence at Toynbee Hall, he succeeded Beveridge as leader-writer on the *Morning Post*. But soon WEA teaching claimed him full time. The articles he published from now until the Great War swept him off were mostly either in the *Highway*, the WEA monthly begun in 1908—six articles, 1909-1912—or in scholarly journals: "Municipal Enterprise in Germany," in the *Economic Review*, 1910, "Economics of Boy Labour," *Economic Journal*, 1911, and two long and learned pieces on "The Assessment of Wages in England by the Justices of the Peace" in a German journal in 1913. In addition, he wrote pamphlets and essays on industrial and educational subjects; his two books on minimum wages; his book of documents, edited with Bland and Brown, which was intended for WEA classes but also won wide university usage; and his classic work of history, *The Agrarian Problem in the Sixteenth Century*. So teaching did not still his pen. In fact he wrote more, and some of it is very good, in the seven years he went around England lecturing to workers, than in any other seven-year period of his life.[52]

Tawney not only lectured to workers but listened to them. His statement that he learned more from workers than at college seems at first a polite exaggeration; as, too, his claim to have learned more from the workers than he taught them.[53] But he probably spoke the sober truth. *The Agrarian Problem*, one of the best books on English history written in this century, was dedicated to Temple and Mansbridge, as officers of the WEA. And though ostensibly a technical treatise, it is also a "book of a movement." In motive and thesis, it issued from the bowels of the WEA as Tawney was shaping the WEA in the formative years before the Great War. Tawney hit on economic history by accident, learned it on the road, and formed his theories on the sixteenth and seventeenth centuries in the course of a quest, begun by Caird's injunction, to see why England had poverty alongside great riches and to do something about it.

Tawney found himself in these years. Barnett had described Tawney's group as "wary of enthusiasm, but . . . expectant of a call which will take it out of itself."[54] The enthusiasm that Tawney could never quite muster at Toynbee Hall now gripped him. In tutorial classes he heard the call that took him out of himself. It could have been a lonely, tough life, but it suited Tawney. He was working things out inside himself, and he had but a dull eye for worldly splendors.

One reason why Tawney became a kind of prophet in the WEA—why a "whole generation carried the mark of his influence"[55]—was that people sensed his dedication, and the self-lessness that was its by-product. Mansbridge enquired of him when the Rochdale class was starting: "really have you thought that the fee of £20 and the fare from Manchester would scarcely cover your expenses if it does that. I know you do not care about that . . . I sometimes suspect that you are trying to kill yourself by work, and you think everyone else must be the same."[56] A measure of realism was pressed upon Tawney, and he was paid £40 per class, but still the money was modest and the work hard (in one season of nine weeks he graded, with elaborate comments, at least 523 essays).[57] Worse, the job was a Cinderella in terms of hopes for a good academic career.

His first two classes were at Rochdale, and Longton in the Potteries (seat of England's Pottery industry in North Staffordshire), but he soon added others at Littleborough, Wrexham, and Chesterfield. First from St. George's Road in Glasgow, and after he married Jeannette, from 24 Shakespeare Street, Manchester, where they settled, he would set out by train on Friday for Longton, teach, put up at the Crown & Anchor pub, go on next day to Rochdale for an afternoon class, and return Sunday, often mingling and chatting on the train with actors and actresses of theatre companies, gaudy with their dress-baskets and stage properties.

Tawney became a legend to his students and a book could be filled with stories and tributes. There was a certain poignant seriousness about the classes. A photo of the class at Chesterfield has Tawney looking unusually spruce; a neat hat, stout boots, moustache; a confident, racy air. His students, all older than he, are done up to the gills, some in boaters, all with vast stiff collars and ties. A general laborer in the Rochdale class, J. E. Henighan, wrote to Mansbridge about its first meeting: "Some forty students met for our first class including three ladies . . . At nearly half-past two Gill [class secretary] entered the room followed closely by a young man wearing the gown; he was the much debated tutor . . . My first impression was one of surprise, first at his youth, and secondly at the sweet affable charm of his presence. There was none of the academic manner about him; none of that air which is so inclined to freeze; he was one of us. We had expected the frigid zone; we were landed at the equator. Tawney is not a teacher: he is a man with a soul."[58]

There was a sense of excitement at new ideas which brought tension to the classroom. Henighan went on: "It was now question time, and an air of calm pervaded the class; most of the students seemed to be feeling their way, before asking questions or offering criticism. Suddenly a murmur arose, one daring spirit was firing a question; he was neatly answered. The effect was contagious, it was the great awakening." Loom-overlooker, spinner, velvet mender—these men had an awe of learning. They went about it, not as magpies picking up pretty bits of glass, but to raise themselves up, and to change England.

E. S. Cartwright (class secretary) captured the sense of intellectual adventure at Longton: "the class meeting is over, and we sit at ease, taking tea and biscuits provided by members' wives. Talk ranges free and wide—problems of philosophy, evolution, politics, literature. Then R. H. T. reads to us Walt Whitman's 'When Lilacs Last in the Dooryard Bloom'd'; this moves a student to give us his favourite passage from the same source: 'Pioneers! O, Pioneers!' Another follows, quoting from a poem of Matthew Arnold that evidently has bitten him . . . And for some of us as we sit listening, a new door opens."[59] It was all very different from universities, where Tawney found that many "make a darkness and call it research, while shrinking from the light of general ideas."[60] Different, no less, from the Working Men's Club at Bethnal Green, where Tawney had not been able to communicate or be communicated to. He had found a way to link life and learning; was not this true education?

Tawney did not look down on these men, for they were

teaching him the facts of economic life. His immense, detailed, correspondence with them—they would list for him the family budget, or describe incidents in the mine—shows Tawney on the way to becoming an economic historian. He was tough with them, insisting they write essays regularly, and some grumbled at this. He would not allow left wing eagerness to excuse error. A student writes that "profit should be done away with". Tawney comments: "Under any 'scientific' socialism, production would be carried on for profit—*necessarily*—tho' the profit is taken by the state for the common good. The only alternative is communism which has enormous special difficulties of its own." Tawney as a wizard with words tried to get the workers to write better: "The *style* of this essay is a bit groggy," he scrawls, "perhaps you wrote it in a hurry"; and he offers suggestions.[61]

The diffident Balliol scholar, from a family ignorant of the industrial north of England, with the added strangeness of the Indian experience, must have been shaken by what he called the "smitings" of blunt Lancashire workers. Greek verse and a Balliol accent cooked nobody's dinner in Rochdale. His letters to Beveridge of 1903, intellectually dilletantish, morally fastidious, might have come from another planet. It was not only a question of learning new facts; though he picked up many, and they gave him research leads, and put wings on his historical imagination. The challenge was existential as well, as it had not necessarily been when Tawney and Beveridge first went to the East End of London. When Tawney took a class, he became not only an educational, but a political figure in the locality. The secretary of the Rochdale class wrote of Tawney in his report for 1909-1910: "Moreover, he has established for himself a position in the town, especially among Labour men, and his withdrawal from Rochdale would be looked upon as a calamity by a far larger circle than the members of the Class."[62]

These potters and weavers were not the woodcutters of Grimm's tales, but Tawney's brothers, with children to feed, Englishmen with rights no less than he. His attitudes and his life-style were dented in his attempt to make learning a thing of fellowship. Tawney and Cartwright became good friends, and on Tawney's leaves from the front in the Great War, the two would go fishing in the Cotswolds. The youngest student in the Rochdale class, A. P. Wadsworth, also became

Tawney's close friend. They were associated through the *Manchester Guardian*, which Wadsworth rose to edit, 1944-1955, and they shared talk on the big themes of history, from the point of view of social moralists, which they both were.

All was not sweetness and light. At Longton, Tawney had trouble securing a place for the class to meet; one official warned him he was starting a "den of iniquity." This class had among its thirty-eight students a nest of members of the Social Democratic Federation (Marxist), who thought Tawney and the WEA were diverting workers, by objective studies, from fighting the class war. Tawney dealt with them as he always dealt with Marxists: coolly, and with argument. He spelled out his reasoning in comments on their essays. He thought them, as he thought Marx, intellectually precocious. He was also amused at their habit of dressing up to the nines, which was not his own. One Longton SDFer came to an evening gathering at a Balliol WEA summer school in top hat and frock coat, garb which his leader, H. M. Hyndman, thought apt for any public talk of Marxism. The air was thick with talk and smoke and nobody noticed, until too late, that Tawney had been blandly emptying his pipe into his ardent student's top hat, upturned on the table beside him.[63] After several years of friendly sparring with SDF critics in his class in Rochdale, Tawney must have been pleased to get this report, in a letter of 1913 from one of his students: "I may say that the members of your class, those whom it was said you were sent to sidetrack etc., are still the staunchest socialists in Rochdale."[64]

Tawney would sometimes grow depressed and also angry at the administering authorities, because of what he thought were sagging standards in the classes. "The work of the classes (except Rochdale)," he suddenly wrote to Mansbridge in the spring of 1909, "has been most unsatisfactory." Tawney felt he had no time to prepare, examine students' essays properly, or spend sufficient time with students to make the classes truly "tutorial." He even wrote: "If I visited the classes as an impartial visitor, I should say that they are humbug, and so I think wld you, or anyone who read the report and knew what we had in our minds." He declared: "I cannot face another winter like the last," and vowed that unless his classes were limited to no more than four each week he would resign. His tone to Mansbridge grew sharp with exasperation at the threat to tutorial classes as he had envisioned them ("there is no call for you to answer this letter, provided that you attend to it").[65]

J. A. R. Marriot, secretary of the Oxford Delegacy, later a Tory member of parliament, was not entirely happy with Tawney's appointment as first tutor, and Tawney's toughness, almost roughness amidst ensuing tensions would surprise those who think of him as genial and absent-minded. Poor Mansbridge wrote back, in January, 1908, to one of Tawney's blasts: "If your letters increase in acidity, you will find me knocking at your door one morning before many days are over." At the end of March he asks why does Tawney "lay down the law so beastly emphatically," and pleads with him not to reveal "your unnatural fighting attitude to your natural enemies. Don't jump on me because I am flat and spiritless already."[66] The issues were not petty or personal but ones of principle, and on issues of principle Tawney could be fiery.

Within the WEA, two outlooks now and then clashed. Mansbridge, a religious man, thought of education as spiritual emancipation of the individual. Others, such as J. M. Mactavish who succeeded him as general secretary, saw education more as a weapon for the political advance of the workers ("I decline to sit at the rich man's gate praying for crumbs. I claim for my class all that Oxford has to give").[67] In its first years, the WEA had on its letterhead: "Unsectarian and Non-political." Soon "Non-political" was changed to "Non-Party in Politics." Class-conscious militants pulled further away from the Mansbridge position, asking full political partisanship. This made some universities nervous about their WEA link.

Mansbridge was terrified that the unions might take over the WEA. In this situation Tawney was a splendidly effective bridge. His scholarly standing made him able to calm the universities, and he kept the intellectual standards of the WEA high. Yet he leaned to the political rather than the cultural view of the WEA's task, especially when the issue came, as it later did, to whether the WEA existed for the workers or for all classes. (At one debate over having middle-class people at classes, someone said, "Of course we should have them, just like any other class; God made the middle-classes," and Tawney enquired: "Are you sure?")[68]

Tawney and Mansbridge often disagreed sharply on both educational and political issues. When a book on adult education was being planned in early 1909, Tawney tore into Mansbridge's proposed outline of a series of essays. These authors "will produce merely pious platitudes about how nice it is for people to be educated. In fact a collection of essays of this kind would be mere gossip, which is not only useless but debauches the mind." This letter to Mansbridge sums up: "The scheme you have drawn up is typical of the worst kind of Dillettantism that has flourished so long in the University Extension Movement, and which will invade the WEA unless you are careful."[69]

Tawney's firmer political commitment and his concern for substance not the package is brought out in another controversy with Mansbridge, over whether or not to appoint Richard Acland to the WEA's executive committee. Tawney's arguments against having Acland are worth quoting at some length. "He would be by far the best-known among us. People glancing at the list wld say, 'Hullo, here's Acland' and forget everyone else." It was not personal but political considerations that motivated Tawney in this disagreement: "as Acland is known mainly as a keen liberal, his inclusion (without the inclusion of an equally *well-known* Labour man) would in fact give us the appearance of having a liberal bias." Tawney made clear in this letter to Mansbridge the difference he felt in their respective standpoints: "as a socialist, which you are not, I hear a great many comments on the WEA which you do not hear. I am sure that, if, on being asked 'who's the best known man on your committee?,' I had to say 'Acland,' we should lose the sympathy of several influential socialists, who might help the cause infinitely more than Acland can." Tawney's parting suggestion is acute and typical of him: "If he [Acland] wants to help us, he can help us a lot quietly without joining our E. C."[70]

During his tutorial class years Tawney made the incalculable contribution of a pioneer, and these years fixed many of his attitudes. His rigorous pattern of classwork became the WEA ideal. The early classes yielded unnumbered fruits. Out of the Longton class, to mention one, Tawney and Cartwright fashioned the North Staffordshire Miners Higher Education Movement. Members of the class carried the work—themselves as teachers—to small villages. Mansbridge wrote to Cartwright: "It really means the beginnings of a Potteries

College." Thirty years later, a letter from Tawney to Cartwright, and another from Tawney to the North Staffsordshire WEA, opened the consultations that led to what is now the University of North Staffordshire.[71]

During five years residence in Manchester, among the happiest of his life, Tawney made key friendships. With George Unwin, the first professor of economic history Britain had, to whom Tawney owed a "debt beyond acknowledgment" for his example of the life of an intellectual, and for counsel, as when Tawney went to spend a night of talk with him before leaving to fight in the War. With Ernest Simon, rich and liberal, who admired Tawney, and found unobtrusive ways to ease his lack of money.[72] With T. S. Ashton, later Tawney's colleague in history at London; D. T. Shackleton, of the Weavers Amalgamation, to which Tawney was friend and advisor; Fred Hall, a Rochdale student, afterwards a professor, and advisor to the Co-operative Union; William Mellos, secretary of the Manchester and Salford Trades; George Mall of the ILP, of whom Tawney remarked that he was "an anarchist who later degenerated into an Alderman."[73]

In Manchester he kept a diary—alas, for less than two years—concerned above all with the march of his thoughts on moral principles and the social order.[74] It is earnest and acute, vigorous in aspiration, sharp in argument, with little of the brittle filigree that gives a ponderous touch to the late Tawney. Experience with the worker-students had planted the seeds of his socialist ideas: "What I want to drive home is . . . that the man who employs governs . . . He occupies what is really a public office"; and inspired an ironic line on the gulf between theory and practice: "The true history of St. Paul: He was offered a Professorship at Athens, which he accepted, and became a distinguished writer on the New Morality, the Conflict between Science and Religion, and the substantial identity between Greek Philosophy and Christian Thought."[75]

He stored up a remark which Cartwright had passed on to him. "I don't know what things are coming to," said an official of Christ Church, where some students from tutorial classes were staying during a summer school. "I saw a letter addressed to my butler the other day, and it had 'Esqre' after his name! I said to him: 'John, what do you mean by receiving letters addressed 'Esqre.'? Kindly see that they are addressed properly in future.' " He reflects on the way "standards" are determined by economic arrangements: "A great many poor people are 'inefficient.' This means that they do not correspond to a standard of efficiency erected by their masters, the rich. Why the devil should they?"[76]

Tawney was finding his values, thoughts, and style. When in the 1930s Bloomsbury lights wrote a manifesto proclaiming their views, and Tawney, asked to sign, declined and enquired "Why should anyone listen to you?," he was blunt because he had learned that only experience of industry gave someone the right to map solutions for industry's problems.[77] Perhaps Tawney generalized too readily from his tutorial class students to the whole English working class; they were in a way an elite. Perhaps he also came a bit too close, in this period, to believing education was the royal road to socialism.

WAR: "I SUPPOSE IT'S WORTH IT"

The last entry in Tawney's Manchester diary was a sustained passage about war and capitalism. "There are no mechanical arrangements by which men who regard society as a struggle for existence can be prevented from fighting."[1] Suddenly he was himself fighting. The marching music, horses, and banners made the war seem exciting at home. Tawney enlisted, declined a commission, and went off as Private Tawney to the front in France, where there was little excitement but much carnage. He joined the Twenty-second Manchester Regiment, though he had already come back to London to be director of the Ratan Tata Foundation, endowed by an Indian millionaire for the study of poverty. For three months he returned to Toynbee Hall, while Jeannette was apparently unwell and elsewhere. Then the Tawneys moved to Mecklenburgh Square and never left it for long. For fifty years in this quiet but central niche in Bloomsbury, Jeannette hovered over a ménage of total chaos, which no one set adrift in it even for a day could easily forget.

Once more Tawney found the world surprising. In the new, far worse arena of war, he saw and felt things, as in the East End and the industrial towns, for which his kind of Victorian upbringing had in no way prepared him. Again he was toughened, again his moral stature seemed to grow. But in between lay bitter things, mental anguish, and injuries which brought him to death's door.

Walter Moberley, who was in the same Greats class as Tawney at Oxford, and who went to war as an officer, recalled: "When it was clear everyone was needed, and not just the suitable people, I went in."[2] Tawney was not a "suitable person" for battle, but he did not hestitate to enlist, because it did not occur to him to doubt that if England had to go to war, he personally must go to war. Tawney was not a pacifist. No perfectionist ethic ever won him. Nor could his mind accept the spectacular gulf the pacifist sets between war among nations, on one hand, and the muted social and economic war within a nation, on the other.

In *Democracy or Defeat*, a stinging pamphlet he wrote after coming back to England, Tawney criticized "patriot" *and* "pacifist." Both "mistake the vehicle for the spirit." Patriotism, as a force nerving men to fight, lasts but a few weeks in the trenches. War drives home to soldiers not their national distinctiveness, but their common humanity. So they feel there must be some *principle* at stake in the war. Pacifism does not recognize that most wars, being more than a mere cockpit of nationalities, involve the issue of what kind of social order men are going to live under. "What will become of the world if Germany is victorious?" an old French peasant asked Tawney, and he was impressed by the question. He thought a war against oligarchic, militarist Germany clarified and sharpened the challenge to build social democracy in England.[3]

The war had to be fought; in an evil world such things come upon nations. But he fought with no sense of exhilaration. The moral peril of fighting could only be justified if England fought not just for England, especially the complacent England of 1914, but for principles that went beyond her national self; for the sake of a new England, which could be the fruit of victory, and was not less the condition of victory. She would win only if she could inspire for the effort, not those "who chatter in lobbies or lounge in clubs," but those "who sweat half-naked in the mine and at the forge."[4] Equally, she would only deserve to win if the peace attained was put at the feet of those in the mine and at the forge, by replacing acquisitiveness with fellowship as the rationale for the social order. One may read Mao Tse-tung and Lin Piao, yet still feel that nowhere is there a better statement of what "people's war" means than in Tawney's *Democracy or Defeat*.

If there was sometimes a trace of romanticism in Tawney's view of workers in the Rochdale and Longton days, it vanished in the war. His belief in the equal value of all men never wavered throughout his life. The slight change is that, after he returned from the Somme, he was never tempted to forget that workers were sons of Adam no less than anyone else. A year with the British worker, Tawney wrote to Beveridge by candlelight from the front in 1915, "has taught me a good deal, among other things that his philosophy, as much as that of his masters, is 'get as much and give as little as you can.' "[5] He saw that being exploited is no guarantee of virtue; that the moral values on which he was erecting his social principles were not the exclusive possession of any single group or class. He poignantly related to Mary Stocks his surprise at finding that in the army, *"No one assumed I told the truth."* He could no longer be sanguine that "nurture" would speedily win all her battles with "nature": "one can't change the habits of four or five generations in a year or two." The war made Tawney firmly realistic about human nature. No shimmering image of an artisan hungry for knowledge above all things, but "Henry Dubb," the unheroic, good-hearted "proletarian fool," is the worker he kept in mind from the 1920s on.[6]

Tawney developed a liking for France. After his negative remarks to Beveridge about British workers, he added: "In France there is not the same problem. For one thing the economic conditions of the peasant proprietor, of whom I've really seen quite a lot at first hand, don't produce quite the same commercial outlook on all human affairs." There was a second reason: "the fact that less than a century and a half ago there was a brief moment when masses of Frenchmen were really disinterested enthusiasts—the charm of the opening year of the revolution—has given a kind of potentiality of [greatness?] which we haven't got." He went on to say, "on the whole I prefer to think of myself as fighting for this country than for England. If I survive and can scrape together enough cash, I would like to settle down in France a bit. They have not 'made a bargain with fate' to the same extent as we have." An aching doubt about what England was fighting for seemed to outweigh, for a moment, the deep feeling he had for his country and his vocation for WEA work and researches in economic history.[7]

His admiration for France endured. "I think that France is the best country," he said after World War II, dining with Lionel Elvin just before Elvin went to Paris as a UNESCO official. "It is the country where they do the best things best. If I think of an ideal peasant, a peasant as such, I think of a

French peasant. If I think of a true professor, as a professor should be, I think of a French professor." But his esteem for the intelligence of the French did not continue to obscure from him the injustices of French society. Being shown over a handsome French estate, in a party of visiting economic historians during the 1940s, Tawney, after listening to an imposing catalogue of its splendors, was asked his impressions. "It was all wrought from the blood of the peasants," he growled.[8]

One day in July 1916, at Fricourt, Sergeant Tawney was trying to organize the remnants of a battered company to rush a trench.[9] It was the first day of the advance on the Somme. Crawling low, he called out to a nearby knot of men: "reinforce." They did not move. Tawney, not knowing they were either dead or wounded, knelt up to wave and call again. A shot went through his chest and abdomen. He thought, "this is death." Groping around, his weak fingers closed on the nose-cap of a shell. It was still hot, and he said to himself, "this is what has got me." A lad wriggled up to him and asked: "What's up sergeant?" Tawney mumbled: "Not dying, I think, but pretty bad." The lad wriggled on. Tawney lay there in pain, his tin hat over his eyes. He called feebly for stretcher-bearers. "Of course, it was imbecile and cowardly . . . But I'd lost my self-respect." Short of water, he rummaged for an acid-drop in his tunic; "the gift, I suppose, of some amiable lunatic in England." It made him feel sick.

From Mecklenburgh Square, Jeannette telegraphed to Beveridge: "Harry wounded Sunday sent base please try ascertain particulars." Beveridge used his government position to send priority telegrams. Tawney had lain in the open for two days, after being hit by a machine gun. Jeannette was summoned to France, but Tawney was a strong man and he survived.[10] Back in an army hospital at Oxford, Bishop Gore came to see him. Not being an officer, Tawney had been put to convalesce in an inferior establishment—a "workhouse" he called it.[11] His bed was a mosaic of books and pipe-ash. The matron found him willful, and was surprised to see a bishop visiting such a scruffy character. Gore said to her as he left: "Remember you have in your care one of the most valuable lives in England." The matron hurried to Tawney's bed and scolded him: "Why ever didn't you *tell* us you were a *gentleman?*"[12]

When Tawney began writing again, he first did several pieces on the war in *Athenaeum, Nation, Westminster Gazette*, and *Welsh Outlook*. This last one, an ardent appeal to make war aims really democratic, so ordinary men could fight full throttle for them, came to Lloyd George's attention.[13] Tawney looked back on Fricourt; 820 Britons had attacked; "we lost 450 men that day . . . and after being put in again a day or two later, we had 54 left. I suppose it's worth it."[14] Standing on a world of graves, Tawney burst with things to say. He sought to make the peace something for which the war could be judged worthwhile. The themes he talked over with Clement Attlee behind hedges in France, he now began to hammer into policies.[15] The next decade was his most vigorous in public activity and political writing. He now became not only a WEA, but a national figure. As a spring-board into the issues, he sought to tie the case for socialism to the impulse for postwar reconstruction. "It is very nice to be at home again. Yet am I at home?" He wondered if English soldiers had not "slaved for Rachel" only to come back and have to "live with Leah." He picked up the themes which had closed his diary on the eve of leaving for France. If the horror of war is to be ended, the horrors of peace must be ended. He addressed his fellow countrymen while the war was still on: "Every inch that you yield to your baser selves, to hatred, to the materialism which waits on spiritual exhaustion, is added to the deadly space across which the Army must drag itself to its goal and to yours." Arbitrary power, greed, "might makes right"—these were evils of industrial life hardly less than of international life.[16]

PUBLIC FIGURE: MINERS AND BISHOPS

After convalescence in various spots—at the bishop of Peter-borough's, with the Simons in Hereford—he worked at the Ministry of Reconstruction and did effective work on its Adult Education Committee. He urged educational reforms: in the Consultative Committee of the Board of Education (which he remained on until 1931); through the Labour party; and in articles in the *Daily News, Saturday Westminster*, and the WEA's *Highway*. H. A. L. Fisher has paid tribute to Tawney's influence on his important Education Act of 1918.[17]

He stood for parliament for the first of several times at Rochdale in 1918. He was not successful, and though the Webbs and others had in mind a political career for him, he probably was not suited for it. Balliol made him a Fellow in 1918, though he never intended to take root again in Oxford, and within two years he had begun his thirty-year stay on the staff of the London School of Economics. In the WEA he was active on the Executive, writing for the *Highway*, and (from 1919) as the association's first resident tutor in North Staffordshire.

His thoughts on the social order crystalizing, he wrote "The Sickness of an Acquisitive Society" for the *Hibbert Journal*. Soon expanded into the famous book, it was a development, in less philosophically idealist terms, of the thoughts on social principles he had confided to his diary and put into a book outline, "The New Leviathan," before going to the war. *The Acquisitive Society* was one of the great books of the 1920s. Margaret Cole called it "perhaps the most powerful of all post-war appeals for socialism."[18] One lady of a deeply Tory family, whose brother was in Conservative cabinets after World War Two, read it by chance and has voted Labour ever since.

Tawney began a long string of tasks as advisor to and advocate for workers, making him the British socialist intellectual best in touch with the unions. Threatened with a miners' strike in February 1919, the government set up a Royal Commission on the Coal Mines. Tawney and Sidney Webb were among the six men representing the labor side. Among many such experiences—he joined the Chain Trades Board the same year—it was the Coal Commission which affected his thinking most. In its thousands of pages of testimony, Tawney can be found probing points that became themes in *The Acquisitive Society* and *Equality*.[19] The commission, chaired by Justice John Sankey, and addressed by every leading authority on the industry in England, turned Tawney into a national figure.

The commission's debates, in which the miners' side argued for nationalization, touched basic principles; its sessions were likened to the tribunals of the French Revolution. Tawney dazzled with an impressive blend of moral sense and acute argument. It is no surprise to find in Beatrice Webb's diary: "Sidney has come out of the Commission with a great admiration for Tawney, for his personal charm, his quiet wisdom, and his rapier-like intellect. Tawney has in fact been the great success of the Commission."[20]

The class character of English society hung in the air as a tangible force. Owners were referred to as "masters," the producers as "men." The chairman, fixing procedures, recognized that the commission could not sit long hours, because people have to get to "their home in the country." Mr. Balfour, of the owners' side, had to absent himself because "My horse fell with me." Smillie, with his rough eloquence, was like an offensive bulldog in such an atmosphere, and Tawney complemented him with learned supplementary questions.[21]

From the problem of getting to their country homes, the owners passed on to talk about the homes of the miners. A witness was asked if miners' homes have bathrooms. "No, that has not been necessary, because in this district we are very short of water." Confronted with the argument that "a bad tenant makes a bad house," Tawney was roused: "Do you suggest that a bad tenant succeeds in reducing a four-roomed house to a one-roomed house?" Tawney poured irony on a spokesman for the owners, Mr. Scott, who, interfering in the business of the commission of which he was not a member, kept quoting the interim minority report, which Tawney happened to have drafted, back at the commission. Tawney drily observed: "I'd go so far as to say I'm even familiar with the report which he's read." When Scott interrupted yet a further time, Tawney referred to Mr. Scott, perhaps with deliberate mockery, as "Sir Leslie Scott."[22]

Years before, Tawney had carried on correspondence about working conditions with miners in Burnley, Padiham, and other places.[23] This labor bore fruit. No one had realized, until Tawney explained it, that in discussing working hours per day, allowance ought to be made for the one to two hours traveling time miners in North Staffordshire needed to get to the pits. He stopped in his tracks a medico who was showing that miners are healthier than most workers; the doctor had overlooked the fact that only the healthier men are able to become miners in the first place; and in 1913, after all, did not an average of three men a day die in the coal mines of Britain?[24]

Tawney argued that economies could be made in production and distribution, which might make it possible to shorten hours without putting up coal prices and losing export markets. Sir Daniel Stevenson objected that if improvements were made competitors would do the same! To which Tawney rejoined: "It was not an argument against putting in a spinning mule, that Germany would do the same."[25] He impaled a representative of the Coal Owners Association on the issue of absenteeism. "Have you got the figures of the loss of output due to management sending the men home for want of work?" Mr. Gibson answered that he could speak only of figures which exist. "Do I understand," Tawney innocently returned, "that the management keeps records of absentee-ism on the part of the men, but keeps no records on loss of time due to faults of management?"[26] Such ripostes were telling, both in the short term, in swinging Sankey against the owners, and in the longer term, in discrediting in the public mind the arbitrary power of capitalists.

One owner argued that high profits are justified, even when wages are very low, because they are due to good management. Tawney enquired whether large profits go to managers or shareholders, whereupon the owner conceded lamely: "Generally to the shareholders." Gradually opinion swung toward the side of labor, and the owners grew surly as Tawney grew cocky. There was but desultory resistance to the case Tawney built up against "functionless property" (to be a major theme in *The Acquisitive Society*). A mining engineer was asked what exactly the mine-owner is paid for. "He is paid for his property." Tawney resumed: "That is to say the royalty is simply payment for a private right quite irrespective of any function which is performed or any work that is done. Is that a fair statement?" The mining engineer could not deny Tawney's logic: "I think that is fair." When Tawney asked whether a man *should* be paid for mere possession, the mining engineer was reduced to an appeal to precedent: "Yes; I have always been brought up under that idea."[27]

Tawney harried another hostile witness on the same issue. A Mr. Rhodes stated that the owner is paid "because under the law of England he owns the coal. That is the reason I gather he is paid." Tawney asked: "Do you think it is a good thing that people should be paid if they perform no function?" Mr. Rhodes was out of his depth: "I should not like to answer that question." As the case for nationalization built up Tawney taunted the owners' side with their bland negativism. Pressing Sir Hugh Bell on alternatives to nationalization, he elicited the response, "I want hearty co-operation between the two parties." Tawney brushed aside the helpless moralism of this "solution," paraphrasing it as "Be good, and you will be happy," and branding it unsuitable for an industrial crisis.[28]

Thirty years afterward Tawney looked back on the commission in a speech before the LSE Students Union: "Our opponents, though forcible people, were not skillful advocates. In fact as far as mere dialectics were concerned, one could go through them like butter."[29] Tawney was amused when the *Saturday Review* claimed, after his performance on the commission, that his teaching at Oxford was "not merely an academic but a national outrage."[30] But he was not amused when the commission's report (urging nationalization) was left to one side for twenty-five years, until the Attlee government at last implemented it. This delay taught Tawney a lesson. He concluded that without political power, the labor movement, no matter how many intellectual victories it might win, would not further socialism.

Tawney also took away from the Sankey Commission a dark view of capitalists, which stoked his socialist passion. Yet the coal-owners were an extreme case, in their social distance from the workers and their ideological myopia, and in the 1920s Tawney may have generalized from them a little too freely. In the late 1930s, when he was on the Cotton Trade Conciliation Committee, Tawney thought less badly of the employers. He found their speech, dress, manners, and some of their views close enough to those of the operatives for progress to be possible. The older Tawney modified not only the picture of workers he got at Rochdale and Longton, but also the picture of owners he got during the struggle sessions of the Coal Commission.[31]

THE LONDON SCHOOL OF ECONOMICS,
WITH DISTRACTIONS

Before settling down as a reader at the LSE, Tawney, in the spring of 1920, made the first of five extended trips to the United States, to lecture at Amherst College, Massachusetts.

Alexander Meiklejohn, president of the college, had gone to England to find three men "to stir us up at Amherst."[32] Tawney followed Ernest Barker. Meiklejohn, born in Rochdale of parents active in the Co-operative Society, admired Tawney, thought his views would be good for the students, and eventually counted him an "adored friend." "No other Englishman I have met," he later wrote, "has seemed to me so enlightened and so powerful."

At Amherst, Tawney lectured in the medieval history course, gave a seminar on "The Control of Social Development" and four public lectures in the Beecher series, on industrial, educational, and religious issues in Britain at that time.[33] Meiklejohn's comment on Tawney's visit could stand for many of his forays to America. His three months at Amherst were "very fruitful" and there were men "profoundly and permanently influenced" by the man and his message. At the same time, Tawney "was not easy in formal social relations. He played tennis with us, not very well, but happily. But casual conversation did not interest him, and, if there were differences of opinion, he often seemed abrupt." Tawney spoke here and there in New England, as at Clark College, in Worcester, Massachusetts, on the British coal industry, and he established connections at Yale, which he visited in May before sailing back to London.[34]

In 1924 he was in the United States again, at Williams College, also in Massachusetts, to deliver lectures which in 1925, by contract with the Williams Institute, were published by Yale as *The British Labour Movement*. The book conveys an effulgent view of its topic. Tawney conversed as a man aglow in the dawn of democratic socialism's great day. And he showed no doubt that Americans would and should take very seriously anything that happened in Great Britain. At Williams, Jeannette was present too. One faculty member recalls that she teased Tawney about his laziness in writing up his research: "Apparently she expected a volume every two years, if not every year."[35]

On religious matters, Tawney's conduct and opinions varied over the years. During the 1920s he was a discriminating satellite in the outer orbit of the Church of England. When he wrote on religion his topic was the church and the social order; no longer doctrine, religious feelings, and the ultimate grounds of Christianity, as in his pre-war diary. The basic issues were for him already settled. His faith is reminiscent of

Carlyle's words in *Past and Present:* "Our Religion is not yet a horrible restless Doubt . . . but a great heaven-high Unquestionability, encompassing, inter-penetrating the whole of Life."[36] His beliefs were uncomplicated. Perhaps for Tawney as for Richard Baxter in the seventeenth century, Christianity meant the Lord's Prayer, the Creeds, and the Ten Commandments. As he grew older, he seemed to believe more and more in less and less. He was a "once-born" not a "twice-born" soul. He seemed to have Heaven in mind when he talked about Earth.

For a time a lay reader, he would frequently but not regularly go to church, often taking his dog, less frequently his wife. From 1917, he and Temple were active in the "Life and Liberty Movement," a campaign to revitalize the church for new social tasks. At the end of the war, he drafted, with Bishop E. S. Talbot and others, the report on "Christianity & Industrial Problems" of the fifth of the archbishop of Canterbury's committees of inquiry. The *Church Socialist* hailed it as a charter for "a revolution in the world of industry"; conservative bishops, such as H. H. Henson at Durham, frowned on it and on Tawney.[37] In 1924 he took part, also with vigor and some impact, in the important Conference on Politics, Economics, and Citizenship (COPEC).

Tawney was a religious man and a social moralist more than he was a churchman, even at this time. His intimacy with Temple no doubt kept him nearer to the organized church than he would otherwise have been. Both of them figures in the WEA, both concerned with the church and the social order, they often talked to each other about things that mattered most to them. Once Temple went to see Tawney at Mecklenburgh Square, when Jeannette was away. Talk consumed the hours, and Tawney, thinking he ought to feed his guest, rummaged behind a shelf of books and pulled out some cold mutton cutlets. These they ate, ungarnished. The evening far gone, Temple went to sleep on two traveling rugs on a bench inside a bow-window of the front room. During the night, a suspicious police officer, seeing the crumpled form in the light shed by the street lamp, thought he ought to investigate. He did not expect to disturb the slumbers of a prince of the church.[38] Thus the informality of the tie between these two quite different Rugby old boys. The mutual influence was great. Intellectually, perhaps Tawney was an even greater influence upon Temple than Temple upon him, partly because Temple was more eager and able to rummage in Tawney's field of social questions than Tawney was to tackle Temple's discipline of theology.

One of Tawney's best religious articles, a review of the "COPEC Report on Industry and Property," was done for Temple's journal, *The Pilgrim*, in 1924. Others appeared in the *Hibbert Journal* ("Religion and Business," 1922) and the *Journal of Political Economy* ("Religious Thought on Social and Economic Questions in the Sixteenth and Seventeenth Centuries," 1923). There were also four articles on similar themes in the *New Republic*, 1921, 1924, 1926, and a piece in the *Manchester Guardian*, signed "An Anglican Layman," on "The Enabling Bill: What it Seeks to Do and Why," 1919.

Tawney was not a movement man, everlastingly in and out of groups. Maurice Reckitt, who was such a man, recalls Tawney's reluctance to get into movements and "talk round in circles."[39] Tawney stuck to the same few channels, and was in this organizational sense a conservative rather than an innovator. Occasionally he would give a speech to a religious group—to missionaries, or to the Student Christian Movement. His topic was often the need to apply Christianity not only to personal morality but to the structures of society. "In my experience," he remarked in a characteristic epigram, "those who say that what they desire is a change of heart usually mean that they object strongly to a change of anything else."[40]

One of Tawney's two most famous series of lectures, seed of an historical classic, was given to a religious audience. Friends of Scott Holland, whose socially aware Christianity had made its mark on Tawney at Oxford, endowed in his memory triennial lectures on "the religion of the incarnation in its bearing on the social and economic life of man." Their choice for 1922 fell on Tawney, and he created, after the usual agonies, a treatise of sustained eloquence on economic practice and religious thought from the Middle Ages to the seventeenth century.

Rejected as dull by the first publisher approached, *Religion and the Rise of Capitalism* (1926) quickly won sales into six figures, and in American, French, German, Japanese, Spanish, Italian, Polish, and Dutch editions became a book of world impact. Its critics have acknowledged its influence no less than its admirers. Professor G. R. Elton has said the book "greatly assisted in the decline of Protestant self-confidence and the consequent revival of Roman Catholicism, in the reaction against capitalism as an economic system, and even perhaps in the West's increasing inclination to relinquish world leadership."[41] In this eloquent essay, Tawney linked his religious concerns with the economic changes he had studied while a WEA tutor. Raising large questions, the book set an agenda for a generation of historical research. Equally, it dared the churches to recover the proper concern of Christianity with the whole range of social and economic life. The challenge to historians produced rich fruit; that to the churches came to little. Tawney's religious themes made more impact on his secular readers than his economic views did on his religious readers.

Tawney's hopes for the church sagged as time passed, and his theology slipped into unexamined corners of his mind. But he kept on trying to influence the social teachings of the church. With Temple, he attended, and read a paper to, the conference of the International Missionary Council at Jerusalem in 1929. There he showed impatience with the ecclesiastical nationalism of Asians, declaring that the Orientals "seem determined to go the European way to hell."[42] He was also a figure at the Oxford Conference on Church and Society, in 1937, writing for its Economics Section a memorandum urging churches to stop pouring holy water on the "counter-religion" of capitalism.[43] At the Oxford Conference, Tawney listened to an involved speech about the doctrine of the trinity by the archdeacon of Monmouth. Emerging from the hall, he said it was dull doctrinal stuff, "but the man did come down at the end in favor of nationalization."[44] The principles Tawney distilled from the gospel were out of line with capitalism; but as much so with communism. He devoted a *New Statesman* piece in 1935 to the latter theme, attacking the "servile cult of the inevitable" and the "doctrine that history is its own justification."[45] On a personal level, Tawney continued to have a religious impact on others, and there are people who say they became Christians through the example of Tawney's humility, selflessness, serenity, and sense of ultimate things.[46]

Yet such were the equivocations of the church on social issues in the 1930s that Tawney doubted it was any longer serving a Christian purpose. He used to complain to Joseph Fletcher, a young American clergyman who went to learn from him about Christian social thought: "You speak as if

Temple is representative of the churches. Unfortunately he is not."[47] Even Temple disappointed him when, elevated to the bishopric of Manchester in 1935, he resigned from the Labour party out of a desire to be impartial. Religion remained for Tawney the great heaven-high Unquestionability. But the job to be done, he felt, was political and economic.

Beatrice Webb was intrigued by Tawney's religion, and his goodness impressed and also bothered her. "What I am always asking myself" she wrote after a talk with him in 1935, "Is R. H. T. a convinced Christian or a religious minded agnostic? He is assumed to be a Christian: I have never had the courage or indiscretion to ask the question!" But she did inquire from him what he prayed about. Margaret Cole, who recalls this, observes: "I don't think she succeeded in getting him to tell her."[48]

In 1937, after the Tawneys had spent a weekend with the Webbs, Beatrice returned to the topic of Tawney and religion and made shrewd remarks: "How far is Tawney a believer in the supernatural? He deems himself to be a Christian and associates with Christian divines on those terms—but in all his sayings and writings, though never denying Christian dogma, he certainly ignores it. Anyway he profoundly dislikes and denounces the worldliness of the Anglican church and its toleration of capitalist exploitation." A year later she was with Tawney in her house when a broadcast came over the radio by a certain Dr. Mathews, "in defence of the Christian faith." Tawney refused to listen to it. "I dislike theology," he observed, and retired into the study with a book. The same weekend, Beatrice asked Jeannette about Tawney's religion, and was told that he "takes the sacrament on Christmas day" but was not a regular church goer. The last of many entries in Beatrice's diary on Tawney's religion finds her still puzzled: "Altogether, in his religious opinions, he remains a mystery to his free-thinking friends."[49]

Jeannette, raised in the rationalism of the Beveridge home, was not religious. Beatrice Webb noted in 1938 that Tawney "has never tried to convert his unbelieving wife to his faith." A few years later, however, it appears Jeannette did become a Christian. In Chicago, where Tawney was lecturing, she came under the influence of an Episcopal priest, Bernard Bell (at one time a friend of T. S. Eliot) and joined the Church of

Tawney at an adult education summer school in Oxford, 1927.

England. Tawney told a friend this was something he had hoped for all his life.[50] During the last years, when Tawney went to church more frequently than for several decades, Jeannette was often with him.

Throughout the 1920s, Tawney did not let his academic duties keep him from politics, journalism, and public activity. In 1921 he joined the Fabian Society executive, and three years later was chairman of the society's fortieth anniversary dinner. Only in 1933 did he leave the Fabian executive, when along with many others he found the society inadequate to the times. Although foreign affairs was not a major interest—until the clouds of fascism and war gathered in the later 1930s—he joined the Union for Democratic Control, and served on the Labour party's Advisory Committee on International Questions.

Twice in 1922 Tawney stood as Labour candidate for Tottenham, at the by-election and the general election. Just before the general election campaign he was so ill (war wounds complicated a gall bladder operation) that Laski wrote to Justice Holmes: "My friend Tawney, whose books you well know, is, I fear, dying; and unless some miracle happens I shall lose the friend that, you and Felix apart, has meant more to me than any men [sic] I have ever met".[51] Tawney recovered, though the war wounds caused bother for the rest of his life. In 1924 he stood again for parliament at Swindon. For the fourth time he lost an election. But not before he held an open-air meeting which chanced, because the road was under repair, to be near a small red flag placed as warning to vehicles. As Tawney spoke, a passing clergyman stopped to listen, hurried on, and in a moment came back with a Union Jack, which he planted with earnest determination alongside the "red flag." Later, in 1935, Tawney was offered a safe seat but declined it.

Opinions varied on his skill as a candidate. Years later Tawney remarked, "Long ago I fought 3 elections, and quite rightly was rejected with enthusiasm at all of them"; and he would warn friends who asked him to speak in their campaigns that he was an "electoral Jonah."[52] Yet once a Tory agent told his faithful not to ask Tawney questions at his campaign meetings, so effective were his replies. At any rate, no one doubted his brilliance as a drafter of Labour party statements. The manifesto for the 1928 election, which Labour won, was essentially Tawney's work. The title, *Labour and the Nation*, expressed his conviction that Labour should boldly present itself as a national, not a class, party, offering its socialism unashamedly as the best ideal the English nation could follow. The title was a landmark, some say a turning-point, in Labour's self-understanding.[53]

For education at all levels, Tawney did an astonishing amount. *Secondary Education For All* (1922), largely Tawney's, and two years later, his *Education: The Socialist Policy*, are among the major education statements in Labour history. Beatrice Webb said C. P. Trevelyan, first Labour president of the Board of Education, got his ideas from Tawney.[54] Yet forty-five years and the Wilson governments later, these ideas had been little surpassed and still not entirely implemented. Since 1920 vice-president of the WEA, Tawney was in demand to speak at educational meetings. In 1922, at Manchester, he addressed a conference of 156 trade union and labour councils, co-ops, guilds, and Labour party branches, attacking the Geddes Report, with its proposed cuts in education spending. "Certain sections of English society," he claimed, regard it as "a kind of absurdity that the children of the workers should be educated for any other purpose than effective industry."[55] He discoursed at Toynbee Hall (1924); to the Association of Assistant Masters in Secondary Schools (1926); to the National Educational Conference (1927). In 1925, at the Northern Educational Conference in Manchester, he called for better education for boys and girls aged eleven to sixteen. The *Times* reported: "Mr. R. H. Tawney raised a controversial point by suggesting that all fees should be abolished in municipal secondary schools, and a system of maintenance allowance, based on subsistence, should be substituted."[56]

With Ernest Barker and Sir Percy Nunn, he was the major formulator of the Hadow Report on "The Education of the Adolescent."[57] Subsequently, he traveled around the country explaining and defending this report, which, with its proposals for a universal system of secondary education, was the basis for the 1944 Education Act. At the Conference of the British Institute of Adult Education in 1926, he gave a lively paper on the meaning of adult education; in 1927 he spoke to the Imperial Education Conference about the WEA. He served on the Education Committee of the London County Council, and the London Library Committee.

Throughout the 1920s he wrote on education a great deal, in the *Highway*, the *New Republic, Manchester Guardian* (some sixty pieces) and, when there was a particular argument to be made, in obscure journals such as the *Schoolmaster and Woman Teachers Chronicle.* Seldom did he decline to write an introduction for someone else's work, however humble the author, if he thought it good and agreed with it.

Tawney's nonacademic activities kept him longer at the level of a reader at the LSE than as a "pure scholar" he would have been. Even when appointed professor, in 1931, he got the title but not the salary; part of his time was left free for activities outside the school. Tawney was at the LSE not only a teacher, but an "authority"; and because he was an authority, he was perhaps a slightly less brilliant teacher than he had been at Rochdale and Longton. The past, for Tawney, was a door to the present. If the historian "visits the cellars," he said in his inaugural lecture, "it is not for love of the dust, but to estimate the stability of the edifice."[58] The students who found him a great teacher were those, of whom the tutorial class members were not the only, but perhaps the supreme examples, who saw historical studies in the context of citizenship. To such students he was an inspiration, and he changed their lives. The older Tawney was less good when the occasion called for spontaneity than he had been in early days, and less good as a listener. Students also changed. In 1913, when he first went to the LSE, there were only 243 full-time students, and 1,789 part timers. Part timers were a bit like Tawney's WEA students; their learning was for living. But later the proportion of part timers dropped a lot.[59]

To all students he was a fine lecturer. He always had a script, done in his cramped handwriting, all loops and hooks, sometimes on the back of notepaper picked up in hotels, and he would declaim its rolling phrases with quiet intensity. He could steer gargantuan sentences safely to harbor because he had an unerring sense of the geography of a sentence, revealed in his meticulous punctuation. At the lectern, ash would drop onto his papers, and sometimes he would, when transported, thrust his still-burning pipe into a pocket of his tweed jacket already stuffed with odds and ends. Moments later, as he was absorbed with the Court of Wards or the cunning of Lionel Cranfield, smoke would issue from him, while students watched in silent consternation. The fire discovered, Tawney would remark: "I see I burn prematurely."

Among students, he liked question-askers more than answer-givers. He was conscientious himself—his papers are full of lists of esoteric articles in many languages, like shopping-lists in a housewife's drawer—and he expected others to be so. But he could be soft with students whose heart was in the right place. Darts of irritation were reserved for those who seemed pretentious or complacent. He liked to talk over with students those questions of values which he thought economic history raised. The historian, in Tawney's view, is biased toward irreverence, for he has a "propensity for treating the most venerable institutions, from capitalism to university curricula, as historical categories." He thought history was a way to broaden the perspective of "the intellectual villager, who takes the fashion of his own day for the nature of mankind."[60]

Periodically Tawney worried if he was not, as an economic

historian, digging small holes and doing nothing to help mankind. Once he doubted to Ashton that his books had been worth the effort; perhaps he ought to have been a clergyman?[61] This sense of constantly questioning the human significance of scholarship Tawney communicated to his students. And he linked history to the streams and dales of the English countryside which he loved. At Rose Cottage, his simple stone retreat in the Cotswolds, he would take visitors from Stroud to the cottage, with its wonderful western views, recounting parts of the Royalist campaign in the Civil War as he walked, etching in local touches drawn from his own knowledge of the soil. To a student in London who needed a break, or a quiet place to work, he would give the key to Rose Cottage and tell him to disappear.[62]

Not a man of fixed method, Tawney spilt little ink on problems of methodology. He made into an art what he could not claim for science. Of the J. L. Hammonds, he said their "brilliance conceals their scholarship from those critics—a great host—who believe that, in order to be scientific, it is sufficient to be dull." Tawney was the same. He carried his erudition lightly. His methodology he came to by experience and reflection. He did not make it explicit, or try to hang it on his students. Discussions of method, he was prejudiced enough to believe, are like a Chinese drama which the spectator, after five hours of curtain-raisers, discovers is over just when he expects it to start.[63]

Tawney was not an economist, though he is often referred to as one. He knew Alfred Marshall's work well, but had little grasp of technical economics, and esteemed it little. "We all respect economics," he purred once to H. L. Beales, "It is a body of occasionally useful truisms."[64] His fight in 1926 (with Laski at his side) against Professor A. L. Bowley's scheme to make statistics a compulsory subject at the LSE was one of many such against "technical" economics.[65]

Among his colleagues on the faculty were Laski, who thought more of Tawney than Tawney did of Laski; Eileen Power (he edited several historical volumes with her) for whom his affection would be hard to overestimate; T. S. Ashton, one of many men he was intimate with despite big disagreements; H. L. Beales, whom Tawney brought to the LSE, but did not support for the chair in 1940 (Ashton got it)—Beales glimpsed an aloof, tough side of Tawney. In later years there was F. J. Fisher, an historical disciple; and Richard Titmuss, whom Tawney thought more highly of than anyone else at the LSE at the time he left it.

When he put his mind to it, Tawney could operate shrewdly in academic politics. "There are academics, with their high ideals," he once observed to Elvin when walking home from a WEA meeting, "and there are politicians, with their sharp methods. One knows both, and can accept both. But the terrible creature is the hybrid, the academic politican whose uses sharp methods while chattering his high ideals."[66] But Tawney was no fluttering purist himself. Over a number of appointments at the school he laid his plans carefully and acted firmly. Thus before leaving for China in 1930, he wrote to Laski at great length to make it clear why there should be no question that the vacant chair ought to go to Eileen Power, and the vacant readership to Beales.[67]

Among university organizations, he became president in 1921 of the new University Labour Federation (ULF). In 1926, he stood (unsuccessfully) under its auspices for the rectorship of Edinburgh University. He urged the USF to be a disturber of the peace of mind of academic institutions, so that universities might become an "intellectual seed-plot of a new and better social order."[68] The academic organization in which he felt most at home was the Economic History Society; he helped found it in 1926 and co-edited its journal, 1927-1934. Tawney stimulated a vast amount of research among members of the society, and himself published in its *Review* six articles, including his reverberating pieces on "The Rise of the Gentry." Due to Tawney's influence, the Economic History Society eschewed big hotels for its conferences, and met in simple surroundings where people could easily talk to each other. In later years, despite rising costs, he obstinately opposed raising the price of the *Review* and paying its editor a stipend. He seemed to think the subscribers were mostly trade unionists who would be unable to afford a penny more. His authority prevailed and only belatedly did the price of the *Review* go up and its editor receive payment.[69]

In the early 1930s, Tawney was twice enticed to China, which country provoked his intellectual curiosity, won his affection, and stirred his pen. The International Research Committee of the Institute of Pacific Relations (IPR) invited

Tawney to make a study of China's agriculture and industry, as a preparation for its Shanghai conference in 1931. By inviting Tawney, J. B. Condliffe of the institute hoped to stimulate a fresh approach to Chinese problems. Instead of perpetuating the prejudice of the missionary mentality, Condliffe felt, an historian versed in the pre-industrial economic history of Europe would provide a fresh angle of vision. Out Tawney went in late 1930, traveled and interviewed in Peking, Tientsin, Nanking, and other places for several months, and wrote a *Memorandum on Agriculture and Industry in China* as an IPR data paper.

His immersion in this subject surprised some of his friends. What fascinated him in studying China was throwing light on how much in a man's character at any point is part of his common humanity, and how much is due to the social structure he happens to be caught up in at the time. This mattered deeply to Tawney. As a moralist he held that men were often set against each other in a jungle of warring interests, and as a Christian he was sufficiently a philosophical idealist to hope that common, conscious ideals could create a "social purpose." Yet as a socialist he was sufficiently philosophically materialist to know that conscious ideals came not out of thin air, but filtered through circumstance.

He felt vitally interested in Chinese achievements which "lend lustre to a humanity which is our own." Perhaps China might show a way of esteeming moral excellence in an age addicted to mechanical efficiency. He also wanted to test a point he had thrown out in *Religion and the Rise of Capitalism:* "The conflict between the economic outlook of East and West, which impresses the traveller today, finds a parallel in the contrast between medieval and modern economic ideas, which strikes the historian."[70] Like Weber, who also wrote a book about Puritanism and a book about China, his eye for China was sharpened by much gazing on the origins of capitalism in Europe. Seeing the apprentice system and child labor in Tientsin, Tawney marveled at such a first-hand encounter with practices he had up till then known only through dusty documents.

In 1932 Tawney published *Land and Labour in China,* which drew on his *Memorandum.* A generally acknowledged classic of sparkling prose ("A general in control of a railway is like a monkey with a watch"; "The furniture of western society, which stands a sea voyage better than its spirit, was unpacked at suitable points on the eastern seaboard.") it was said by Sir Keith Hancock in 1946 to be "the best short book ... which any scholar of this generation has written about another country."[71] In China it was serialized in *Ta Kung Pao* and other organs, and had, according to a Chinese economist at Nankai University in a position to know, "a tremendous impact on the thinking and outlook of Chinese intellectuals and the enlightened Chinese public."[72]

Land and Labour in China had weaknesses. It stressed too much the role of intellectuals, was impatient with Chinese nationalism, and took insufficient note of cultural factors in economic development (such as expensive weddings and funeral rites). But on land problems it was frequently brilliant. "The revolution of 1911," ran one prophetic passage, "was a bourgeois affair. The revolution of the peasants has still to come. If their rulers continue to exploit them, or to permit them to be exploited, as remorselessly as hitherto, it is likely to be unpleasant. It will not, perhaps, be undeserved." So it *was* possible, even in 1931, to foresee the Nationalists' crucial weakness; Tawney did so. He judged, at the very time Mao Tse-tung was turning from the cities to build a movement deep among the peasants, that if China "may borrow its tools from abroad, for the energy to handle them it must look within. *Erquickung hast du nicht gewonnen, Wenn sie dir nicht aus eigner Seele quillt*" (you have not gained refreshment if it does not come out of your own soul).[73] Two years later, in his Earl Grey Memorial Lecture at Newcastle ("The Condition of China"), Tawney applied his view on the land issue to the appeal of communism (at this time very few people, in China or outside, thought or said anything at all about Chinese communism).

Tawney's second visit to China, September to December, 1931, was as educational advisor under the auspices of the League of Nations. At the request of the Chinese government, the International Institute of Intellectual Co-operation, instructed by the League's council, appointed a mission of four to go to China: Carl Becker, of Berlin; Professor P. Langevin, of the Collège de France; Professor M. Falski, of the Polish Ministry of Public Education; and Tawney. Through Eileen Power, Tawney had met Ludwig Reijchman of the League, who was greatly struck with him and placed

The Tawneys with Mrs. Franklin Ho in China, 1930.

him on the mission.[74] Tawney was by now fascinated with China, not its land questions alone, but its culture too. The monuments not yet improved out of recognition; the happy lack of "pert amenities"; the concrete earthiness of Chinese peasants. He also needed the money that would come as a fee. It seemed apt that in going back to China he should look at education, for the last sentence of his *Memorandum* had said that the "indispensable condition" of all he had urged for China was "the creation of a National system of Public Education."

Tawney later doubted the value to China of short visits by notabilities, though the mission's report, *The Reorganization of Education in China,* is thorough. Its members, however (Tawney not least), overestimated what could be achieved by a slow drizzle of education, in the absence of a thunderclap of political change. Tawney's total of eight months in China led to many less formal writings. Nine articles in the *Manchester Guardian*, charming excursions of an historian let loose in a new country; pedestrian pieces in the *Highway* and the *China Weekly Review*; an edited volume for the Institute of Pacific Relations on agrarian China, at the end of the decade.

In China he was quite a spectacle. Billed as a professor, but looking like an English squire, he would stride out to inspect a cow or test a bamboo rake. But as usual he had the style to move with the elite, even if he preferred to amble with the peasants (he considered himself a "peasant displaced from the soil"; so much for the industrial revolution). It seems that he carried himself in China just as he did in England. Despite the terrible heat of Nanking, he always wore tweed suits and resisted all suggestions that he buy light clothing, because that would mean *new* clothing. Seeing coolies hauling heavy carts in the street, he would provoke astonishment by seeking to lend a hand. Tawney came to be widely respected in China, but perhaps not widely understood. Yet he developed many associations, and when his friend Richard Rees visited China in the late 1930s, Tawney furnished him with references to an array of the Westernized elite, including Hu Shih, the liberal essayist, and Ting Wen-chiang, the geologist.[75]

Jeannette reveled in the East, as if something from her Indian past now sprang to life within her. Before the two of them sailed from Shanghai, she scoured the shops and pounced upon numberless trinkets—"antiques"—hoping to sell at a gain those she could not spread around at Mecklenburgh Square. Pearl Buck, in whose house the Tawneys lived at Nanking, recalled Jeannette's recurrent shopping sprees, and her own vain efforts to steady Jeannette's impulses by sending a Chinese woman with her on each expedition to the shops. To disguise her purchases from Tawney, Jeannette would deploy them about Miss Buck's house to make it seem they belonged there. When the day of departure came Tawney was furious on discovering the truth, and he watched in stony silence as twenty-seven boxes were filled with all manner of trumpery. Alas, Jeannette's judgment was as bad as ever. The ornaments turned out to be Birmingham brass, exported to China, worth nothing. The fee Tawney needed to pay his debts lay transmuted into useless bric-a-brac.[76]

3   SQUIRE OF HOUGHTON STREET, 1932-1942

POLITICAL TROUBLES

Politically, the 1930's were frustrating for Tawney. Tom Jones (his friend from Glasgow days, now a government aide) went to see him in March 1933. Jeannette was in Brighton convalescing, and Tawney made tea, borrowing three pennies from his visitor to put in the gas meter. Europe, Tawney said to Jones, was in the grip of a war of "Economic Religion." Between the drought of a toughening capitalism and the flood of communism, where could a social democrat and an educator stand? "Bridge-building, intermediate organisations like the W.E.A.," Tawney complained, find it harder to get support.[1] Unhappy with political trends, he lost prominence as a public figure. He spent more time on education matters, on historical research, and as an honorary peasant at Rose Cottage.

Political leadership lay with three mediocre men. Ramsay MacDonald, Tawney had long known and distrusted. The feeling may have been mutual. MacDonald is said to have dismissed urgings (in 1922) that he put Tawney in the House of Lords, as education spokesman, with a scornful remark about Tawney's shabby appearance.[2] McDonald did appoint Tawney to his Economic Advisory Council in 1930, but, though star-studded, the council proved ineffective. Few attacks on MacDonaldism were more influential than Tawney's essay of 1932, much reprinted since, "The Choice Before the Labour Party." Personally, the two men were as chalk and cheese: MacDonald, the insecure plebian, reaching up; Tawney, the unafraid patrician, reaching down. In Baldwin and Chamberlain, Tawney saw no hope (despite the curiosity that Baldwin's speeches now and then contained quotes from Tawney; the work of Tawney's friend and Baldwin's aide, Tom Jones). Churchill he came to admire, when foreign policy took pride of place; and he thought quite well of Lloyd George, whom he, together with Laski and the Webbs, used to meet through Haldane, when Lloyd George was prime minister.[3]

But, as usual, the faults of the children of light worried him as much as those of the children of darkness. It was the Labour party's lack of a creed, in Tawney's view, that was shown up in the debacle of the second Labour government; in the wild oscillations to the extreme left of fine idealists, during the "long silly season of the 1930s"; and in some Labour politicians' unsavory taste for "titles and such toys." His blasts against "labour honours" in the 1930s were angry. How can the Labour party persuade the nation it stands for an alternative society when its leaders "sit up, like poodles in a drawing-room, wag their tails when patted, and lick their lips at the social sugarplums tossed them by their masters"?[4] He did not talk about why he refused a peerage from Mac-Donald. To talk about declining honors would almost be like accepting them. But the note he sent back to MacDonald's offer must be one of the curtest notes a prime minister has ever received from a notability.

One of Tawney's major books, *Equality*, along with *Religion and the Rise of Capitalism* and *The Acquisitive Society* his best known, appeared in 1931, after originating as the Halley Stewart Lectures for 1929. Through the ribs of the English establishment, with its "religion of inequality," Tawney passed the rapier of irony more mercilessly than in any other work. *Equality* offered a principle for socialist policy to adhere to. Welfare-state incrementalism, Tawney thought, was no substitute for a socialist commonwealth. But though he was, as always, clear and strong on goals, the ideological polarization of the thirties found him lacking a strategy. *Equality* did not tell social democrats what to do about the thorny issue of cooperation, or not, with Marxists. Nor was it a guide to the problem of fascism. Was war the least evil course; were the communists key allies against fascism; should there be a *union sacrée*, to first ward off England's enemies?

In fact, mind and heart tugged at Tawney in different ways in the thirties. In the third, revised edition of *Equality* in 1938, Tawney came quite near to Laski's quasi-Marxist analysis of capitalism's crisis. Yet his disposition remained entirely social democratic. In sum, amidst the ideological polarization

The author of *Equality* at work on WEA affairs, early thirties.

of the Pink Decade, a gulf yawned between the goals Tawney set out in *Equality* and the way to get to them. Though the book sold well before World War II, it had meaning mostly for the postwar reconstruction, when the left re-embraced democratic methods. And Tawney acknowledged, in its fourth, revised edition of 1952, that the Attlee governments had made England a more equal society.

Equality was dedicated to the Webbs, whom Tawney saw much of in the 1930s. He had met them in 1904 or 1905, at 41 Grosvenor Road. He left their house wearing by mistake the bowler hat of John Burns. Beatrice, who was then cultivating Burns for some Fabian purpose, sent Tawney next morning a scorching letter about his laxity.[5] He and Sidney grew close during the Coal Commission, and over the years Tawney was often at Passfield Corner, where a social visit became a well-conducted seminar. In earlier days, Tawney felt the Webbs, especially Sidney, put too much faith in "mechanisms," and too little stress on the moral bases of socialism. Tawney did not think that fact-gathering plus the movement of history would together bring socialism. "No amount of conjuring," he noted in his Manchester diary, "will turn a fact into a principle."[6]

Later, he refused to follow the Webbs into the well-lighted abyss of Stalinism. In both areas it was his Christian basis, as distinct from their utilitarian basis, which made the difference. Yet Tawney learnt a lot about social investigation from the Webbs. And he was abidingly drawn to them because "each possessed the fire at the centre without which great things are not done."[7] With Beatrice he had even more affinity than with Sidney. She and Tawney both knew a certain turbulence of soul which apparently passed Sidney by. Tawney considered Beatrice a mystic, and said she never gave up prayer.[8]

During the weekend house parties there would be determined walks. The Webbs, observed Tawney, had the appetite for physical exercise "of a gryphon in the wilderness." At table, their appetite was evidently more modest. Tawney referred to "the famous exercises in asceticism described by Mrs. Webb as dinners." He pictured Beatrice, skirts turned back and crouching over the fire, admonishing, "Beware of dilettantism"; and Sidney, full-length on a sofa, with: "Above all, no intimacies."[9]

For her part, Beatrice records high regard for this "old friend of ours." "Tawney, with all his indecisions and contradictory aspirations," she wrote after a weekend they spent together in 1935, "has a noble and inspiring influence." In the 1920s, she had realized that Tawney's " 'proletarian' sympathies" much exceeded hers or Sidney's. In the 1930s, Tawney, anxious about the state of the Labour party, wondered to the Webbs whether he should leave the safe haven of the LSE and go into politics. By then Beatrice saw that he should not. "His task is that of a discoverer and an expounder of the new faith (economics based on service of man rather than exploitation of man by man) not that of a maneuverer or politician or even an administrator." She then put her finger neatly on a Tawney trait. "He is far too sensitive and fastidious . . . he always retires or resigns when he disagrees with or disapproves of the person with whom he is working." Later, she observed that Tawney was acquiring a pontifical touch, from long years of dispensing knowledge to students.[10]

Tawney did not agree with the Webbs about the Soviet Union. Never an anti-communist, he hoped the Webbs were right, but feared they were wrong, when they published their painstaking monument to Stalin, *Soviet Communism: A New Civilisation?* in 1935 (two years later it came out again without the question mark in the title). Beatrice claimed in her diary for 1938 that Tawney "is a warm admirer of our book [on Soviet communism]." But the judgment is seen in perspective when she adds that he "demurs to its cool acceptance of the cruelties of the liquidation of the rich peasants."[11] Tawney had an eye for the interests of peasants, which the Webbs had not (he visited Russia on the way back from his first trip to China). And he did not have the kind of mind that functions as if it had the agenda of history furled inside itself. He could not gaily mortgage present well-being for future glory.

In 1940 Beatrice had a "bitter tiff" with him over whether Moscow Radio lied more about the West, including the Labour party, than the BBC and the Labour party lied about Russia. Tawney admired the high degree of collective purpose in Russia, but he greatly disliked its bureaucratism and lack of freedom of the mind. "Tawney's contempt for our ruling class is more intense than ours," Beatrice poignantly and astutely summed up, "but he does not share our faith in Soviet Communism." Postan says that Gaitskell, Durbin, and himself, may have kept Tawney from "pro-Russianism." It seems more likely, given chronology and what is now known of Tawney's views, that *he* influenced Gaitskell and Durbin on this issue.[12]

In 1942, when the Webbs sent him their new book, *The Truth About Soviet Russia*, Tawney, thanking them from Washington, brilliantly predicted American hostility toward Russia.[13] Expecting the Cold War, and having limited faith in Russia, he was less shattered by the postwar polarization than were Laski and Cole. But he never became a Cold Warrior. His mind had no room for an ideology (as distinct from principles). And he would not follow Orwell into an abstract attack on so-called totalitarianism. "How does Orwell *know* Russia is so bad?" he said to Rees.[14] Of course, Orwell did not know much about Russia; he built (almost) a social theory on the basis of the mental posture of a tormented intellectual. Tawney was totally disinclined to do that.

A grey footnote finishes the story of Tawney and the Webbs. The Webb Trustees invited Tawney to write a biography of Sidney. Tawney accepted, and by the spring of 1949 he had collected much material. With his retirememt from the LSE imminent, he faced the task with some spirit. He had done two fine essays on the Webbs. "No one living," said Laski, was "so fitted" to do the "life."[15] But Margaret Cole, one of the trustees, had under way, unbeknown to Tawney, a biographical volume on the Webbs. When Tawney found out, he erupted, and gave up his project.

In June 1949, he wrote to Mrs. Cole, "astonished at your procedure." He felt that a trustee, when a party to an invitation to someone else to write the "Life," ought not herself to produce a book on the subject. "It was open to you," he reasoned, "to take the obvious course of asking my opinion on your project of producing a book on the Webbs, or, if you did not wish to do that, to inform me at once of your decision to produce one. You did neither." Mrs. Cole had, in assembling her volume, asked contributions, in the form of memoirs, from people who were to be among the major sources for Tawney's biography. Upset, Tawney wrote sharply to one of Mrs. Cole's associates and defenders of the "limits of my capacity to swallow humbug." His anguish is clear in his exchanges on the subject with his old pupil and confidant, Wadsworth, editor of the *Guardian*.[16]

Tawney, after all, had known the Webbs intimately, whereas the Coles had not always got on well with them. He may have felt, as Laski put it to him, that "Mrs. Cole has taken over [the Webbs] legacy as a permanent source of income." Laski ended his letter of sympathy to Tawney: "I am sure that could they [the Webbs] have been asked they would have felt that you more than anyone else were fitted to undertake that work and would have felt quite a special pleasure in knowing that you had done so."[17]

When Mrs. Cole's volume appeared, later in 1949, it had the title *The Webbs and Their Work*. Incredibly, in the circumstances, she had taken, letter for letter, the title of Tawney's own 1945 Webb Memorial Lecture! Tawney found mistakes in the biographical index at the end of Mrs. Cole's volume. He passed details of these on to Wadsworth, who commented, in his own review of the book, on its "fantastic errors." Three years later, in 1952, Tawney gave another lecture on the Webbs, published by the University of London, and he decided, with gentle assertiveness, to call it "The Webbs in Perspective."[18]

Turning to the political scene, we find Tawney dormant in the 1930s. In 1934 he drafted the Labour party's election manifesto, "For Socialism and Peace."[19] When friends asked him to campaign for them, as Patrick Gordon Walker did in the 1935 election, he seldom refused. Yet the tune of politics was not on his lips, as in the 1920s.

No political event swept him into participation as the General Strike had done in 1926. In those buoyant days he was in and out of the miners' (and other unions') offices. He claimed with glee that he started the General Strike. For one day in 1925, alone except for secretaries at the miners headquarters, he took a call from northern colliers asking whether they should go down the pits for the next nightshift. "No," said Tawney. The ensuing stoppage formed one link, he liked to think, in the chain that brought the General Strike.[20]

He wrote no book on political ideas in the 1930s to match the three of the previous decade. If he joined the Socialist League, he was hardly, like Stafford Cripps, a crusader for it. It was more significant that he left the Fabian executive in 1933, after twelve years on it, and that he wrote few political articles because he was not quite sure what to say. He declined endorsement for the safe seat of Clay Cross at the 1935 general election.[21]

It was the decade of Tawney as teacher. At the LSE; in the WEA; entertaining at his city flat or his country cottage. He hammered away at the seventeenth century, as fresh waves of students filled his famous seminar, "Economic and Social England (1558-1640)." Armed with Tawney's questions, they took up his historian's torch and lit new corners of Tudor and Stuart times.

Postan took Gaitskell and Evan Durbin to meet Tawney.* This group, with others (Eileen Power, sometimes Patrick Gordon Walker), would go to Tawney's flat and toss around the great issues of social democracy. Tawney wore his sergeant's jacket. His pipe he would empty into the cuff of his tweed trousers. Bits of half-eaten food sat among piles of books. Now and then a mouse would hop over the one to get at the other. But Tawney's imperious bearing was not shaken. This emperor of the realm of social values was as tolerant of small scandals as he was intolerant of big ones. Margaret Cole remembers Gaitskell washing teacups at Jeannette's bidding. Postan relates: "In [Tawney's] company we were prepared to sit and listen, amused by the wit and aptness of his language and enraptured by the image of the man himself, to us the greatest living Englishman."[22]

For Gaitskell and Durbin, Tawney was the best exponent of democratic socialism they knew. Tawney liked them because he thought they had character. Durbin, but not Gaitskell, shared Tawney's religious position. Both men thought for themselves, unlike some "automatic" people who shouted socialism from the rooftops. Both were unequivocally democratic. In 1938, when Professor Nef asked Tawney to recommend an economist whom the University of Chicago might hire, Tawney raised three eminent names: Lionel Robbins, D. H. Robertson, and Henderson. Then he put all three aside and urged either Gaitskell or Durbin, despite their youth. "Both, while good economists, have a humane outlook and wide interests. Neither is ambitious or on the make."[23] It tells us much of Tawney in the 1930s that, in an age of revolutionists and pamphleteers, the group he gathered round him were social democratic teachers. They

---

*Said Tawney on greeting Gaitskell: "Your face seems familiar somehow." In fact, during the General Strike, Margaret Cole had enlisted Gaitskell, then an undergraduate, to drive the activist Tawney from one appointment to the next, in Gaitskell's little car. (Postan, conversation with author, Cambridge, England, February 11, 1970.)

were not flashing comets of the 1930s, but after the war, when Labour had a chance to do something constructive, they were in the front rank. Thirty years later, Gaitskell looked back on his association with Tawney. He recalled, above all, Tawney's combination of learning and passion; his perfectly natural modesty; and that there was "nothing neurotic" about him.[24]

There was no Bloomsbury smartness about the gatherings in Mecklenburgh Square. Nor did they brim with ideological zeal. Nor, again, were they bands of intimates who peered into each other's souls. Tawney was too forbidding for that. Like others who came down the mountain of Victorianism, Tawney could be impersonal with others and a bit ignorant of himself. Rather, the talk was of history, economics, and how to change England without wrecking it. Tawney assumed, too readily, that his companions shared his underlying values. Perhaps it was bad form to probe them. It was as if an agenda existed—social tasks—and the unity of the group arose from the agenda. To go beneath or beyond the agenda may have put an end to the unity.

Tawney was not a clubman. Rather than sit in a club with his peers, he preferred to fraternize with random human beings. No matter what strata of society they were meant to belong to, or how unpremeditated the situation, Tawney would strike up a conversation which blended homely nothings with philosophic issues. Political views did not obscure a man's humanity from Tawney. The list of his friends is no sound clue to his own political (or religious) convictions. He liked Jack Horner enormously, without sharing the miners' secretary's communism; he liked Sir Arthur Steel Maitland, whom he roped into the LSE (eventually as chairman of the governors), despite Maitland's Burlington Club Toryism.

Many of his friends were liberals, like Ernest Simon in Manchester. There was, too, a cluster of socially aware historians who were close to Tawney. These men—Wadsworth, J. L. Hammond, among others—were not socialists. But they were moralists, and they sympathized with the working man. To these binding ties, a third was added. Tawney simply found them nice people, by which he meant people without humbug.

It was because he found them nice people, not for consonance of views, that he grew close to T. S. Ashton and

The Tawneys at their rural retreat, Rose Cottage, in Gloucestershire, during the thirties.

81 *Teacher, Colleague, Watchdog of Education*

Richard Rees. He would stay with Ashton near Oxford. Rees, who introduced Tawney to Orwell, talked with him of literature and religion. Pressing on Tawney books by T. S. Eliot and copies of *Criterion*, Rees found he had "excellent literary taste." He persuaded Tawney, in the 1930s, when Tawney no longer read much religion, to read Simone Weil, on whom Rees was an authority. Tawney was impressed. Rees parried a little; Weil was not an orthodox Christian, of course . . . Tawney came back: "The Christian religion is for bad people like me, not for good people like her."[25]

If Tawney was open-hearted to nice people he could be aloof to others. With the spectacular exception of Eileen Power, he did not warm to intellectual women, as Barbara Wootton recalls.[26] He seemed to prefer the company of dogs and fish to that of people he considered puffed-up or complacent. At Rose Cottage the "displaced peasant" in him emerged. Even history then became a thing not of books but of the soil; of dales and ridges, of old churches, of the serpentine memory of a shrewd Gloucestershire farmer. Out he would trudge with his sheep dog, to trade yarns at the Stroud pub. Professor Elaine Carus-Wilson, an LSE colleague of Tawney's, invited to Rose Cottage, reached Stroud, then set off on foot for Elcombe. Soon she spotted a roguish farmer sitting on a stile. It was Tawney, come, with his dog, to meet her. As the two of them strolled to the cottage, Tawney explained the links between local topography and the Royalist campaign of the Civil War.[27]

The cottage was a charming slum. There being no automatic toilet, a patch of ground near the dwelling could give off terrible odors. Tawney would draw necessary water each morning from a well. Jeannette in her usual fashion blended luxury with squalor. Postan remembers her overordering on strawberries and cream by a factor of ten; as the feast proceeded, dogs ate scraps from the floor. At her best and with circumstances favorable, Jeannette was no mean cook. Patrick Gordon Walker learned at the cottage to make an excellent omelette. In the outdoor henhouse Tawney kept his books. During the war, Tawney heard of working-class friends with no place to live, and telegraphed them to come to Rose Cottage. They came, with an unexpected bevy of children, and lived in the henhouse.

Tawney loved to fish. He used to stand with rod and line in long wet grass, wearing Jeannette's brocaded bedroom slippers. Characteristically, he preferred fly-fishing; shabby he might be, but his fishing style was aristocratic. Fishing gave him many a literary image. Criticizing Toynbee's analysis of civilizations as units, in a review of *The Study of History*, he observed that it is "not easy to put a hook into the jaw of these leviathans."[28] With villagers Tawney had cordial, equal relationships. Wadsworth's daughter, Janet, who helped the Tawneys move when they finally left Rose Cottage in 1955, remembers going with Tawney to say goodbye to a neighbor. He was a former miner from Wigan; proud, independent. As they shook hands there seemed a total equality in the tie between them. "The embodiment," Miss Wadsworth remarks, "of what equality has meant to me ever since that day."[29]

In London, academic and WEA matters claimed Tawney. Membership in the British Academy (1934) pleased him. It perhaps symbolized his increased preoccupation with scholarship, and his reduced activism in industrial and political matters. In 1932 came his inaugural lecture, "On the Study of Economic History." Two years later, with routine help from Jeannette, he did for the *Economic History Review* a study of employment in Gloucestershire in 1608, which showed that rural society and agricultural society are not at all synonymous terms. In 1936 he was Ford Lecturer at Oxford. On the basis of the manuscripts for this series, Tawney wrote up two major articles that appeared after war began. Meanwhile, he busied himself, often at the Public Record Office, with research on the career of Lionel Cranfield that only twenty years later issued in his last historical book, *Business and Politics Under James I.*

In the 1930s he also did much to help place refugee academics from Central Europe. Leo Strauss, to name one of many, came to Tawney with a recommendation from Henri Sée.[30] Tawney helped get him a temporary post at Cambridge, then later another at the New School in New York. Considering Strauss "the best scholar among the refugees whom I have had to do with," Tawney persistently tried to get the University of Chicago to appoint him. There was resistance, eventually overcome. Odd that a socialist should have helped a conservative theorist of natural law to reach his professorial pinnacle. Yet it was Tawney's habit to put a man's need and quality above his point of view. From the 1930s to the end of his life, Tawney continued to help refugees regularly, as his correspondence testifies.[31]

If in historical scholarship, 1540-1640 was "Tawney's century," in the WEA the 1930s was Tawney's decade. Elected president, replacing Arthur Pugh, in 1928, he held the office for the next fifteen years. He became the leading figure in adult education in England. With the WEA as his platform, and later as chairman of the Council for Educational Advance, he did a lot for the 1944 Education Act. His public voice pressured the government to act, as it had done with the Fisher Bill of 1918. His private counsels, offered to R. A. Butler and sometimes sought by Butler, shaped its action.[32]

With his pen he reinforced both approaches. He had once writted to Wadsworth: "The *Guardian* ought to do more on education. I don't care who does it, so long as it is you or I."[33] As it turned out, Tawney, at Wadsworth's instigation, became the *Guardian's* authority on education. Between his election as WEA president and the Butler Act sixteeen years later, Tawney published ninety-odd articles on education in the *Guardian.* Most were unsigned leaders; many helped sway public opinion on their theme; some had the impact of a grenade in the packed trenches of the educational establishment.

During the thirties he also wrote a string of long essays on education and public policy. Some were given as presidential addresses to the WEA. At this annual highlight of the association's life, Tawney would by turns lash, charm, and tickle his audience. These speeches he would memorize, disappearing to his hotel room the night before to do so, reappearing next morning to speak with hardly a glance at his text. Other essays were written to back up campaigns for educational progress; yet others were memorial lectures—the Sidney Ball Lecture in 1934 ("Juvenile Employment and Education"), the L. T. Hobhouse Lecture for 1938 ("Some Thoughts on the Economics of Public Education").

There were two frequent themes: he urged people who worked in education to be missionaries for educational advance, not just functionaries of the system as it stood; and he argued that you cannot have democracy without convictions, that education should help people to arrive at their own convictions. "If heads are empty," he said of the crisis in parliamentary democracy in his 1934 WEA address, "it matters little whether chairs are empty or full."[34] In 1937, as the lights began to go out all over Europe, he reminded his countrymen: "A bad system, with a high degree of vitality, will always defeat a better system without it. The source, and the only permanent source, of vitality is conviction."[35] Where better to foster it than in voluntary education?

More than any president in its history, Tawney was a working president of the WEA.[36] Ernest Green, general secretary while Tawney was president, would hear from Tawney the Monday morning after an executive meeting, and together they would plan how to carry out the decisions made. When he felt like it, as he often did in the WEA, Tawney could show a great mastery of detail. He was the key strategist in many struggles within the association. He forestalled Richard Livingstone's plan, which Temple and Cole supported at first, to build an adult education group that would not be specifically working class. Seeing the plan could not realistically be opposed, he shrewdly did not try to kill the proposed adult education group at birth, but castrated it later, by pushing it into a nonproviding role, as a harmless umbrella organization which did not itself give classes.

At a meeting early in his presidency, he got rid of a lady researcher whom he thought poor value, although the general secretary, Firth, backed her. Moments afterward he said to Green, who was at that time Firth's deputy, and, like Tawney, not impressed with Firth: "We've done one dirty job, Green, what about the other?" Green asked in a bland tone: "What do you mean?" Tawney said: "I mean Firth." Tawney had a plan; he went to talk with Firth; soon Firth resigned on grounds of ill-health.

The flat in Mecklenburgh Square became a WEA center. Green recalls transacting business there with Tawney at the lunch table, as Tawney, with measured concentration, tossed bits of liver from his plate to the waiting mouth of one of Jeannette's cats. One reason for Tawney's penury was indiscriminate gifts to the WEA. A check arrived for a *Guardian* article. Jeannette pounced on it, but Tawney intervened: "Oh, no, that's for the WEA"[37] (He also induced his American friends to send checks to the WEA.)

Chairing WEA meetings, Tawney's heart could get the

better of his head. He would not shut a workingman up, no matter how obvious the need to do so, and his sense of time was medieval. He was excellent, however, at summarizing a discussion. As a debate went on, Tawney, gazing into space, his glasses perched on his forehead, would scribble a resolution; then, amending it as fresh points were brought up, present it as the debate ended and thus pull coherence out of apparent chaos. He did not have a good sense of what could be expected of office staff. It was ironic—not Tawney's kind of irony, so he missed it—that he should keep a young typist in the office half the night dictating to her a memo on the need for better opportunities and conditions for juvenile workers.[38] On the telephone he was impatient. "Harry," Rees used to say to him, "you're a bastard on the telephone."

What Tawney above all did for the WEA was to keep its standards high, and to keep it a workers' movement. He would not let its classes become leisure-time dabbling. He declined to substitute propaganda for learning. He kept a link between education and the social emancipation of workers.

TO AMERICA

In the spring of 1939 Tawney went to lecture for three months at the University of Chicago. Surprising, perhaps, that he should have left England at this critical time. But Tawney was near despair at political trends. And arguments for socialism seemed to many people a distraction, when fascist dictators were breathing threats at half of Europe.[39] So Tawney was not unhappy to accept the invitation of Professor John Nef, the economic historian whom he had known since 1922, to lecture to Americans on the seventeenth century and British social democracy.

He also needed the money, as he remarked to Beatrice Webb, to pay off debts that he and Jeannette had incurred.[40] On this and two subsequent visits to Chicago, Tawney bargained rather keenly over the fee to be paid him; a change from Rochdale and Longton days. Everything was made more complex, financially and in other ways, by Jeannette's condition. Heat reduced her to collapse; she could sleep only in a bedroom of her own; reaching Chicago, she was immediately *hors de combat* with a corn. The suite at the

Windermere Hotel, at $7.50 a day, Jeannette's chiropodist, and her impulsive purchases, must have eaten into the generous $5,000 which Chicago paid Tawney for three months.[41]

Tawney enjoyed himself and made an impact. He did not, however, take Americans in general very seriously. The *Chicago Tribune* ("that work of romance") fascinated him, with its bombast and its comic-strips. "How is little Annie?" he wrote back to Nef from London. "I left America at a critical moment in her life, and have often wondered how she escaped from that villain in a frock-coat." For its part, Chicago University liked him enough to offer him a permanent professorship, which he declined; then to ask him back in 1941 to receive an honorary degree.[42]

Two years later, Churchill and the Labour party were at the helm, and Tawney was more in step with public events. His flat had been bombed into inhabitability, but he thought light of it ("slightly knocked about," he reported to Nef). He was charged with a new spirit, now that narrow Tory rule had given way to a government determined to fight a "people's war" to the end against fascism.

Tawney joined the Home Guard, and firing a rifle for the first time since the fateful day on the Somme, he purred with pleasure at getting "several bulls."[43] He suddenly became active again as advisor to men in government, frequently using Creech Jones as a channel for his widely heard and accepted suggestions.[44] He also took up the pen to explain the war. His "Why Britain Fights," written for the *New York Times* at Tom Jones's urging, had influence in the United States and much success in Britain as a Macmillan War Pamphlet.[45] He argued that the war was being fought for democracy, as well as for Britain's survival, and that it *could* also be a war for socialism (the second theme was stressed in the British, but not in the American version).

For Tawney's visit to receive the honorary degree in 1941, Chicago proposed both a term as a visiting professor and participation in a seminar, "The Place of Ethics in the Social Sciences," planned as part of the fiftieth anniversary celebrations of the university. Tawney declined the former. If he was to spend time in America, he now felt, he should not be bottled up in one university, but go round the nation, especially among labor groups, to speak about the war. Coincidentally, just after he explained this to Chicago, the British government asked him to go to Washington as labor advisor at the embassy.[46] He told William Crozier and Nef he had no choice but to accept; "orders are orders" in such circumstances. Yet from what he said to Beatrice Webb he was pleased to be summoned to an official role in the war effort, and his correspondence with Arthur Creech Jones shows that Tawney took initiatives to get himself a government job. As Tawney left England for America, a farewell from the sergeant of his Home Guard platoon touched him and expressed the spirit of the hour: "Of course it is your duty to go, but we are all very sorry because you may miss the invasion."[47]

With Jeannette, he flew out, via Bermuda, to Chicago, and after a short stay for the ceremonies, went on to Washington in October 1941. He was too rushed to do justice to the seminar on ethics.[48] Arriving with nothing prepared, he merely gave a vote of thanks—after Jacques Maritain, Robert Hutchins, and C. H. McIlwain of Harvard had spoken—on which he tried to hang some weighty remarks. Never diplomatically acute, he panicked when he found three Rockefellers at the seminar. Was he not supposed to be a labor attaché? He phoned Nef at 6 A.M. to get a promise there would be no reporters present. Precautions were taken. But at the end of the morning disaster struck as photographs were taken. Tawney flapped: "It's happened, Nef; I've been photographed with a Rockefeller!" Yet five minutes later Tawney, deep in animated conversation, hopped gaily into a limousine to drive off for lunch with Henry Luce on one side and Marshall Field on the other. Muttered one of the Rockefellers, seeing this and pondering the morning's fuss: "The man is mad."

To say the British ambassador in Washington was unprepared to make use of Tawney would be an understatement. Lord Halifax had no idea why labor advisors were appointed to embassies (the Washington post was one of three). On arrival, Tawney found himself listed as a typist and consigned to a gloomy wooden hut in the embassy grounds. By unlucky chance, the Tawneys' luggage, following them in a cargoboat, had been torpedoed. Having few clothes, and wishing to spend much of their American money on food-parcels for English friends, they hunted for second-hand garments. Jeannette found a local Catholic charity which raised money

Tawney during his fourth visit to the United States, 1941-1942.

by selling used clothes. (It was called the Christ Child Opportunity Store; when she telephoned a voice would answer: "Christ Child speaking.") Thus were the Tawneys reclothed.[49]

Tawney wrote to Beatrice Webb that his work was "at first distressingly indefinite."[50] Criss-crossing the country, he spoke about British labor, now to union groups, now to the Union for Democratic Action, now at colleges. For the Foreign Office he kept an eagle eye on American labor. In July 1942, he reported on the visit of Walter Citrine, general secretary of the Trade Union Congress, and the next month did a solid, well-informed memo on American labor and the congressional elections of 1942. His third report was a 40,000 word analysis of the American labor movement. It is a blend of pedestrian survey and brilliant *aperçus* on why labor is characteristically an "associate" not a "critic" of capital. Strains of British paternalism are evident; he did not doubt that American labor will in the fullness of time tread the political path British labor has trodden.[51]

Tawney interpreted Britain's war effort well, made some friends, and impressed those he chose to unbutton for. Yet he did not engage with America enough to overcome the inherent tedium of saying the same thing again and again. "I have come to hate the sound of my own voice," he confessed to Nef in January 1942.[52] With Pearl Harbor he felt that the justification for his assignment had largely disappeared. When he accepted the job he had been promised that he might resign after six months. In fact he stayed just under twelve, returning to London in September 1942, to teach, write prolifically for the *Guardian*, and begin his brilliant campaign for education reform.

One reason why Tawney was not wholly suited to embassy work lay in the nature of the British foreign service at that time. He made astute comments about it in a letter to Creech Jones soon after his return to London. The Foreign Office, he observed, was staffed too much by "gentlemanly amateurs, who know little of the life either of their own country or of those in which they serve."[53] It seemed to him that diplomacy was increasingly breaking up into a series of specialisms, and that the "public school-Oxford & Cambridge young man whom one meets on the staffs of embassies knows as little about such matters as he does about astronomy." Through Creech Jones and other channels, Tawney made several suggestions to improve the situation.

At every important British embassy, he urged, there ought to be a labor attaché, with adequate staff and status, well backed up from London (none of these things he enjoyed in Washington). The foreign service in general, he said, should be recruited exactly as were other departments of the civil service, without reference to family or social connections. After their appointment, all candidates should spend at least one year in advanced study on a special subject related to their future work, and there should be periodic refresher courses, and seconding of embassy officials for spells of service with other departments of government. Tawney mounted a minor campaign to have the foreign service brought out of its aristocratic past by reforms such as these. (He had parallel criticisms of the "young cubs" in that "awful show," the Ministry of Information. He observed to Creech Jones: "When someone asks me 'what did you do in the great war, daddy?' I shall reply, 'I did *not* get a job in the Ministry of Information,' and feel that the answer is adequate.")[54]

He made one more visit to the United States, again to Chicago, as visiting professor in the spring of 1948. The sponsor was the Committee on Social Thought, whose efforts to cut across disciplines and grapple with value questions he admired. His historical lectures were repeats of 1939. But he also gave vigorous public lectures defending the Attlee government's "peaceful revolution." Professor Frank Knight was stirred by these to puzzle loudly how a great historian could be so wrong on current politics. The two men exchanged letters, and Tawney put into his last lecture a conciliatory passage on Knight's position. Seeing Knight at the lecture's end, Tawney asked him pleasantly what he thought of the passage. Knight became enraged and denounced Tawney to his face. Leaving the hall, Tawney said to one of his hosts: "You know, Nef, a university is the next thing to a lunatic asylum."[55]

Tawney did not like the United States enough to try and understand it on its own terms, as Graham Wallas and Harold Laski did. A sojourner, he liked some particular things, but not the tone of American life, and he looked down on American culture. He appreciated its freedom from a caste system; a sense of natural equality won him to the Midwest especially. But he complained to Beatrice Webb of "self-righteousness" and "publicity-mongering," and "so much pretence that fourth-rate work is first-rate."[56] He did not find in the American worker the "modest sagacity" of the European worker. Among intellectuals, there was "more intelligence than wisdom."[57]

Politically, Tawney oversimplified his picture of the United States into an admirable progressive period under Franklin Roosevelt, preceded by a capitalist jungle, and succeeded by a bout of ideological self-righteousness during the Cold War. (Ironically, the areas of America where the "natural equality" he liked was most evident became most afflicted from the late 1940s with anticommunist ideology.) Even after Churchill had become prime minister, Tawney considered Roosevelt "certainly head and shoulders above any other political leader in the world today." The next sentence of this letter to Nef nevertheless hints at condescension: "It is satisfactory that his stature should be recognised by his countrymen."[58] *Recognized;* Tawney apparently did not think the issue was the American people's to *determine.*

It is a clue to Tawney's views that he did not regard Americans as wholly foreigners, but as Europeans manqués. So he did not realize that British ethnocentrism kept him from entering into the different reality that is America. He expected more empathy with the motives of the British war effort than could reasonably be expected of the United States. He quite failed to foresee how little account America the superpower would take of Britain after the war. Having taken British influence on America for granted, he did not relish American influence on Britain.

Of academic life in the United States he had dimmer views than he chose to express while a visitor. "Your news about the decision as to a Rockefeller grant is distressing," he wrote in 1951 to a young Australian scholar he had tried to help. "What damned pedantics American sociologists are! I blame myself for not having reflected that they would probably be frightened of research into any subject more extensive than the number of fleas per square inch of army blankets. It would have been quite easy to word your subject in such a way as to satisfy even these myopic intelligences."[59]

Tawney's prejudices suggest that he was not really interested in America. It was for him a place; not a civilization. He seemed to go there in good spirits but with half his mind turned off. Yet when his cultural prejudices did not overwhelm him, when prejudice was a gloss, and not a veil, upon the truth, Tawney's judgments were shrewd. To Beatrice Webb, in July 1942, he observed that Americans were becoming friendly to Russia because Americans admire success and the Russians were winning battles. Then he added: "What the attitude will be after the end of the war is another question. There are signs that an American imperialist mentality is developing, which will be prepared to tell the whole world how it should behave. We no doubt, shall be its first target; but Russia will be the next."[60]

It was a brilliant prediction, and his analysis of the Cold War mentality when it arose was no less impressive. He wrote to Wadsworth in 1950 about the current "paroxysm of self-righteousness": "Recurrent fits of hysteria are necessary to the health of Americans. They reassure them as to their superior virtue, which they cannot resist asserting yet cannot wholly believe in. This attack looks like being a bad one. It will not last, for the world is insufficiently wicked to provide an inexhaustible supply of scapegoats, but it will probably continue long enough to do some damage that will take some time to repair."[61] Unmoved by America's qualities, he had a sharp eye for its flaws.

Now over sixty, Tawney felt the strains of wartime living. Back from his American perambulations, he could not slip into a settled daily pattern; nor did he have a proper place to live. His LSE classes took place at Cambridge, and for a while he commuted daily. But trains were erratic so he soon accepted an offer from Peterhouse College to stay a couple of nights a week. His London program was full: WEA business; journalism and committees on educational reform; contact and correspondence with scholars in all continents; in odd hours, on the corner of a table, historical research.

The flat in Mecklenburgh Square was a dusty shell. He and Jeannette tried various expedients before moving into two chickenhouses near Russell Square. Approached by steps behind the Russell Hotel, this new Tawney nest had the outward appearance of a public toilet and the splendid name "The Colonnade." Tom Jones was shocked by the "chaos" when he visited in 1944 and had to prop himself up on a divan bed.[1] Once a message boy came with a huge bouquet of flowers for Jeannette from a French dignitary who knew Tawney. But when the boy saw the entrance, and Jeannette in dressing-gown, her hair like an unpruned privet, he suspected a mistake. "But it's from a *Frenchman*," he repeated, and handed over the bouquet only when proof of identity was produced.[2]

Tawney did not mind the squalor, only the lack of space for books. He remarked when he moved in: "I never knew hens lived so luxuriously." In 1950 when Oxford made Tawney an honorary doctor of letters, the Public Orator included this remark in the Latin presentation, and said Tawney could leave Diogenes standing when it came to leading the simple life.[3] But in such circumstances Tawney let his health go, and influenza led to a congested lung in 1943. Jeannette as usual was intermittently ill, with phlebitis among other ailments, and was sometimes in hospital and often at Rose Cottage. For both of them the war years took a toll.[4]

WAR A SPRINGBOARD FOR SOCIALISM?

Tawney had learned from World War I that the time to plan for after a war is during the war. In the WEA and the Labour party, in speeches and articles, he talked of reconstruction, linking the case for socialism with war aims. He wrote in the *Economic History Review* an article on "The Abolition of Economic Controls, 1918-1921" which rammed home the missed opportunities of 1918; postwar energies and wartime governmental experience were not tapped for a leap forward in social justice. He spun the same theme in numerous essays and pamphlets, and in speeches, among them a prescient address at his old school, Rugby, on "Post-War Policy," as early as 1942. Tawney saw "new conceptions of the social contract" implicit in the national fellowship of the war effort.[5] Was there not a springboard here, from which England might turn its back on the acquisitive society and set its postwar face toward a functional society?

Tawney's American experiences disposed him to speak also on Anglo-American ties. No sooner in the door from Washington, he found a telegram from William Crozier, editor of the *Guardian*, asking for a leader on this topic.[6] Tawney saw many Americans, including the United States ambassador, John Gilbert Winant, who told Kingsley Martin soon after his arrival that the person he most wanted to meet in England was Tawney (Martin invited them both to lunch, and also David Low, after which Tawney said to Martin that Winant seemed "too good to be true").[7] When dealing with policy issues, as distinct from handing down cultural impressions, Tawney held a balanced, by no means unfriendly view of the United States.

In its social order, Tawney wanted Britain to map a middle path between Russian communism and American free enterprise. He hoped this would set an example for other smaller countries. But he never questioned the alliance with the United States. This got him into trouble with the Labour Left, who attacked Bevin's foreign policy and opposed NATO. Tawney was not anti-Russian. He went there in 1945,

The Tawneys pottering at Rose Cottage, during the forties.

with Julian Huxley and others, and liked much of what he saw (though he felt very negative about Russia in the early 1950s, when Zhdanov's policies put a muzzle on his Russian historian friends).[8] He thought Russia, which had good reason to fear the West, had a right to group Eastern Europe into a bloc. By the same token, he thought the West had the right to form a bloc too. To put it mildly, Tawney was no socialist visionary when it came to international affairs. Men were evil enough; nations more so; morality could only occasionally come into the picture.

Tawney was a major figure on the postwar British scene. In the 1945 election, he campaigned for many of his younger friends, including Durbin, and Lena Jeger (whose electorate embraced Mecklenburgh Square). In 1950 he again spoke at election meetings, praising the Labour government's achievements. He was announced, he told Wadsworth with some amusement, as an ancient who had hobnobbed with the socialist giants of the 1890s. "By the next election they will describe me as a former Chartist."[9]

Tawney saluted the steps toward communal provision, and the modest shift of power that nationalization and economic equalizing had effected. He did not wring his hands at moral loss, but rejoiced at practical gain, when enactment of a bill removed an issue from the arsenal of socialist demands. He did regret the bureaucratism of the government's idea of socialism. People's solidaristic energies had not been evoked; industrial relationships had not been altered; the public schools still cried out privilege and snobbery. When once again Labour leaders offered him Honours, he realized sadly that socialist politicians had still not renounced the toys of their opponents.[10]

He was among the few who predicted the 1951 Tory victory.[11] It was almost as if he thought Labour did not deserve to win again. The Labour movement—he often said "movement" rather than "party"—had great moral significance for Tawney. Its appeal could never be mainly to a man's purse. If it failed to inspire a majority with the superiority of a socialist commonwealth over capitalism, it *could* not and *should* not win.

Tawney wrote two much-read articles about the situation of British socialism after the smoke of Attlee's first four exciting years had cleared. One was for an American symposium, *The Christian Demand for Social Justice* (1949), the other in 1952 for *Socialist Commentary*. He reapplied his socialist principles, found good things had been done as well as other good things left undone, and transcended effectively certain left-right feuds which turned on methods or personalities alone. As the disputes within the Labour party of the mid- and late-fifties flared, he put party unity above almost all other considerations and opposed those—whether on the left or the right—who seemed to take party unity too lightly.[12]

On the other hand, some of his criticisms seemed nostalgia's bastards. He was upset that a smart young woman doctor, when he showed her the place where J. J. Mallon and he had run the Anti-Sweating League, asked him: "What is wrong with sweating?"; she knew not the word's meaning.[13] In his mind he knew this was progress, but emotionally he was saddened by what he suspected was a loss of social outrage. Later, his objections to the Common Market seemed more in debt to the past than the future.

When he criticized the materialism of some workers, he was being nostalgic for the transitional generation he had known in Rochdale and Longton. These men could not be duplicated in a society of wide and general opportunity. Nor could Tawney see that it is less impossible for a Victorian patrician like himself to despise the outward circumstances of life, than for a man of simple origin with little cultural security or breadth of vision.

But if Tawney sometimes carped, he always practiced what he preached. He treated the local, voluntary work of the Labour party with seriousness. At campaign committee rooms he would turn up for menial tasks, and to the end of his life he went to branch party meetings, poring over its business as if an empire hinged on it. Since he never succumbed to "professionalism" himself, his denunciations of it greatly embarrassed those who had.

With Lionel Elvin, Walter Moberley, and other friends, Tawney sat on the University Grants Commission (1943-1948). The UGC had financial power; its discussions were not speculative but about hard cash. Tawney proved tough and shrewd in pushing for democratization of British universities.

He wanted them thrown open to working-class students. But how to arrive at a figure for the increase in student numbers to be asked of the universities? "The difficulty with academic committees," said Tawney, "is that they are too intelligent. Everyone insists on having his own opinion, and where figures are concerned the possible alternatives may run into thousands." One evening he was chatting with a UGC colleague (later chief scientific advisor to the government). Both agreed discussion of the right figure threatened to be endless. Suddenly Tawney exclaimed: "Why not double the blasted thing?" Due not least to Tawney's vigor, this expansion was achieved in less than ten years. First the universities suggested they could manage a 30 percent increase, then 50 percent; finally, under further pressure, 92 percent at the end of ten years. "We said 'Good enough',," Tawney recalled, "and closed on that."[14] Actually the performance turned out better even than the high commitment.*

Tawney kept up his stream of leaders and reviews on education for the *Guardian*. There were also pieces in the *Highway* and essays and introductions in WEA publications. But these latter sometimes convey disenchantment with the WEA (he stayed on for five years as vice-president, after Harold Clay succeeded him as president in 1943). "Every movement goes wrong after thirty or forty years," he observed to Elvin, and though he was referring to the Salvation Army, the remark was made as they walked home from a WEA meeting. "Either there is a redefinition of purpose, or it just drifts on, and ought to be abolished."[15] In part, Tawney's reduced keenness for the WEA was a matter of sheer tiredness, mixed with a twinge of doubt as to the value of his own vast expenditure of time in its service. Just before relinquishing the presidency he wrote to Creech Jones: "I can't help feeling that I should have influenced more people to think sensibly about educational and social things, if I'd spent on writing the time which the WEA requires me to spend on committees, memoranda, interviews, deputations and so on."[16] From the WEA's side, no less than from his own, he felt it was time for a change.

---

*Tawney's shrewdness stopped short at personal matters. After its last meeting one year, the UGC members went off to eat in the gloom of a West End restaurant. The meal over, Tawney could not remember where his overcoat was or what it looked like. The only clue, he told the attendant, was that the pocket contained a confidential cabinet memo. Other patrons watched with some interest as Tawney and the attendant went through the pocket of every coat in search of a cabinet memo. (Elvin, conversation with author, London, January 28, 1971).

He hit out, in private, against the timidity of the WEA in bringing in fresh blood: "Its future depends on its getting able young men to work for it *before* they become known . . . If it does not do so, it will inevitably go down hill. Hence my dislike of the policy of embalming aged mummies, which I gather, is contemplated in my case."[17]

But differences over issues had also arisen within the WEA. Tawney wrote to S. G Raybould in 1948 of his unhappiness that WEA classes contained fewer workers than previously; that tutorial classes, the most intellectually ambitious of WEA activities, had been downgraded; that many members had little sense of the association's purpose. Tawney did not think the WEA's specific purpose was furthered by classes on butterfly-catching and medieval monasteries. He was against "begging people to join" classes "whether they mean business or not;" as if quantity made up for quality. He wanted students challenged, not catered to. Education should make socialist citizens out of them.[18]

He hammered away at various educational causes—better teacher training, a leaving age of sixteen, more money for the local education authorities—in the Council for Educational Advance, of which he was president, and the Society for Research in Education which, with Mallon and H. C. Barnard, he became a vice-president of in 1945. He ardently supported comprehensive schools. On this he clashed with Richard Crossman, when they both sat on a Labour party education committee; Crossman then wrote a caustic piece called "The Comprehensive Child."[19] To the end Tawney agitated for better and more egalitarian schools. Weeks before his death he badgered his WEA associate Harold Shearman, "What are they doing about the primary schools? They are always getting forgotten."[20] Without alert young citizens, how could the best legislation in the world achieve socialism?

ACADEMIA: HOOD, KNIFE, PEN

Due to retire from the LSE in 1946, Tawney stayed on with reduced duties until 1949. The next year the school presented to him his portrait, and in response he made a speech of unusual warmth and simplicity.[21] Claude Rogers had done the pencil sketch, Tawney said, with tact as well as grace. Three things, he remarked, caused him to love the LSE. One was its intellectual dynamism. Frontiers between disciplines were not seen as immutable; LSE scholars had made a healthy habit of redrawing them. A second was its informal, egalitarian social atmosphere. "It is agreeable to belong to an institution which does not inherit traditions but makes them."

The third was its sense, derived from Webb, that the purpose of learning is ultimately to make a more just society; the school exists not for itself but for the public. Tawney was comparing the LSE favorably, in this respect as in the others, with Oxford and Cambridge. The bidding prayer in use at the older universities, he recalled, spoke of "serving God in Church and State." The LSE did not talk that way, but it acted that way.

He did not yet retire from history, though a string of honorary doctorates threatened to bury him alive. Manchester had been first (1930); coming early, not as a shroud but as a spur, it meant much to him. Others piled up: Chicago (1941); Paris (1945); Oxford (1950); Birmingham (1951); London (1953); Sheffield (1953); Melbourne (1955); Glasgow (1961).

But if these were pretty hoods, there were also sharp knives. An historical controversy simmered, which he had started with his wartime articles, "The Rise of the Gentry" and "Harrington's Interpretation of His Age." By turns it amused, irritated, and bored him. A gargantuan literature now exists on this "storm over the gentry."[22]

Tawney's class interpretation of the causes of the Civil War was challenged by H. R. Trevor-Roper, who questioned Tawney's categories and use of statistics, and provided exceptions to Tawney's generalizations (1953). Trevor-Roper also criticized Lawrence Stone (1951), who had set forth a pattern of a declining aristocracy that complemented Tawney's theory of a rising gentry (1948). Tawney came back at Trevor-Roper with a "Postscript" (1953). J. P. Cooper later made further detailed criticisms of Tawney's theory (1956). J. H. Hexter and others took issue with Tawney's concern for high-level theories of historical causation; in particular, economic theories.[23] The issues spiraled on, but Tawney said no more in public about them. He saw no further value in controversy, he told Nef just after Cooper's article appeared.[24]

Tawney and his close colleague T. S. Ashton, during the fifties.

Tawney began the ferment. That is important, for Tawney felt his highest historical task was not to settle issues, but to raise them. Over the gentry, as over the first great debate he triggered (on puritanism and capitalism), Tawney expected to be superseded and *hoped* to be superseded. The tone of the attacks on him however he did not like. Why should an historian who takes a step forward pant in furious criticism of all previous steps forward? "An erring colleague," Tawney suggested, "is not an Amalakite to be smitten hip and thigh."[25] Was not historical scholarship in the last analysis a cooperative enterprise; were there really any "final solutions" to the seventeenth-century issues which justified the "unpleasing asperity" of self-righteousness? His mutterings to Nef about "historical Scribes and Pharisees"[26] expressed one objection he had to certain of his critics.

Tawney did not think he erred on any matter of substance. One striking impression of the debate, indeed, is that none of its able leading protagonists did so. The differences lay primarily in values, and in what relation study of the past has to the historian's present existence. If Tawney reached for a theory of the Civil War, it was because he thought men must make patterns of the past if they are to responsibly face the future. If he had a keen eye for an exploiting class in history, it was because he sympathized with the underdog in his own time.

If his search for a theory and his feeling for the underdog led him to essentially economic explanations, it was in part because of the *time* at which Tawney labored in the vineyard of history. "The economic problem" predominated in Edwardian public life; yet history was being written in terms of kings, battles, and constitutions; Tawney tried to adjust scholarship to life. At the end of *The Agrarian Problem in the Sixteenth Century*, laying out the value questions involved in the topic of the book, Tawney confessed: "Such differences lie too deep to be settled by argument, whether they appear in the sixteenth century or in our own day."[27] That was also his view of the gentry fuss.

Tawney did not, as some critics may have thought, resolve research problems by reference to ideology.[28] His socialist principles suggested questions, and offered possible organizing vehicles for data. Often this proved fruitful; a striking pattern emerged. But sometimes it did not, as in his Cranfield biography. Those who flayed Tawney as an ideologue may be surprised to hear Tawney's private words on Cranfield. He began the book, he wrote to Beveridge in January 1961, "with a prejudice against [Cranfield] as a capitalist on the make. I ended with a respect for a man who, without being overscrupulous in business, was in courage and public spirit head and shoulders above the awful gang of courtly sharks and toadies with whom, as a minister of the crown, he was condemned to mix, and sacrificed his career for the service of the state."[29] Tawney did not, to put it mildly, press Cranfield into a proscrustean bed of socialist theory.

The accusation about ideology boils down to differences on how the past relates to the present. Hexter says the historian brings to bear on data from the past "whatever may seem enlightening and relevant out of our own day. And what may be relevant is as wide as the full range of our own daily experience." Tawney would have agreed, but Tawney's daily experience was not the hymn to privatism which Hexter has told us his is. Hexter declared that his own present awareness, which he brings to bear on past data, has "precious little to do with the Great Crises of the Contemporary World."[30] But

Tawney *did* feel in his own bones the crises of the contemporary world. His perspective from the present to the past was not, as Hexter says his is, a household routine, but the struggle of working-class Britons for a socialist commonwealth. Facts are least of the issues between two such historians. Two views of man's priorities in life stand opposed.

Hexter, if I may still take this able scholar as example, was a characteristic historian of that brief interlude labeled by some utopians of stability "the end of ideology." Tawney was different. If ideology means a formulation of and quest for the *summum bonum*, Tawney would have said the end of ideology means the end of compassion and responsibility. He once said of a book by an English historian (not Trevor-Roper or Hexter): "The only thing wrong with X's book is X himself." I think Tawney would be happy to have the kernel of that remark applied—whether positively or negatively—to his own work.

Tawney's pen had one more book in it, his eleventh. To Nef he wrote in March 1958: "I wonder how your writing work goes on? I have virtually finished, except for proofs, index, etc., a tedious work on London business and public life under James I as illustrated by Lionel Cranfield. I am ashamed of it, and wish that I had never begun it."[31] At last *Business and Politics Under James I*, started more than twenty years before, was done. F. J. Fisher, long Tawney's friend and amanuensis, helped get the final draft in order. Tawney once remarked to his fond and remarkable housekeeper: "Lucy, I think this is my masterpiece." Why then did he tell Nef, after finishing it, that he thought it hardly worth while?[32] The contradiction cannot be resolved, but Tawney's double attitude can be explained.

The book deals with that "seductive border region where politics grease the wheels of business and polite society smiles hopefully on both"; the arena of Tawney's lifelong professional concern.[33] This time, Tawney, rather than reaching for general explanations, dealt concretely and biographically with his usual seventeenth-century themes. He proved, if further proof were needed, that he could write both kinds of history well. Indeed, using "people" rather than "trends" as a point of departure was in some ways Tawney's natural bent. He did not think that focusing on the concrete, the nuances, obviated the need to try and find patterns. Nor that to flourish an exception was to demolish a generalization.

However, Tawney did think the Cranfield study less *important* than his works which drew large patterns. Less demanding to do; less a contribution to the major tasks of history. That did not mean professional historians may not consider the detailed study his masterpiece. Nor that Tawney, who could be sensitive to attacks on his technical scholarship, may not have *wished* them to so consider it. Cranfield done, Tawney said to Janet Wadsworth that he felt guilty about spending so much time on a pocket of history, and was now anxious to apply himself for a while to matters of current importance.[34]

In sum, Tawney felt that, in terms of the dialectic between past and present which is history, he had in his Cranfield book let the proper tension sag, and dug a hole in the past which took him too far from the light of general ideas. The overview of the seventeenth century, long projected, which *both* Tawney *and* the scholarly reviewers may have considered his masterpiece, was never written.

Little time remained. In 1953 he had collected some of his essays on war, religion, and politics, in *The Attack and Other Papers* (dedicated to Richard Rees). He planned a second volume, mainly on education and politics, but it was finished only after his death, edited by Rita Hinden as *The Radical Tradition*. He published articles in the *Economic Journal* (1955) and the *Economic History Review* (1959) and reviews in the *Times Literary Supplement*. Tawney's last published piece (1960) is a splendid portrait of Lawrence (J. L.) Hammond, an historian after Tawney's own heart. It is a study rich on Tawney's views as well as on Hammond's work.

Hammond's politics, Tawney wrote in a passage no less true of himself, "were based on moral premises, not on economic expediency or on visions of future Elysiums to be purchased at the price of present wrong." That was the path which Tawney, too, tried to hew between capitalism and communism. He added words that showed how his own hopes had dimmed: "In a world in retreat, not only from particular principles, but from the very idea that political principles exist, it is natural that such convictions should seem a remote and worn-out creed."[35]

Tawney traveled for academic events in his last decade. He did not go a fourth time to Chicago, as he would have liked, but he lectured in Denmark and Sweden in 1951, and went often to his favorite foreign country, for Anglo-French historians meetings, or to look for things in the Bibliotheque Nationale. In 1955, he flew to Australia with Jeannette to spend five months at the University of Melbourne, in whose School of History Tawney's work had long been fed generously to students.[36] He lectured, to thunderous applause, on seventeenth-century subjects, the British Labour party, George Unwin, and voluntary associations. Small discussions he enjoyed; also walks in the Australian "bush," which so appealed to him that he declared he must have been an aboriginal in a previous incarnation.

He sensed and liked a radical strain in Australia, eclipsed though it was in the 1950s. This vast sun-baked country seemed freer than most from the "imprisoning social prejudices" he had fought in the name of socialism. In the Australian Labour party he took a lively interest. It was pleasing to use the "improprieties" of Labour governments in Australia (and New Zealand) to "beat the heads of American critics and to reassure ourselves."[37] Jeannette amused her hosts, not least by her enquiries into prostitution. "How much do the girls charge in Melbourne?" she asked an Australian professor, as he, with his wife, drove in the Dandenong mountains with the two Tawneys.

"THE ROOTS ARE LOOSENED"

Into the 1950s, and his seventies, Tawney began to lose personal mastery. If still active, he was seldom original. He was without the will for fresh initiatives, and not up to the overall rethinking that would justify a big new book on politics. He was now a man doing things when and because he was asked to do them. Requests dictated the agenda of his working life. Problems of his personal life intruded endlessly on his larger concerns.

Jeannette was more often ill than not. Tawney ran a never ending race to overtake unanswered correspondence. He would reach for a book, then remember Jeannette had sold it. The landlord hovered over him for rent, which he could

Tawney and M. M. Postan, the historian, in the garden of Postan's
Cambridge home, 1959.

not always pay. He was unable to plan ahead, for he was not
sure his health would let him keep long-range commitments.

It was as if he never had the time, or maybe the heart, to
draw back from the grind and do and say what was most in
him to do and say. He wrote one preface after another for
other people's books. But his great unwritten work on the
seventeenth century lay in unfulfilled fragments, beneath
piles of circulars, bills, committee minutes, and letters from
enquiring young scholars. His work for the *Guardian* was now
mostly reviews, rather than leaders, and February 1955, saw
the last of those.

His friends died one by one, like lights going out along his
own personal highway. He was constantly writing obituaries
for them; a drain on his time, but more on his gaiety. The
death of Eileen Power in 1940 took more punch out of him
than any other.[38] She had been his intimate friend, as Jeannette well knew, and at times an inspiration. Then Hobson,
Temple, Cartwright, Mansbridge, Clay, Wadsworth,
Hammond, all predeceased him; such losses left him less sure
of touch. Companions gone, landmarks repositioned, he
could not strike out into the deep as a thinker any more.

Little things showed him faltering. In 1952 he put "1652" at the top of papers (a charming inadvertent rebuttal to J. H. Hexter's charge that Tawney was not "history-minded" but "present-minded").[39] He put every imaginable address on letters to Janet Wadsworth except the correct one. Asked to speak, he doubted that he had anything new to say. He called himself "senile" only half in jest.[40] After the mid 1950s his handwriting lost its round, bold flourish; it became limp; by 1960 it was spidery. In letters to friends a poignant phrase recurred: "I hope to catch a glimpse of you some time."[41] The man who shaped events was now dependent. The man who spanned diverse worlds was now a bit alone.

Jeannette's death, in January 1958, sharply reduced Tawney's mastery. Annette Jeanie Beveridge, daughter of Henry Beveridge, I.C.S., brother of William, and Harry Tawney's wife for half a century, was not a simple woman, yet hardly a distinguished woman. She was in some ways a trial to Tawney; yet her death brought a void.

Jeannette was not a housewife to go scrubbing in every corner. Her house was a mess, not only because Tawney was untidy, but because of her own impulsive, distracted ways. Many a visitor saw her empty tea leaves into the stockpot. Her habits of dress were unschematic. "It doesn't matter what men wear," she would say, but was she unaware that her spreading, sprouting second-hand hats stopped people in the street; that her colors clashed like fighting cats? Her muddle had its explanations. Her father, who once asked for jam and tea in the middle of a six-course dinner at a smart London restaurant, was not a conventional man. The family had grown used, in India, to a bevy of servants. But after she married Tawney, if boots got muddy, there was no one anymore to clean them but herself; and her health was poor.[42]

Her untidiness was less of a problem for Tawney than her stunning extravagance. Her eye for expensive products was sharper than her eye for products of quality, and her spending outran Tawney's purse. It also taxed her brother's more ample purse. Tawney wrote a book called *The Acquisitive Society*, Kingsley Martin remarked, and Mrs. Tawney illustrated it. A glance at Jeannette's correspondence with her brother William during the late 1930s confirms the aptness of Martin's sharp remark.

In April 1937 she asked Will for £12-12-0 she says he promised her the previous Christmas. In September she wrote: "It occurs to me that in your house removing you may have mislaid my wireless account so I am sending it to you again. You may feel like sending it with my September 15 gift." An October letter spelled out a birthday request: "I should love to have an armchair for the cottage . . . I know you are at the moment extra well equipped to select me the perfect armchair." In January 1938 she enquired: "Now I want to ask you if you want to keep up your good habit of giving me a Xmas present?" She suggested money for a type-writer.[43]

Later in the year she complained of her brother's long silence! But she was back in business by February 1939: "Thank you so much for saying you will contribute towards the new fur coat. Please add it to the wireless account." In October yet another need presses: "Thanks so much for saying you'll give me a birthday gift. It so happens that my much beloved handbag has given way irreparably and I am without a good bag." In December she requested a sewing-machine.[44]

Both Tawney and Jeannette were upper-middle-class, but Tawney was unconsciously so and Jeannette self-consciously so. She did not like it, though he did not care, when, during Tawney's furloughs from the war, they would be refused rooms in good hotels because Tawney was not wearing an officer's uniform. Her letters are full of upper-class anxieties: bother with servants, jewelry matters, where to store things, complications arising from having two places to live in. Yet (and here lay her dilemma) Tawney did not lead the life, socially, of an upper-class man. The WEA crowd were quite another cup of tea. So Jeannette was torn between her husband's principles and her own social origins and impulses. She wanted to shift to Oxford, she told Beatrice Webb. But most of what Tawney cared for was in London.[45]

Yet Jeannette did have a feel for Tawney's principles. She was kind. She threw herself enthusiastically, if indiscriminately, into good causes. They had met at a receiving house of the Children's Country Holiday Fund. She was one of the first woman factory inspectors in England. She was on the governing board of several schools. She would help a WEA student to learn French; though, God knows, her own was fickle. She bombarded Wadsworth with letters—too eccentric for publication—on drifting Hungarians, neglected Aboriginals. She would make excerpts from documents for Tawney, and type for him.

There was, however, a vagueness to Jeannette's good intentions which made her a somewhat pathetic woman. There was little Wadsworth could do about the matters in her flapping letters. Her causes were the distant, exotic kind (which Tawney himself thought unworthwhile because of the yawning gap between passions felt and the possibility of effective action). For a church bazaar at St. Bartholomews, in Grays Inn Road, she swung into action, yet she brought *milk-bottles* to be sold! She had a degree and read books. At parties she could irritate Tawney by loudly (and correctly) remarking: "Harry and I both got Seconds, you know." She had, at Bishop Gore's urging, edited a selection from Richard Baxter's *Christian Directory* in 1925.[46]

But there was something inconsequential about her flailing intelligence. Driving to Rochdale for a WEA meeting with Tawney, Ashton, and others, she pecked away at the subject of the uses to which urine is put in rural China. Scraps of fact she had, but her chatter seemed to hang suspended in the air like a feather without source or destination. Sometimes she would choose, when visitors were in the house, to converse with Tawney in fractured German. In this way she imagined she could make discreet remarks or ask delicate questions— "Is there enough food to give them lunch?" "Do they know where the bathroom is?"—but her guests, alas, often commanded better German than she. She wrote a novel, and bits of articles. But the prose was stiff, the touch flawed by naivety, and her jejeune manuscripts gathered dust amidst her trinkets. She was not an intellectual woman like Eileen Power. She was not a practical woman like Lucy Rice, the Tawneys' housekeeper in later years. She was intelligent, she was kind, but she was a scatterbrain.[47]

For Tawney's life and work, marriage to Jeannette had its consequences. There were no children, as there were none in William Beveridge's marriage. What lay behind her obsession for talking about sex—in vivid terms—I cannot judge, but of her obsession little doubt is possible. When she suddenly observed to Pearl Buck in Nanking, "Your husband; he looks as if he must be a beast in bed; is he?" it was a remark startling for Miss Buck but typical of Jeannette. Jeannette's household methods, extravagance, and frequent ill-health, meant that Tawney's own health sometimes suffered, as did his routine of work, and his finances. Socially, Jeannette's attachment to upper-middle-class ways (and again her ill-health) probably reduced Tawney's intercourse with working-class people, and with intellectuals outside the university. Her views, and probably also her judgments, had small effect on Tawney. Jeannette's do-goodism was of the paternalistic, individualistic, drawing-room kind which Tawney put behind him when he turned to socialism.

On the other hand, Jeannette was immensely loyal to Tawney, which sustained him when he doubted himself or despaired at the world. Though he could not always conceal his impatience with her, he felt affection for her too. When she died Tawney sent Janet Wadsworth a photo of Jeannette ("I hope you will forgive my inflicting it on you").[48] It is an attractive, open face. A vulnerable face; so different from Tawney's, which was well within itself, giving nothing away. Hair tossed up, a fur at the shoulders, thin-rimmed spectacles. The mouth is drawn in, as if in resignation. The eyes are slightly wild; there is kindness in them, and bewilderment; and perhaps the record of suffering.

As Tawney's eightieth birthday approached, a few friends, with Creech Jones, Lady Shena Simon, and Harry Nutt (of the WEA) active among them, took steps to honor him. The first idea—a volume of his shorter writings from earlier years—was eventually set aside. Tawney dragged his feet out of doubt that the material bore publishing. Lady Simon favored a book limited to educational topics, while Creech Jones had in mind "representative pieces of writing on his approach to society in a variety of divisions." Tawney's quiet resistance to the projected volume being identified too much with the WEA also complicated matters, since the WEA office seemed the logical base for the organizational and editorial work involved.

After long months of letters, meetings, and tentative dealings with Tawney, who did not make it entirely clear what he would or would not approve, the book project was essentially abandoned (some of its possible contents appeared after his death in *The Radical Tradition*). The group decided instead

Tawney as sketched by Vicky of the *New Statesman*, 1960.

on a booklet about Tawney and a dinner for him at the House of Commons.[49] A fund was privately launched, which climbed above £750, enough to pay for the dinner, the booklet, and gifts for Tawney of an armchair, books, pens, and a wireless (the Tawneys used to have a wireless, but Jeannette's brother paid the wireless bills, and the set was sold after Jeannette died). Richard Titmuss wrote the thirty-page booklet con amore, helped by J. R. Williams, Fisher, and others who sent in bits of Tawniana.

To the dinner came one hundred and thirty-six people, including historians (Beales, Carus-Wilson, C. K. Webster, Ashton, Fisher); WEA men (Green, A. E. Emery, H. C. Shearman, J. H. Thomas, H. Nutt); politicians (Attlee, James Griffiths, Pethick-Lawrence, Ray Gunter, Fred Peart, Shirley Williams, Creech Jones, Dalton, Brockway, James Callaghan, Chuter Ede); unionists (Clay, Frank Cousins, Vic Feather, H. R. Nicholas, J. Wray, Woodcock); educationalists (P. S. Noble, S. Caine, H. L. Elvin, Charles Morris); and friends of different spheres and vintages (Shena Simon, Richard and Kay Titmuss, Janet Wadsworth, Father John Groser, Kingsley Martin, Mrs. Laski, Richard Rees, Mary Stocks). Tawney was embarrassed when he got wind of the proportions to which "this ridiculous celebration" was swelling.[50] But he managed, through Rees, to add some working-class people to the invitees, including Lucy Rice, the housekeeper, who came. "Have I got to dress up?" he enquired.

At the dinner, Titmuss spoke about Tawney as a university man, George Woodcock on Tawney and the trade unions, Sir Charles Morris on Tawney's instinctive understanding of the ordinary man and his needs. Lord Attlee said British socialism owed Tawney "an immense debt of gratitude" because he set forth the "highest principles" for which it stands. Ernest Green, longtime general secretary of the WEA, said Tawney had guaranteed the association's high standards and independence from pressures. Tawney's greatest fault, Green observed, was impatience. As WEA president, he used to urge on Green the principle: "Get on with the job—you can consult the Committee when it's done."[51]

Tawney had not intended to say more than a paragraph of thanks. But in looking back he touched some cherished themes: the British worker's preference for democracy, the humanistic basis of British socialism, the pity of squabbling in the labor movement, the need in the Labour party for more political education in the meaning of socialist citizenship.[52]

He rambled a bit, and did not fire his listeners. After the dinner he wrote a typical mocking and self-mocking note to Creech Jones about the occasion and his speech: "I cannot honestly say that I enjoyed being the victim on the altar, whom you butchered to make a happy holiday for all; indeed when I think of the idiocies which I uttered and have not yet managed to forget, my blood runs cold, and I feel surprised at having escaped alive." The irony did not seem to be only at his own expense: "That, however, was, I suppose, part of the comedy which you planned, and it is possible that the audience was sufficiently callous to enjoy even that part of the sport."[53]

The press rediscovered Tawney; there appeared an editorial in the *Times* ("Puritan Militant"), and features in the *Guardian* ("Prophet of Equality"), *Daily Herald* ("the major prophet of British Socialism"), and dozens of other papers, in London and in provinces where Tawney had taught. For the *New Statesman*, Crossman compiled a splendid "Tawney Anthology." From abroad there were many messages, among them a cable from Nef and Edward Shils in Chicago.[54]

One message Tawney especially liked came from the children of Eastleach primary school. Fisher had under way, a little late for the birthday, a *Festschrift* volume, essays by sixteen historians on themes Tawney had pioneered, which came out in 1961 under the title *Essays in Honour of R. H. Tawney*. None of this went to Tawney's head, but it eased the growing loneliness of the four years between Jeannette's death and his own.

Tawney sank to his end at the apex of Macmillanism. Its key slogan was: "You've never had it so good"; a government's invitation to an equally complacent citizen's slogan, "I'm all right Jack"—polar opposite of Tawney's ideal of socialist morality. But Tawney's political work was done; his gaze had now become a longer one. Often he went to church, and he talked with the vicar about religion more than he had with anyone since Temple died.

He went out now and then, carefully planning his bus route, for his energy was limited, and he disliked being too long among whizzing cars. Now to a meeting of the Carlyle

Club; or to yarn with Beveridge—whom he was close to again—at the Reform Club or at the House of Lords (where Beveridge now sat as a peer). He prepared a few speeches but seldom, when the evening arrived, felt like making them. At the top, in a crabbed hand, he would write: "Not Given." He read new books on history and on socialism. C. A. R. Crosland's *Future of Socialism* he took up with interest, and put down "with some anxiety." Friends who glimpsed him in the street were sometimes taken aback at his shabbiness. He was conscious of this in a half-amused way, as in a letter thanking Creech Jones for a gift of cigars: "I am told by a candid friend that, before smoking in public so superior a cigar, I must buy new clothes, or I shall be suspected of having stolen it." During 1961, Creech Jones, Rees, and other friends tried to despatch him on a sea cruise—using the remainder of the birthday fund money—but Tawney did not quite have the will and energy to get himself organized for it.[55]

The winter of 1961-62 was tough on him, and on Saturday, January 13, he went into a nursing home in Fitzroy Square. He took *War and Peace* with him, and two books by Stanley Weyman. He was happy to be still in Bloomsbury, near, he observed, where Shaw had lived. But his friends found no good portent in reports that he was being a model patient. "We old people are an awful nuisance," he murmured to a visitor with unwonted pathos.[56]

Once before he had faced death. Of that day on the Somme he wrote: "By a merciful arrangement, when one's half-dead the extra plunge doesn't seem very terrible. One's lost part of one's interest in life. The roots are loosened, and seem ready to come away without any very agonising wrench. Tolstoi's account of the death of Prince Andrew is true." It was that way. On the Tuesday afternoon he died peacefully in his sleep, Tolstoi on the bedside table. Tawney as he had been known was no more. Lucy Rice wrote to Ashton: "the biggest jobs are the books and papers. I am glad that he didn't leave any work undone. He was always working against time."[57]

Perhaps Tawney did not cling desperately to life because he seldom clung desperately to anything during his life. Building an individual kingdom of his own—money, power, esteem, a network of exclusive ties—did not interest him. What he wrote in his diary in 1912 as aspiration could, fifty years on, have been his epitaph.

Tawney in his last years.

The greatest mistake that we make with our own lives is to *snatch* at the particular objects we desire . . . If we realized the riches that lie within everyone of us we should know that we can all afford to be spendthrift of nine-tenths of the possessions which we treasure; success, praise, and good opinion among men, achievements, and still more material well-being . . . Never be afraid of throwing away what you have. If you *can* throw it away it is not really yours. If it is really yours you cannot throw it away. And you may be certain that if you throw it away, whatever in you is greater than you will produce something in its place. Never be afraid of pruning your branches. Trust the future and take risks. In moral, as in economic affairs, the rash man is he who does not speculate.[58]

This profound nonacquisitiveness of spirit must have taken some of the sting out of death for Tawney. If he was nothing else, Tawney was an *unafraid* man, and death no doubt holds reduced terror for those who have not feared life.

Only a few intimates were at Highgate, in high wind and rain, when Tawney was buried at Jeannette's side under tall poplars. Gordon Huelin, vicar of St. Bartholomews, spoke of Tawney's religious faith, as he saw it in the last, brief years he had known Tawney. A worker threw on the first earth. Two weeks later a large and astonishingly varied congregation attended a memorial service at St. Martins-in-the-Fields.[59] Psalm 15 was read, which praises "he that putteth not out his money to usury, nor taketh reward against the innocent."

Few were left who could have spoken intimately of Tawney. What would Gore or Temple have said; Wadsworth, or Hammond, or Ernest Simon; E. S. Cartwright, or Webb, or George Unwin; Lord Sankey of the Coal Commission; the nameless man who was beside Tawney on the Somme: "the kindest and bravest of friends . . . a bricklayer by trade . . . the man whom of all others I would choose to have beside me at a pinch; but he's dead"? It was Hugh Gaitskell who spoke: "I think he was the best man I have ever known." Tawney left £7,096, all of it, after certain small gifts, to the WEA.[60]

Part Two. Tawney's Socialism

5 EQUALITY

If men are to respect each other for what they are, they must cease to respect each other for what they own. They must abolish, in short, the reverence for riches, which is the *lues Anglicana*, the hereditary disease of the English nation. And human nature being what it is, in order to abolish the reverence for riches, they must make impossible the existence of a class which is important merely because it is rich.
(*Equality*, p. 87)

The strange English version of equality . . . with its courageous assertion that all incomes of equal dimensions, whatever their source, were equally respectable, acquired the prestige which belongs to success.
("Lectures on Seventeenth-Century English History"; LSE)

For Tawney, socialism stood opposed to two phenomena of capitalism: privilege and tyranny.[1] Privilege pertains to the circumstances of social and economic life. It is the special advantage of wealth and status enjoyed by certain groups in a capitalist society. Tyranny pertains to the distribution of power. Against privilege, Tawney set equality. Against tyranny, he set dispersion and control of power.

ASPECTS OF EQUALITY

Four conceptions of equality may be distinguished from Tawney's. First, unlike Rousseau, who wrote, "From the moment one man needed the help of another, equality disappeared," Tawney did not consider that all inequality has its source in social organization as such.[2] Nor did he think man was in any way better off isolated than bound up in the web of society.[3] Rousseau set himself against the oppressive weight of authorities that stifled a person's life. Tawney, heir to the doctrines of positive liberalism of the socialistically inclined followers of T. H. Green, set himself against social anarchy, which exposed a person's life to the consequences of an impersonal economic mechanism. The inequality which Tawney denounced was, he considered, a product of specifically capitalist social organization.

Second, Tawney did not espouse any sharp form of quantitative equality; he did not urge equal incomes for all Englishmen. "Differences of remuneration between different individuals might remain," he said in describing the equality he proposed, "contrasts between the civilisation of different classes would vanish." On occasion Tawney appeared to severely downgrade the importance of equal incomes. "What is repulsive is not that one man should earn more than others, for where community of environment, and a common education and habit of life, have bred a common tradition of respect and consideration, these details of the counting-house are forgotten or ignored." To put it briefly for the moment, Tawney did not have an arithmetical but an algebraic notion of equality.[4]

Third, Tawney did not embrace proportional equality any more than quantitative equality; he transcended both. As Isaiah Berlin has conceded, proportional equality boils down to "fairness." People should be treated on the basis of rational and relevant criteria, and not arbitrarily.[5] Equality viewed as fairness has something but not much to do with Tawney's equality. To eliminate illogical and capricious inequalities may leave society with even greater, if rational inequalities.

Moreover, equality viewed as fairness is not based upon an evaluation, central for Tawney, of the equal worth men possess simply by virtue of their common nature as men. It is true that Tawney favored differential treatment for different people; "equality of provision is not identity of provision." But this would be founded, not on hierarchy of deserts, but mainly on the different kinds of needs men have. Analogous to "a doctor who prescribes different regimens for different constitutions, or a teacher who develops different types of intelligence by different curricula."[6] Tawney's position thus differed from proportional equality at two points. He was concerned not just with the principles according to which people are treated, but with the *social results* of the treatment people receive. He did not totally reject quantitative equality; he went beyond it. And his views on human nature set severe limits, in terms both of needs and deserts, to the scope for differential treatment of different people.

Fourth, Tawney's equality was not the same as the most widespread conception of equality, "equality of opportunity." He took an historical approach to equality of opportunity. It was a liberating cry only when the overriding task was to remove legal and political inequalities. Richard Wollheim has tried to focus on the principle of equality "as it is"; Berlin to "isolate the pure ore of egalitarianism" from alloys with which it is frequently mixed.[7] For Tawney this enterprise is only partially possible. *Equal rights* may be thus pinned down, but equal rights was no longer the nerve center of equality. The twentieth-century question was equal rights to *what*.

Equality as an absence of disabilities was apt during the struggle against the privileges of kings, nobles, and priests. But now equality hinged on the presence of abilities. The struggle was no longer for legal and political equality, but for economic and social equality. If as Tawney believed, "economic realities make short work of legal abstractions," equality of opportunity, under certain economic conditions, amounts to little more than "the impertinent courtesy of an invitation offered to unwelcome guests, in the certainty that circumstances will prevent them from accepting it."[8]

In the struggle against feudalism, equality of opportunity was an important idea (the United States, whose traditions Tawney admired more than most British socialists, was its incarnation).[9] Capitalism, however, posed a new set of problems. The "claim for an open road to individual advancement" was no longer a progressive cry. The principle of equality now called for "collective movements to narrow the space between valley and peak."[10]

In sum, Tawney saw three objections to equality of opportunity. It had been overtaken by events in the economic life of Britain; it established no relation between opportunity and the prospects of human self-fulfillment; it said nothing about the *relationship between people* which would result from equality of opportunity.

EQUALITY AND EQUAL WORTH

Now we confront Tawney's equality, which rests on three pillars. The first is his Christian view that all men share a common humanity. Contemplate the infinitely great, and human differences seem infinitely small. Tawney saw a link between the decline of religion and England's new religion of inequality. A diary entry in 1913 reads:

> What is wrong with the modern world is that having ceased to believe in the greatness of God, & therefore the infinite smallness (or greatness—the same thing!) of *man*, it has to invent or emphasise distinctions between *men*. It does not say "I have said, Ye are Gods!" Nor does it say "All flesh is grass." It can neither rise to the heights or descend to the depths (these meet in a spiritual exaltation which may be called either optimism or pessimism). What it does say is that *some* men are Gods, & that some flesh is grass, and that the former should live on the latter (combined with *pate de fois gras* & champagne). And this is false.[11]

Here is the basis of Tawney's lifelong insistence that "man as man" has value and traits that transcend all differences.

By contrast, Aristotelian equality seems hardly about equality at all. Berlin, though he appeared to accept as a starting point "common humanity," went on to state: "Then, given that there is a class of human beings, it will follow that all members of this class, namely, men, should in every respect be treated in a uniform and identical manner, *unless there is sufficient reason not to do so.*"[12] The italicized phrase entirely begs the question from Tawney's point of view.

Tawney at once claimed less and more than Berlin. He did not claim uniform and identical treatment, yet he plunged into the problem of "sufficient reason." Is there sufficient reason, he asked, to treat people unequally, and his answer was no. It is here that Tawney's doctrine of common humanity applies. He went beyond equality as "equal consideration" (a conception embraced, in effect, by the present South African government, which claims it gives equal consideration to white and black). He went beyond equality as "treating people in the same circumstances equally" (embraced, in effect, by the government of the Third Reich, which argued the Jew did not find himself in the same circumstances as the Aryan). In a word, he sought to close a crucial trapdoor to inequality, generally retained by the various proponents of proportional equality.

But what is common humanity? It is not a question of equal capacities. "I do not share the illusion that all men are born with equal endowments," Tawney said ironically in a speech to the WEA in Ramsay MacDonald's time. "If anyone does, let him deal for a short time with the great ones of this world and I guarantee a lightning cure."[13] But it is more than a mere hope that a common humanity is attainable if men are good and wise enough to pursue it steadfastly. Tawney thought history and common observation bear out the Christian view that all men have marked, common limitations. None are so pure that they part company morally altogether from their fellow mortals. None are so irredeemably wretched that other men cannot see in them, as in a mirror, basic attributes of the human condition which command a minimum of respect.

This amounts to an assertion of the equal worth of all men. It has roots in experience, but it cannot stand without a foundation in mere faith, that since God values each man as an end in himself, therefore men share a common humanity more basic than any differential that divides them. "It is the truth expressed in the parable of the prodigal son," Tawney declared, "the truth that it is absurd and degrading for men to make much of their intellectual and moral superiority to each other, and still more of their superiority in the arts which bring wealth and power, because, judged by their place in any universal scheme, they are all infinitely great or infinitely small."[14]

Tawney also made an argument, still on Christian grounds, that human identity is the basis of obligation. His diary records: "a belief in equality means that because men are men they are bound to acknowledge that man has claims upon man."[15] From this, there stem several branches of Tawney's case against capitalism. Nothing can therefore justify one man using another as a tool. The personality of man, not wealth, or power, or numbers, or learning, is the yardstick with which to test the social order. Compulsion, Tawney reasoned, is not really the basis of order. Equality is. For mere compulsion, as in capitalist industry, produces not order but disorder; in the end, revolution. Order will prevail only when people freely recognize their obligations—and obligation is only recognized where there is identity of nature.

Where did Tawney's view of human nature come from? Not only biblical teachings ("He hath put down the mighty from their seats, and exalted them of low degree") but experience of the English upper classes, in the army, at Oxford, and through his family's Indian connections, disinclined Tawney to respect the high and mighty.

From the battlefields of France during the Great War, he wrote to Beveridge of "these great little men [who] stamp and fume and gnaw their moustaches and abuse their subordinates for their mistakes."[16] The well-born British officers were simply incompetent. "The worst of the military system [is] one can never bring one's superiors—the men who make the really big blunders—to book . . . they escape scot free, or with nothing worse than a peerage." The more he saw of the British elite the emptier seemed its self-image as a class born to rule.

In war, its leadership mystique was at the mercy of its very human lack of courage, and its very aristocratic "ignorance of the ordinary affairs of men." In India, only a thin thread of circumstance, unrelated to any natural distinction, put pompous Englishmen in authority over Indian peasants. At Oxford, only rarely did privileged students, whom money and position alone had singled out above the miners of Wales and the millhands of Manchester, possess moral worth to match their social and economic worth. A story Tawney told of William Temple sums up Tawney's mischievous depreciation of the snobbery of the social elite. He says to a visitor: "Take a chair, Mr. Jones." The visitor responds: "Mr. *Montague*-Jones, if you please." And Temple says: "Indeed? Take two chairs."[17]

Tawney discovered that few seemed worthy of great place. He also discovered, in London's East End, in Manchester, and among the workers of his tutorial classes, that ordinary folk were as capable and virtuous as those who, in the name of economic freedom, ruled industry and thereby ruled the "hands" which stoked the furnaces and worked the looms. The men at Rochdale, summarizing British economic history in grubby notebooks, their pencils gripped in rough hands with dirty fingernails, proved, despite their tiredness after a day's work, to have minds no less capable than the sons of their bosses at Oxford. "If I were asked where I received the best part of my own education," Tawney reflected after fifty years of the WEA, "I should reply, not at school or college, but in the days when as a young, inexperienced and conceited teacher of Tutorial Classes, I underwent, week by week, a series of friendly, but effective, deflations at the hands of the students composing them."[18] These men taught Tawney as much about the practical conditions of industry as he taught them about the past and about theory.

Certain socialist intellectuals of Tawney's generation romanticized the working class. "The men of my age know it very well," Sartre has observed, "that the great reality of their lives, more important even than the two world wars, was their encounter with the working-class and its ideology. This offered us an inattackable vision of the world and of ourselves."[19] One may wonder how concrete was Sartre's encounter with the working class. Perhaps Orwell was franker: "But is it ever possible to be really intimate with the working-class? . . . I do not think it is possible."[20] In the case of Tawney, his opinion of the working class was based upon concrete knowledge. Asked what had made him a socialist, he replied: "Going out into the world and meeting working people."[21] If Keynes regarded the bourgeoisie and the intelligentsia as "fish" and the proletariat as "mud," Tawney rejected this moral and mental distinction.[22] He simply found working people impressive; in all that mattered they seemed the equal of those men considered their "betters."

But Tawney did not romanticize the working class. Personal experience suggested to Tawney, not only that working people were equally as talented and sensitive as the middle and upper classes, but that they were also equally frail. A Christian view of man was confirmed by (or built upon?) Tawney's own observations. War experience dented the Cairdian idealist view of political man in Tawney's mind, and strengthened the Christian realist view which is characteristic of his mature writings. He began to use "Henry Dubb" ("common, courageous, good-hearted, patient, proletarian fool") as a paradigm of the worker.[23]

Biographically, then, there existed ar experiential root to Tawney's Christian view that all men are of equal worth. This view set limits to the differences of treatment due different individuals. But what limits? The idea of equal worth was vague. It ruled out certain inhumanities, and is thus a far from useless principle, since inhumanities are common enough; Aristotle's proportional equality was compatible with slavery. But what did it positively require? Did the equal worth of all children mean that a dullhead would have fifteen years of free education just as a Newton?

Equal worth may appear to leave Tawney leaning to quantitative equality. He was not content with equal rights. The result of the exercise of rights concerned him even more than the nature of the rights. And he did not separate his belief in equal worth from empirical tests. He saw limits to how good were the good, both morally and intellectually, and to how bad were the bad. Somehow, he appeared to endorse an idea of equality as equality of condition. Was he asking, not merely that people be treated equally, but that they be treated to equal portions?

EQUALITY AND SELF-FULFILLMENT

These issues posed, consider the second pillar of Tawney's equality. It is a doctrine of self-fulfillment. Society should be so organized that "all its members may be equally enabled to make the best of such powers as they possess."[24] Tawney liked to say that he agreed with F. A. von Hayek (the two had basic disagreements) on one important matter: the highest political good is freedom. Tawney, however, unlike Hayek, invested his understanding of freedom with the idea of the self-fulfillment of the individual, and also with the idea, reminiscent of Milton, that freedom carries the connotation of freedom to do one's duty.[25]

If brilliant man and plodder are each alike enabled to fulfill themselves, will not the result be inequality of condition? Not according to Tawney's Christian theory of equality, for there is enough "gold" in every man, however diverse its forms, to ensure that the application of the doctrine of self-fulfillment will reduce inequalities.* Self-fulfillment (like respect) becomes an egalitarian idea the moment the argument that men as men are equal is accepted. Thus harnessed, the two together provide clearer guidelines for policy than the idea of equal worth by itself.

H. A. Bedau aptly observed that it is unreasonable to declare that an "inequality is an equality merely because it is justified."[26] If the application of the doctrine of self-fulfillment does not lead to a diminution of inequality, there is no good reason to consider it an egalitarian doctrine (numerous nineteenth-century political thinkers held the doctrine of self-fulfillment without egalitarian implications). There may be societies in which an application of the doctrine of self-fulfillment could actually have an antiegalitarian implication.

But Tawney's England was not such a society. Millions remained fulfilled in basic ways. Health and education were manifestly purchasable commodities. In such circumstances, what people need takes on a sharply different meaning from that given it in abstract discussions of equality. Bedau used the case of distributing free tickets to a theater performance to demonstrate that need has got nothing to do with equality. One person, one ticket, would seem the egalitarian doctrine. But suppose, Bedau reasoned, one man did not care for the theater, and another wished to bring a friend with him? Such a case has very little to do with the problem of inequality as Tawney wrestled with it. The need for theater tickets is subject to more mercurial fluctuation than the need for food and shelter. Tawney met this point, in dealing with Burke's statement that all men have equal rights, yet not to equal things:

> But, unfortunately, Nature with her lamentable indifference to the maxims of philosophers, has arranged that certain things, such as light, fresh air, warmth, rest, and food, shall be equally necessary to all her children, with

*Tawney thus encapsulated the evolution which liberalism was undergoing in the late nineteenth century. Democracy posed for liberalism the challenge of equality. Inheriting liberalism's values, it went on to proclaim them the legitimate aspiration, not of the upper and middle classes alone, but of every man. Tawney provided a firm theoretical base for this challenge to liberalism.

the result that, unless they have equal access to them, they can hardly be said to have equal rights, since some of them will die before the rights can be exercised, and others will be too enfeebled to exercise them effectively.[27]

Self-fulfillment, though it may lack egalitarian implications when the question is theater tickets, did not lack them when the question was economic and social policies in Tawney's England.

Yet we are still in a realm of imprecision. If Tawney was not content with equality as what Friedrich called "appropriate differentiation," or what Benn and Peters called "impartiality," it is not clear *how* near Tawney came to accepting quantitative equality, or upon precisely what basis he would have done so.[28] Sir Francis Chichester, being of equal worth to any man in England, and standing in need of self-fulfillment by means of sailing around the world in a small boat at great expense, may demand an income from Tawney's state far in excess of that which a miner, even if he has ten children, could claim on the basis of the same two principles. How are conflicting claims to be weighed up, in a way that avoids what Tawney eschewed as sensational inequalities, and also the crude arithmetical method of actually distributing to each person the same amount of society's benefits?

EQUALITY AND SOCIAL FUNCTION

Social function stands as the third pillar of Tawney's equality. *Distribution should never fall out of relation to service rendered to the community.* Reward follows function. Once again Tawney transcended quantitative equality. "Inequality of circumstances is regarded as reasonable in so far as it is the necessary condition of securing the services which the community requires."[29] Nevertheless, it is clear, more so with function than with self-fulfillment, that severe limits on inequality of circumstance will result from its application.[30]

This is especially true when two of Tawney's subsidiary arguments are added. Function is related to reward, not only by the idea of service to the community, but by the requirement that reward should be commensurate with what a person needs in order to perform his function properly. And a limit is set on possessions by denying the right of any man to have more things than he can *use*. (There are biblical roots to these notions, and a certain puritan austerity occasionally attends Tawney's expression of them. "If a man has important work, and enough leisure and income to enable him to do it properly, he is in possession of as much happiness as is good for any of the children of Adam."[31])

Tawney's conception of social function offers a "common good" argument which tightens his idea of equality. Discussions of equality frequently see it as one among various goods that have to be calculated, and seek to separate its "pure ore" from other goods. But Tawney's view of equality is relational; he approached it in a dialectical rather than a calculative manner. Calculative discussions of equality generally assume a liberal concept of equality. Men should start equal, and their efforts should be rewarded on a competitive basis. But the argument of common good circumvents the factor of competition. Prospects for wealth and status do not hang in abstraction from social realities, nor are they unlimited. Self-fulfillment sets some limits to competition. Social function sets more.

"A country, when it becomes socialist," wrote Plamenatz, "may be no less but more competitive than it was before." The poor may contribute some bright sons to good positions, but, said Plamenatz, "once they get these jobs, they may be cut off" from their roots. "As they rise socially," as they "pass from groups of lower to groups of higher status" they will lose communication with their fellows.[32] Plamenatz was talking about equality of opportunity. He assumed an atomistic society. Tawney hit at the whole notion of rising in society, and his theoretical basis for equality obviated it.

The social depths and heights from which people might rise or to which they might fall would be limited by tying distribution to talent, character, and service to society. And the individualism which alone gives meaning to competition would be similarly limited (as concerning wealth). If material allocations were tied, for example, to social function, the factors determining individuality would be other than economic factors. Competition would attain full vigor in realms other than those of getting bigger incomes and amassing bigger fortunes.

Half a century later it is easy to underestimate the extent to which Tawney's equality carried a radical challenge to British society. Plamenatz wrote: "The principle that privileges should correspond to services is recognized in all societies." But in Tawney's Britain this principle was not accepted (nor is it fully accepted today). Tawney's appeal to social function was as radical in the context of the moment as the appeal to antiquity was radical on the lips of sixteenth-century theorists, or the appeal to natural rights at the time of the English Civil War. In 1938, two thirds of the aggregate wealth of Britain was still owned by one percent of the people.[33] Women had no vote in the years when Tawney wrote most of his books, and the burden of election expenses and the power of the hereditary House of Lords detracted from political equality. Tawney's last writings acknowledged a lessening of inequality in Britain since he had first written on the subject in Edwardian times; it would have occurred more slowly without his own efforts.[34]

Unlike liberal equality, Tawney's equality is not purely negative. Benn and Peters wrote: "Claims to equality are thus, in a sense, always negative, denying the propriety of certain existing inequalities."[35] This statement seems to be anchored in liberal assumptions. "A positive egalitarianism," the authors believe, "demanding similar treatment for all, irrespective of *any* difference, would clearly lead to absurdities." Tawney maintained a positive egalitarianism, but it was not so crude as this mechanical and arithmetical notion raised up and put down by Benn and Peters. He had something subtler in mind than to "sweep away all distinctions" and thus "commit injustices as inexcusable as any under attack." It is positive egalitarianism in the sense that it grounds equality in a total view of social justice.

Observe first that its cause does not come to an end, as Tom Paine's may appear to, when a particular set of oppressors have been eliminated. Tawney warned: "It is idle to urge that any alternative is preferable to government by the greedy materialists who rule mankind at present, for greed and materialism are not the monopoly of a class . . . So, in the long run, it is the principles which men accept as the basis of their social organization which matter."[36] Nor is Tawney's equality properly realized if wealth is momentarily equalized by an all-powerful dictator, or a sudden arithmetical redistribution. Tawney offered an algebraic not an arithmetical version of equality. Equality was to be built into the central and permanent processes of society. It will exist, he was fond of saying, when anyone will be able to say to anyone else "Go to Hell," yet no one will want to, and no man will need go when it is said.

Equality was defined by Tawney, then, in terms of right relationships between people. It was sought for the sake of fellowship. It stood upon the three pillars of equal worth, self-fulfillment, and social function. Viewed historically, the second and especially the third pillars extended the notion of equality from the legal and political realm to economic and social life. Everyone lauds a tradition after it has been created; thus with legal equality. It is perilous to create a tradition, as Tawney did in the case of social-economic equality; yet the two categories are consanguine. The case for both legal and economic equality hinges upon abstracting people in some degree from various unequal environments. "The legal equality before the law," says Friedrich, "is in a sense the secular version of the creaturely equality before God."[37] Tawney derived an idea of social-economic equality from the same source (equal worth), by linking it to self-fulfillment and social function, and viewing it historically.

Conservatives, though once convinced that legal equality was as monstrous and anarchic a doctrine as they still thought economic equality to be when Tawney wrote, did eventually abstract the individual far enough from the effects of environment to accept equality before the law. Tawney applied the same principle to contemporary social and economic conditions. His claim was that "the existence of differences of personal capacity and attainment is as irrelevant to the question whether it is desirable that the social environment and economic organization should be made more conducive to equality as it is to the question of equality before the law."[38]

THE FRUITS OF EQUALITY

Tawney expected from equality certain fruits, which would characterize socialist society. The wastefulness of capitalism would be reduced. On grounds of equal worth, self-fulfillment, and social function, children of twelve should be kept in school, for example, and not given to industry which "needed" them. The result, long and short term, would be less personal waste and less national waste.

The need for maximum national war effort had caused some in the 1940s to see a value in social and economic equality they had not seen before. "The crisis," Tawney drily remarked of a radical editorial in the *Times* during 1940, "for a moment set Saul also among the prophets."[39] The impact of wartime experience, on the public, politicians, and civil servants, made it easier for the Labour government to introduce equalizing policies after 1945. But Saul did not long remain among the prophets, and Tawney's case for an equality that would advance a common culture extended beyond the need for national strength in emergencies. "Sharp contrasts between economic standards and educational opportunities of different classes," he noted, "have as their result, not a common culture, but servility or resentment, on the one hand, and patronage or arrogance, on the other." Tawney regretted the attitude of the working-class to the upper-class almost as much as he regretted the converse attitude. Privileges produce "callousness in those who profit by them, and resentment in those who do not."[40] The value of equality lies in removing both evils.

A common culture is thus a new creation, not a leveling down to the existing working-class mentality or a leveling up to the existing middle-class or upper-class mentality. Individual character, diverse and even eccentric, will flower when personality, rather than wealth, is the badge of a man's social position. "Individual differences, which are a source of social energy, are more likely to ripen and find expression if social inequalities are, as far as practicable, diminished."

In so far as wealth generates power, a further fruit of equality would be elimination of concentrations of power which are fatal to the mobilization of cooperative effort. The freedom of the majority is enlarged. Tawney acknowledged that, as "freedom for the pike is death for the minnows," so is effective freedom for the minnows death for the pike *as pike*. Social and economic equality would destroy the aristocracy as a class. Tawney's three pillars for equality gave his justification for that. But in the measure that freedom is undermined not only by tyranny but by inequality (privilege for some to hold sway over others) an advance toward equality is an advance toward freedom.

Tawney carried the discussion of equality, in a novel way, from the plane of distributive justice to the plane of social relationships. Not only equal rights, but the result of equal rights and egalitarian institutions interested him. The implication of equality (and inequality) for the richness of man's common life was the paramount issue. Equality, in the sense of identity of nature, was also the only sound basis for the claims of one against another. Thus it became for Tawney the ground of obligation, and ultimately of order.

"Equality has no importance in itself," Mao Tse-tung said to Malraux; "its importance springs from it being the natural mode of those who have not lost contact with the masses."[41] This distinction was crucial in Tawney. He wanted to see in Britain an egalitarian social atmosphere, with people naturally in easy communication with each other, respecting each other without regard to birth, wealth, or reputation. Equality as the *condition* of disparate individuals (which is the sense of quantitative equality) was less important, for Tawney as for Mao, than equality as relationship.

In a talk at the LSE when his seventieth birthday portrait was unveiled, Tawney hinted why he preferred the LSE to Oxford and Cambridge:

> its simplicity, its *terre à terre* quality, its freedom from formality and inhibitions which is the note of its social atmosphere. People talk of the advantage of traditions . . . but I regard them as ornaments which it is more pleasant to admire or criticise in other people than to wear oneself.

Such an atmosphere he not only found more congenial, but more productive than that of the universities with an aristocratic past:

> There is [at LSE] a natural and easy give and take between students and staff and different members of the staff. People stand on their merits, and do not, as at some universities, acquire a status of undeserved inflation from the dignity of the institution to which they belong. A natural and unlaboured equalitarianism is the best atmosphere both for work and for young people.[42]

Tawney delighted in this unlabored egalitarianism. He helped reproduce it in the Economic History Society, by holding conferences in halls of residence, rather than in luxury hotels where people never meet each other, in his classes, where the idea, not the teacher was sovereign, and at Stroud, in Gloucestershire, where he used to trade yarns with villagers about their work and local folklore. In the WEA, he refused to call people by their titles, or himself be called by his academic title. In the Labour party, he railed against "Honours" (of peerages: "Cruel boys tie tin cans to the tails of dogs; but even a mad dog does not tie a can to its own tail."[43]) Egalitarianism, too, marked his relations with people who worked for him—he insisted on his housekeeper attending his eightieth birthday dinner at the House of Commons.

Tawney wanted "unlaboured equalitarianism" and the "*terre à terre* quality" to exist throughout British society, not just in isolated pockets where socialists created anticipations of socialism by special initiative. "A common culture cannot be created merely by desiring it. It must rest upon practical foundations of social organization."[44] That meant, in the first place, breaking down social and economic inequalities, so that Englishmen would respect each other for what they were, not what they owned. They would be encouraged to cherish and act upon the basis of the common humanity which united them, rather than the external circumstances which divided them. *The Great Learning* of ancient China contained the ultimate point of Tawney's equality: "To centralise wealth is to disperse the people, to distribute wealth is to collect the people."[45] Tawney wanted equality in order to collect the people.

We arrive at the centrality of fellowship in Tawney's socialism. Each of the three pillars of equality has its roots in fellowship. The equal worth of all men is derived from a Christian belief in the fatherhood of God. Men are of equal worth because of their common condition (brotherhood) as sons of God. Self-fulfillment is seen, not in hyperindividualistic terms as with the nineteenth-century philosophers of success, but in social terms. Education ("the process by which we break down the barriers of our individual isolation, and become partners in a kingdom of ideas which we share with our fellows"), furthers self-fulfillment conceived in terms of fellowship.[46] Its proper provision, too, is impossible except upon fraternal assumptions. The third pillar, social function, ties equality very closely to fellowship. It relates rewards to social purposes, and requires rewards to advance, not hinder, egalitarian social relationships.

Tawney's "equality for the sake of fellowship" is quite different from liberal views of equality. One searches in vain for commentators who treat equality as other than one component (competing with other components) of justice toward the individual. Dewey observed: "Equality denotes the unhampered share which each individual member of the community has in the consequences of associated action." Plamenatz laid down: "champions of equality have been concerned above all to preserve or to enlarge the following things: personal security, symmetry or due proportion, freedom, decency, and dignity."[47] This list does not touch, nor does Dewey's definition, what is important about equality for Tawney.

Tawney was interested not only in the treatment of individuals, but also in the consequences for the health of the whole society of the way individuals are treated. It was in the realm of social relationships that he bid for equality; equality was a means to the paramount good of fellowship.

6 DISPERSION OF POWER

A conception of Socialism which views it as involving the nationalisation of everything except political power, on which all else depends, is not, to speak with moderation, according to light. The question is not merely whether the State owns and controls the means of production. It is also who owns and controls the State.
("Christianity and the Social Revolution," *The Attack*, p. 165)

When Birmingham and Manchester and Leeds are the little republics which they should be . . .
(*The Acquisitive Society*, p. 121)

Men exercise only the power that they are allowed to exercise by other men, whom, when their clothes are off, they much resemble; so that the strong are rarely as powerful as they are thought by the weak, or the weak as powerless as they are thought by themselves.
(*Equality*, p. 159)

"The alternative to religion," observed Tawney in his Burge Lecture, *The Western Political Tradition*, "is rarely irreligion; it is a counter-religion."[1] Into the vacuum rush new gods. "The apostasies waiting to succeed are legion; but the most popular claimants to the political throne have commonly been two. They are the worship of riches, and the worship of power." The consequence of the first is privilege, of the second, tyranny. As religion lost its sway over social norms and institutions, Britain inclined more to the worship of riches than to the worship of power. Nevertheless, Tawney was much concerned with tyranny, and the interconnections between economic power and political power.

THE THREAT OF AUTHORITARIANISM

Equality may exist under a variety of political regimes. "Diffused wealth is expedient for governments," declared the monarchist Francis Bacon. The authoritarian Hobbes favored equality because it would make easier control of the citizenry. The early Bentham, no democrat, favored equality because it would facilitate scientific administration.

For Tawney, socialism was not concerned with economic and social conditions alone. The "horizontal" shape of socialism is equality. The "vertical" shape of socialism must be control and dispersion of power.

It is a curiosity of Tawney's career that he faded somewhat from the scene during the 1930s, the decade supposed to constitute a peak of influence for socialist intellectuals. He published less in this decade (the decade of the Left Book Club and thousands of socialist pamphlets) than in any decade of his sixty mature years. After *Land and Labour in China* (1932), indeed, there was no book for twenty years. Tawney was depressed, and intellectually a bit paralyzed, by the intensifying concentration of irresponsible governmental power and the rise of totalitarian ideologies all over Europe.

The young Tawney, as we know from a document among his unpublished papers, found a focus for his concern with political thought in an attack on mechanistic and organic notions of the sovereign state, acknowledging no higher principle than its own existence, unresponsive to the moral purposes of its citizens.[2] This was during the Great War. Within twenty years the subject of this unpublished paper, "The New Leviathan," became increasingly a reality. In all countries where democracy had been a recent growth, authoritarian rule smothered it. Even in Britain, democracy as a political form was gravely threatened, not only from without but by concentrations of various forms of power within.

Like other thinkers of his time, Tawney saw Europe in the grip of a single crisis. A "frantic dervish" such as Hitler got Germany to "truckle to hoary sophisms."[3] But Stalinism, as Tawney said from the start, was only marginally better. The democracies, moreover, seemed likely to follow one or the other if, "prizing property above freedom" they remained a "democracy in form, and plutocracy in fact." And it was not only in Berlin and Vienna that intellectuals "held up a candle" to tyranny. Closer to home, they seemed to forget, as Tawney would not, that the supreme political good is freedom.

Had it not all happened before? In the hundred years between the dissolution of the monasteries and the civil war—

"Tawney's Century," Trevor-Roper called it[4] —there was in political thought a "marked shift away from questions of legitimate authority, with their connotations of a stable political world, to *questions of power*, or the ability to exert mastery by controlling an unstable complex of moving forces."[5] In this period political thinkers had to grapple with the problem of disorder (or wickedness as it seemed to Calvin). They became preoccupied with the question of how to strengthen government discipline, for the purpose, urged on the sovereign prince by Bodin, of repressing disorder. Tudors, Valois, Habsburgs—all helped to sculpt the modern state. Machiavelli, Hooker, Calvin—all directed special attention to justifying authority. Political will burst through against higher sanctions. If the medieval conception was that law is *discovered*, the Tudor conception was that law is *made*. More's view that the purpose of society was the moral improvement of the people was soon a relic of the past.

Too much should not be made of any historical parallel, yet Tawney was both a leading British historian of the sixteenth and seventeenth centuries *and* a noted social philosopher of the twentieth-century crisis. He did not become an historian of the origins of capitalism by accident or inheritance. He "found the world surprising" and turned to the sixteenth century to understand it better. Armed with questions and values formed in Edwardian England, he dug into Tudor and Stuart history not with mere parallels in mind, but to lay bare the shaping forces of modern England. In some respects, he considered the disasters which unfolded in the period dating from August 1914 to be culminations of certain developments of the sixteenth and seventeenth centuries.

Tawney felt that the concentration of irresponsible governmental power, and the theory of untrammeled political will that went with it, were only possible in a society from which religious authority had largely disappeared.[6] In Tawney's terminology, the "vacant throne" of religious authority was occupied by totalitarian power theories and the secular messiahs who incarnated them. The removal of the restraint of a higher religious authority was a crucial development toward what in 1939 he called "the monstrous doctrine of national sovereignty, which, in 1919, was preserved by loving hands, like some rare and fragrant flower, but whose principle is murder."[7]

By then nationalism and the idea of sovereignty were harnessed, and in combination enjoyed a dangerous potency that separately (as, for example, in Burke's version of nationalism, unaccompanied by a theory of sovereignty) neither possessed. The rise of political ideologies saw two essential streams. A rationalist-utopian response to industrialization and other aspects of modernization, and a romantic-conservative response. In Tawney's time, the two streams could be observed in bolshevism and fascism respectively. Both were totalitarian ideologies, supreme expressions of the autonomy of politics.

To be sure, it had been the autonomy of economics as much if not more than the autonomy of politics that Tawney had analyzed in his historical work, expressed in his famous dichotomy between mechanism and purpose in the social thought of the sixteenth century. But the two doctrines were creatures of the same genus when viewed, as Tawney viewed them, from the standpoint of religious sanctions in the first place, and true social democracy in the second place.

What occurred during the "era of tyrannies" (the three or four decades after 1914) as the totalist ideologies flourished was a shift of emphasis from economic to political categories. In contrast to the major social philosophers of the nineteenth century, those of the early twentieth century took the view that society could not be properly analyzed nor cohesion won by means of economic categories alone. Within communism the difference between Marx and Lenin was testimony to the change. "The central point of Lenin's argument," Wolin aptly observed, "was the refutation of an assumption common to classical liberalism, early socialism and Marx as well: the primordial importance of economic phenomena."[8] The same was true of Fascism. Nietzsche's affirmation, "I am the last anti-political German," turned out a prophecy.

Where is Tawney in the midst of this? Peculiarly sensitive to this outburst of the triumphalism of political will, he looks at times like a latter-day More, forlornly trying to uphold a moral conception of politics in the face of hopeless odds. Unlike some on the left, he possessed a basis of historical discernment on which to oppose "half-insane ideologies masquerading as revelations," even when they came out of the rationalist-utopian tradition of the nineteenth century.[9]

His criticisms of Calvinism, which made "Geneva a city of glass, in which every household lived its life under the supervision of a spiritual police," are remarkably similar to his criticisms of the Soviet dictatorship, and he likened the religious wars and conflicts of the sixteenth century to the "creedal war" of the twentieth century.[10]

The trend toward concentration of power was first discerned by Tawney in the agricultural changes of the sixteenth century.[11] As he mapped the shift from subsistence to commercial farming—open strips to enclosures, small copyhold to large leasehold properties—his value judgments were visible. A wide dispersal of land among independent smallholders, and avoidance of landlordism and landlessness, seemed to him the best economic basis on which to secure the highest political good—freedom. But wealth and power did not long remain thus dispersed. Referring to the United States, where Jeffersonianism had expressed much that he favored, he observed regretfully: "The magnificent formulae in which a society of farmers, merchants and master craftsmen enshrined its philosophy of freedom are in danger of becoming fetters used by an Anglo-Saxon business aristocracy to bind insurgent movements on the part of an immigrant and semi-servile proletariat."[12] Tawney hankered, in a way, for Jeffersonianism.

THE NATURE OF POWER

Socialists have seldom analyzed profoundly the nature of power. Perhaps the first generations of socialists, like their eighteenth-century progenitors, were so opposed to the state power of their day that it was difficult for them to analyze power dispassionately. Later, when the anarchist and syndicalist versions of socialism were swept aside, both Fabian collectivism and Leninism—the two major forms of socialism after the collapse of the Second International—swung far in the opposite direction, lauding the strong state as the proper vehicle for socialism.

Tawney was not impressed with anarchism, or with schemes for implementing socialism through model communities in pristine isolation from the levers of state power. Nor was he ever really a guild socialist. But he did not entirely agree with Webbsian collectivism either, especially in early years. His diary records his rejection of collectivism and guild socialism. "How state management deadens spiritual life is evidenced by the Church of England. How syndicalist management fosters corporate selfishness is shown by the bar and by Oxford and Cambridge."[13] Nor did Tawney opt for the Leninist notion that concentrated power is fine so long as the working class wields it.

Not only socialist views of power, but liberal views seemed unsatisfactory. Tawney's intellectual roots lay in liberalism, but he saw that its bases—economic individualism and faith in progress and a natural harmony of interests—had lost credibility and relation with each other. Even the reformed liberalism of Hobhouse seemed, after the cataclysm of the Great War, drained of the promise it held in prewar days; when Leonard Woolf had set out for Ceylon with ninety volumes of Voltaire as his reading matter; when, as Kingsley Martin recalled, young thinkers felt that the world was "an oyster to be opened with the sharp sword of Cambridge intellectualism"; when Keynes described his circle as being like "water-spiders, skimming gracefully, as light and reasonable as air, on the surface of the stream without any contact at all with the eddies and currents underneath."[14]

Tawney confronted the eddies and currents. "The rule of liberty," Hobhouse had written in 1911, "is just the application of rational method." The "common good" sounded like something a well-run debating society would arrive at without too much difficulty. Though it wrenched his intellect and emotions somewhat apart, Tawney had to part company with this "harmonic conception"[15] of Liberalism. He found it too rationalist, optimistic, and atomistic to cope with the social conflicts engendered by agglomerations of economic and political power.

"Power," wrote Tawney, "may be defined as the capacity of an individual, or group of individuals, to modify the conduct of other individuals or groups in the manner which he [sic] desires, and to prevent his own conduct being modified in the manner in which he does not."[16] Tawney then made the startling statement that the "ultimate seat" of power is "the soul." How can this be?

Rejecting the "formal-legal" (constitutional) conception of power as being what governments possess, Tawney offered a social conception. Power in society, unlike physical power, is dialectical. It cannot be understood apart from the response it elicits or seeks to elicit. Therefore, to destroy it, "nothing more is required than to be indifferent to its threats, and to prefer other goods to those which it promises." Tawney appears to have overstated the matter here, but that need not hide his point. If power is awful, it is also fragile. It is dependent on hopes, fears, and values.

Three characteristics follow. Contrary to theories of sovereignty which, as in Austin, make of sovereignty a juristic doctrine, Tawney did not think that power resided in a determinate place. It was volatile, less a fact than a capacity; and a capacity which changes as "the interests which move men" change.

Second, power in society, like energy in physics, has multiple sources and multiple expressions. "Formal-legal" analysis is wrong to take power as political power *tout court*. Marxism is wrong to assert that all forms of power are, in the last resort, economic. For "men are so constituted as to desire other than temporal goods and to fear other than economic evils." At various times and places, power "has had its source in religion, in military prowess and prestige, in the strength of professional organization, in the exclusive control of certain forms of knowledge and skill, such as those of the magician, the medicine-man, and the lawyer." Nevertheless, at the end of a century in which England, as Tawney saw it, had bowed before the god of industrialism, the most important (and unacknowledged) source of power, which needed to be exposed and controlled, was that which Marxist analysis highlighted: property.

Third, it followed that one form of power could be transmuted into other forms of power. To be sure, not indiscriminately; many rich men failed to wring a peerage out of Disraeli. Yet Tawney demonstrated that economic power was being turned into political power, and it became a vital argument in his socialist case. Neatly inverting the formula of Saint-Simon ("The government of people becomes the administration of things"), he declared in a book which took the declaration as its major theme: "Property in things swells into something which is, in effect, sovereignty over persons."[17] The result is tyranny. "Lord Melchett smiles, and there is sunshine in 10,000 homes. Mr. Morgan frowns, and the population of two continents is plunged in gloom."[18]

POWER MUST BE DISPERSED

Tawney did not see power as an absolute evil. Socialism could not be built without utilizing power. Nor would the problems arising from the exercise of power all disappear under socialism. His idea was to disperse power. His socialist landscape would be a decentralized one. Its rationale lay in an appeal to right relationships. Power dispersed, people will be prevented from tyrannizing over each other. Any man may, as it were, say "go to hell" to another without fearful consequences. On the positive side, when power is dispersed people feel encouraged, by the trust reposed in them, to exercise their creative capacities. Not least important, when power is dispersed people may, by the habit of cooperation that is rendered normal and necessary, be led to see and believe in the common humanity they share with others (which either a hierarchical or a junglelike society obscures).

The starting-point of these notions was Tawney's view of man as a mixture of good and evil—similar to that upon which Niebuhr based his argument for democracy in *The Children of Light and the Children of Darkness.*[19] Every man has enough quality to be given some responsibility, none so much that he should be given absolute dominion over his fellows. None being angels, few being *vauriens*, men are by nature fitted for the cooperative life which a pluralist arrangement of power affords and requires.

True, some thinkers (among them Bodin), equipped with a theory of sovereignty, have denied that political power can be dispersed.[20] Tawney, however, had a comprehensive conception of power. Even Bodin upheld the inviolability of private property, and conceded that the sovereign was subject to the higher authority of God. If a comprehensive theory of power is adopted, which takes account of the economic sources of power, it is difficult to maintain, on the basis of Bodin, that "sovereignty" is in fact undivided. For what if the right of private property should clash with the will of the ruler? Or if the ruler were to make an order that contravened God's law?

In modified forms, and allowing for the fact that the will of God often has its modern counterpart in the will of the people (expressed in sometimes extraparliamentary challenges to the government, such as Chartism, or CND) these were precisely the kinds of conflicts which Tawney tried to accommodate in his approach to power. In other words, the question of whether power can be dispersed becomes a question of the definition of power. The strength of Tawney's position hinged upon his demonstration that power has multiple sources and expressions.

The case for equality and the case for dispersion of power are related. Since wealth in the capitalist system transmutes itself into power, inequality of circumstance generates inequality of power. Tawney believed in frustrating this process through death duties, progressive tax, nationalization, and by starting government-owned enterprises. Though he would not reduce inequality of circumstance to the point of arithmetical equality of income and possessions, he would erect an absolute barrier against concentration of wealth which generates "sovereignty over persons." Thus private wealth would not be permitted to prejudice litigation; it would be forbidden to spend unlimited funds on election campaigns; industry would be reorganized to do away with the "new feudalism" of fused economic and political power.

Tawney argued that democracy can only justify its claims in conditions of dispersion of power. "Democracy is unstable as a political system, as long as it remains a political system and nothing more."[21] Tawney wavered on whether democracy meant a method of government or a type of society, but it is consistent with the overall pattern of his thought to take the former view, and to treat his more expansive observations on democracy as observations on the *conditions* necessary to the effective working of democracy. The alternative interpretation is unfruitful, and ultimately leads to the unsatisfactory conclusion that Tawney meant by "democracy" what he meant by "socialism." Why is dispersion of power a necessary condition for the effective working of democracy?

It is a commonplace in the 1970s to deplore the concentration of power. It is not always clear, however, except when the criticism comes from anarchists, on what ground power is deplored. For Tawney, power was important not only as an instrument of certain policy objectives but also for its good or bad effect on social relationships. Thus concentrated power, even if it is supposed to be enforcing socialist policies, is bad. Widespread participation by the people in decision-making is desirable in itself and a basic tenet of socialism.[22]

Of course, power will inevitably be concentrated to some degree in a government. But there is the special problem of *irresponsible* power; power which lies outside the processes of government. Mill said that among the cases where representative government cannot work is that "in which a small but leading portion of the population, from difference of race, more civilised origin, or other peculiarities of circumstance, are markedly superior in civilisation and general character to the remainder."[23] That has generally been taken to apply to racial minorities, such as the *colons* in French Algeria.

Tawney showed that "peculiarities of circumstance" could take other forms too. For example, parts of English society were so cut off by differences of wealth and power from other parts that the relationship between them was effectively that of lord and servant. In such conditions democracy as a method of government could not be genuine. The arrangements of power provided by political mechanisms were swamped by concentrations of power flowing from extrapolitical sources. Tawney said "responsible" power (that which stands in a line of democratic accountability) should always be greater, at any point of time and at any place in the body social, than "irresponsible" power (that which stands outside any line of democratic accountability). To ensure this, concentrations of irresponsible power must be avoided, especially those which stem from property.

Mill said that where his condition of unity was not fulfilled, dictatorship would have to be the form of government. In the same way, Tawney thought that, in practice if not in theory, where the concentration of economic power was sufficiently great to bend democratic forms to its own contours, the result would be dictatorship. Mill proposed for such conditions a "constitutionally unlimited" (i.e. authoritarian) government. Tawney considered the alternative in the 1930s to be either advance to a truly social democracy, or descent to fascism. As World War Two began, he predicted:

Either democracy will extend its authority from the political to the economic system, and be established more firmly, because on broader foundations; or it will cease to exist, save in form, as a political institution. In Scandinavia and the British Dominions, present tendencies point to the first alternative being followed. Fascist Europe has not only established the second, but has made it a state religion, with an inquisition to enforce it. In Great Britain, France, and the US, the issue remains in doubt. In Russia, which has known no democracy, it has hardly yet arisen.[24]

Dispersion of power was necessary to democracy; it was also necessary to peace. Tawney saw international relations neither as a mere extension of the class struggle, nor as an entirely autonomous realm where balances are struck and games are played without any link to domestic social realities. In Tawney's view, what a nation was in its social system, so it would essentially be in its international conduct. Just before going off to the Great War he wrote in his diary: "War is not the reversal of the habits and ideals we cultivate in peace. It is their concentration."[25] Prussianism was but one instance of the arrogance of unbridled power. Not class, but power lay at the center of Tawney's analysis of war. By contrast, most socialists of Tawney's generation saw no link between socialism and international relations. When Woolf set out to write a book on war in 1913, his friends, including Keynes, thought of the subject as meaning just "arbitration." Reckitt recalls that in August 1914, the Fabian Society held a weekend conference "without anyone mentioning international politics at all!"[26]

Tawney saw the impulse to unlimited economic expansion, oligarchic power, and the notion of the unbridled sovereignty of the nation-state as causes of war, in the twentieth century as in the sixteenth. But like all socialists in the 1930s, Tawney sat on the horns of a dilemma. Fascism seemed to be basically a degeneration, in particular circumstances, of capitalism. The domestic cure for fascism in countries like Britain seemed to be an advance to socialism. Yet internationally the fascist powers had to be stopped, and the capitalist powers, Britain and France, were crucial to the military task. Therefore socialists, with varying degrees of conviction and consistency, fumbled toward a *union sacrée*, viewed as an intermission after which the struggle for socialism within each capitalist society would be resumed. Such a solution involved many (Laski is one) in a rapid modulation from a class theory of international relations to a girding of the loins for patriotic war.[27] Their resultant theory was a honeycomb of contradictions.

Tawney did not have to recast his position in 1939 or

1941. He had written in 1921: "Yet all the time the true cause of industrial warfare is as simple as the true cause of international warfare. It is that if men recognise no law superior to their desires, then they must fight when their desires collide; for though groups or nations which are at issue with each other may be willing to submit to a principle which is superior to them both, there is no reason why they should submit to each other."[28]

The alternative to a naked power struggle was submission to a higher authority or principle, stronger than any of the contending agglomerations of power. This was an answer to both domestic and international ills. Tawney declared in his diary on the eve of World War I: "There are no mechanical arrangements by which men who regard society as a struggle for existence can be prevented from fighting. There is one way and one only: to abandon the standards of good and bad, success and failure which are expressed in the existing arrangements of industry, property, and social life. And to seek to make society, when it is at peace, a field in which mere power, ruthlessness, ambition, can *not* override the merciful and gentle."[29] Socialist democracies will not be absolutely peace-loving, as Marxism guarantees socialist democracies to be, but they are less likely to start war than capitalist states. And capitalist states, when democratic like Britain, are in turn less likely to start war than fascist states. Tawney also argued that a socialist democracy would be able, in war as in peace, to perform more nearly at the height of its powers, other things being equal, than other kinds of states. Where wealth and power are concentrated in a privileged elite, the people are less likely to perceive the government's commitment as their own, and to rise to superlative effort.

The acquisitive society was not only the antithesis of socialism; it was also a threat to peace. It permitted men to plunder the freedom and dignity of other men. It permitted nations to do the same to other nations. It made of society a jungle which honors power, instead of a fellowship which honors personality.

PURPOSE AND POWER

The question "Where does power lie?" is close to the question "Where does a society find its unity?" Tawney had a strong sense of the need for social unity. Dispersion of power was not meant to reduce society to localism or privatism. Thinkers on the left seldom make frequent use of the idea of authority; Tawney was an exception. He did not leave the term to the traditionalists and the totalitarians, but claimed it for democratic socialism. Was it inconsistent to embrace both the idea of authority and that of dispersion of power?

Tawney could approve "inequality" of power if three conditions were fulfilled. If the exercise of power was not arbitrary; if the commission could be revoked; and if power was used for a social purpose approved by the people.[30] The first two conditions are standard features of the checks on power of the Lockean liberal tradition. With the third condition, Tawney moved beyond liberalism to lay a keystone of his socialist edifice.

Like Marx, Tawney viewed 1789 as a vital watershed, and felt the need to explain its relative failure in such a manner as would keep alive the hope of its principles.[31] Unlike Marx, Tawney did not conclude that the key problem was who should be the *bearer* of revolution. Tawney asked himself under what social and economic conditions the political principles of 1789 could be made to work. He spoke of common good, but in no historicist sense. It was an empirical notion, to be determined by what people say they *want*, not by what some vanguard may say they *need*. Tawney frequently used the word "will" where one might expect him to have said "power." "Given, in short, the *will* to make an end of economic inequality and industrial autocracy, the technical and administrative difficulties involved present no insoluble problem."[32]

To be sure, there are puzzling features of this usage of "will." It owes too much to the moralism of the early Tawney to be a fully democratic notion. ("We have . . . to *make* the public opinion which will support us in taking the right line.")[33] Yet it is significant. Tawney believed that capitalism would only be done away with by means of a will to socialism among the majority of the English people. The will would be generated by persuasion. The ideas of 1789 provided the definition of goals which socialism would concretely fulfill. The working class would be the leading force in the task of creating patterns of socialism, though not necessarily the leaders of a future socialist society. The will of which Tawney spoke *is* power. "There *is* no creative force outside the ideas which control men in their ordinary actions," Tawney noted in his diary. "There is no *deus ex machina* which can be invoked, though men are always trying to discover one."[34]

In twentieth-century English intellectual history, Marx's historical materialism is frequently accepted yet at the same time bolshevist political strategy and the dialectic are rejected. Kingsley Martin recalls of his youth: "I was converted to the 'materialist conception of history,' but not to the need for a proletarian revolution."[35] Tawney is part of this tradition. He differs deeply from Marx, not on economics but on politics, particularly on power. Given his view of the nature of power, Tawney could assert not only that economic power *may* determine the political system, but also that in certain circumstances political power may *remake the economic system.* Tawney believed Marx's greatest shortcoming was that he did not appreciate the possible effect of political democracy on social development.

For Tawney, democracy was a conception of the power arrangements in society. There were not various kinds of democracy, as C. B. Macpherson argued, rudely twisting the meaning of the term to cover the Soviet Union and Ghana as well as Britain.[36] If power was not dispersed, responsible, and controlled, a political system was not in Tawney's eyes democratic, no matter how egalitarian or populist might be its program or its vision of the future. In the Socialist League, the view was held—by Stafford Cripps among others—that democracy was *a path* to socialism. There may be other paths, and there were vigorous discussions about which path was best. For Tawney, democracy was not a path to socialism, but *part of socialism.*

In a passage which bears a superficial resemblance to the position of Cripps and others in the Socialist League, Tawney also makes his difference from that position clear:

> a conception of Socialism which views it as involving the nationalisation of everything except political power, on which all else depends, is not, to speak with moderation, according to light. The question is not merely whether the State owns and controls the means of production. It is also who owns and controls the state. It is not certain, though

it is probable, that Socialism can in England be achieved by the methods proper to democracy. It is certain that it cannot be achieved by any other; nor, even if it could, should the supreme goods of civil and political liberty, in whose absence no Socialism worthy of the name can breathe, be part of the price.[37]

Some of Tawney's socialist colleagues in the 1930s *were* eager to nationalize everything except political power. Though Tawney went on to talk as if democracy was one path to socialism, he separated himself from that approach by saying not only that no other path can bring socialism, but that the so-called path is actually part of the destination. Socialism is not a goal which exists the other side of problems of power. The problems of power are permanent. Rule by a new class (the proletariat) will not eliminate them. The creation of "will" in a continuous way is an aspect of socialism in action.

Tawney's approach to power differed not only from Marxism but also from the liberal view which, as Franz Neumann put it, is "solely concerned with the erection of fences around political power."[38] By its nature, Tawney felt, power is something not just to be fenced but to be used, for its limitless source is the energy of free people.

Locke defined political power as a right of making laws "for the Regulating and Preserving of Property, and of employing the force of the Community, in the Execution of such laws, and in the defence of the Commonwealth from Foreign Injury, and all this only for the Publick Good."[39] Tawney's conception of the scope of politics was enormously broader than this. The scope of politics was no less than all those endeavors which men are unable to pursue in isolation and therefore pursue in association with their fellows. If Locke allotted to politics the purely negative function of *preserving* property and the inviolability of the nation, Tawney allotted to it the positive function of *generating* corporate moral purposes on the part of the citizens.

Moreover, whereas the Lockean view of power was legalistic, Tawney's was social. The "force of the community" was just a juristic notion to Locke, whereas for Tawney the phrase was an expansive one. Potentially, the force of the community encompasses all the social energies and social purposes of the people. To return to the question, "Where does a society find its unity?": for Tawney it was not found in legal forms any more than in economic mechanisms, but ultimately in common purposes.

Sheldon Wolin, at the end of *Politics and Vision*, lamented the loss of the "political" from modern Western politics. To revive the "integrative experience" of man, he observed regretfully, has seemed in the twentieth century "an invitation to totalitarianism."[40] Tawney offered another, democratic, way of binding up the fragments of an industrial society that had lost all directing principle. Cooperation of free and equal citizens, generating common purposes, making their will the effective power of the state.

Weber had three notions of authority: traditional, charismatic, legal.[41] Tawney sketched a fourth kind of authority: the authority of common purpose emanating from a community. Political thought and practice alike have since Weber's death been dominated by the legal ideas of authority, expressed in the liberal-capitalist states, and the charismatic idea, expressed in the totalitarian states. Tawney tried, amidst this polarization, to keep alive a socialist idea of authority which does not part company with liberal values.

He pointed to Chinese civilization as an example of an entity whose unity cannot be analyzed in economic or legal terms. China's unity has traditionally been "the unity of a civilisation rather than of a political system." Such unity can be just as meaningful and powerful for its citizens as juridical unity. To assume that "political unity is the sole unity which counts" is to confound "the spirit of a civilisation with one, and not necessarily the most significant, of its consequences."[42] Tawney cited Germany as a negative example. Why did Hitlerism "interpret unity in half-tribal terms of race and blood," finding it "in the mere physical attributes of a human herd?" Partly because "there is little in German history to remind them that there are loftier planes on which unity can be achieved." If the sources of power are more than juridical, so are the expressions of community. "A community can remain a community, even though it lacks the marks of what the thought of another epoch called a *societas perfecta.*"

These pages have examined the democratic character of Tawney's socialism. Democratic socialism, he thought, should attack the worship of power as well as the worship of riches. The triumphalism of power of twentieth-century ideologies, like that of sixteenth-century despotisms, was incompatible with humanistic politics. Whether "left" or "right," it could have nothing in common with socialism. Democracy is not a mere tactic, but a central socialist value.

Setting aside the naive harmonism of liberalism, and the utopianism of those strands of socialism which expected to bypass or transcend the state, Tawney took the problem of power seriously. Yet he saw power as a volatile capacity, with multiple sources, transmutable into various forms. Ultimately power is will. If Marxism correctly assesses the turning of economic power into political power, it fails to see the reverse possibility.

The reverse possibility is the power of common purposes emanating from a community of free citizens. Power is what a free people make of it. This gives meaning to Tawney's presentation of socialism as a moral vision and to his work in education. Since human nature is a speckled thing, concentrations of power are dangerous. Since human beings have the capacity for fellowship, cooperative initiative in conditions of dispersed power is best.

Power must not be so concentrated, or so removed from the lines of democratic accountability, that power over things becomes power over people. If power is not dispersed, but concentrated, or if economic power is permitted to turn itself into political and social power, democracy is unstable or even unworkable. Concentrated, irresponsible power leads to tyranny. Internationally, the resulting concentration of arbitrary power is likely to express itself in war.

Dispersion of power makes of power an instrument of constantly renewed moral purpose. "In the interminable case of *Dubb v. Superior Persons and Co.*, whether Christians, Capitalists or Communists I am an unrepentant Dubbite."[43] Dubb is the end to which all political systems are a means. Opinion is the only rightful source of power.

7 SOCIAL FUNCTION

The question of our day is by what *right* is the control of industry
vested in the hands of those who control it today.
(Diary, February 27, 1914)

All rights, in short, are conditional and derivative, because all power
should be conditional and derivative. They are derived from the end or
purpose of the society in which they exist . . . If society is to be healthy,
men must regard themselves, not primarily, as owners of rights, but as
trustees for the discharge of functions and the instruments of a social
purpose.
(*The Acquisitive Society*, p. 51)

[Of the Great War] The war seems to have caught us halfway in a transition to democracy. We have not the kind of strength Germany has.
Nor have we the kind of strength which we should have if the mass of
working people felt that the war was their war, not an enterprise for
which their rulers want their arms but not their minds and hearts.
(Tawney to A. L. Smith, December 27, 1917, Balliol College Papers)

Tawney wrote not only about how wealth and power should
be arranged, which could be called the Shape of Socialism,
but also about behavior and motivation, which could be
called the Life of Socialism. He criticized collectivism
because it neglected the dynamics of socialism. "However the
socialist ideal may be expressed," he remarked late in life
when pointing to the limitations of the welfare state, "few
things could be more remote from it than a herd of tame
animals with wise rulers in command."[1] Tawney could not
agree that arrangements from above, however excellent, alone
guaranteed socialism, for socialism was also a way of life. By
the same token, he criticized communism for its faith that
the social psychology of socialism would be taken care of by

a once-for-all transfer of power. Because his socialism was about right relationships, its dynamic, psychological component was crucial.

Tawney's view of socialism as a way of life was reflected in his imagery. He often spoke of "path," "way," "road," and other words of journeying, and a metaphor of movement provided the title for three publications with which he was connected: the *Highway*, organ of the WEA, the *Meteor*, magazine of Rugby School, and *Pilgrim*, a quarterly edited by William Temple.[2] He felt that democracy in England had so far meant only changes in the political system, but not a transformation of social relationships and motivations. The socialist society Tawney envisaged would be not an organism, certainly not a machine, but rather a *process*. The next two chapters are devoted to this Life of Socialism. For society as a whole, the key ideas are "function," "purpose," and "service" (for the individual and his ties, the key idea is "citizenship," which topic I pursue in the following chapter).

Today, sociology and social anthropology give "function" its meaning, but its roots lie in mathematics (where Leibnitz originated it) and the biological sciences. The mathematical meaning of function, as a variable in relation to, and defined by reference to other variables, has found its social science echo in expressions like "functional interdependence" and "functional relations." The biological meaning, as a process essential to an organism, speaks of this or that cultural custom as "necessary" to the health or stability of an entire society.

Tawney did not use function in these objective senses of the term. Three distinctions are apparent. For Tawney the idea of function is inseparable from those of purpose and service. He does not identify the three terms, but he links them sufficiently to mark his usage of function off from usage with roots in biology and mathematics. Second, Tawney uses function, not so as to put a premium on adjustment to a given order of things, but as a principle to test the status quo. There is a tendency in functional analysis, Robert Merton says, "to focus on the statics of social structure and to neglect the study of structural change."[3] This arises from the common habit of taking anything that is functional to a society as important to that society. (Kluckhohn can even write: "The at present mechanically useless buttons on the sleeve of a European man's suit subserve the 'function' of preserving the familiar, of maintaining a tradition."[4]) It would be tidy, but inaccurate, to conclude that Tawney meant Merton's "manifest" function (which has conscious motivations) as distinct from "latent" function (which refers to objective consequences). But Tawney did not think of function purely as *conscious* function. He followed Hobhouse who thought performance of function could also be unconscious.[5] The central question is: functional in regard to what? For Tawney, the answer was: functional in regard to the *total life of society*. The test of an institution or a policy was its function in the life of the whole British nation.

It is instructive to notice how Tawney differed at this point from G. D. H. Cole and J. N. Figgis.[6] Like other pluralists, Figgis and Cole felt oppressed by Mill's and Spencer's spectacle of man on the one hand, the state on the other hand, and nothing of theoretical consequence in between (so was Tawney, in his own way). Figgis, concerned with churches, attributed inherent rights to groups. For Cole, the state was just one association among others; the test of them all being the functions they perform. Where pluralism and functionalism were thus put together, the consequent functional theory of democracy quite rejected representative democracy as it existed in England. Tawney did not embrace this pluralism or its associated idea, functional democracy.

Like Laski and Russell, he held to the individual as the fundamental unit for weighing liberty and representation.[7] He did not exalt groups as Cole and Figgis did. He feared the antidemocratic implications of pluralist and guild socialist notions. Closer to an orthodox Fabian position on the state than to guild socialism (with which he is often overidentified), he was not prepared to allow the rights of trade unions, churches, or other groups to cut across the basic vertebrae of democratic responsibility through territorial parliamentary representation. He applied the principle of function to the *whole society;* its referent was the common good.

Looking at Tawney alongside his contemporaries, it is hard to call him a functionalist at all in the usual sense of the term, and it is best to break down his idea of function into two other ideas: purpose and service. It is the *overall purpose of the society and the particular service contributed by each person to that purpose* which provide the foundation for rights in Tawney's socialism.

PURPOSE

Staggered by what he saw of English society in the East End of London, and in North Staffordshire and Lancashire while teaching tutorial classes, Tawney set himself to understand the roots of the fanatic, Faustian industrialization that had, as he thought, subordinated human values to the exigencies of material progress. Thus he became an historian of the origins of capitalism, turning first to the agricultural transformations of the sixteenth century, later to the social and economic factors behind the Civil War, and to the relation between religious thought and the dominant social philosophies which accompanied the commercialisation of agriculture and the growth of modern industry.

Tawney considered that the industrializing process, not by necessity but from want of human wisdom, had occurred in such a way that mere economic mechanisms had taken the place of social purposes. He cited Robert Crowley to characterize the society taking shape in the seventeenth century which cleared a path for arbitrary power and functionless property. It is the work of "men that live as thoughe there were no God at all, men that would have all in their owne handes, men that would leave nothyng for others, men that would be alone on the earth, men that bee never satisfied."[8] There stands the whole catalog of evils against which Tawney's political thought is deployed: uncreaturely arrogance, possessiveness, acquisitiveness, separation of man from man.

In Western societies of the 1970s, straitjacketed as they seem to be in directions imposed by technological and bureaucratic "realities," it is difficult to appreciate the concern of those who, in the late nineteenth century and early twentieth century, saw England drifting without corporate direction, in need of a conception of what was sometimes called a "social form." Socialist thinkers (like their sociologist forerunners earlier in the century, such as Comte and Saint-Simon) tried to establish principles and institutions which would replace the social fragmentation brought about by industrialization with a new social cohesion. It is in this perspective that I view Tawney.

As Machiavelli enunciated an autonomous politics, Tawney analyzed the rise of an autonomous economics. Once, "economics had been a branch of ethics;" it gradually became, however, a sovereign mechanism beyond the effective influence of values.[9] The eventual effect was the erection of a means into an end. Industrialization was carried out in such a manner that it became what Tawney called "industrialism."

> The burden of our civilisation is not merely, as many suppose, that the product of industry is ill-distributed, or its conduct tyrannical, or its operation interrupted by embittered disagreements. It is that industry itself has come to hold a position of exclusive predominance among human interests, which no single interest, and least of all the provision of the material means of existence, is fit to occupy . . . [This] obsession by economic issues is as local and transitory as it is repulsive and disturbing. To future generations it will appear as pitiable as the obsession of the seventeenth century by religious quarrels appears today; indeed, it is less rational, since the object with which it is concerned is less important.[10]

The true purpose of industry is "the conquest of nature for the service of man."[11] For production and accumulation to become ends in themselves was an aberration.

Tawney compared industrialism to militarism. Militarism was the trait "not of an army, but of a society."[12] Similarly, industrialism was the trait not of factories but of society's estimate of the importance of factories. The magnates who emerged from the smoke of industry to become the real rulers of England, "talk as though man existed for industry, instead of industry existing for man, as the Prussians sometimes talked of man existing for war." Thus, to take an example, opposition to the raising of the school-leaving age was mounted on the ground that the "small fingers" of young children were indispensable for work in northern mills.[13] "What the military tradition and spirit did for Prussia, with the result of creating militarism," Tawney asserted, "the commercial tradition and spirit have done for England, with the result of creating industrialism."[14]

As well as erecting a means into an end, industrialism degrades human relationships. Tawney admired the ambience of a society of small property-holders. "Whatever the future may contain, the past has shown no more excellent social order than that in which the mass of the people were the masters of the holdings which they ploughed and of the tools with which they worked."[15] Industrialism withered the working man from a whole human being into a hand. "Politically a citizen, in industry he is neither a citizen nor a partner, but a hand."[16]

In Tawney's view of the purpose of industry, the labor of men should employ capital in enterprise designed for social good. That seemed the right relationship between people and things. "Labour consists of persons, capital of things. The only use of things is to be applied to the service of persons."[17] Yet such was the triumph of industrialism that a reversal of this scheme of priorities had become the conventional wisdom. "Capital 'employs' labour," Tawney raged, "much as our pagan ancestors imagined that the pieces of wood and iron, which they deified in their day, sent their crops and won their battles." Englishmen were being used as tools, as Plato thought a fit use only for slaves.

The psychology of industrial relationships was thus hopelessly poisoned. Rentiers lounged like lizards in London salons during June, went after pheasants in October, to Cannes in December, while workers toiled, degraded by their status and resentful to an extent which tragically threatened to make the trade unions as bereft of social purpose as the owners. The best performance was not evoked from the workers; morale was sagging in pit and factory. For if the public "allows workmen to be treated as 'hands,' it cannot claim the service of their wills and their brains."[18] Hence it was impossible for the true purpose of industry to be fulfilled.

A society in which production and accumulation have become ends in themselves, Tawney called an "acquisitive society." A society in which industry is established on the basis of social purpose, to which production and accumulation are means, Tawney called a "functional society."

But what is social purpose? Could England have a single purpose? When uncertainty arises, who is the arbiter of the social purpose of industry? It was made clear in discussing manifest function and latent function that Tawney did not have in mind conscious aims alone. Rather, he meant purpose in the sense of raison d'être. "What is the purpose of coal-mining in Wales?" That is the kind of question Tawney asked. If the answer is, broadly speaking "To make money for the owners," to that extent England is an acquisitive society. Concrete empirical tests could determine the answer: are decisions about production schedules, expansion or contraction, safety in the mines, made by criteria other than profit for the owners? If on the other hand, the answer is, broadly speaking, "To get coal to further the munitions industry so that London may be defended against bombing by foreign aircraft," to that extent England is a functional society.

Social purpose is dialectical, not determinate. Industry has a social purpose when the public interest is served. It is possible to give a measure of objective content to the notion of public interest. Where disease is rampant it is in everyone's interest that it be stopped, even among the poor, for infection knows no class restraints. In Tawney's day, it was not hard to draw up a long list of reforms, especially in health and education, which were indisputably covered by the idea of public interest. Children were, after all, said to be starving daily in the public elementary schools when Tawney was a boy.[19]

After a century in which the working of society was viewed predominantly in mechanistic terms, the first task was to convince people that the public interest was a notion relevant to politics.[20] Tawney asserted that social policy should be tested by whether it is functional to the public interest *which Englishmen consciously define for themselves.* In the universe of Adam Smith, even more so in the "biological" universe of Herbert Spencer, an activity was considered functional (or dysfunctional) to the whole society in a manner that had little to do with the striving of men, and little to do with politics. For Tawney, it was the business of politics to crystalize, pursue, and enforce the public interest.

Social purpose can also be identified by the breadth of the

interests or needs served. Here Tawney found criteria by which to support the bill which led to the Fisher Education Act of 1918, abolishing exemption from school attendance for children under fourteen, against the opposition of the Federation of British Industries, which declared: "A period of eight hours a week taken out of working hours [i.e. for the education of the children] would impose a burden upon many industries which they would be *quite unable to bear*.[21] Tawney found the interest of children a broader interest than that of the factory owners.

A further guideline for social purpose is self-fulfillment. Tawney's notion of self-fulfillment was dealt with in the chapter on equality. What is its relationship with the idea of public interest? Human beings have an instinct for fellowship; a cooperative life is congenial to man. Self-fulfillment is therefore in part a social question. It is attained only when the whole company of Englishmen are in right relationship with each other. It therefore implies corporate purposes.

Notice that Tawney was not offering a theory of general will. The ultimate test of social purpose is empirical: the expressed will of the people. Recall, too, the distinction between Tawney's idea of function, and the sociological idea of function derived from mathematics and biology. The latter is neatly consonant with a theory of the general will. Certain actions or roles are "natural to" or "required by" or "in harmony with" the organism or the mathematical model. Here is available a ready-made distinction between conscious will and the kind of "true" will which Rousseau and Bosanquet postulated. Tawney's idea of function does not admit of two radically different kinds of relation to the social whole, or of any radical distinction between the expressed will of the people and some esoteric will. We can now give a fuller answer to the question, "Functional in regard to what?": in regard to social purpose freely expressed or consented to by the people through democratic procedures.

The keynote of Tawney's practical activity was an attempt to generate social purpose through political education. Hobbes said that the "generation of the commonwealth" occurs when the citizens "confer all their power and strength upon one man," the "mortal god." The seventeenth century theorist believed that "it is the unity of the representer, not the unity of the represented, that maketh the person one" [i.e. makes society into one person].[22] Tawney had another method of generating the commonwealth. Social unity comes not from concentrating power on one man, but from concentration of purpose among the citizens. Tawney often spoke of the need for a new "authority" in British industry. But there is ultimately no other authority than the purposes men hold in common. And from those purposes spring rights.

SERVICE

If one side of function is social purpose, the other is participation in furthering that purpose. Tawney called such participation "service." Industry, as he defined it, "is nothing more mysterious than a body of men associated . . . to win their living by providing the community with some service which it requires."[23] Tawney contrasted *performance of service* with *pursuit of profit* as the two basic possible dynamic principles of industry.

Purpose has to do with the raison d'être of an industry. Service has to do primarily with its psychology. The two are not entirely separable—purpose affects morale, and the principle of service affects basic decisions concerning the direction of industry—but it is useful to distinguish them analytically. To take an example, some may question whether prostitution qualifies as a social purpose. However, by the criterion of service, it is the prostitutes themselves, since they perform the service, and not some absentee middleman, who should receive the rewards and decide the arrangements for the industry.

Tawney's application of function to property—they had not been linked before—is among his most important ideas. He assailed the notion that poverty is the "fundamental cause of present malaise."[24] It was no more fundamental than (we may suppose) he would consider "race" or "cities" the fundamental problems in the England or America of the 1970s. He considered two factors fundamental; they were the twin serpents in the garden of social thought and practice. One is arbitrary power, the other is functionless property. The entire corpus of his socialist writing was pitted against arbitrary power and functionless property. No socialism would be worthy of the name if it did not dispose of them. They link his historiography and his political writing, as they link both with his basic beliefs about human nature.

My concern now is with functionless property, and its companion doctrine, the unconditional rights of property.

It may seem strange that a moralist should have become an economic historian. Tawney gives two reasons, and both suggest why property was to him a central concern. The first was his reaction against a false but prevalent conception of spirituality, which shriveled Christianity into a spiritual sanctifier of the status quo. He saw it in the second generation of Puritans who were "convinced that character is all and circumstances nothing."[25] Thus Baxter had brought himself to approve enclosure, "done in moderation by a pious man," for the reason that a master can exercise a moral discipline over his servants which they might otherwise lack. "If they lose as peasants," Tawney summed up ironically, "they will gain as Christians." Then he commented: "Opportunities for spiritual edification are more important than mere material environment. If only the material environment were not itself among the forces determining men's capacity to be edified!"[26] For Tawney, to study the history of property relations was to illumine a branch of morals which western Christianity, forgetting that it was a religion of the Incarnation, had largely neglected for three hundred years.

The second reason was related to the first. When Tawney became an historian, the Whig interpretation of history, of which Macauley was the saint and George Trevelyan the contemporary star, dominated Tudor and Stuart studies. Possessed of a vision of English liberty, it saw the 1640s and 1688 in terms of a battle to establish the rule of law and the liberty of the individual citizen. Its implicit theory of social causation seemed to involve ideas alone. Kings and constitutions were its staple subject matter. Social history there was, but social meant costumes, chairs, and drinking habits, more often than it meant working conditions.

Tawney confronted this august tradition with "a few ill-mannered questions" concerning the data to be focused upon, and the theory of social causation implicit in the chosen themes and data. Tawney took up the study of the history of property relations because he saw in them a clue to policies and behavior fraught with consequences for the lives of simple men, women, and children. "English liberty" as understood in the Whig tradition, he did not much esteem. A man's existence as a worker was likely to be more important (to himself) than his existence as a citizen. History, too, was not the record of men's intentions but of their actions. "The supreme interest of economic history," Tawney reflected in the preface to his first historical book, "lies in the clue which it offers to the development of those dimly perceived presuppositions as to social expediency which influence the actions not only of statesmen, but of humble individuals and classes, and influence, perhaps, most decisively those who are least conscious of any theoretical bias."[27] Like Dag Hammerskjold in diplomacy, Tawney entered a discipline which the observer might suspect he would find too dry and secular. But he entered it with a moral purpose. The thousands of pages of notes on wool prices, wage rates, beneficial leases, and custom of the manor, were his chosen pasture because he decided that here were crucial roots of social change.

On the nature of property Tawney tended to follow three streams of thought: traditional Christian theories; a version of the labor theory of value (which he considered heir to Christian theory: "The last of the Schoolmen was Karl Marx");[28] and the rather hazy views of Ruskin and other anti-industrial romantics. St. Thomas and St. Ambrose had seen property as a stewardship from God. The idea existed, though perfunctorily, in Locke, but it had been buried in the demolition of natural rights by utilitarianism. For Tawney, it was essentially a weapon with which to deny the absolute claims of property—hardly a guide to specific social policies.

In Tawney, the association of property with the labor and life of man is closer than its association with God. Wealth is produced in social ways; thus it has a social character. Also, as St. Antonino put it, riches should exist for man, not man for riches. This latter idea Ruskin developed, summarizing it as "There is no wealth but life.."[29] When Tawney applied the principle of function to property, he carried forward all these lines of thought. The basis for his views, however, was psychological rather than aboriginal.

Tawney linked property with personality. Property was not good or evil independent of its impact on human creativity. The writer who said that "private property is the foundation of civilization, agrees with Proudhon, who said it was theft, in this respect at least, that, without further definition, the words of both are meaningless."[30] What Tawney offered was a dialectical view of the relation between property and work and life. He was concerned with the *function* of property. He found ground both to praise property *and* to condemn the way property was generally held and regarded in the England of his day.

The nature of the ownership of property had changed since St. Thomas and even since Locke. "To defend the property of the peasant and small master is necessarily to attack that of the monopolist and usurer, which grows by devouring it."[31] Again Tawney underlined the change: "The considerations which justify ownership as a function are those which condemn it as a tax." He was not opposed to private property: "If by property is meant the personal possessions which the word suggests to nine-tenths of the population, the object of Socialists is not to undermine property, but to protect and increase it."[32]

In fact ownership was not the heart of the problem of property. Ownership remains a static concept. Public ownership does not in itself produce social solidarity. Instead of stressing the static concept of ownership Tawney stressed the dynamic concept of function. It followed that Tawney was flexible about problems of state ownership, as became clear in the 1950s when he surprised some people by not going into the left-wing camp during the nationalization controversy within the Labour party. Tawney's attitude toward ownership resembled his attitude toward merit as the criterion for incomes. It is too static and individualistic. The idea of function is dynamic and solidaristic. Rewards are to be based on the performance of a service which furthers a social purpose. Cooperative activity is thereby encouraged.

The Christian (and Marxist) argument concerning the social character of property does not always or necessarily lead in a socialist direction. The idea of stewardship, for example, can be interpreted to mean that some are appointed to be stewards of great things and others of small things. As for the labor theory of value, there is no necessary logical link between it and any particular pattern of distribution. Ruskin's thought reminds us that an acute sense of the responsibilities of property-holding can be accompanied by political conservatism which asserts, in Ruskin's forthright words, the "impossibility of Equality."[33] It is when *the ideas of service and social purpose are linked to the position of property in society* that Tawney's originality emerges. This becomes clear in three areas: distribution of the social product; the governance of industry; the basis of rights.

Since few people perform functions hundreds of times more socially valuable than other people, a system of rewards based on social function is likely to be egalitarian. Such a dynamically induced equality seemed to Tawney more attractive and more realistic than an arithmetically determined equality. In so far as incomes affect social relationships, people would be kept within reasonable social reach of each other by virtue of participation in social purposes.

In Tawney's England such an approach generated the rationale for great changes. In 1910, it was estimated that 5½ percent of the population took 44 percent of the pecuniary income, while the lower 94½ percent took only 56 percent.[34] Many of the 5½ percent received their reward without performing any service at all. Thus could Tawney talk of the "alchemy by which a gentleman who has never seen a coal mine distils the contents of that place of gloom into elegant chambers in London and a house in the country."[35] Mineral royalties and urban ground rents were the most striking examples of payment without service. They were nothing less than a "tribute paid by those who work to those who do not." Tawney would deal with mineral owners and absentee landlords "as Plato would have treated the poets, whom, in their ability to make something out of nothing and to bewitch mankind with words, they a little resemble, and crown them with flowers and usher them politely out of the state."

Tawney implied that function was an even more important principle in a society of scarcity than in a society of abundance.[36] Yet beyond the question of standard of living, he rested the case for the superiority of a functional basis for income on considerations of social dynamics. There seemed to him something admirable and conducive to a quiet mind in a society where people might say, with the Book of Proverbs: "Give me neither riches nor poverty, but enough for my sustenance.."[37]

The governance of industry is the second area where we see how Tawney linked property to social purpose and service. Tawney found "English liberty" to be an equivocal term because it had not yet been applied to industrial life. "Englishmen have not expelled arbitrary power from the throne in order to see it re-established in the factory and the mine," he somewhat hopefully told an American audience.[38] In Edwardian years British industry faced a crisis of organization. Characteristically, Tawney defined it as a crisis of authority, and called for a new constitution for industry. His view was that authority could only be re-established on the basis of purpose. The dictatorial authority of Victorian years was out of the question; the unions were too strong to permit it. The standard collectivist approach to industry carried the threat of bureaucratism. The syndicalist solution was fraught with tendencies of a reverse dictatorship; the consumer may be little better off if the unions got arbitrary power than when the owners had it. Just as economic freedom was the goal, in Tawney's idea of industrial reorganization, so function was to be its principle of operation.

Function offered an alternative that cut across both the collectivist and the syndicalist solutions. It meant bodies like trade boards. Control went to the participants, and they were to be responsible to the public for whom the industry was being carried on. Within the industry itself, the method of securing the application of function was to treat every trade as a profession, just as the practice of law or medicine is a profession. The provision of food was to be organized on a professional basis just like the provision of health; the making of munitions no less than the firing of them.

The idea of unprofessional conduct would extend to industry. Trades would be responsible for setting standards and for prohibiting certain kinds of behavior; as, for example, medical doctors are prohibited by their professional associations from advertising. Just as teaching had progressed, in a century, from a "vulgar speculation upon public credulity"[39] to a profession about whose motives and even standards the public may feel reasonably at ease, so this change may occur in more and more trades. They would come to be seen in functional terms, as enterprises serving a social purpose. Tawney expected such a change to correct the twisted priorities of industrial life.

THE BASIS OF RIGHTS

The basis of rights in society at large is the third area where the linking of service and social function to property is important. If rights were based on social function, England would cease to be Disraeli's "Two Nations" and attain a "principle of unity." Despite a note in "The New Leviathan" which may suggest the contrary, Tawney was not restoring the eighteenth-century idea of rights (in this same fragment he criticized the eighteenth-century idea on the ground that it lacked a "supernatural reference").[40] Rights were seen in psychological rather than in aboriginal terms.

True, Tawney's views on men's equal worth amounted to an argument about natural rights. The traits of human nature, however, included some evil ones. Tawney's theory of rights was not merely a cry for the clearing away of restraints, as was Paine's. Just as in industrial life function imposes obligations on trade unions as well as on owners, so in the wider sphere of the application of function not only rights but *duties* are implied. Indeed, the performance of a kind of social duty (service) is the necessary condition for the possession of rights.

There is also, with function, more ground for dealing with conflict in society, when social purpose fails to be as widely shared as may be hoped, than with natural rights. If everyone has absolute rights, other criteria must be found upon which to arbitrate competing claims. But the principle of function presses closer to the bone. Not everyone all of the time serves a social purpose. Room exists to encourage intensified service by discriminating between conduct of varying social usefulness.

Is not social purpose a kind of utility? No, it is more dynamic and more solidaristic than the idea of utility. Bentham approved many rights which were unaccompanied by service (as well as many which were). Bentham made of property rights something which Tawney found indistinguishable from natural rights. Consider Bentham's case of the piece of land which, after being submerged under water, becomes dry; who shall have it? Bentham gives it to the adjacent landowner.[41] Tawney's idea of function would make him concerned with the *use*, rather than just the ownership, of the new land. Would he not give it to someone who was landless, or to the state so that it may be prepared for communal use?

The Great War influenced Tawney's search for a principle of unity for English society. He was almost obsessed by war, partly because of biographical and historical coincidence. His own life was deeply affected by the two world wars, and the life of England no less so. It was also partly due to a realization, arising from his historical work, of a vital connection between war and social change. References to war and illustrations from war abound in his writings. Recalling that the English political scene has often been transformed by war, from the fifteenth century onward, he added that the Great War "revolutionized British industrial organization, political divisions, and social and political thought."[42]

"The New Leviathan" contains an interesting note on the impact of the 1914-1918 war: "It is remarkable how the idea of 'Right' has been banished from political and social discussion in the nineteenth century. Contrast eighteenth. *But it is being restored by the war*, and its application will not be limited to international affairs."[43] What did Tawney mean by this? Perhaps he saw the British war effort as a paradigm, however imperfect, of the principle of social function at work. Even more completely, for the mass of the people were more directly involved, he saw the World War II effort as a paradigm of function. In 1919 he made this analysis of war and society:

> War is always shocking; but its remoter influence upon domestic policy and social organisation depends, to no small extent, upon the motives to which it has appealed for support. If domestic reaction was the natural consequence of the arrogant nationalism which was the note of Germany in 1870, and of England in 1793, it is not too sanguine to believe that the liberal and humane ideals which, whatever may be true of governments, have been a spell to bind the common people of England and France to a hateful duty, will be a potent force for internal reform when they lay down their arms . . . Right as the basis of human association, freedom for weak as strong, the moral law in public affairs—such ideas have a reference to social organisation as well as to international policy.[44]

The wartime national effort provided a ready-made social purpose which few questioned (fewer still in World War II). Performance of service in furthering this social purpose offered a motive which people could understand and accept as normative.

The term "service" gained rich meaning in wartime. "In what are described *par excellence* as 'the services,' " Tawney recalled, "it has always been recognized that *esprit de corps* is the foundation of efficiency . . . The power upon which the country relied as its main safeguard in an emergency was the professional zeal of the navy and nothing else."[45] Here was the professional spirit which Tawney thought could be made to infuse industry. England was socially melted down by the Great War. Key sinews of the complacent, hierarchical, snobbish social order of Edwardian England were snapped. Tawney saw both an opportunity for social transformation *and* a social dynamic for achieving it (which would also provide the basis for a whole theory of rights).

By what method, after all, had the war brought about change in Britain? According to Tawney, "economic mechanism, which seemed so ponderous and rigid, has been transformed in three years by a *collective act of will*, because there was a strong enough motive, which was not an economic motive, to transform it."[46] It was not a quest for profit, but a widely shared social purpose which fueled the war effort. It had proved more powerful than anyone expected. It was strong enough to serve as the basis for rights and duties. A revolution in communal psychology had in effect brought into view a new basis for rights: rights based upon social function. In this sense did the war restore the idea of right.

Did Tawney take the war situation merely as an analogy, or as a manifest presence of a functional society? It seems as an analogy. He attempted to find a point of generation in peacetime for the fellowship that wartime purpose evoked. Social purposes will vary over time. They should always be sufficiently shared purposes for Englishmen to find fellowship in pursuing them.

This chapter has begun to examine the dynamics of a functional society, Tawney's alternative to an acquisitive society. Tawney saw socialism not only as structures, but also as dynamic principles. Function was a principle for society's overall operation (as citizenship was for the role of the individual). Function was not a purely objective or static notion, as in sociological theory. Nor did it exalt small groups, as in the work of pluralists. It was a dynamic principle for the whole society; its referent was the common good.

Tawney's idea of function meant, first, social purpose, and, second, service performed in furthering social purpose. The task confronting Britain was to regain social purpose, after having permitted the mechanism of capitalist industry a destructive autonomy. Industrialism, like militarism, was the erection of a means into an end. Tawney held an expansive yet flexible view of the public interest; it was democratic and included the idea of self-fulfillment.

If purpose denotes the raison d'être of industry, service denotes its proper psychology. Tawney attacked functionless property because it yields a reward without requiring service. Likewise he attacked unconditional rights to property, because rights should not be absolute but derivative from purpose and service. The centrality of property in Tawney's socialism springs from his reaction against a false spirituality, and his concern with the concrete life of ordinary people, whose material existence is the proper subject matter of spiritual values and socialist relationships.

At the same time, ownership is not the heart of the question of property; function is (or lack of function). When purpose and service are linked with property, there emerges a basis for distribution of wealth and income and for the governance of industry which cuts across both collectivism and syndicalism. Similarly, Tawney drew from function a basis for rights in society generally. It is a clearer basis than natural rights. It enables society to link rights with positive moral force and social purpose. It requires (from all) duties as well as granting rights. Rights based on function would give a sadly needed principle of unity to British society. Of the operation of this principle Tawney saw the Great War as a half-fulfilled paradigm. Then were men brothers, because they were serving a common purpose which ordered priorities and spurred cooperative effort.

In the transition to political democracy, this country . . . underwent . . .
no inner conversion. She accepted it as a convenience, like an improved
system of telephones; she did not dedicate herself to it as the expression
of a moral ideal of comradeship and equality, the avowal of which
could leave nothing the same. She changed her political garments, but
not her heart. She carried into the democratic era, not only the institutions, but the social habits and mentality of the oldest and toughest
plutocracy in the world . . . She went to the ballot-box touching her
hat.
("The Realities of Democracy")

A Democracy is impossible without democrats.
("Podsnappery in Education")

The more I take part in social movements and observe my fellows who
do the same, the more I realise that large amounts of those engaged in
them are intellectually enslaved to the very principles and order of ideas
they are struggling to overthrow, and that only those are effective in
action who are independent in mind.
("Fragment on Education," Public Lectures Given in Chicago, 1939;
LSE)

A PLACE IN THE HOUSE OR A NEW HOUSE?

Certain socialist theorists, like the British collectivists or
Lassalle, have put preponderant emphasis upon the state as
vehicle of socialism. Others, like the British guild socialists or
Sorel, have been inclined to see industrial organization as
decisive. Tawney was interested in socialism as a comprehensive manner of life. To be sure, he considered state power
and economic institutions the indispensable vertebrae of socialism. That is clear from his ideas on dispersion of power

and equality. He also thought socialism required that industry be conducted with a single eye to social purpose and
service. When that is said, it remains distinctive of Tawney's
socialism that relationships in society were considered as important as those in industry or those which tie men to the
state.

British socialism did not arise directly from the mass of the
people (though Tawney said it did).[1] It could as nearly be
said to have arisen from the middle class (in the 1880s).
There was of course, from the early 1800s, a mass working-
class movement in Britain. It was the first in the world and it
could boast an impressive pride, confidence, and cultural
vigor.[2] Yet after the abortive climax of Chartism, no strong
working-class movement existed for thirty years. When it revived, there was no longer at its heart a serious, confident bid
to remake English society.

The unionism of the 1880s was sectional in outlook and
pragmatic in aim. The slogan "an eight-hour day" about
which Engels complained was paradigmatic. Piecemeal industrial goals were pursued, and the height of the unions' political vision was to replace one set of conventional politicians
with another. It was primarily the middle-class leadership of
the socialist societies—not the unions—which wished to
mount a bid to remake England. Alert working-class figures
put their hope in industrial action (and what political hope
they had was often placed in the Liberal party), rather than
in a quest for a socialist commonwealth. Glasier tells of a
meeting in Glasgow in 1884 addressed by William Morris on
the subject "Art and Labour," after which an old veteran
remarked to Glasier: "Ah, young man, I heard a' that kind of
thing frae Robert Owen and Henry Hetherington fifty and
more years ago. They were going to bring in the New Moral
World, as they ca'd it, but they found human nature too hard
a flint to flake. Na, na, it hasna' come in my day, and it'll no
come in yours; and it'll no come at a' if you're going to
wreck the Liberal Party as some o' your friends are trying
their best to do."[3]

In sum, though the British working-class movement remained extremely strong, it did not evolve the *hegemonic
way of thinking*—aiming not just at sectional gains for its own
members but at a new moral world—which its early nineteenth-century scope and vigor foreshadowed. And as British

socialism got shaped by the mood and requirements of the trade unions, the vision of British society remade in its totality, evolved by intellectual socialists at the end of the nineteenth century, was itself frequently eclipsed by narrow pragmatic concerns.

Tawney was steeped in the presocialist radical and utopian tradition of Lovett, Owen, and Cobbett. He was also imbued with the reconstructed liberalism which stemmed in part from the philosophy of T. H. Green. From the radical working-class movement of the early nineteenth century he drew an emphasis upon comradeship, cultural vigor, and the bid to transform Britain socially. From idealism he drew an emphasis upon the moral significance of political activity. Both predisposed him to try and provide for British socialism a hegemonic way of thinking.

That is to say, he was not content that the working class be ushered into occupancy of a house already constructed upon the ground plan of a bourgeois world view and bourgeois industrial and political ways, the values of the household already settled in the grooves of Benthamite psychology. In clamoring for a place in the household of the British constitution, it was all too easy, Tawney thought, for the working class to overlook the basic question: *what kind of house.*

"A constitution," J. H. Thomas observed in 1924, "which enables an engine-driver of yesterday to be a Secretary of State today is a great constitution."[4] Here, from the mouth of a key Labour leader, was the antithesis of Tawney's way of thinking. Thomas saw socialism in terms of getting a larger share of the industrial and political cake for the working-class and its representatives. Of socialist social relationships he had little sense. But for Tawney socialist social relationships were a crucial part of true socialism.

What Tawney had in mind was not an ideology handed down by intellectuals, but a comprehensively radical way of thinking generated among the working people themselves. He sought to revivify the "heroic culture" of the early nineteenth century, and give it a philosophic underpinning derived from idealism and Christianity.[5] Marxism never took deep root among the British working class (when they were most available for it, in the third and fourth decades of the nineteenth century, it was only just being born). Idealism, as Adam Ulam pointed out, failed to establish ties with the labor and socialist movements of the late nineteenth century.[6] Perhaps Tawney among British socialists has come nearest to providing a truly hegemonic philosophy, transcending sectional claims, bidding to remake British society by democratic means.

The idea of citizenship is vital to Tawney's hope for the remaking of British society. If fellowship is the heart of Tawney's vision of a new Britain, and function is the dynamic principle of socialism in its overall economic and social pattern, the dynamic principle for the individual is citizenship.

DEPARTURE FROM A VICTORIAN TRADITION

In Tawney's socialist society power is dispersed, and a line of accountability runs from powerholders to the rest of the people. The principle of rewards emphasizes men's common humanity; people will all be within social and economic reach of each other. Citizenship takes on its meaning in this context. In the simplest terms it is equality in action. It is the relationship of self-reliant, self-respecting equals, in a society where the absolute claims of personality are respected. It is marked by initiative, responsibility, freedom, and a new conception of good manners.

It contrasts with the combination of deference and contempt which in Tawney's view marked the relationships of unbridled capitalism. A "hand" is not a citizen. A man is not a citizen if he can make or unmake others by virtue of his wealth or the exercise of arbitrary and irresponsible power. Citizenship can be facilitated and encouraged by social arrangements. Its full operation, however, is a matter of positive energy which ultimately depends upon the quality of the people. Citizenship for the university scholar means a way of life that continuously applies knowledge gained to the improvement of society. Citizenship for the WEA student means, not only that he be a recipient of the instruction of the WEA classes, but that he join the association, further its purposes, and himself become a missionary of wider educational opportunities for all.

Citizenship can carry two meanings: as membership in a territorial unit, or as personal social performance. In the ancient world citizenship had primarily the personal sense. Later it took on the territorial sense; within the circumstances of modern democracy this interpretation comes close to eighteenth-century theories of civil and political rights. Tawney considered this kind of citizenship to be a pale thing unless it also embraced economic rights, for the nineteenth century had seen intermittent tension between the claims to citizenship and the realities of social class.[7] He went beyond the territorial sense of citizenship in a further way: he dealt not only with relationships between the individual and the state, but with those among individuals, whether or not the state is involved in them.

The sense of citizenship as personal performance enjoyed its renaissance in the later nineteenth century as a reaction against the territorial sense of citizenship which eighteenth century theories of rights had embodied—hence the refurbishment, by the idealists, of the largely Greek notion of public mindedness. There appeared in late Victorian and Edwardian times a large literature on the subject of citizenship, suffused with tones of moral and religious uplift. As well as being a reaction against the eighteenth-century stress upon rights, citizenship as personal performance owed much to profound modifications in the meaning attached to the Christian gospel. Beatrice Webb aptly summed them up: "I suggest it was during the middle decades of the nineteenth century that, in England, the impulse of self-subordinating service was transferred, consciously and overtly, from God to man."[8]

Tawney was exposed to the idea of citizenship as lofty personal performance, inspired by religion though directed toward society. It began with his birth at Calcutta; continued at Rugby; at Balliol under Caird; at Toynbee Hall with Canon Barnett. Yet he left this style of life and thought behind him.

On the public schools, which he considered monuments to inequality and snobbery, he delivered one attack after another. He seldom missed an opportunity to compare Oxford unfavorably—for its social rather than its educational attributes—with the University of London. One of the most interesting of his early unpublished memoranda—"The Expense of Education in Oxford"—showed how hard it was for the son of a poor father to fit into Oxford life and recommended drastic changes.[9]

The entire enterprise of church charity work he came, as if with a mental sigh, to esteem very little. It seemed "mere ambulance work for the victims of class privilege."[10] He urged the churches to turn from philanthropy to the rediscovery of a prophetic stand against injustice. "Character can no doubt overcome circumstances," he observed in an undated note, "as those who have had few unfavourable circumstances to overcome are never tired of reminding us. But is it [reasonable?] to suggest that men are more likely to listen to a creed which calls them to a life of service and self-sacrifice, if the social environment in which they live is dominated by a ruthless economic egotism?"[11]

Comparisons suggest themselves with T. H. Green. Green harnessed religious impulse for a kind of civic religion. The Christian vision was made immanent in a society moving in upward moral progression. Citizenship was not merely the *expression* of a Christian life; it was *itself* the Christian life. By contrast, Tawney never sought to blend socialism and Christianity together into a civic religion. The evangelical aspect remained, as is clear from the quotation about character in the last paragraph. A just social order, Tawney implied, will be a better witness to Christ and a better garden for the flowering of Christian life. But a just social order is not itself the Kingdom of God. The Kingdom finds fulfillment only beyond history.

A second comparison follows the first. G. M. Young observed that though the leading spirits of the Victorian age were not satisfied with the world as it was—"they were all, in their way, reformers"—nevertheless they felt themselves on a path which was leading to a satisfactory world.[12] Creature of that epoch, Green was greatly more optimistic about human nature than Tawney. In a letter to Scott Holland, he explained why the antithesis between religious and secular would no longer do: "The rational movement of mankind has got beyond it." In the measure that Tawney ever held such a belief in progress and rationality as principles of the universe or society, it was knocked out of him by his experiences in the Great War. "The sense of Sin is very much an illusion," Green reassured his contemporaries. "People are not as bad as they fancy themselves."[13] In Tawney's view they were nearly always worse than they fancied themselves—hence the prominence of irony in his style.

Tawney declined to absolve the proletariat of "sinful" proclivities. They were the offspring of no immaculate conception. They could be expected to behave no worse, but no better, than other classes which had preceded them in exercising power. One is conscious of dark clouds of irrationality and conflict in the writings of Tawney; not in Green. If the characteristic stylistic mark of Green is earnestness, of Tawney it is irony ("Most persons believe in free competition as long as they are confident of competing successfully").[14] In Green the notion of citizenship carries the sense of men swimming with the tide. Tawney felt no such harmonic sense.

Furthermore, Green's note of paternalism is absent in the more structural concerns of Tawney's socialism. The Victorian tradition of service did after all assume the supremacy of the servant! One did not risk one's superior status by going out to serve. True, there took place under the influence of Green and others an important shift of focus, from serving in the dizzy realms of imperial glory to serving in England's own shabby backyard. Green had, to the horror of some of his contemporaries and the puzzlement of others, proclaimed the condition of ordinary people the central stuff of politics. If Milner went to serve in Egypt, Barnett also went to serve in Whitechapel.

But to Tawney both varieties of service seemed paternalistic. Both failed to accommodate the *power* challenge Tawney encouraged the exploited to mount against imperialism and industrialism. Paternalism often goes hand in hand with a moralistic agenda for reform. So it was with Victorian idealism. If Green was perhaps less moralistic in his choice of issues for social action than the young parsons he inspired to plunge with high intent into England's slums, his preoccupation with the "drink question" nevertheless epitomized the tendency.[15]

Tawney reacted so firmly against it that he seemed to smile on whatever conventional opinion considered unrespectable. The prevailing code of respectability seemed to him largely a shroud of mystification cast abroad to keep workers in their place. To demand special feats of moral athleticism from the poor, as Victorian charity was wont to do, appeared an almost vindictive demonstration of the powerlessness of the poor.

Tawney altered the agenda for social reform by turning a piercing searchlight on the infrastructure of capitalism. The very virtues of English life at the height of industrialism—thrift, money-making—he reinterpreted as "vices more ruinous to the soul than most of the conventional forms of immorality."[16] In departing from the paternalism of Victorian idealism, and from its special interest in the moral condition of the working class, Tawney effectively departed also from the conception of citizenship which Green had brought to a splendid theoretical and practical crystalization.

Tawney's idea of citizenship was not one of high performance on the part of a sensitive and privileged few toward needy masses in India or Whitechapel. It was not one of performance at all, but of relationships; between people for whom service would have a meaning which did not imply inequality. In 1909, James Bryce wrote *The Hindrances to Citizenship*, which is a finely turned gargoyle on the edifice of Victorian paternalistic, moralistic, optimistic, public-minded idealism. The three hindrances were indolence, personal self-interest, and party spirit. Here par excellence was citizenship as personal performance. To Tawney, personal self-interest and indolence were not failures at the level of personal morality, but turbine and by-product respectively of the capitalist system. As for party spirit, it was close to being the pearl of great price. How else but through party was the working class going to effectively organize itself?

Tawney's citizenship was a political and not a merely cultural notion. Not pleasant, toothless leisure-time pursuits designed to keep people amused; not the habit, which J. B. Priestley found a clue to England's greatness, of meeting "in a thousand places to consider Alpine plants, migrant geese, or sixteenth century madrigals."[17] Tawney's idea was fully and centrally political. In Green's civic activity there was an almost exclusive concern with local affairs. The practice of Green's citizenship, as his own admirable life suggests, seemed most natural at the level of the town council where the scale is small and the ties intimate. Much less so at the impersonal level where the stakes are national power and national policies. Tawney did not limit citizenship to activity practised on a small and intimate scale. The political imagination must also grasp the social system as a whole, he considered, and seek to reform it as a system.

Nor was there in Tawney any special attachment to participation for its own sake, as a kind of therapy which is good for people even if it leaves society unchanged. The claim to merely participate can have an aura of unjustified meekness, as if people are allowed to take some part in the affairs of the nation as a concession to their restless spirit, rather than as a basic right and duty. If their conception of politics was as broad as Tawney thought it ought to be, the activity of citizens was no less than creating their own new world out of the "molten" social condition to which Lloyd George had referred in 1917.[18]

EDUCATION, MYTH, AND CITIZENSHIP

To a WEA gathering in Manchester, where his "five years as a citizen" were among the happiest of his life, Tawney spoke about the politics of citizenship.

We may prefer of course to live in a state of innocence untroubled by [political] issues. We can if we please resign the discovery of solutions for our problems to the superior wisdom of persons who are delighted, if we will allow them, to do our thinking for us. We can again evade them by taking refuge in the illusory consolations of dogmatic ideologies which, by claiming to possess a prefabricated formula for all situations, are dispensed from the necessity of grappling seriously with any one of them. But, if we reject both these primrose paths to futility ... only one alternative remains. It is that we should resolve for two or three hours out of the one hundred of our waking week to consider those issues of public and general importance with somewhat the same seriousness that we bring to our private affairs, to do what we can to ascertain essential facts, and, since none of us can hope to travel far towards truth alone, to seize every opportunity to correct our limitations and enlarge our horizons by cooperative study and discussion with our fellows.[19]

Here was, in part, a sketch of the vocation of the WEA. It was especially in workers education that Tawney formed his ideas of citizenship. To "free the minds" and "straighten the backs" of ordinary people through education seemed to him crucial to the prospects of socialist citizenship. Here was the informing and energizing force which could snap the working class out of mesmerization by capitalist myths. The WEA was both a paradigm of citizenship in action and an instrument to lay foundations for a broader and deeper citizenship.

Tawney was no theorist of education ("Books on education . . . belong to a type of literature which, I am sorry to say, I cannot read").[20] He saw educational policy as in every case *social* policy. Imaginatively handled, it could make England a juster society. It was a means of breaking down the possessive individualism of capitalist culture. Tawney criticized as a "ladder" concept the liberal view of education as a means by which working men, one by one, as they prove worthy, are permitted to become inheritors of the full life of society. Through education, he wrote, "men transcend the limitations of their individual [perspectives] and become partners in a world of interests which they can share with their fellows."[21] Education ought to be a vehicle of that social solidarity which socialism partly requires and partly creates.

Like Plato's idea of citizenship, Tawney's speaks of a shared life (and is thus less individualistic than prevalent Victorian ideas of citizenship). Yet compared with Tawney's, Plato's citizenship is almost purely moral. What is shared in the *Republic* is moral intimacy; but nothing is shared that has to do with the levers of power and the making of political decisions; that is left to the "superior wisdom" of an elite which alone can aspire to a science of politics. For Tawney, on the other hand, citizenship was less an ideal than an operative relationship, creating a continuing political dynamic, sweeping into its ken all the values, purposes, and interests of the common life of men.

Tawney made a comprehensive attempt to reinterpret the meaning and scope of politics for a democratic era. For most of history, politics had had no meaning for most of the people; they were only its objects. Again and again—starting with the Greeks—visions of citizenship fell short of being universally political in that they pertained to the life and activity of an elite alone, or allotted to ordinary people a participatory role that was merely therapeutic. But now it was possible, Tawney thought, to sharply advance the "social equality and practical freedom of the mass of mankind."[22]

Rousseau understandably remarked that Plato's *Republic* was hardly a book on politics at all but a great book on education. In Tawney there is seldom a blurring of the line between education and politics. He did not allow his profound concern with education to eclipse his concern with power. He did not expect education to "work the miracle" that Baron d'Holbach expected of it—automatically bringing eventual happiness to society—for he did not have Holbach's faith in the rationality of man.[23] Closer to home, Tawney did not share the rationalist optimism about education which Kingsley Martin considered a prevalent error among British intellectuals before World War II. They relied, as Martin put it, too much on nurture, and they underestimated nature.[24] Tawney's Christian realism held him back from doing this. He disbelieved in the perfectibility of human nature.

Tawney accused British capitalism of mentally bewitching and enslaving humble folk with myths, seducing them from their proper inheritance as citizens. The result was "a kind of collective hypnotism."[25] Tawney's appeal for demystification of British society was perhaps his most influential; it evoked his most intense feelings; there is nothing more passionate in his writings than the blistering attack on "Honours" in the Ramsay MacDonald years.[26]

What Tawney had to say about mystification can be usefully compared and contrasted with the ideas of Walter Bagehot. Tawney knew only too well that, although everyone knows where Buckingham Palace is, "if you tell a cabman to drive to 'Downing Street,' he most likely will never have heard of it"; and that British women "care fifty times more for a [royal] marriage than a ministry."[27] Tawney, however, unlike Bagehot, *deplored* the gulf between the "efficient" and the "dignified" aspects of the English constitution. It was the means by which the working class was enthralled in deference to its superiors.

Bagehot crystalized a political ideology for the middle class at the height of industrialism. He was contemptuous of crown and aristocracy, as well as of the masses. They all seemed to him mere stage scenery for the activities of the business and political classes. But the sun went in a little on Bagehot's world even before the appearance of the second edition of *The English Constitution*. The 1867 Reform Act brought the threat of proletarian intrusion into the nicely calculated stability of a middle-class order. For Tawney, the entry of the masses was no threat, but an opportunity for a new politics of citizenship.

The English constitution is chameleonlike, and it grants the blessing of permanent ascendancy to no class. A problem to Tawney was that the shroud of mystification inordinately prolonged the ascendancy, especially the social ascendancy, of the type of men who ruled Victorian England, even after a string of Reform Acts and two Labour governments. This god of "Mumbo-Jumbo" inhibited socialist citizenship, and the working class was as much at fault as those who sat nearer to the throne of Mumbo-Jumbo.[28] Some leaders of the working class were more to blame than anyone. These were the ones who combined socialist political success with social capitulation to the hostesses of London society; who would "sit up, like poodles in a drawing-room, wag their tails when patted, and lick their lips at the social sugar-plums tossed them by their masters."[29]

Mumbo-Jumbo meant the prevailing set of myths about British society, which Bagehot had correctly identified as functional to the Victorian system. Tawney urged that the methods and findings of anthropology be fed into the study of economics and economic history. Anthropologists regrettably turned their tools only on primitive societies, overlooking the rich possibilities of Mumbo-Jumbo in Britain. "An anthropologist who investigates the life of a primitive people gives due weight to the utterances of the elders of the tribe, but he devotes his main attention to such impersonal facts as its family system, its class structure, its customs as to property, its methods of organizing the activities needed to provide its livelihood. In studying civilized societies, the right procedure is the same."[30] Writing an introduction for an anthropological study of the New Zealand Maoris, Tawney concluded with the hope that "an equally gifted Maori anthropologist should write an equally faithful account of the people of Great Britain."[31] If that were done, casualties would surely result at the court of Mumbo-Jumbo.

The myths of Mumbo-Jumbo hid the flaws and inhumanities of economic fundamentalism. An anthropologist might challenge the notion, held as gospel in Bagehot's England, that economic forces were autonomous—that to organize society as a cooperative commonwealth of equal citizens, whose own best values were put at the center of the industrial system, would wreck the delicate and inscrutable machinery of the economic system. To the economics of Benthamism, "man" meant "middle-class man." Comparative anthropological investigation might show that Victorian industrialism had mistaken a particular instance for a general truth; that it had thought natural to man what was merely convenient to one class or generation of men.

Tawney did not consider the myths of British capitalism sacrosanct. Unless they were stripped away, socialism could never be a *way of life* in England. To be sure, economic science could and did make progress of its own accord; it eventually left fundamentalism behind. To be sure, collectivism might replace the more junglelike aspects of capitalism. But what of that "servile respect for wealth and social position" which, Tawney judged in 1935, "remains even today the most characteristic and contemptible vice of large numbers of our fellow-countrymen"?[32]

Especially did the peculiar British custom of Honours seem incompatible with citizenship. It set up barriers between people which had no basis in function or personality. The idea of citizenship assumed that men as men were worthy of respect, and capable of showing respect to others. If people are to esteem others as persons, they must not esteem others for what they possess, or for the largely irrelevant adornments of status which mirror a feudal past. Honours also tended to poison the internal relationships of the labor movement. "Those who think that acceptance of them does no harm," Tawney vowed, "have been mixing too long with blasé politicians. They should attend their local Labour Parties, and listen for a change to the views of ordinary men and women."[33]

At the University of London, in civic organizations, or attending local Labour party meetings, Tawney practiced cooperative and egalitarian citizenship. Perhaps he saw the relation of the labor movement to socialism somewhat as Protestant theologians have seen the relation of the church to the Kingdom of God. It was supposed to be a laboratory for the practice of a socialist way of life, and a witness to society at large of what that way of life might be like. Socialists and especially Labour parliamentarians of Tawney's time did little to explore practical socialist citizenship. The outlook of

J. R. Clynes was more common: "As we stood waiting for His Majesty, amid the gold and crimson of the Palace," the Labour leader wrote of one of his royal moments, "I could not help marvelling at the strange turn of Fortune's wheel, which had brought MacDonald the starveling clerk, Thomas the engine-driver, Henderson the foundry labourer and Clynes the mill-hand, to this pinnacle beside the man whose forbears had been kings for so many generations."[34] British Labourites have indeed often "taken to [tradition] in the way that lapsed puritans take to drink or sex—far more devotedly than the more expected addicts."[35]

There is in China a parallel to Tawney's assault on the mystification which hindered socialist citizenship. In China as in Britain, the bonds of *society* seemed even more important, in obstructing socialism, than the regulations of the *state*. In such circumstances, socialism could not be fully attained by a transfer of state power alone. If Mao Tse-tung sought to implant socialist values in the homes and even the spirits of his people, believing that Lenin failed to do this in Russia, Tawney wanted at least to see socialist values implanted in the daily relationships of the people (spirits were another matter). His attack on "collective hypnotism" was a call for cultural revolution.

It would be straining an analogy to depict Clynes as the Liu Shao-ch'i of Britain, yet one can see why Tawney felt that Labour leaders like Clynes or J. Hodge, who saw their political success in terms of Fortune's wheel and were so enthralled by monarchy that to brush shoulders with a King was to reach life's pinnacle, needed to be tempered by a socialist cultural revolution.[36] Just as Mao Tse-tung exhorted the Chinese people to fight against the "Four Olds" (features of the social pattern of Chinese feudalism), Tawney urged British workers to achieve in their minds a total independence from the hangovers of feudal Britain. For Tawney as for Mao, it was necessary to destroy the attractiveness of the old in the minds of the people; as Tawney said, "to [deprive] inequality of its sting by stripping it of its esteem."[37]

Tawney, like Mao, impetuously beckoned young people to reject what they don't like and build anew. Mao offered them the formula: "It is right to rebel." Tawney proclaimed: "the first duty of youth is . . . to make a tradition not to perpetuate one."[38] Like the Chinese leader, Tawney feared that simple folk might be unduly impressed by the models of social life their former masters practiced; that hair-splitting intellectuals wielding esoteric pens might divert simple folk from utilizing their own creative resources. That did not mean that socialism was easy. Rather that it had to be rooted in the self-reliant life of working people confident of their own traditions and capacities. Tawney (again like Mao) thought that the "party" could get soft and that socialism could be made to seem *too* easy.[39]

A SOCIALIST WAY OF LIFE

Before the London Advisory Council for Juvenile Employment, which had received complaints about the manners of juveniles, Tawney gave evidence in these terms: "What is probably true is that manners are different from what they were, e.g. children do not say 'Sir' so often and are more independent and sure of themselves . . . To myself the change seems an improvement."[40] He delighted in the breaking down of patterns of manners that were based elsewhere than on the claims of personality. In the shops, the subtle class-based system of manners—whereby one lady customer is "Madam" and the next is "luv"—was starting to weaken. Toward the end of his life, Tawney remarked with satisfaction that though there was yet much "loathsome and beastly" respect for the canons of Mumbo-Jumbo, "At least shopkeepers are less polite."[41]

It would be absurd to conclude that Tawney thought personal relations unimportant. He believed the basis of good manners to be respect and self-respect. How could these flourish when industry knew its people as "hands"? When some men received enormous salaries? "It is said that among the barbarians," Tawney scathingly wrote, "where wealth is still measured by cattle, great chiefs are described as hundred-cow men." The man with $400,000 a year "might similarly be described as a hundred-family man, since he receives the income of a hundred families."[42] Tawney called huge salaries ungentlemanly; they implied to him disrespect for the worth of fellow-workers. By contrast, a functional society "would cultivate the *esprit de corps* which is natural to young men, and would make them feel that to snatch special advantages for oneself, like any common business man, is, apart from other considerations, an odious offense against good manners."[43] These were the good manners of socialist citizenship. It was not a question of refined or moralistic rituals and had less to do with attitudes to property (and property-holders) than with attitudes to personality. Tawney hoped for the day when those who liked to "pick over the treasures of earth and heaven for a piece they can put in their purses" would be called ill-mannered.[44]

There were times when Tawney feared the Tories might cling indefinitely to their long-standing social hegemony. Even when Labour governed, and despite the immense power which the unions came to have, Tory norms continued to dominate the social and cultural world of England. The working class seemed all too ready to occupy an appointed niche in this unsocialist world. In Beer's terms, they were ready to settle for functional representation instead of aspiring to a socialist commonwealth. Socially and culturally, the effort to attain a socialist manner of life was aborted. Too many workers desired "not a social order of a different kind, in which money and economic power will no longer be the criterion of achievement, but a social order of the same kind, in which money and economic power will be somewhat differently distributed." Too many were timidly deferential toward the way of life of their superiors, "staring upwards, eyes goggling and mouths agape, at the antics of a third-rate Elysium, and tormenting their unhappy souls . . . with the hope of wriggling into it."[45]

Tawney saw these problems reflected in trade union attitudes toward education and culture. In 1927 the *Cotton Factory Times* criticized a paper of Tawney's on "The Possible Cost of Raising the School-Leaving Age." The newspaper argued that to raise the age would impose an intolerable financial burden on working-class parents. It was rare for Tawney to be criticized in a working-class journal; he chose to reply. He presented an argument, which seems sound, that the diminution of the supply of low-paid juvenile labor will actually tend to increase the earnings of older workers, and thus obviate economic loss to the family. He then burst out: "But I must say, at once, that, even if I did not anticipate that result, I should still be in favour of raising the school-leaving age. I know only too well the cruel dilemma in which thousands of parents are placed today. I am well aware they often are anxious to keep them at school till fifteen or longer, but they know that, if the elder boy or girl remains at school, instead of going to work, the younger brothers and sisters will suffer, and they hesitate to impose on them a sacrifice from which they would not shrink themselves. But I refuse to accept as inevitable the existence of this vicious circle which binds poverty in one generation to lack of educational opportunity in the next, or to acquiesce for ever in a situation in which the low wages of parents are at once subsidised and perpetuated by the earnings of children who ought to be at school."[46] Tawney wanted to lift union eyes above industrial issues, to the task of bringing in a socialist commonwealth and fashioning a way of life fitting to it.

For Tawney socialism was not the same as proletarianism. Compare him on this matter with Sorel and with Marx. Both Tawney and Sorel invested politics with a pronounced spiritual dimension. But Sorel made an ideology out of the moral superiority of the proletariat. Whereas for Sorel the spirituality lay in the quality of the workers and their struggle, for Tawney the spirituality lay in a perspective which transcended the nature and interests of the workers.

Tawney was unequivocally committed to classlessness. One could define his idea of citizenship as the social relationships of a classless society. But what is the connection between classlessness and the access to power of the working class? In the realm of culture most Marxists identify the two. That is fairly clear in Soviet practice. Even in Marx and Lenin, though the dictatorship of the proletariat is supposed to be a temporary thing, there is nothing that explains how socialist culture will differ from proletarian culture. It seems strange if a classless (socialist) culture is the same as the culture of one particular class (the proletariat). Yet that is the implication.

By contrast, Tawney offered a picture of socialist social dynamics that is truly beyond class. He saw that the proletariat had been forced by the exigencies of capitalism into a narrow, one-sided social existence, and that its values inevitably remained partial by the standards of classless values. If the arrogance of the "hundred-family man" must be superseded, so must the smouldering resentment of his erstwhile employee. Power is not safe with any class. "If those who have the will to make a better society have not at present the power," Tawney reflected poignantly in 1921, "it is conceivable that when they have the power they too, like their predecessors, may not have the will."[47] Thus only principles count in defining the good society. Only citizenship based on humanistic principles which have an objective existence apart from any group or class interest can give meaning to socialism as a way of life.

Tawney put his finger on the problem of the lack of inner assurance of British Labour governments: "They are portentous over trifles, scrutinise farthings under microscopes, and balk at hedges which their opponents would take in their stride, with a laugh or a curse. [The Tories] have been brought up to believe that they are the elect, and are not troubled by the thought that they may possibly be mistaken. If they decide to throw money away, they throw it away with a hearty gesture; if they think it advantageous to pass an unworkable Act, they pass it, and damn the consequences. They listen to criticism politely enough; but, except in the merest details, they are not deflected by it. They know that, once in the saddle, they can do what they please . . . That attitude of tranquil assurance is a considerable asset."[48] Here is a brilliant glimpse of the tragic psychological situation of Labour governments in a country which has had a political revolution (a long time ago) but not a matching cultural revolution—where a socialist party may be in power, but socialism has not become a way of life.

One solution lay to hand. A Labour government could be strengthened by a continuous upsurge of enthusiastic citizenship from the people. If the Labour party trusted the citizenry, and prepared in advance of office a socialist temper among them, evoking and welcoming their constant efforts, Labour governments would develop a new kind of assurance. Then the "territory" that is claimed may indeed be "effectively occupied." A military image is employed: "In attacking the oldest and toughest plutocracy in the world, Labour is undertaking, on any showing, a pretty desperate business. It needs behind it the temper, not of a mob, but of an army."[49]

TRUSTING THE PEOPLE

Tawney saw in totalitarianism an attempt to freeze history at a certain supposedly optimum point. That might do for communities of ants and bees, which are not subject to change, but not for human beings like "Henry Dubb," whose soul is his own, whose community is subject to more than biological change. Tawney's Christian position made him immune to political claims which implied the freezing of history. Possessing a Christian hope that lay beyond history, he was unlikely to allow a *political ideology* to assume a position beyond history; his mind had no vacancy for an eschatology. He could acknowledge no laws of history independent of the minds of men, envisage no final destination at which conflicts and imperfections would be absent from social life.

Tawney, unlike Laski, Strachey, and most British socialist thinkers of that generation, had no Marxist phase in the 1930s. He had always admired Marx, but he thought some of Marx's followers had made a "theory of the processes of history do the work of a political philosophy."[50] His case here against Marxism rests on the same premise as his case against capitalism. "The one view of Man which is fatal both to Christianity and to any social revolution worth making is that which regards him, not as a being with a capacity, if he will use it, for autonomy and responsibility, but as a machine or a slave." Industrialism treated man as a "hand"; Stalinism treated him as a "cog." In both ideologies, Tawney argued, ends and means were juxtaposed and human creativity squeezed out.

To a lesser degree, Tawney raised a similar objection against Fabian collectivism. He spoke (at a Fabian dinner!) of pundits who can "answer every question except how any child of man could endure to live in the paralytic paradise promised by [the Fabians]." He felt some Fabians were too enamored of their political system for its own sake (and again he used a static image pejoratively). At the same dinner he confessed: "One whom I revere, Beatrice Webb, once froze my blood by remarking casually that what she most desired was to establish for the benefit of her long-suffering fellow countrymen what she called 'a regimen of mental and moral hygiene.' " Nor could he approve Sidney Webb's talk of society as a machine. Democratic socialism, he insisted, was concerned with releasing energies as well as harnessing them.[51]

It is easy to see why Tawney never flirted with utopianism. In so far as utopias (or anti-utopias) are predicated upon an assumption that history can or will stop at some point, they contain authoritarian implications. For who will do the thinking and make the choices after that climactic point? Presumably some wise elite. One way of measuring the horrors of the twentieth century is to compare *News From Nowhere* with *1984*. The closed, ideological view of history that saddened Tawney seemed orchestrated to a *götterdammerung* in Orwell's negative utopia. Here, in Orwell's words, is a "huge, accurately planned effort to freeze history at a particular moment of time."[52] Here man is reduced to an instrumental role as comprehensively inhuman as that of "hand" and "cog" combined.

In so far as utopias seek to subsume religious values and authority to the realm of politics, Tawney was opposed to them for this additional reason. Orwell carried the tendency to the point of nightmare caricature. There is "thought-crime," an equivalent to sin, and there are continuous demands for an "act of submission" which is "the price of sanity" (as in a religious system submission is the price of salvation). "You will be hollow," Winston is told, "We shall squeeze you empty, and then we shall fill you with ourselves" (a parallel to the emptying of self followed by inflowing of the Holy Spirit). "We make the laws of nature," says the cadre (comparable to the church's claim to be the fount of all truth). Near the end O'Brien brings the analogy home to the crucial area of authority: "We are the priests of power."[53] Here was a religion of politics, objectionable both to Tawney's religion and to his politics.

If Tawney's religious position kept him from flirting with dictatorships of the kind Orwell caricatured, the basic principles of his socialism also provided early-warning signals against their glittering claims. Oceania was not capitalist or socialist. Neither an apologist for capitalism, such as Hayek, nor an apologist for communism, such as Strachey in the 1930s, possessed the conceptual apparatus to demonstrate its true inhumanity. Tawney did. He would have none of this "paralytic paradise" (even before it was caricatured), for the *same reason that he would have none of the theories of Hayek and Strachey:* their failure to recognize that only the social purposes of a free and equal citizenry are the proper well-spring of the state.

Is there occasionally a trace of utopian thinking in Tawney? If so, it is a utopia different from prevailing twentieth-century forms. The latter (whether negative or positive) consist of the aspiration to *attain full control* over nature and/or men. In Tawney there may be traces of a utopia which aspires to *avoid* certain manifest evils of modern society. It is in the tradition of More and Morris, interested not in control but in *right relationships.*

Orwell showed remarkable prescience about the imminence of political systems which treated human beings as things; he saw aspects of them which Tawney did not. Yet long after Orwell had lost hope in the struggle for a socialism married to liberty, Tawney continued it and with some success. It seems to have been Orwell himself who spoke in *1984:* "But no advance in wealth, no softening of manners, no reform or revolution has ever brought human equality a millimeter nearer."[54] Tawney did bring equality nearer in England.

Although he lived in Bloomsbury, Tawney did not mix much with intellectuals, and often threw out deprecatory (and self-deprecatory) remarks about them. He did not care for the characteristic approach of intellectuals to politics, especially during the "era of tyrannies." He thought the "false sense of participation," which, according to Mannheim, marks the approach of intellectuals to politics, predisposes them to squeeze the human beings out of their blueprints.[55] As Tawney watched some of them proclaim an end to the "openness" of history, and clasp antidemocratic ideologies to their mental bosoms, he feared democracy and socialism might lose each other in the dark night of ideology. He doubted the full seriousness of these "paladins of paper revolutions," not for any lack of sincerity on their part, but because their political center of gravity lay in abstractions rather than in intimate contact with "Henry Dubb."[56] They filled their essentially democratic minds with the authoritarian principles of communism, fascism, and other species of positive and negative utopia.[57]

Tawney kept a simple belief in the wisdom and all-round capacity of working people. Speaking of the period between the start of World War II and the attack by Hitler on the Soviet Union, when there was "a certain amount of chatter among self-styled revolutionaries as to the wickedness of cooperating in a capitalist war," he acidly remarked: "The rank and file of Labour [who] remained quite unaffected by [this chatter] . . . know the limitations and defects of British democracy a good deal more intimately than the melodious intellectuals who harrow cultured audiences with tearful cries of stinking fish."[58] Behind such views lay Tawney's insistence that the point of socialism was *not the building of a tidy governmental system, but the unleashing of the latent energies of the people.* Even the maintenance of the Labour party should not be regarded as the purpose of citizenship—but the converse.[59]

To the comparison of Mao Tse-tung's concern with cultural revolution and Tawney's concern with socialism as a continuous manner of life, a point of contrast has to be added. If Mao's key motto in the Chinese cultural revolution was "Serve the People", Tawney's characteristic motto was perhaps "Trust the people." In the last analysis, Mao's motto is an authoritarian one which implies the Leviathan many Chinese intellectuals half a century ago desired in order to make China once again wealthy and powerful. Tawney had seen and rejected the Victorian liberal paternalistic notion of "serving the people"; he had no more taste for an idea of serving the people which implied authoritarian politics and a closed view of history.

British socialism has recently shown more concern for the social relationships of socialism (as distinct from questions of industrial organization and questions of state power) than when Tawney was writing. During the postmortems of the 1950s, there began an attempt to cast the net of socialist theory more broadly than factory and husting. Crosland's *The Future of Socialism* (1956) was the first notable book of this tendency. If Crosland's work showed that the right wing of the Labour party felt the need to proceed beyond economic issues, the same was also true of the left wing. Three volumes of essays from the left all revealed an emphasis upon issues which could broadly be called "cultural": *Conviction* (1958), *Out of Apathy* (1960), and *Towards Socialism* (1965).[60]

Some of the writing reads like a return to Tawney. Both streams quote Tawney, finding in him a basis for their concern with the whole range of social relationships (few if any other socialist figures are quoted so evenhandedly by both the contemporary Labour left and right). However, Tawney's idea of socialism as a comprehensive manner of life differs in some respects from both these left and right varieties of "cultural" socialist theory, and two of them are germane to the question of citizenship and the masses.

Unlike Crosland, Tawney thought the problem of a socialist manner of life to be much more than a problem of distribution. Crosland (taking an overly optimistic view of the prospects of the British economy) argued that, since basic economic problems were now largely solved, greater resources should be devoted to cultural pursuits. Tawney saw culture in expansive terms as "an energy of the soul."[61] It was not one segment of social life but the whole activity of ordinary people in their daily life. "Our object," he told the WEA in a presidential address, "ought to be not merely to increase the number of persons with access to what is conventionally described by the rather depressing word culture. It should be to create a new culture drawing its materials from the experience and outlook on life, not of a leisured minority, but of the mass of the people."[62]

From the quasi-Marxist position of writers such as Ralph Samuel, Perry Anderson, and E. P. Thompson, Tawney differed in his attitude to the working class. There is a similarity, which contrasts with Crosland, in the way cultural problems are considered integrally with the entire complex of economic and political problems. But from Tawney's point of view, these leftists have too little respect for "Henry Dubb." Their dismay at the apparent contentment of the workers in a consumer society reveals interesting differences from Tawney. There is no evident underlying view of human nature in their socialist theory. They slip somewhat by default into assuming (or demanding) an extraordinary approximation to perfection from the common man, without saying just why he can be expected to perform so much better in the future than he has habitually done in the past. And there is a touch of contempt for the "material" which Tawney hardly shared. It is difficult to imagine Tawney trying to spiritualize the working man out of the pub to the art gallery, or away from the television to the sterner pastures of socialist literature. Any hint of a socialist culture being implanted by advanced intellectuals was foreign to him.

Tawney's citizenship was a child of his unwavering humanism. "What is civilized?", "What is fit for men?", were his guiding questions. At the boiling point of ideological controversy in 1935, he surmised that "the division of the future will lie, perhaps, less between different forms of political and economic organization than between different estimates of the value to be put on the muddled soul of Henry Dubb."[63] In 1973 it seems a wise remark, now that politics is caught up in problems posed by bureaucracy, the human dilemmas of "technetronic" society, and demands for various kinds of cultural revolution and meaningful participation.

One of Tawney's last speeches reveals how he was questing for new patterns of socialist life after the legislative spurt of the Attlee governments and the following lull. He wondered whether "we do not think too much of evils to be abolished and too little of positive goods to be achieved; . . . too little of energies to be released; too much of a man's income and too little of quality of life; too much of the goods which can be measured, counted, and weighed, and too little of the humans which can't."[64] Tawney was not belittling the achievements of the Attlee governments; the same speech warmly praised them. He was combining "commonsense Labourism" with the rocklike humanistic base of his thought, and the combination does much to explain his influence on Britain and socialism.

9 FELLOWSHIP

[The aim of the Labour party is] to diminish the temptations of the rich, and to make it somewhat easier for them to cultivate, in a practical form, the difficult virtue of fraternity.
(*The British Labour Movement*, p. 160)

The noblest aspect of popular movements in this country was expressed by Morris . . .: "Forsooth brethen, fellowship is heaven, and lack of fellowship is death: and the deeds that ye do upon the earth, it is for fellowship's sake that ye do them."
("Christianity and the Social Order," *The Attack*, p. 191)

During the war, we are all brothers.
(*Democracy or Defeat*, p. 11)

RECOVER FRATERNITY?

As the rationalist political thought of the Enlightenment passed its zenith, two notions arose to complicate and, by the twentieth century, to dominate political thinking: *class* and *nation*. The socialism of Tawney can be seen as a struggle against the imperious demands of both.

Democratic socialism has sometimes been squeezed into impotence, between bolshevism which puts class at the center of its analysis, and conservatism (or fascism) which puts nation at the center of its analysis. Much of the thought of the eighteenth-century revolutions was later wrenched from its moorings by the pull of one or other of these magnetic poles.

"Liberty and equality have usually in England been considered antithetic," Tawney complained, and "fraternity has rarely been considered at all."[1] Why had the third element of the trilogy been neglected? It seems, as often in the strangely discontinuous history of political thought, that a political concept arose because a social "interest" bore it up on the wings of a claim made by that interest to a place in the political order.

In England, liberty had its champion in the broad coalition of forces that opposed the arbitrary power of the crown, and then during the nineteenth century in the middle-class challenge to the residual political power of the aristocracy. The great Whig cry of "Liberty" was rooted in a concrete struggle.

Equality, too, had its natural sponsor. After rationalist and utilitarian liberalism had won legitimacy for "rights," it only remained for the rising artisan class to extend the same arguments into a claim to *rights for all*. The narrow base of Bagehot's constitution proved vulnerable before an appeal to political equality. In the Acts of 1867 and 1884 the town workers and agricultural workers respectively found this appeal a usable ticket to their place in the sun of the English constitution.

But who was to speak *in tones that hinted a power challenge* for fraternity? True, themes approximating fraternity were common during the surge of working-class organization and agitation in the 1820s and 1830s; these were passionate years. But the idea of fraternity at that time was limited, and its season turned out for good reason to be short. It was not a fully *political* notion. Either it was an exotic plant designed to flourish in a model community set apart from the mainstream of British life, or it was a spiritual quality which marked the internal dynamics of working-class movements. It is tempting to say it was the fraternity of an essentially preindustrial socialist impulse.

As soon as the working-class movements turned to direct pursuit of political power, the emphasis on fraternity disappeared. This tendency began in the 1840s with Chartism; by the time working-class organization revived in the 1880s it was very clear. Fraternity lived on as a way of life within the labor movement. But fraternity as a value *all* social relationships in Britain should be made to express was largely lost.

Yet what the labor movement abandoned others took up. The major vehicle of fraternity as a hegemonic idea in the twentieth century has been fascism. If the ideas of liberty and equality came to be deeply colored by notions of *class*, the idea of fraternity came to be deeply colored by the notion of *nation*.

To be sure, this was a severe distortion of *fraternité* (as "English liberty" and "socialist equality" are perhaps distortions of the other two key ideas in the Declaration of the Rights of Man). After World War I this distortion approached its terrible apogee. Fraternity now existed only at the gut level of national feeling, especially where national feeling was harnessed to the politics of national resentment or imperialist expansion. Fraternity had become by default the possession of sentimental vitalists (Stefan George, Barrès, d'Annunzio). They recoiled before the strain of trying to reconstruct industrial society on the basis of liberal values, and sank back to fondle the easy certainties of irrational nationalism.

Tawney sought to reclaim fraternity (or fellowship as he usually termed it) for socialism. It is paradoxical to find fellowship at the heart of the thought of a man who emphasized liberal values, including the sanctity of the individual personality. What meaning could fellowship have for this formidable patriarch of British socialism? He conceived fellowship not as a matter of *feelings*, but as a matter of *right relationships* which are *institutionally based*.

"The production of a true social form," wrote an editor of Ruskin's works in 1891, "has been the supreme task given to the nineteenth century."[2] To see the meaning of Tawney's socialism we must first understand the problems to which it was a response. The fundamental one was that the liberal capitalist order no longer provided social cohesion. A new social form had to be found which would overcome the social fragmentation of industrialized Britain.

The loss of social cohesion was in part a matter of the facts of industrial sociology. A man's life was more of a unity when he practiced a craft under his own roof or tilled his own land, with his family and neighbors alongside him, than when he went out of the neighborhood daily to work for someone else in a factory. In part it was a matter of the moral and philosophic bases of prevailing social theory. "Economic man" was an abstraction whose almost religious authority in the Victorian period—despite notable critics— testified that it was the logic of Smith's and Ricardo's economic mechanism, rather than broadly social considerations, which was considered the source of whatever systemic unity British society possessed.

In *Religion and the Rise of Capitalism* Tawney had sought to explain how social theory that acknowledged the autonomy of economics had replaced the organic social theory of Christendom. Bagehot, from his standpoint as an apologist for Victorian industrialism, had no disagreement with Tawney's point that political economy as a cosmology was an upstart science. It had only recently replaced that older genus of social theory which took social values to be more fundamental than economic values. In *Physics and Politics*, Bagehot conceded that there had formerly been "a sort of pre-economic age when the very assumptions of political economy did not exist, when its precepts would have been ruinous and when the very contrary precepts were requisite and wise."[3] That dark age was now happily past. Political economy now did service as political philosophy. Until the appearance of idealism at Oxford, its sway in Britain had been challenged only by the brief innings of Owenism, and sporadic assaults from literary figures who were not always clear whether their target was laissez-faire political economy or industrialization as such.

The liberal ideology of industrialism was triumphant. Tawney called it "a kind of religion," and in one respect this was true.[4] It embodied a faith that the acquisitiveness of individuals would harmonize to produce the good of all. Buttressed by biological analogies, this rather attractive faith delayed the realization that *social* problems were piling up which could not be coped with either by the political system as then constituted, or by social theory which could admit no serious tension between economic individualism and the claims of social justice.

As often with triumphant ideologies, the first doubts about it came only when its practical capacity declined. What the accusations of Ruskin and Carlyle could not do, economic depression, the rising competition of Germany (after the Franco-Prussian war) and the United States (after its Civil War), and later the diplomatic challenge from France, gradually began to do. "I sometimes fear," Benjamin Jowett confessed to Lady Amberley midway through Victoria's reign, "that with all our great wealth and commerce, we are only an orange going to be sucked by France or America."[5]

Imperialist success and the myths surrounding it delayed national doubt and softened for a time the acuteness of latent social conflicts. But with the Great War the liberal ideology collapsed. Victorian industrialism in theory and practice alike seemed to have no answer either to the need for a peaceful international community of nations, or to the demands for a social transformation within Britain itself. There were many problems, and the basic one may have been the relative economic decline which Britain entered upon around the 1880s and in some ways has never recovered from. But the problem which preoccupied social critics was the apparent loss of social cohesion.

Britain had become musclebound with her industrial and imperial mechanisms. When, during years that coincided with the first signs of deflation of the diverting Jingoist spirit, her social body was examined by Seebohm Rowntree in York and Charles Booth in London, it proved to be emaciated and neglected.[6] One fifth of the country was in poverty, and the working class was sick, hungry, undersized, demoralized, and cut off from the great institutions, activities, and values which were assumed to be nationwide but in practice were limited to the upper and middle classes. Not surprisingly, the Edwardian years brought mounting industrial unrest, and the Great War led to a tremendous impulse to reconstruct society. The war climaxed the realization of the loss of social cohesion, in part because in translating men from factory bench to battlefield it brought a searchlight to play upon their alienated and apathetic condition.

Poignant that these bewildered men, knowing little fellowship in British society, should find it on the fields of France, fighting for democracy. Hardly surprising that many should rejoice in the first stages of the war, since it brought a sense of social cohesion born of common endeavor that they did not find at home yet evidently craved. Tawney lashed out at this after returning wounded to England. "For an army does not live by munitions alone," he bitterly accused his countrymen, "but also by fellowship in a moral idea or purpose. And that, unless you renew your faith, you cannot give us. You cannot give it us, because you do not possess it."[7] This was the year when Tawney's regard for England sank low; the irony of a fellowship limited to the business of killing abroad and absent from the business of living at home grew insupportable.[8]

In political thought there were two broad responses to the loss of social cohesion. The conservative response appealed to authority and nationalism. In Europe it frequently took an irrationalist and iconoclastic turn, resulting in what has been called an ideology of resentment (Moeller van den Broeck is its most notable exponent.)[9] In England it leaned essentially upon the feudal traditions of the past (as in Lord Hugh Cecil).[10] The radical response appealed to equality and internationalism. Both responses rejected the political economy of liberalism. Both had to accommodate loss of faith in a natural social harmony. Both felt the pressure to reach beyond the individualism of liberalism and to bind up society with ties more affective than the sinews of the cash nexus.

Eventually both dethroned reason from a central place in political analysis. This was not true of the radical response before the collapse of the Second International. But when, with the founding of the Comintern in 1919, bolshevism became the predominant strain of socialism, the left's break with the rational and liberal tradition was nearly complete. In the wake of the Depression, the conservative and radical responses to the breakdown of the pre-1914 order confronted each other in their ideologized forms as fascism and Stalinism. By then the judgment of the historian J. B. Bury in 1913 echoed as a mockery: "The struggle of reason against authority has ended in what appears now to be decisive and permanent victory for liberty."[11]

There were evident both organizational and vitalistic ways of "binding up" society. The distinction cut across the terms "radical" and "conservative." On the left were organizationists ranging from Fabians to Leninists, as well as liberal evolutionists like J. A. Hobson who called for a "science of social progress." But the left also contained "vitalists" (for whom sentiment or solidaristic impulse was the path to socialism); notably syndicalists and guild socialists. William Morris's *News From Nowhere* was a book written by a vitalistic radical as a rebuttal to the utopia of an organizational radical (Bellamy). The artist with medievalist sympathies pitted his vision of socialist fellowship against what he called the "scheme of the organization of life" presented in *Looking Backward.*[12]

On the right, W. H. Mallock in his *Limits of Pure Democracy* (1918), sought to reassert order in an anarchistic situation by an appeal to the "oligarchic principle." It was mainly in Europe that conservatism took a vitalistic form, but the fascism of Mosley, like other fascisms, owed much of its uncanny power to catch well-meaning people off balance to an ingenious combination of the vitalistic and the organizational.

The cross-fertilization of styles of thought on the left and right seems testimony to the depth of the antiliberal consensus which gripped political thinkers. No one epitomizes the uncertainty of the categories of right and left more than Sorel; and no one is more deeply and totally antiliberal in his quest for a new fraternity. It is the one immovable rock in the landscape of his intellectual career.

UP FROM LIBERALISM

How were these currents of thought meaningful for Tawney? Ernest Barker recalls that at Balliol around the turn of the century "most of us" were "Liberals in politics"; Tawney was no exception.[13] His liberalism was idealist in its philosophic underpinnings and moralistic in tone. The "disorders of modern society" then seemed to him "the inevitable result of a particular way of looking at the world." The lack of a "supernatural reference" flawed laissez-faire capitalism and collectivism alike. Liberty was defined (evidently following Acton) as "the opportunity to do one's duty." Tawney never fully expounded these views in published form, which is significant (and perhaps not regrettable). Even before they were gathered for the outline of a book, he had begun to edge away from the assumptions that made them a unity.[14]

Tawney first grappled with the problem of the loss of social cohesion as a problem within the world of thought itself. The fragmentation of the intellectual monism of European thought (which Mannheim has described as the backdrop to the emerging possibility of a sociology of knowledge), bothered young Tawney. He was searching, he said, for a "general philosophy of life"; it is reminiscent of Mannheim's search for a "total conception," which would integrate the fragments of man's knowledge of himself and society. At this stage, Tawney attached great importance to ideas, much less to institutions. Explaining why the creation of a "generally accepted philosophy of life" was his prime task, Tawney noted in his diary in 1914: "There *is* no creative force outside the ideas which control men in their ordinary actions."[15]

Tawney never formulated a general philosophy of life, and before he was forty he had abandoned the effort to do so. His search for cohesion was transmuted from a problem about knowledge into a problem about politics. Instead of a philosophy of life he worked out a philosophy of socialism. The total conception that he came to advocate went through various mutations until it was less a philosophy for the minds of men than a polity for the British nation (and for other nations).

Two key experiences led Tawney to make concrete his quest for cohesion. The first was his personal encounter with industrial problems (which in turn led him into economic history). The second was the Great War. These experiences brought Tawney to see the "disorders of modern society" in an organizational framework. It began to seem a little less important that men adopt a right way of thinking, and a little more important that Britain adopt the right structures of society. Concern for virtue was edged aside by concern for justice. He indeed became concerned with *social* cohesion.

It is possible to trace in Tawney's successive writings his evolution away from philosophy and toward politics; toward a notion of social cohesion made concrete by a pattern of institutions. The clearest crystalization of the idealist, moralistic position occurs in the diary and the outline "The New Leviathan"; of the materialist, structural position, in *Equality*. In some important respects *The Acquisitive Society* stands midway between the two positions.

At all stages he rejected the notion that economic mechanisms could provide the required unity for society. But whereas in "The New Leviathan" it is people's conception of things which is expected to master and redirect economic mechanisms, in *Equality* politics has become the master science. The power arrangements of society are the central concern (*Religion and the Rise of Capitalism* had contributed to the change; he had concluded, unlike Weber, that economic factors were more decisive than ideas in the transformations of 1540-1640).

In "The New Leviathan" the theories of *The Acquisitive Society* existed in embryo, but they were suffused with a Miltonic idea of Christian liberty. The functional view of industrial relationships was qualified by the imperative to do one's duty (ultimately before God). A secularization has taken place in *The Acquisitive Society;* the service of society is the crucial test of conduct. But *The Acquisitive Society* was still more about industry than about politics.[16] It also differed from *Equality* in the criteria that were used to determine the distribution of the social product. In *The Acquisitive Society*, the stress was on need; in *Equality* on just reward. Moreover, in *The Acquisitive Society*, more importance was attached to function than in *Equality*. Tinged with guild socialism, *The Acquisitive Society* presented service and purpose and function as the key dynamic principles for the whole society. In *Equality*, these were sometimes transcended by another, higher principle: politically rooted fellowship. It would not be true to say Tawney had replaced a vitalistic with an organizational quest for social cohesion, but he had placed a vitalistic hope (as Morris did not do) within an organizational framework.

INTERLUDE OF POSSIBILITY

The formative period of Tawney's life coincided with a notable interlude of fluidity in the state of political thought, extending from the outbreak of the Great War into the 1930s. This interlude was marked by an expansive quest for a new social cohesion under democratic auspices. The dominion of liberal ideology lay in the past. It had proclaimed utilitarianism, yet also held as an inarticulate premise a certain evolutionary optimism. Interference with the structures of the socio-economic order was thought unwise if not impossible.

In the future, soon to put an end to this interlude in which it seemed possible to make almost any pattern out of the social fragments of the wartime experience, lay three forces that clipped the wings of political thought: the rise of the ideologies of fascism and Stalinism; sceptical sociology; and pessimistic philosophies of history. All three posed acute problems for Tawney. His own interlude of fluent, creative social thinking was severely checked by them. The ideologies generally seemed either vulgarized or irrationalist: the manipulative authoritarianism of Stalinism, the alternatively emotive and cynical eclecticism of the fascism of Mussolini and Alfred Rosenberg.

If, in retrospect, the theoretical political discussion in Britain during the later 1930s seems brittle and derivative, it is because the debate did no more than echo in a muddled way the clash between totalitarian ideologies. These ideologies were largely irrelevant to Britain. This seemed plain when the reconstruction of the 1940s proceeded not according to the "new religions," but according to Beveridge, Fabianism, Macmillan's "Middle Way," and the liberal Yellow Book, *Britain's Industrial Future.*

A second development which helped end the interlude was the quick advance of sociology, with its deflating realism about the nature of groups, elites, bureaucracy, and the behavior of the working class. The first generation of political sociologists, among them Pareto, Michels, and Mosca, threw doubt on the attainability of certain social goals widely sought by thinkers of the interlude. This doubt Mannheim tried to systematize in his sociology of knowledge, but the doubt seemed more real than the attempt to systematize and thus transcend it. In the work of the sceptical sociologists, the rationalistic optimism of the nineteenth century was totally eclipsed. The happy ending which Marx posited to the unfolding of history was dropped, and in its stead is Michels' bitter remark: "It is probable that this cruel game will continue forever."[17]

A third development was the ascendancy gained by the somewhat pessimistic philosophies of history of Toynbee and Spengler, and the dawn of a realization that the torch of social progress might soon pass from Europe's hands to America, to Russia, and through Russia to the peasant revolutions and nationalistic self-consciousness of Asia.

These three developments came to weigh heavily on Tawney as an Englishman born at the high noon of Victorian liberalism. The pall they cast on the later Tawney strengthens the impression that Tawney's fruitful work on social theory was done in an interlude of seemingly open possibilities in the second and third decades of the century. This interlude was not a moment, but a situation, which came at different times for different societies and different thinkers. Thus a totalitarian ideology was already established in power in Russia well before the interlude of creativity in social philosophizing in Britain was ruptured by the rise of the ideologies and the shadow of World War II. The interlude was nonetheless real and its nature may help in understanding Tawney.

In Britain after the Great War, there seemed to be wide scope for remaking society. Laski began his *Grammar of Poli-*

tics (1925) with the declaration: "A new political philosophy is necessary to a new world."[18] The widespread vogue of the terms "new order" and "reconstruction" justified his mood. The "molten state" which Lloyd George sensed in Britain's social condition seemed paralleled in political thought.[19] Rockow's *Contemporary Political Thought in England* (1925) conveyed an intellectual landscape of real ferment if little profundity. Norman Angell and the Union of Democratic Control persuaded many people that the chance to secure international peace once and for all was at hand. Churchill himself told the House of Commons a few years before he took the helm to fight the high priests of fascist authoritarianism: "Either there will be a melting of hearts and a joining of hands between great nations which will set out upon realizing the glorious age of prosperity and freedom which is now within the grasp of the millions of toiling peoples, or there will be an explosion and a catastrophe the course of which no imagination can measure and beyond which no human eye can see."[20] It is a haunting illumination on post-1945 Britain that there ensued neither a melting of hearts and joining of hands nor an irredeemable catastrophe. Instead the interlude was transmuted into a deadpan collectivism at home and Cold War abroad that no one between the wars remotely foresaw.

The confusions of the post-World War I period have been cited as a testimony to the psychic cost of Victorian optimism.[21] Yet now we can see that the optimism had not totally vanished. It was still thought possible for men to reason together and produce a just society out of their efforts. Laski described the social good as "the product of co-ordinated intelligence."[22] There existed that faith in reason which true socialism shares with liberalism. There was during the interlude sufficient sense of crisis to force a return to first principles, yet sufficient hope to generate an enthusiastic search for solutions.

On the left this was the heyday of the "socialist generation" on whose capital the Labour party lived through its post-World War II successes.[23] Political thinkers were convinced that 1914 had brought a point of no return for the liberal order. Yet they had by no means thrown in the sponge before the fake triumphalism of the ideologies. Laski could call democratic government "a final form of political organization," and say in passing, "for Western Europe, at least, democratic government has become a common-place beyond discussion."[24]

Progressive political thinkers were convinced of the inadequacy of nineteenth-century individualism, even in the reconstructed form given it by T. H. Green. Yet they claimed to possess a sociology radically more optimistic than that of the sceptical sociologists, Michels, Pareto, and Mosca. Sociology was still widely and naively thought to be a kind of science of progress, albeit not the serene and inevitable progress that made the 1890s resemble a permanent summer afternoon. What J. A. Hobson had written in 1901 remained the hope of the many thinkers who tried to fashion a new sociology in the 1920s: "sociology, by the distinctive intellectual operation of enabling individuals to realize society as an elaborate interaction of social forms and forces, and so to understand the worth of social conduct, *will alter the scale of human values and desires.*"[25] These progressive political thinkers, although they felt the spiritual illness of a Europe which had killed forty million people in an unnecessary war, quoted Spencer frequently and Spengler never, believed in the League of Nations, and (the socialists among them) thought the hope of social democracy all over the world rested in the virile lap of the British Labour party.

Tawney was fully part of this fluid interlude of mingled crisis and hope; yet he transcended it in important ways. His idea of socialism as fellowship is explicable as a product of the interlude, yet it retained validity beyond World War II. His 1924 lectures at Yale, published as *The British Labour Movement,* strike a jaunty, earnest, vigorous, slightly complacent note which is characteristic of the interlude. After 1918 Tawney saw a new epoch at hand: "the parliaments of England and France will be as powerless to revive the past as the Romanoffs were to maintain it."[26] Britain had great problems, but nothing too intractable for the socialism of the Labour party to handle. The springboard of postwar idealism made the sense of crisis exhilarating rather than paralyzing.

Underlying his work was a sense of open options which looks strange and alluring to those who have been wrenched, moulded, and subdued by the ideological polarizations of the Cold War. The basic ingredients for successful reconstruction existed after 1918: awareness of its necessity; belief that the problems were amenable to rational procedures; an available political force (the Labour party) freshly apprised of its capacity to win political power.

All this was a far cry from the situation in Tawney's eighth and last decade (the 1950s). By then socialism and left-liberalism had lost confidence. The traditionalism of Oakshott and the empiricism of Weldon possessed greater prestige and influence. The Labour party was sunk in internal dispute and self-doubt which made it seem that the socialist generation was spent. The party leader himself (Gaitskell) proposed that nationalization, for many the Crown Jewels of the socialist kingdom, should be done away with. Orwell was an intellectual hero, and his political books were devoured by people who found in them a suggestion that all socialism, and even liberalism, was stained with the sins of totalitarianism. Not least, the bomb cast its pall of cosmic pessimism.

Yet Tawney had not lost relevance for midcentury, as had most thinkers of the interlude:

1. He had long built a dyke against the seductions of the totalitarian ideologies by his insistence that among things which must be "nationalized" political power was crucial.[27]

2. He anticipated the major theses of the sceptical sociologists. His sense of history, his sobriety about what could and could not be expected of human nature, kept him from predicating his socialism on an assertion of the moral superiority of the working class. It kept him, too, from that naivety before the snares of bureaucracy which supposes that *who* rules is the only crucial question for socialist theory.

3. The survival in amended form of capitalism, despite the wide expectation during the interlude of its spectacular demise, did not leave Tawney naked. His socialist hope was not (like that of some Fabian collectivists) based on a proof that capitalism was inefficient or (like that of quasi-Marxists) on a prediction of capitalism's collapse. Although his ideas on socialism were complex, their only final rationale was that socialism is morally superior to capitalism.

4. Tawney was not greatly shaken by the pessimistic philosophies of history, because the Christian myth in which he believed accommodated his pessimism without rendering him an *historical* pessimist. Well before he read Toynbee and Spengler he had settled with the gods of gloom in the course of coping with the Great War.[28]

5. He was not torn apart as some were by the tension between vitalistic and organizational conceptions of socialism and the way to achieve it (with which the 1950s debates within the Labour party had something to do). For he had elaborated a stable relationship between the two. Socialism would not come only from the heart (vitalism) or from the top (organizationalism) but from both. So if Tawney was indigenous to the interlude, there were also good reasons why the end of the interlude was not the end of Tawney.

THE KEY IS FELLOWSHIP

Now to explore the centrality of fellowship to Tawney's socialism. The four key ideas this book has set out all contribute to the ideal of fellowship. First, dispersion of power is meant to prevent one man or group "lording it over others." It makes people more accessible to each other than a system where power is highly centralized and society is a tapestry of authoritarian links. Second, though equality has never been linked with fellowship in a theoretical way, any consideration of Tawney's equality which does not see that it is built on an argument from fellowship must miss its point. Tawney was concerned not only with *how to treat individuals,* but also with the *consequences for society* of the way individuals are treated.

Third, the idea of function, too, is inseparable from solidaristic values. I suggested that Tawney's idea of function breaks down into "purpose" and "service." There is nothing particularly socialist about "purpose" unless some ground is found to pitch purpose at a level higher than personal or sectional interest. Everyone has purposes even if they are as antisocial as killing a neighbor or making ten million pounds from the toil of others. Tawney reached the idea of a social purpose common to the whole society by means of the high value he put upon fellowship.

Fourth, Tawney's citizenship centered upon a certain quality of human and social communication. Equality and dispersion of power are its preconditions. It is the lubricant of good government. It is also valuable in itself, for the rich quality of relationships it represents (not only between the citizen and the state but among the citizenry). It is a matter not of super-public-spirited performance by moral athletes, but of cooperative life among equals who respect each other's common humanity.

Tawney's social fellowship was not sectional but all-encompassing. In British working-class and socialist tradition, fellowship generally meant one of two varieties of sectional fellowship: intimate personal bonds in a model community, or comradeship within the labor movement. Drawing upon a much broader heritage of social philosophy and range of involvements than communitarians such as Robert Owen or self-made messengers of comradeship such as Robert Blatchford or J. Bruce Glasier, Tawney sought fellowship that would embrace all of British society.

Here it is interesting to compare Tawney with Matthew Arnold (who influenced him) and T. H. Green. Arnold's desire to "rise above the idea of class to the idea of the whole community" was shared by Tawney. But while Arnold merely mounted a moral appeal for men to think bigger than class (or disregard class), Tawney did not believe in any rising above class short of abolishing class. Arnold is able to refer patronizingly to "our working class"; Tawney revolted against the very idea of there being a distinct working class.[29]

The comparison with Arnold is more than between two sets of ideas, like two wines on the mind's table. Tawney's social and intellectual roots lay in Arnold's England, and it may not be fanciful to see a threefold progression from Arnold, to Green, to Tawney on the question "how can social unity be attained?" Arnold observed in *Culture and Anarchy:* "Everywhere we see the beginnings of confusion, and we want a clue to some sound order and authority." The search for such a clue also busied Green and Tawney. Arnold found it in the cultural realm, where there could be spun "perfection," resembling a mantle of equality to be laid over existing socioeconomic inequalities.[30] With Green the central concern was no longer culture but social service. A political dimension had appeared, though it remained essentially paternalistic. Tawney had both Arnold's concern for culture and Green's for social service, but he subordinated both to an argument that social unity could only be attained by socialist reconstruction.

We should not overlook Tawney's antipathy for the nineteenth century. Like that of Morris (whose antipathy was stronger than Tawney's) it was partly based on the feeling that the social unity talked about by Victorians was, behind its dulcet tones, a mystifying and hypocritical ideology.[31] It tells us something about Tawney's belief in fellowship as an over-all principle that he admired Elizabethan England as much as he disparaged Victorian England. He did not defend the Elizabethan age as one of conspicuous humanity or enlighten-ment, but it had a "zest" evident "not only in the high places of poetry, but on the level plain of intimate letters and casual conversations, and which finds its way into literature because it is already in life." It was a "loosely knit, decentralized society, whose pattern of existence was a round of individual activities in a framework fixed by custom." Attractively, "most men worked for themselves, not for a master." Tawney saw a people in frank and easy communication with each other, expressing themselves naturally and forcefully, unintimidated by superior persons. The hallmark of everyday life at the Elizabethan high noon, he concluded, "was a ge-nial, passionate vulgarity." This he liked. "Whatever the crimes of the Elizabethans," ran a swipe at the Victorians, "respectability was not among them."[32]

Above all, the presence of something close to a common culture struck and won him. "In literature, painting and scholarship, the patron plays an important role; but culture is popular, in the sense that it draws on a body of experience which is not the monopoly of a single class, but is, in some degree, a general possession. It voices the outlook on life, not of an elegant *élite*, but of the world of common men." There was a common manner of speech which sadly lacked in his own England. Elizabethan, like Athenian, drama, was an "eminently social thing"; later it was to degenerate into a comedy of manners, "which turns on the contrast between 'the good form' of the fashionable world and the 'bad form' of everyone outside it," with "smoking-room guffaws or drawing-room witticisms in place of humour." The secret of Elizabethan zest lay in "energy working in an appreciative environment," and in its degree of excellence being "not ex-clusive, but widely shared." In sum, an extraordinary enthusi-asm pervaded Tawney's treatment of the Elizabethan age. He did not identify his socialism in any serious manner with agrarian yeoman society; yet, although the "shape of social-ism" did not then exist, Tawney saw aspects of the "dynam-ics of socialism." He discerned an imperfect but genuine para-digm of fellowship embracing the whole society.[33]

Communalism and totalism were not what Tawney had in mind by fellowship. Totalitarianism bids for a kind of "togetherness of the entire society"; how did Tawney separate himself from this notion? His avoidance of atomization was crucial. It is generally agreed that the accessibility to totalitarian appeals of masses, whose participation in intermediate groups is weak, is an important ingredient in the success of totalitarian elites. As William Kornhauser found: "Those with the fewest social ties are the most receptive to mass appeals."[34] Tawney's "citizenship" would severely reduce the availability of non elites to mass appeals.

Tawney's fellowship here contrasts with an apparently similar notion in Rousseau, who believed the state of nature a "golden age, not because men were united, but because they were isolated." Far from having praised isolation, Tawney envisaged socialism as a network of cooperative relationships. "Each, in giving himself to all," wrote Rousseau, "gives himself to no one."[35] Tawney mentally shuddered at this mystical communalism. He eschewed the notion that fellowship is a result of communal excitement evoked from masses who find in the corporate life of the state some missing aspect of their personalities. Sentiment played little part in Tawney's idea of fellowship; indeed, it would be hard to find a less sentimental writer in the history of socialist thought. Rather than "togetherness," Tawney proposed easy, egalitarian communication, facilitated and encouraged by institutional arrangements. Wolin nicely observed: "What Luther aspired to in man's relationships with God, Rousseau transferred to man's relationships with his fellows."[36] Not for Tawney. The sons of Adam had a heavenly destiny, but their spirituality was contained in decidedly earthen vessels. Human society could not provide salvation.

Although Tawney quoted Morris on fellowship as "heaven," there is a difference between them on this point. Morris put into the mouth of John Ball a connection between heaven and society which is one of immanence: "For I say to you that earth and heaven are not two but one."[37] For Morris, fellowship is *literally* heaven. But Tawney did not believe heaven could be realized on earth. To try and bring down heaven on earth was probably to raise hell. Tawney is kept from Morris's "heaven upon earth" utopianism by drawing from Christianity a strong sense of order (unusual in a socialist thinker).[38] Equality, he argued, far from implying anarchy, is "the one foundation of human subordination." Tawney's point is that order involves obligations. And obligations are only recognized where men see their identity with other men. We have no duties to a tiger or a fish. We do have duties to each other because all men are of equal worth in God's eyes.[39]

There is a suspicion in theories of fellowship based on sentiment that compulsory enthusiasm is being prescribed for the citizens. The twentieth century provides melancholy examples of societies based upon "organized enthusiasm." People are punished in these societies not just for doing wrong things but also for failing to do right things. None of this marks Tawney's ideas. The raw material of fellowship, as it were, will exist in socialist society. People will not want to tell each other to "go to hell." Yet if they feel like doing so, this would not be dangerous or criminal.

Tawney's temperament—reserved, upper-class Englishman, "squire of Houghton Street"—may have contributed to these views. Fellowship based on sentiment has been the favorite dream of uprooted, alienated spirits sprung from the lower orders. Yet the fundamental reason for the unsentimental character of Tawney's idea of fellowship is that he clung to the individual as the ultimate unit of value in socialist society. E. M. Forster, a contemporary of Tawney's who went the Cambridge path to Bloomsbury, religious scepticism, and privatism (as opposed to the Oxford path to social idealism), wrote after the Great War: "I have no mystic faith in the people. I have in the individual."[40] Tawney would not say that. Yet as we look back from Beer's "Collectivist Era," the measure of agreement which Tawney has with Forster seems important. There is no holism in Tawney; neither the mystical kind, nor the organizational kind that struts across the late twentieth century.

Tawney's collectivity is made up of individuals; truth's seat remains each man's conscience. Unlike Rousseau, Tawney does not reach for a general will over and above the particular will of each person. Unlike the organizational holism of today, Tawney's fellowship does not see its component individuals as grey nonentities satisfactory in inverse proportion to their idiosyncrasy. But Tawney disagreed with Forster on the nature and possibilities of politics. Partly because he was so much concerned with working-class people, Tawney saw the individual as drastically subject to the effects of political decisions (or the lack of them), and he could not agree either with the underlying factual assumptions of Forster's privatism or with its morality. The individual was not an autonomous island but a participant in a social fellowship which may not be able to "make" him but could certainly "break" him.

Leonard Woolf, who like Tawney was born in 1880, provides a further illuminating comparison. Though he stood on the political fringe of Bloomsbury, Woolf's way of thinking (not his way of acting) was close to Forster's. Quite unlike Tawney, Woolf felt that the Great War simply pulled the rug from under all that was civilized. It was the fate of particular individuals (all of them intellectuals) that brought this home to him. As he pondered their tragedy he burst out: "Happy the country and era—if there can ever have been one—which has no politics."[41] The difference from Tawney boils down to a question of whether it is *some* individuals or *all* individuals who are considered ends in themselves. "Politics" spoiled the lives of some after 1914, yet it enriched the lives of many more. Bloomsbury thought civilization the affair of an elite; Tawney's idea of equality seemed to them ridiculous. Woolf remarked of a servant he once had: "Lily was one of those persons for whom I feel the same kind of affection as I do for cats or dogs."[42] Friendly, well-mannered, totally patronizing, the remark is an epoch apart from Tawney's attitude to working people.

When all that is said, Tawney shared with Forster and Woolf, and almost all thinkers of his generation, the view that the individual is an end in himself, and that the social good was to be defined in terms of the lives of individuals.[43] Tawney confided to his diary a sharp attack on English socialism for swallowing the Benthamite criterion of public well being. Slavery, sweating, cannot be ruled out on the basis of majority good. "There is a law higher than the well-being of the majority, and that law is the supreme value of every human personality as such. This is what is meant by saying 'It were better that a mill-stone should be hanged about your neck . . . than that ye should offend one of these little ones.' "[44] In sum, Tawney clung to certain central liberal values despite rejecting the liberal analysis of history. His view was like Bernstein's: "as far as liberalism as a world historic movement is concerned socialism is not only temporally but spiritually its legitimate heir."[45] The early socialists of the nineteenth century had not stressed individual personality; it was from liberal roots, and from Christianity, that Tawney drew this central concern of his socialism.

WITHIN REACH OF EACH OTHER

In a speech at the London School of Economics in 1956, Tawney remarked of the Webbs: "there is a sense in which the fact that they were socialists is less important than the kind of socialists they were."[46] The same is true of Tawney. He was a socialist who made little use of the label "socialist" in self-description or in titles for his writings. He thought of himself as an Englishman who tried to stand for what was just. There was also the practical consideration that socialism was even in his own time a tree of many branches.

Of socialism as *order* he was not enamored. Bellamy's vision of Boston as a superbly organized symmetry of things, Fourrier's plan to regiment the passions until no psychological stray ends remained, did not move him. (It is difficult for any "socialism of order" to outlast its own epoch; how commonplace Bellamy's machines seem to a generation which put men on the moon, and craves respite in the countryside to keep its serenity.)

Toward socialism as *conquering nature* Tawney made no bow. Ulam observed: "Ever since the beginning of the nineteenth century all political theories have had one great target—the complete domination of man over his physical environment."[47] Tawney was an exception. Laski wrote in *Faith, Reason, and Civilisation:* "We must begin with the assumption that the sole method open to mankind by which he can improve his lot is an increasing mastery of nature."[48] Such a sentiment is missing in the author of *The Acquisitive Society.*

With socialism as *efficiency* Tawney was not taken either. One stream of British socialism, rooted in utilitarianism, has put efficiency on its intellectual altar. To some degree the Webbs were of that stream. Noel Annan has asked of Beatrice Webb's infatuation with the Soviet Union late in life: "Where else could her secular mysticism lead other than to worship of power?"[49] Though Tawney revered the Webbs, he asked Annan's question. His doubts rested on a realization that the thirst for efficiency could be quenched by many an evil brew.

Tawney was not prepared to put even *equality* at the center of his socialism. Too static and soulless would be a socialism only "about equality." And equality, Tawney came to see, could be secured by methods which took freedom as their price. For Tawney the deeper and logically prior value was *fellowship as right relationships among free and equal individuals.*

Beer claimed that for the socialist generation which surfaced after 1918, fellowship "would be the social force that made the Socialist Commonwealth a viable society; it would be a principle of socialist economics."[50] That was true for Tawney, who in *The Acquisitive Society* probed as far into the psychology of industry under socialism as any Briton has done. Fellowship was also an end in itself for Tawney. It was the right condition of life for human beings. Its value was independent of its results, whether in production of goods or in the strength and grandeur of the state.

Such value placed on fellowship is normally found among conservatives who are nostalgic for the hierachical fellowship of feudalism; thus T. S. Eliot. But Tawney's fellowship had no truck with hierarchy. Only equal relationships could produce fellowship. The gulf between social groups which quasi-feudalists consider conducive to fellowship (everyone keeps to his station) was the key *target* of Tawney's theory of equality. The gulf was the evil thing, not the deprivation itself. This dialectical relationship between equality and fellowship is one of Tawney's major contributions to socialist thought.

Fellowship would be *made possible.* It would not actually be *made.* Some organizationists propose to organize fellowship. Some vitalists propose to whip it up. Tawney went no further than to facilitate and encourage it. The power arrangements of society would not themselves require fellowship; that way lay totalitarianism. Power arrangements were not neglected. But their importance was more for what they prevented than for what they guaranteed. Nor was fellowship to be found in the sentimentality of Burke's fixed and hierarchic platoons. Platoons there may be. But they would be voluntary, ever-shifting, cooperative formations, which people would move in and out of according to interest and temperament.

In Morris's *A Dream of John Ball* the voyager in utopia describes an encounter with an official on a horse: "The man soon came up to me, but paid me no more heed than throwing me a nod."[51] Here is a glimpse of Tawney's socialist society. It was not natural or necessary that a relationship of superior before inferior, powerful before powerless, be established between the two men. And the voyager was not bound to get entangled with the official; the choice for social engagement or nonengagement was open. So with Tawney's fellowship: domination of one man by another was prevented. But communion was not compulsory. The citizens would simply be *within reach of each other.*

Tawney's fellowship implies a view of human beings (to caricature) neither as *gods* nor as *cogs*, but as what Christianity knows as *creatures.* There is not the unqualified optimism about human beings which throws them into full, unstructured, and constant communion with each other and then expects harmony. Nor the contempt for human beings which views them as malleable material to be "constructed," or charismatically sucked into some ingenious corporate design.

Human beings are viewed as various in type and imperfect in quality, yet capable of a rich social life, and (even when they perform badly), of ultimate value as persons. And the possibility of right relationships in society is considered an inescapably political possibility. The fellowship Tawney proposes makes no claim to be postpolitical, or apolitical, or suprapolitical. The "life of socialism" cannot properly exist unless the "shape of socialism" exists. The entire society, not one pocket of it, is the arena of fellowship. Conflict will never be eliminated but only controlled. The social life of men will be compounded of their interests and their ideas and values. It will break down if either interests or ideas is permitted to totally eclipse the other. Fluidity, even crisis, is permanent in a healthy society, and so the blunt but essential instrument of politics is permanent. No one group or policy will ever achieve finality and be justified in bringing down the curtain on the rest.

In short, politics will not be subsumed into economics as Tawney found it to be when he started his career. Nor into religion or its surrogates as totalitarians appear to wish. Nor into the harmony of direct communalism, as Morris and other romantics yearned. Nor yet into the smooth and scientific "certainty" of administration, with which we are threatened by fanatics of stability in the 1970s.

Tawney kept the idea of fellowship loose, and this may have been deliberate, because he had in mind open-ended fellowship. Its point was not a collective design as such, but the chance for personality to flower and social relationships to produce their natural ferment. At bottom, Tawney was urging that obstacles to human creativity be cleared away, that first things be put first, that nothing be allowed to eclipse the final importance of intercourse among men. What he had always fought against was the artificial and capricious *gulfs* that capitalist industry and social class set up between people. The point of socialism was to bridge these yawning, inhibiting, chilling gulfs. To be sure, people may then edge toward new kinds of separation from each other. But these, at least, would be freely chosen, the fruits of personality not the involuntary result of the tyranny of wealth or the tyranny of power. Despite its indirect character, Tawney's socialism as fellowship brought, and yet brings, a revolutionary thrust to policy choices: the mutual relationships of all the citizens should be the yardstick for all social and economic decisions.

Part Three. Tawney Today

10 VULNERABILITIES

Since previous chapters have seldom paused to make substantial criticisms of Tawney's ideas, I will now draw together those which are basic. The reason for speaking of vulnerabilities, more than of errors, is that part of the explanation for the reduced relevance of aspects of Tawney's socialism today lies in recent changes in our prevalent assumptions and concerns. To be sure, Tawney did not avoid contradictions and he had his blind spots; these will be scrutinized. Beyond these, however, he also stands vulnerable before certain subsequent shifts in the prevailing political terms of reference.

THE PROBLEM OF COMMON ENDS

Social cohesion results from unity about social ends, Tawney thought. It is true that he climbed down some distance, over the years, from the misty peaks of idealism. In *The Acquisitive Society* (1921) the central stress is no longer on a general philosophy of life (as in "The New Leviathan"), but on principles for the organization of industry. In a further modulation, the centrality of the theory of social function is reduced and Tawney's mature position is that loosely knit, cooperative fellowship is the ultimate socialist value. The dignity of individual personality, and right relationships between human beings sharing a common humanity (rather than agreement about ends) becomes the source of rights and obligations. Still, the theory of function remains one of the five ideas of Tawney's socialism, especially important for his views about incomes and industrial legislation. Belief in common ends appears here and there in nearly all Tawney's work.

In *The Acquisitive Society* Tawney defined society as "a community of wills which are often discordant, but which are capable of being inspired by devotion to common ends."[1]

But what is the nature of the inspiration? Is the discordance to be overcome momentarily on particular issues, or once-for-all by agreement on a single comprehensive common end? Tawney was influenced by the unity and purposefulness of medieval England (and by Greek notions). Has he imperfectly integrated medieval *religious* common ends with *social-political* common ends?

In the passage above from *The Acquisitive Society*, common ends are set over against the absence of defined ends in a society viewed as an economic mechanism. But "ends" in this sense do not have to be "common." The alternative need not be economic mechanism or common ends. There may be *diverse* social ends, all of them worthy or useful, to which productivity per se is subordinated. Even shared ends may not be common ends; parallel activities may be pursued by people acting not together but separately, in small groups scattered throughout a decentralized society.

Or do common ends have to do with the universality of social and economic benefits? Activities and products that enrich large numbers of people (like public parks) may be preferred to those which enrich very few (like luxury yachts); the state should ensure that the former are provided and the latter discouraged. Passages in Tawney suggest that this is the meaning of common ends. It arises from a dichotomy between public interests and private interests, which led Tawney to expose the contrast between "private opulence and public squalor" (a phrase he used in 1919, and which some have attributed to J. K. Galbraith who used it in *The Affluent Society* without reference to Tawney).[2] But private ends may be overruled by ends benefiting millions which are however not common ends. Ends determined by democratic processes may be various; may vary greatly in moral or aesthetic quality; and vary also through time. Few of them could be called common ends.

In *Religion and the Rise of Capitalism* common ends were loftily defined in terms of the suprahistorical destiny of all men as children of God. Tawney found in preindustrial England a "universal and all-embracing" purpose that was in "sharp contrast to the modern temper, which takes the destination for granted, and is thrilled by the hum of the engine."[3] But it was a religious purpose, "set by the divine plan of the universe." Consensus on ultimate questions may facilitate widely accepted social policies. It is another thing, however, to make religious belief the explicit authority for policy, as happened when the church still excercised practical and legal authority over society. Although Tawney was opposed to churchly authority over society, nevertheless he liked the idea of a society bent upon common purposes by virtue of shared religious beliefs. Yet it is not easy to see how the theory of function can relate to religious purpose.

Sometimes Tawney meant by common ends merely a consensus about the nature and principles of the good society. He could simplify the matter disturbingly: "What gives unity to any activity, what alone can reconcile the conflicting claims of the different groups engaged in it, is the purpose for which it is carried on. If men have no common goal it is no wonder that they should fall out by the way, nor are they likely to be reconciled by a redistribution of their provisions."[4] The greatest difficulty with this position arises in the international sphere. No single standard of values covers the whole world, yet competing claims and priorities have to be adjudged. The problem is less, but not negligible, within national units that are assumed to be autonomous. If there are areas in which all Britons have a common goal (defending their territory, countering disease) there are others where they do not (what goods to produce, what political ideas to teach children).

Elitists of right and left may not be greatly worried by this issue. The conservatism of Oakshott implies a single tradition within the nation. The vision in Lenin's *State and Revolution* is likewise predicated upon acceptance by all of a common end for society ("The whole of society will have become a single office and a single factory").[5] In those circumstances Tawney's theory of function could have a neat application.

But democratic socialists cannot assume a consensus of opinions about the nature and principles of the good society. In a nation which was a "single office," how could "Henry Dubb" change his job? Perhaps common ends can only exist (and the theory of function which depends upon common ends can only be applied), without loss of liberty, in entities smaller and more coherent than nations. I also wonder what, in a nation pursuing common ends, would be the source-springs and mechanics of *change* in the ends desired. (Tawney acknowledged that the medieval synthesis was static; that there was "no question of progress, still less of any radical social reconstruction."[6])

The gravest question is this: what authority interprets and backs up the common end? Tawney viewed authority not as determinate, but as generated by the expressed social purposes of an alert citizenry. Yet alongside this pluralist notion stands the idea of common ends, with its centralistic, even authoritarian implications. Praising Elizabethan England, Tawney remarked upon "an outlook on life which was surprisingly homogenous."[7] Yet he also liked the "loosely knit, decentralised" character of Elizabethan society. This hopeful coupling of spiritual unity with organizational decentralization runs throughout Tawney's work.

While criticizing the preindustrial pattern of social control—its demise was a "victory for tolerance"—Tawney did not say how else twentieth-century people, under normal conditions, can be drawn into a homogeneous outlook on life (of course they may be forced into it through what Halévy calls "the organisation of enthusiasm").[8] Within a single office a common outlook is possible without detriment to liberty, but in British society as a whole in the 1970s a common outlook is inconceivable, even were the authority for it purely moral, not legally sanctioned.

To this conclusion I enter one qualification. In wartime a common outlook is possible. War resolved the tension between Tawney's hunger for common ends and his respect for freedom and spontaneity. Marshaled against an enemy, the British people attained a self-generated spiritual unity. Far from scoffing at moral leadership, they showed an extraordinary appetite for it. Within a month Churchill shook off the rags of the politician for the mantle of a prophet.

In his passionate essay "Why Britain Fights," addressed to Americans in the summer of 1940, Tawney described this impressive oneness: "We are not fighting in obedience to the orders of our Government. Our Government is fighting in obedience to our orders"—an absurd notion in normal conditions, yet perhaps plausible in those electric weeks after the debate on Norway, when Churchill stepped up to power.[9] Tawney here expressed his idealistic politics of common ends. "The country feels that at last it has got a Government to its mind—a Government which is single-minded in the prosecution of the war." The problem of combining spiritual unity with organizational pluralism, which Tawney never solved in theory, was resolved in wartime practice by a widespread and single-minded adherence to common ends.

Clear once again is the immense influence of war on Tawney's thought. Only in the special conditions of war could Tawney's idea of common ends be valid and consistent with the rest of his democratic socialist position. Agreement on common ends is not necessary to cooperation, or to equality, citizenship, or fellowship. It could be inimical to dispersion of power. "Social purposes"—understood as a plurality of shifting purposes, democratically arrived at—was a valid part of Tawney's socialism, taking its place alongside his general Christian anthropology, democratic theory, and liberal and egalitarian values; but not common ends.

A general ambiguity in Tawney's socialism is reflected in this particular weakness. Like others before and since, Tawney grappled inconclusively with the rival claims of "good" and "free." He cited William Lovett looking forward to "a Parliament selected from the *wise* and *good* of every class, the most *efficient* means for advancing the *happiness* of all."[10] The key words in that sentence have all become problematic or ambiguous in British politics today. In Lovett's age the struggle for freedom seemed also a struggle for equality. But the two ideas are only occasionally partners. In Tawney there lingers an Arnoldonian yearning for perfection. It sits easily with the Christian strains that pushed him in a solidaristic and moralistic direction, but not with the strictly political, partly utilitarian strains that pulled him in the direction of the welfare state.

Perhaps his doctrines about human nature could have provided a framework for a more integrated vision, but Tawney had no appetite for systematic abstract thought and did not attempt it. So the tension remained. Futilities, he wrote, "are not more edifying in a million wage earners than when displayed by a handful of monopolists, speculators, and urban landlords";[11] yet "Henry Dubb" has shown a taste for "futilities."

Few things reveal this vulnerability of Tawney's more than the opinion or consumer survey, now an important institution in the political process. The survey, and the trembling attention paid it alike at Westminster and in corporation boardrooms, is a monument to the dignity and freedom of the individual. It registers *each man's* taste and views. Ordinary people thus speak more precisely of their wishes than in the entire history of democracy. How relevant is it to preach about the perfection of the individual, the development of his personality, or what is fit for men, when the surveys relentlessly reveal what people consider good and necessary and fitting?

Tawney's "elitism" is not, as with Arnold, an elitism of quality, so much as one of morality. If in Arnold it was an appeal to cultural distinction that diluted his democratic proclivities, in Tawney it was the moralist's appeal to right relationships. What led Tawney to this position? It was in keeping with the atmosphere of the interlude after the Great War to seek a new set of principles whose acceptance would bind up a society broken by the cracking of liberal harmonies and certainties. In reaction to laissez-faire political economy, much naivety was indulged about the whole populace uniting around common social goals. Residual idealism obscured certain institutional problems. And idealism was theoretically ill-equipped to find a balance between liberty and authority in industrialized society.

Tawney's historical perspective (materialistic) pulled against his political perspective (tinged with idealism). Though he put the momentous changes of the sixteenth century down to changes in the material circumstances of life, he seemed confident that in the twentieth-century crisis, ideas and principles could mould a new Britain. Purpose had lost out to mechanism during the rise of capitalism, yet it was expected to prevail during the decline of capitalism.

The idealistic strain thus remained anomalously strong in Tawney. It led him into uncertainty concerning the lessons to be drawn from the nature and demise of the medieval synthesis, for it encouraged him to admire what industrialization had destroyed, without weighing the full import, for his politics, of the causes of the destruction of the medieval synthesis.

Tawney spoke with two voices, one cherishing "good" and the other "free," because he was fighting two enemies posing diverse threats. Against the economic expediency which ruled supreme in the jungle of capitalism, Tawney wanted to exalt the idea of common ends. But against the worship of power of the ideologies, Tawney wanted to exalt the dignity and individuality of the ordinary workingman. During his life-time, battles were won against capitalism, but ground was repeatedly lost to totalitarianism. Tawney's response was to reinforce the doctrines of dignity and individuality, while leaving the idea of common ends not well-adjusted to the rest of his thought.

BRITAIN AND THE WORLD

Tawney harbored few doubts that Britain could build so-cialism if the British people willed it, unprejudiced by deci-sive pressures from outside the country. So much did Tawney take the autonomy of Britain for granted that, except in wartime, he gave little attention to international relations. He found the Russian revolution interesting; toward America he was, until the New Deal, vaguely curious, open-minded, and a shade condescending. But neither country impinged upon Tawney's Britain, which he saw as a fixed "Middle King-dom."

Reflecting on his own career, Harold Macmillan concluded: "Nothing has altered more since my youth than the relative strength of the British economy."[12] Macmillan's testimony suggests the vulnerability of Tawney's idea that Englishmen could arrive freely at their own socialism of common pur-pose. On the crowded road of international economic inter-course it is not only the purposes of Englishmen which deter-mine the possibility of a socialist commonwealth, but those of Britain's creditors, and those of international firms increas-ingly prominent in the British economy.

After World War II, Tawney's comments on Britain's inter-national economic position seemed shallow. "I know no evi-dence," he told a meeting of the St. Pancras Labour party, "confirming the suggestion that the US has used either loans or Marshall Aid as a lever to induce the British Government to abandon or modify socialist policies."[13] But overt pressure was a less important barrier for a British socialist government than a complex web of international economic interdepen-dence, compounded by the role of sterling as a reserve cur-rency.

By the mid-1960s even overt external pressure was a fact of life for the Labour government. The wishes of foreign creditors were decisive in the imposition of the wage freeze in 1965, and the deflationary package which followed devaluation in 1967. What was required, and Tawney had not offered it, was socialist theory which incorporated the international aspects of Britain's existence. From the *Fabian Essays* of 1889 to the 1960s, British socialists had more than a trace of Mr. Podsnap's attitude to England ("blest, sir, by Providence, to the direct exclusion of such other countries as there may happen to be").[14] They wrote as if Britain was her own world. Tawney shared this insularity, and it weakens his message in an era when the British have necessarily had to transform themselves, as Kingsley Martin put it, "from Romans into Italians."

Tawney also believed that British social democracy, in finding a middle path between American capitalism and Soviet communism, could set an example that other countries might follow. "If we fail," he said in reference to the Labour party's mission, at a campaign meeting for Evan Durbin in 1945, "then, I think, darkness descends—for how long no man can say. If we succeed, other countries will follow, and a new age will begin."[15] Lecturing on British socialism in Scandinavia, Australia, and other countries, Tawney spoke, and was probably expected by his audiences to speak, as if Britain was to a greater or lesser degree a possible model for international application.

It would be superficial to dismiss this as flagrant error. What happened to the open-ended possibilities of the interlude did not have to happen. The question of models does not pose itself as a purely theoretical one to any society; models which are promoted on the wings of imperial power have a better chance than models that speak with a small voice. Britain's imperial and economic decline reduced the liklihood of British socialism being followed as a model; that touches little on the merits of the model.

Moreover, the interlude was brought to an end (by the war, and the Cold War) in an unexpected manner which transformed the political options in all nations other than the superpowers. World War II replaced the social struggle with a *union sacrée*, and thus posed long-term practical and theoretical problems for British social democracy.

The Labour party in the 1930s had been unsure whether patriotic war or social transformation was the proper method to combat what seemed a rising tide of fascism and reaction all over Europe. The coming of the war, and the patriotic coalition, resolved that issue and really ended the liklihood that the Labour party would remake Britain in a fundamental way. Then came the Cold War polarization.

Where was the middle path? To be sure the social policies introduced in the 1940s, beginning during the wartime coalition, could be said to mark off a middle path between unbridled capitalism and communist dictatorship. But increasingly it became difficult for the Labour party, as for social democratic parties throughout the Western world, to carve out distinctively socialist policies that could not be labeled pro-communist.

The welfare stateism of the 1940s was not a miserable thing; and Tawney praised it. But it did not come through a transformation of values for which the left could take credit and from which it could derive new spiritual power. It came partly through the objective collectivizing pressures of wartime planning. The Labour party had governed well, but by the early 1950's it hardly seemed, even to the party's own leaders, that what it had been implementing was a philosophy which remained a living torch in the party's hands, and which might yet light up dark corners of the Western world.

These considerations suggest that the fading power of British socialism as a model was not due to its own errors or failures alone. Nevertheless, its power did fade. By the late 1950s it was more common to speak of Scandinavian social democracy as an example for a Britain tied down by past practices and myths, than of lessons Scandinavia might learn from Britain. Wales and Scotland, to the dismay of a Labour party always strong in both places, threw up powerful movements which accused London of having little relevance even for *them*.

There are other changes in Britain's international situation which have reduced the relevance of Tawney's socialist thought. The chipping away at national sovereignty is hardly conducive to Tawney's vision of socialism. In few countries, other than giants like Russia, America, and China, is it easy to envisage the establishment of radical socialism without the attempt becoming the occasion of an international convulsion. Tawney did not confront power other than military power spilling over national boundaries in decisive ways. His discussion of industry cannot accommodate the realities of the international firm; nor can the facts of nuclear technology and their implications be easily fitted into his views on British-American relations.

When Tawney was thirty-four years old, some 85 percent of the earth was ruled by white men. In Asia only Japan and Siam were independent and in full control of their territory. Large patches of the world map were colored red, "British" red. But during the era of tyrannies, war, fascist expansion (as Japan in Asia) and the reverberating impact of the Russian revolution, reversed the tide of empire until, by the time of Tawney's death, Europe had become just one region of the world among others. The West no longer seemed like a fixed center, from which the non-European world could be considered as an object of various operations—or ignored. Not only had Europe's power shrunk, but its values seemed problematic to much of the rest of the world, and even to Europe's own youth.

Tawney took European supremacy and the centrality of European values for granted. He made a partial exception of China. He greatly admired Chinese civilization, declined to put China's problems down, as many did, to innate disabilities, or to believe that Chinese economic and political development would or should follow European patterns.[16] Yet he did not see the significance of Chinese nationalism. Brilliant on Chinese peasant life, Tawney was nevertheless impatient with the intense national self-consciousness of the Chinese intellectuals whose leadership the Chinese peasantry required if the socio-economic changes Tawney himself urged were to be effected.[17]

No more than other British socialists did Tawney apply socialism to the question of empire. In *Religion and the Rise of Capitalism* he criticized the medieval church for failing to seriously confront the issue of serfdom: "apart from a few exceptional individuals, religious opinion ignored it. True, the Church condemned arbitrary tallages, and urged that the serf should be treated with humanity. True, it described the manumission of serfs as an act of piety, like gifts to the poor . . . True, villeinage was a legal, not an economic category; in the England of the fourteenth century there were serfs who were rich men. *But to release the individual is not to condemn the institution.*"[18] This resembles his own failure to confront the issue of colonialism. He tended to espouse reform of the empire rather than to demand its speedy, total dismantling as an institution.[19] Though he urged the working class within Britain to mount a power challenge against its masters, he did not urge the proletarian nations to do the same against their colonial masters. We may paraphrase Tawney's words: "apart from a few exceptional individuals, socialist opinion ignored the issue of empire." "Function" and "equality" were not applied beyond the national unit. The younger generation today hungrily quests for international justice; if such a thing exists Tawney offers few clues to it.

In the reaction of the Third World against the West—as the Chinese case shows—nationalism became the orienting value for the indigenous leadership, and ideological values had to find their place within nationalism. Tawney did not anticipate or understand the causes of the nationalistic cast of Asian socialism, so in an era when the cutting edge of socialist thought and practice has passed from Europe to Asia some may find his thought parochial. By mid-twentieth century, which saw the Chinese revolution and the Korean War, the focus of world political struggles and tensions shifted considerably from Europe to Asia. Socialism, too, had become a predominantly non-Western phenomenon. Tawney wrote fine prescriptions for Chinese education and agriculture, but it did not occur to him to seriously analyze Chinese socialism (or socialism in or for any other non-European area); hence there is relatively little in his socialist thought of interest to those outside the West.

His style betrayed the narrowness of the ground on which he stood. Strangely, his wit and irony sometimes blunted his anticapitalist invective; his background gave him control over his passions. So he stopped far short of being brutal in political attack. There were times when people who were the butt of Tawney's arguments sat back and *enjoyed* his speech as an oracular exercise. Wit was a by-product of the control he kept. Irony implied a common language with his listeners and readers. But since the collapse of empire, socialist debate rides on an open sea of divergent cultural and political currents. The British socialist, unless he is willing to become alienated from his *own* society, feels alien from the conceptual and stylistic world of Che Guevara and Ho Chi Minh. Yet, in a reversal from the direction of the transmission of political ideas and images in Tawney's lifetime, it is these Third World socialists who capture the imagination of many young western idealists in the 1970s.

Tawney, who liked his own country and its culture, felt at home in it, and sat about in a sergeant's jacket of the British army, was quite incapable of grounding his socialism in drastic alienation, and was not disposed to select distant heroes as his models. Tawney's generation confronted Disraeli's "Two Nations," yet great as the social and economic gulf was, the two were in fact one nation, sharing the same national traditions, literature, customs, and language. Being a socialist intellectual did not prevent Tawney from remaining British to the bootstraps. With biblical and classical allusions, snippets from Shakespeare, Milton, Burns, and Tennyson, he could offer his readers familiar landmarks, however opposed they were to the socialist opinions he was expressing. Today, because socialist discourse takes place upon no settled cultural arena, even in Britain, Tawney's style must inevitably seem too narrow and complacent to the alienated utopians who have fallen heir to the socialist tradition. Stylistically he seems too adorned with the enemy's clothes, too familiar with the enemy's mode of life.

MARXISM'S CHANGED POSITION

If changes in Britain's position have undermined Tawney's socialism, so too have changes in the position of Marxism. The period in which Tawney thought out his socialism saw open-ended debate about what kind of society Britain should become. Marxism, along with other theories, was weighed up as a set of ideas. It had its chance and won adherents. It was not yet the grinning mask of circumstance. It presented itself as a challenge to the mind, rather than as a fad, or as the approved and required creed of a great power or bloc of powers.

Tawney took Marx seriously, and he chose his direction more than once under Marx's influence. He studied the French Revolution the better to understand the heritage which confronted the young Marx; he wrestled keenly with what Marx had to say about religion. But Tawney felt no compulsion to make Marxism the orienting point of his view of history or of his socialism. Nor did political pressure or intellectual fashion draw him into either blind adherence or obsessive hostility to Marxism.

For Tawney's first forty years, socialism knew no bifurcation into Marxist parties and social democratic parties. English Marxists went under a social democratic label (SDF), and Lenin himself was content with the title "social democrat" (until 1917). Fabians and Marxists seemed, by virtue of their shared evolutionary and economically rooted rationalism, to be prophets of the same science of society. Tawney felt able to criticize them both with the same arguments in his pregnant outline "The New Leviathan."

In the 1930s a new situation arose, as capitalism appeared doomed, fascism rattled forward, and the Soviet Union alone, holding the magic key of "planning," seemed to exhibit economic rationality. In the atmosphere of crisis, Marxism became the natural ideology of British intellectuals (though not of the labor movement). Keynes gave remarkable testimony on how fully Marxism entered the mainstream of British political life. He said to Kingsley Martin in 1939: "There is no one in politics today worth sixpence outside the ranks of liberals except the postwar generation of intellectual communists under thirty-five . . . Perhaps in their feelings and instincts, they are the nearest thing we now have to the typical nervous nonconformist English gentleman who went to the Crusades, made the Reformation, fought the Great Rebellion, won us our civil and religious liberties and humanised the working classes last century."[20] Yet although the 1930s saw a fundamental debate about the social order, political thinking was brittle and derivative, with the flavor of ulterior motives. Marxism's brief triumph was ideological rather than intellectual. The tragic fate of Marxism in the Cold War years was already prefigured in the 1930s.

The appeal of Marxism became inflated by two special considerations extrinsic to the content of Marxism. First, it was for reasons of *foreign policy* that many turned to Marxism. The rise of fascism and the horror of war, more than anything else, lifted the Left Book Club to its amazing success, and gave Orwell (some) reason to say: "For about three years . . . the central stream of English literature was more or less directly under Communist control."[21] As Kingsley Martin recalled, "an alliance with the Soviet Union, which the Tories treated as a pariah country, offered the only hope of defeating Hitler with or without war."[22] This is why there was such an imbalance between the enormous number who supported the Soviet Union and the far smaller number who supported the British Communist party. Many Marxists were red-painted Marxists, Marxists-of-the-crisis, rather than Marxists red all the way through.

Thousands also turned to Marxism as a reflex action, amidst their revulsion from a Western civilization that seemed to have lost its spiritual strength as well as its economic efficacy (though not for Marx's reasons). Middle and upper-class intellectuals felt a cultural guilt feeling. "When the Cambridge undergraduates take their inevitable trip to Bolshiedom," Keynes wondered in 1934, "are they disillusioned when they find it all dreadfully uncomfortable? Of course not. That is what they are looking for."[23] Here were those nervous nonconformist gentlemen, wrestling with their consciences.

A loss of hope in the future somehow had to be made good. A cultural malaise which existed owed more to offenses against the taste of the intellectuals than to offenses against their political convictions. Orwell railed against the age, but his indictment was as much cultural as political. He was able in the same breath to condemn Hitler and tinned food; secret prisons and aspirins; concentration camps and Hollywood films.[24]

To ponder those who "went red" in the 1930s, Spender, Strachey, Caudwell, and their like, is to feel that Marxism was in fact used by a generation of British intellectuals who panicked about the state and future of Western civilization. Strachey frankly said at the end of *The Theory and Practice of Socialism* (1936) that Marxism "offers the sole way of preserving Western civilization."[25] It was not an identical motive to that of the Comintern. The men of Moscow had no burning zeal for Western civilization. Indeed in the "Eurasian perspective" of Stalin, the Bolshevik revolution came to seem a wedge driven between the fatherland of socialism and Western civilization.[26] And Orwell's brand of antifascism was even less attuned to the *Zeitgeist* of the Comintern. The Five Year Plans did not come upon the earth to save sensitive spirits from tinned foods.

For his part, Tawney was unmoved by the brittle Marxism of the thirties. Though Marxism as an ideology meant little to him, he retained the substantial degree of Marx's historical materialism which he had long before incorporated into his general socialist philosophy. He urged Britain to ally with the Soviet Union in collective security against Germany. But this foreign-policy imperative did not refashion his views on socialism. In 1935 he criticized the political system of the Soviet Union as "police collectivism."

As for doubts about and revulsions against Western civilization, there are two things to say of Tawney. He did not feel the cultural alienation from his own society, or from the West, of the tortured literary spirits who filled the pages of *New Signatures* and *New Country*, fought in Spain, and went with heated pulse as pilgrims to Russia. His political and social analyses during the 1930s, though often dire, remained separable from his equable views about the cultural tradition of the West. The second point is that Stalinism did not seem to him to offer any acceptable or workable solution to these political and social problems. He thought Britain must use the best methods and values of its own tradition to move ahead to socialism. Yet, if Tawney was often correct on `he major controversies of the 1930s, his satisfaction was purely negative. He did not make a fool of himself and have later to recant, like some British socialists. But neither did he see accomplished in practice, or accepted in principle, the things he thought essential to democratic socialism.

The changed position of Marxism provides a clue to the later Tawney's loss of buoyancy. The Marxist wave had proved a cul-de-sac. It diverted the development of British socialism, and discredited the British intellectual left, before the trade unions and the public generally. The question of Marxism had become entangled with the international power position of the Soviet Union. Socialism could not in the West be pursued on its merits, or even discussed on its merits, because the fatherland of socialism appeared to be threatening the very existence of the West—its workers no less than its bosses. Irrelevantly, but inexorably, the attitude of a British socialist to communism became the point of orientation for his entire political position. The shadow of Marx hung over the "Clause Four" (nationalization) controversy, and the shadow of the Soviet Union hung over the "Unilateralism" controversy (concerning disarmament).

Sheer confusion, together with cheap exploitation in bad faith of this confusion by the right-wing, compounded the dilemmas of the left. But the dilemmas were rooted in two facts. The Bolshevik Revolution had effectively killed the prospects of Marxist parties in the West. And the failure to avert World War II (since a result of the war was to add the dimension of power to the hitherto essentially ideological tension between the Soviet Union and Western Europe, and since the War smothered democratic socialism under the circumstantial success of war collectivism) boxed British socialism in both at home and abroad. By the 1950s, the position of Marxism presented a double, ironic difficulty for British socialism. As a theory it was irrelevant to Britain's problems. Yet as a factor in power politics it stood at the center of almost every major political controversy.

How did this reduce Tawney's force? Tawney was influenced by Marxism, but not seduced by it (as were many in the 1930s) or intimidated by it (as were many during the Cold War). The "seduced" generation, for whom, as Orwell said, communism had been the "patriotism of the deracinated," embarked in the late forties and fifties on discussions of socialism which Tawney felt no part of because they centered obsessively on the issue of communism.[27] Once seduced by communism, it seemed difficult to avoid being seduced by anticommunism.

Untouched by the psychological traumas of the former communists, Tawney had grounded his thought in a Christian anthropology, and he continued to argue his case for socialism in terms of what was "fit for men." He felt no need to define socialism in terms of its difference from communism—like the ideological revisionist theorists on the right wing of the Labour party in the 1950s. Why, Tawney reasoned, be intimidated by a creed no longer offering anything relevant to Britain, and morally battered throughout Europe? But events had overtaken Tawney. Despite the unappealing character of the socialist ideas of the "seduced" and the "intimidated" generations, it was true that Russian communism and American capitalism, by virtue of their power in the world, necessarily furnished the context for postwar political debate in Britain. Tawney had not foreseen that the United States and the Soviet Union would emerge overwhelmingly dominant after the war. In fact he expected, in 1942, that after the war the United States and *Britain* would be "the only two great nations still standing."[28]

Quarrels centering on Marxism may, as Tawney thought, be unhelpful to British problems. Yet because of the ideological overtones of the international struggle in the Cold War years, and because Britain, shorn of her empire and now a second-rank power, could not, without a major mutation in her national mood, stand aside from this struggle, it seemed unavoidable for democratic socialists to constantly recite their attitude to the social systems of the two superpowers.

The polarization into ideological camps seemed to mark the end of Tawney's hopes for an integration of liberal values into a socialist philosophy. In his *History of European Liberalism*, Guido de Ruggiero had in 1926 written hopefully of how socialism and liberalism were beginning to learn from each other.[29] Yet far from helping or teaching each other, socialism and liberalism (in de Ruggiero's sense of the terms) were rent entirely asunder in the years dominated by authoritarian ideologies, and continued their mutual isolation in the years of the Cold War. The widespread hope in the 1920s of a synthesis between them was shattered within a decade.

The ideological enthusiasms of the 1930s could not hide the fact that liberalism was bankrupt, and able to move only to the right, or that adherents to the fashionable varieties of socialism had lost any conviction about liberal values and were building an ambiguous and ultimately disastrous liaison with Stalinism. The polarization of the postwar period was a predictable consequence. Tawney's comments of the mid-1930s on Stalinist dictatorship and capitalist oligarchy are also quite apt as comments on the social systems of the two superpowers in the 1950s.[30]

Tawney did not strike the right note for the 1950s. Speaking at meetings, he could not hide his feeling that the moment of opportunity for a socialism of fellowship had passed. He wearily acknowledged that the contours of the postwar world gave little room for maneuver to democratic socialists.

It was an index of the importance of the changed position of Marxism that influence lay disproportionately with émigres, who came to Britain and shouted the praises of a liberal capitalist order which seemed splendid to them only because they had fled from Stalinism. Orwell objected to left-wing intellectuals: "They can swallow totalitarianism *because* they have no experience of anything except liberalism."[31] One might turn his words around and say of the émigres who became, after the war, passionate believers in the liberal West: "They can swallow liberal capitalism because they have no experience of anything except totalitarianism."

These fanatical moderates had no appreciation, as Tawney had, of how the sad separation of socialism and liberalism in the democracies had come about, or of the bankruptcy of a mere restatement of liberalism as if socialism had not arisen. They had spun an image of the liberal West out of their own biographies as victims of totalitarianism, and had made an ideology out of it. But they, and not Tawney, struck the right note for the 1950's, because the centerpiece of their politics was an attitude to Marxism: a shrill rejection of it which admirably suited the trend of international politics.

POLITICS, RATIONALITY, and INSTITUTIONAL CHANGE

In his inaugural lecture as director of the Ratan Tata Foundation in 1913, Tawney addressed himself to the relation between social research and social change. To study the long list of social ills for which remedies exist, but which remain untackled "is to have a tragic lesson in the impotence of knowledge to alter conduct." Tawney did not, like the archetypal Fabian collectivist, see a necessary relation of cause and effect between knowledge and progress. Yet the Ratan Tata lecture is rationalistic in two respects. Rational observation and calculation had made the agenda clear. Tools of rationality were the resource for persuading the government and the public to reduce inequality, end industrial anarchy, and introduce comprehensive social services.[32]

Those who possess the power to remove social evils, Tawney told his listeners, "have not the will, and those who have the will have not, as yet, the power." Tawney assumed that the Asquith government lacked only the will; he was not worried that it might not know what to do. The phrase, "as yet," suggests Tawney's expectation that before long there would be a British government with both the power and the will. "Social evils" would then be "removed". The wrong people may have the knowledge and the wrong people may have the power. The knowledge may lie unapplied. Yet the knowledge is there and no reason exists why it cannot be translated into policy.[33]

But today many people feel there are political problems beyond the reach of the tools of rationality. The agenda for social betterment is not always clear. Nor is it obvious that, in mobilizing the will for social change, reason is an effective resource. If Tawney was unconvinced that knowledge would necessarily lead to progress, he did believe in a necessary relationship between *will* and progress. Today even that is occasionally in doubt.

Tawney defined democracy not only in terms of certain institutional arrangements, but in terms of "certain attitudes, habits and standards of political conduct among the general body of citizens."[34] His social democracy called for the free cooperation of rational, equal citizens. But what if the people do not know their own best interests? Or if their trust in rational cooperation is undermined by a drastically reduced sense of political and military realities? What if they lose hope in any future logically related to the present? In such circumstances Tawney's prescriptions are possible of fulfillment only by an elite of exceptional citizens, not by "Henry Dubb," who, tasting the benefits of welfare socialism, may lose his sense of historical grievance, and thus of historical aspiration, and become a happy consumer "outside of history."

Thirty years ago, Schumpeter summarized the changes that democracy has undergone since its classical formulation, and asserted that generally speaking "the will of the people is the product and not the motive power of the political process."[35] Tawney was aware of the increasing importance of Schumpeter's manufactured will, but the only solution he proposed was education, which he thought would not only reduce the gulf between classes, but also increase the alertness and self-reliance of each mind and spirit.

The relation of education to the virtues of citizenship can no longer be what Tawney hoped. Tawney could assert that the WEA "knows that the convictions which wear are not those which are accepted merely as a matter of habit . . . but those which are reached, after enquiry, after hearing the most that can be said against them."[36] But Tawney was speaking of a special breed of workers, in whom adversity had aroused a zeal for education as a path to a wider, richer life. "The first essential condition of the formation of an alert, critical, and well-informed body of opinion," Tawney said of democracy, "is a general belief in the importance of education." Yet not every kind of education, in all historical situations, involving no matter what sort of people as students, contributes to alert, critical, and well-informed opinion.

Tawney believed there was a close link between knowledge and virtue. It was a Victorian belief (which Tawney may have got from Caird), yet as Macauley observed in discussing Machiavelli, it is hardly a belief to be found in every time and place.[37] Today it has shrunk to vanishing point, and with it shrinks Tawney's view of the social significance of education and the rationalistic foundations of the dynamics of his social democracy.

Tawney's idea of an overarching social purpose must also be called into question. It leaned upon rationality in assuming people can know their own and society's best interests; in requiring that the peoples' interests will be clearly and relevantly made known to those who formulate and execute policy; and in supposing that people have enough hope in a future logically related to the present to consider social purpose something other than the cruel joke of a computer or an all-wise guardian.

In 1945 Tawney felt able to point out, with justifiable self-satisfaction, that those socialists whom he had disagreed with in the 1930s had been wrong in talking "as though political democracy were impotent to effect serious social changes."[38] In the 1970s, however, a new generation has doubts about political democracy for reasons quite removed from those of authoritarian leftists under a Marxist spell (rationalistic socialism is hardly less bankrupt in their eyes than liberal capitalism). If the vogue in the 1930s was to see class as the rock upon which political democracy foundered, the equivalent vogue in the 1970s is to proclaim that political democracy is a casualty of urban, industrialized life itself. In the measure that Tawney put "who" problems at the center of his political thought, he cannot help a generation that sees "how" problems at the center of politics. In the measure that the aim of socialist politics was for him to bring the underprivileged into the big, time-tested House of Britain, fitted with its obvious benefits and qualities, he has less to offer those who call the nature, quality, even the existence, of the house into question.[39]

Tawney's discussions of instrumental problems were essentially concerned with the moral economy of socialism, and could be disposed of by enunciating moral principles rooted in given traditions of values and rationality. He offered a path to those hungry for justice; not to those hungry for meaning. He saw moral complexities, but not philosophic complexities, or metaphysical challenges to socialism, such as those of today's curates of anarchism who simply feel no impulse to improve society.

H. G. Wells recalled an early Fabian meeting: "They all felt and spoke as if they were in an absolutely fixed world, even if they thought that it was a world in which stable social injustices called aloud for remonstrance, resistance, and remedies."[40] Wells himself was a rootless outsider, whose being cried out against the idea of a fixed world. But Tawney, for all his differences from the Fabian collectivists, had some of their equanimity in him—as if the task was to get new trains but in no sense to pull up the tracks. Tawney also assumed that the organization of industry would remain the ordinary man's chief problem, and he had little to say about the character of socialist responsibility in a "post-scarcity" situation, where work is peripheral and leisure central. What does "function" mean in such circumstances? How is "dispersion of power" to be made operative when the key source of power of men over other men lies in realms of fantasy, taste, the media, and entertainment? What are we to say of "fellowship" in an overpopulated, leisure-oriented world in which people may become anxious to have as little to do with each other as possible?

Tawney's life seemed to parallel the decline of key British political institutions. A group of eminent figures in 1969 put its stamp of acknowledgement on a "fundamental and comprehensive awareness of a new need to examine our *worn and often ineffective institutions as a whole*, in the light of new social and economic conditions and a dawning new relationship between government and the governed."[41] It is rare for the British to examine their institutions from the roots up. During the 1930s there was iconoclasm, but it was highly ideological, and much of it turned out ill-based. British institutions are "worn and ineffective" less because of the bankruptcy of the capitalist system as such (the view in the 1930s), than because they are institutions created in the heyday of Victorian capitalism.

The key institutions of British politics—parties, civil service, public schools, the reformed parliament—crystalized in the second half of Queen Victoria's reign. A basic influence on their shape and temper was the call of empire. If the mood of the Victorian period (optimism and progress) ended with the onset of World War I, and key ideas of the period (liberal individualism and social Darwinism) were buried in the inter-war years, only later were the key *institutions* of the Victorian period first called worn and ineffective. They were designed for an age when Britain's position in the world, social structure, and mental modes were vastly different from what they have become in an age of Little Englandism, welfare democracy, political irrationality, and media which reach intimately into every living room.

Balfour said of Gladstone that he was "a Tory in everything but essentials."[42] Tawney was a Victorian in everything but essentials. If the Bloomsbury circle seemed anti-Victorian in style yet Victorian in their cultural ideas and confidence in reason and the individual, the converse was true of Tawney. His socialism was built upon a rejection of the major political ideas of the late nineteenth century. But his style and some of his inarticulate assumptions about the norms and procedures of public life did not change, after he left Balliol in 1903, as his political views did. He despised Victorian capitalism, but he did not despise the political institutions that grew out of its effortless, complacent triumphs. He did not question the viability of parliament, the civil service, or the parties. He could tell an American audience that "in England, which is incurably politically-minded, all doctrines pass sooner or later into the arena of the House of Commons."[43] He never dallied, as the Webbs did, with schemes for changes in the basis of parliamentary representation. He was not among those socialists who thought the civil service stood as a brick wall between the Labour party and the achievement of socialism. A party man, Tawney was convinced, despite imminent schisms, proposals for new formations, and doubts about the trade union basis of the party, that the Labour party was the one proper vehicle for socialism.

He had the party man's faith in rationality and the power of persuasion. Gaitskell recalled a talk with him in 1961: "He said he had been to his local Ward Party meeting where there had been discussion about the constitutional relationship between the Annual Conference and the Parliamentary Labour Party." After telling Gaitskell he thought the idea of conference dictating policy to members of parliament absurd, Tawney asked: "But where are the documents on all this? I feel I did not put the case sufficiently cogently."[44] Here was Tawney at eighty, demonstrating his faith in democratic political institutions by arguing particular points at his local party meeting.

Tawney was in institutional matters a Victorian, which reduces the value of aspects of his thought for late twentieth-century socialists. To leftist youths, who seem to feel themselves back in a state of nature, wondering what, if any, social contract they may be prepared to enter, parliament seems a dusty anachronism; they are not even interested in the reform of parliament. In few circles of any generation is reform of parliament the hot issue it was in the early 1960's. Some talk of developing "alternatives" at the grassroots level to parliamentary politics. It is no longer true that all the political doctrines of the hour "pass into the arena of the House of Commons."

Bright young men who would in Tawney's day enter parliament or the civil service, may now think first of careers in technology and the communications industries. International business is a better and more exciting prospect than the Foreign Office or the Colonial Office. The BBC is a better platform for preaching to Britain than a parish or a seat at Westminster. Even parties may turn out mortal. Are there not other vessels and other strategies, both more ancient and more modern, for getting political results: the Fabian strategy of converting leaders, the strategy of local self-help, the economic strategy of industrial militancy, the separatist strategy of Celtic nationalism?[45]

Today the political rationality of late Victorian England seems an historically specific, not a universal rationality. History grants the blessing of permanency to no set of institutions, no mode of thought, least of all to those subject to the winds of change that blew in Tawney's long lifetime. Britain learned liberty first, democracy later. Even the quest for socialism seemed to be a matter of winning an extension of the benefits of existing treasures to more people. But representative institutions and their supporting administrative structure are now under considerable strain. Victorian style "was to make big things seem small, exciting things boring, new things familiar."[46] This bland depreciation was the fit temper of an age which hid its prevailing rationality (even from itself) beneath the glow of a massive confidence in Britain's imperial mission. How hard for ancient nations to change! And for people. Not in doctrines, but in institutional presumptions and political psychology, Tawney's world was in a way the world of Bagehot's *English Constitution.*

REDUCED ROLE OF CHRISTIANITY

The tradition within which Tawney spoke included Christianity. Confronting a church of shrunken vision and narrowing influence, Tawney hoped to see it recover its mission by reformulating and implementing the social-political dimension of its creed. His socialism assumed a Christian context in three respects. In notes for a speech on "A Christian World Order" he defined Christianity as "a body of doctrine which affirms that the nature of God and man is such that only insofar as men endeavor to order their lives in accordance with the principles expressed in the life and teaching of our Lord will they realize the highest values of which human beings are capable."[47] Tawney saw self-fulfillment in this light. Fellowship and equality were derived, not from a science of society, but from a faith about man. He argued for common purpose, not because it was a convenient or efficient point of orientation for social theory, but because the nature of man made common purpose possible, and superior to purposes confined to the individual.

A second aspect concerns the strategy for pursuing socialism. Tawney did not equate the task of the church with the quest for socialism, nor urge the church to declare its allegiance to the Labour party. Nevertheless, he thought a proper statement of Christian social principles would carry strong socialist implications. As a practical matter, he saw the church (for most of his life) as a possible force for social justice; just as, since accommodating to the economic philosophy of capitalism, it had very often been a positive force against it. He was an active exponent of Fabian methods in the outer orbit of the Church of England. Many church reports proved distasteful to conservative bishops partly because of the influence upon them of Tawney. His aim was to recall the church to the radical nature of Christianity. If it is not certain that he derived his socialism wholly from Christianity, he *located* it within Christianity, and found it worth-while to spend time appealing to church people.[48]

Discussing the virulence of patriotism and the feebleness of internationalism in the 1930s, he saw the church as an important potential force. "Historically the greatest of non-national institutions is the church, and it seems to me that its mission involves a perpetual warning to its members that when national institutions and Christian morality collide, it is the former which must give way."[49] Though Tawney's attitude to the church is frequently a mixture of hope and despair, it seemed to him an important social institution, capable of affecting political attitudes and choices. He saw the church as a society (rather than a purely mystical body), and presumed its conduct as a society to be a notable example, for good or evil, to the nation.

A third Christian aspect of Tawney's socialism was the residual Christian belief he assumed in the populace at large when designing his socialist arguments. Like Ruskin, he characteristically recalled his audience to a light they at least dimly knew. If people seemed to him to have mistaken notions of the good society, still they thought there was such a thing and felt a responsibility to promote it. Tawney poured the new wine of socialism into the existing bottles of Christian conscience. In putting this case to Christians, Tawney could summon up a rich historical tradition. He demonstrated that the social philosophy of the medieval church, and even, contrary to a widespread view, of the early reformers, was less reconcilable with the norms of the acquisitive society than those of Church of England leaders of the eighteenth and nineteenth centuries. Conventional church opinion might exalt Dean Tucker, of whom Warburton said that religion was his trade and trade his religion, but Tawney would reach two centuries back and point to the catechism of the archbishop of St. Andrews, of 1552, which denounced usurers, covetous merchants and landlords.[50]

In either case the appeal was to a religious authority or precedent, which had meaning, but could only have meaning, for an audience that chose to define itself as Christian. When Tawney, addressing a meeting on "Christianity and Social Order," challenged the churches to corporately "throw their weight against the obvious evils" in British society, he used Christian ideals as measuring rod for what was evil and what was not. Such was his hidden cargo in urging that the "principles on which [the] economic order is founded should justify themselves to the consciences of decent men."[51]

Aspects of Tawney's socialist appeal have consequently lost their power with the decline of Christianity. In expressing the social and political meaning of Christianity, Tawney assumed allegiance to the fundamentals of Christianity. He blew a bugle whose sound was recognizable.[52] Not only has religion declined; so has the church's authority over its own members. Tawney thought the church had "a right and a duty to reject those of its members who habitually and wilfully disregard its moral standard." In British churches today such discipline is out of the question. Tawney called Christians to rally to teachings from "Christian thinkers of undisputed authority." But it is doubtful that there remain undisputed Christian authorities; even the scriptures are sometimes taken casually within the churches.[53]

Tawney asked that forms of social organization which hindered the Christian way of life be condemned. "It is the obligation of Christians," he judged, "to replace them by others which may cause an approach to it to be less impeded by environmental obstructions than it is today."[54] Now a minority, even of one, can condemn, but it takes a majority or something near it to replace in a democratic way unsatisfactory features of the social and economic order. Yet the dwindling of church membership and attendance has been almost continuous in the twentieth century. Tawney's endorsement of Gore's call for "fewer Christians, if need be, but better Christians" implied no alarm at the dwindling of church membership; indeed it could only further it.[55] By what means, and by what right, could a small minority of Christians replace those institutions repugnant to their consciences?

Turning from strategy to theory, further questions arise. If men are not intrinsically of equal worth, as Christianity teaches, why should rewards not go to the brightest and best citizens, without regard for the resulting gap in living standards between them? And why think it bad, as Tawney did in stressing dispersion of power, that certain people should have the power of life and death over others?

If it is not in men's nature to need and cooperate with his fellows, why put special value on solidarity, and why consider it regrettable that people are not within reach of each other? If there is no reason, based on the doctrine of God the Creator, for man to respect nature as sacred, why should he not endlessly exploit nature for material progress, at least until he has so fouled his cosmic nest that prudence dictates curtailment?

Christian belief gave a vital margin of meaning to a number of Tawney's ideas. He felt direct evangelism was no longer a desirable, or even possible, activity for the church.[56] Christianity's credibility had to be demonstrated by witness on social problems; then perhaps more men would believe. But "social Christianity" was not really separable from the basic doctrinal deposit of Christianity. Tawney took the doctrine for granted (he was taught it by a more evangelical generation). By the 1950s, Christian social action had lost the connection with Christian doctrine that it had when Tawney first encountered Toynbee Hall and the Charity Organisation Society. The question was no longer evangelism *or* social action. If it was not both, it could not be either. Because Christian belief had withered, social Christianity had less to offer socialist thought.

Ironically, it was the ordinary working man who had probably more than any other element in British society lost his Christian belief and commitment to Christian morality. Those who were supposed to be the first born of the socialist kingdom no longer burned with the faith which in part gave meaning to the struggle to win the kingdom. Perhaps Tawney would feel, if he could look back from the 1970s, that the acquisitive society squeezed Christian values out of Henry Dubb more completely than he realized.

11 TAWNEY'S IMPORTANCE

Tawney confronted three partially successive, quite different challenges before which British socialism has defined itself. They were not mutually exclusive, nor equally serious enemies of democratic socialism. The first was unbridled capitalism, with its anarchies, inequalities, and waste. It formed the overwhelming challenge of the first third of the century. The second was the challenge (primarily in the 1930s) of the authoritarian ideologies, which threatened democratic procedures, the dignity and freedom of the individual, and peace. The third was the challenge (in the 1950s and after) of collectivism, which, despite the securities it offers, seems, with its bureaucratism, apathy, and materialism, a miscarriage of socialism.

Unbridled capitalism involved economic tyranny; the ideologies involved political tyranny; and collectivism involves the twin tyrannies of impersonal administration and moral torpor. The second came in part as an attempt to cope with the first, and the third came in part as an attempt to cope with the dangers and excesses of both the first and the second.

Tawney, although he varied his exposition for each challenge, met all with essentially the same arguments. His own theory was not just built up dialectically, as a way to protest against existing arrangements or other theories. It was also like a lamp, with its own source and fuel and definition, which from an unwavering center sent out beams across the political landscape of each successive period.

THE CASE AGAINST CAPITALISM

Tawney thought capitalism was breaking down. "Though it still works," he wrote in 1921, "it works unevenly, amid constant friction and jolts and stoppages, without full confidence even in itself."[1] This view was widespread during the interlude, and it is less notable that Tawney held it, than that it was one of the least of his arguments against capitalism. He also believed that under capitalism man has no effective control over his corporate life. There is a jungle situation, in which an almost superstitious deference to a supposedly logical and self-sustaining mechanism prevents men taking hold of their own lives through social purposes. In consequence control of society goes, by default, to property owners, and the materialist values surrounding property-holding come to be normative all through the society. Even when serving no function, property bestows wealth, power, and prestige.

Capitalism, Tawney held, erects production and the making of profit, which should be a means to certain ends, into ends in themselves. The ultimate confusion of means and ends is that labor (people) is considered by capitalism to be used as an instrument by capital (things). It follows from this, and from Tawney's Christian view of man's nature, that capitalism encourages the wrong instincts in men (acquisitiveness) and goes against the grain of the instinct for service and solidarity which exists in men and can be drawn out by different social arrangements.[2]

In addition, for Tawney capitalism is inhospitable to culture. Downgrading the common life of men, exalting inequality, it arrives at a notion of culture as a kind of possession. "A species of private entertainment to which a coterie of the right people [receive] an exclusive invitation."[3] Tawney did not like capitalists, nor did he like the "alternate subservience and rebelliousness" induced in their victims. An insidious feature of capitalism for him was that it beats down the morale and undermines the morals of those it exploits. Tawney faced this point frankly, and it led him to insist that it was the principles of capitalism not the character of capitalists, or the fact that the "wrong class" was in charge of Britain, that was the major evil to be tackled.[4]

Tawney considered that capitalism is prone to make war. While not denying that socialist countries could start aggressive war, nor holding that international relations were simply a matter of class relations, Tawney thought that the anarchy of a society in prey to the mechanisms of capitalism made it more likely than a socialist society to stumble into war.[5] Tawney also argued that a capitalist economic system would always be in tension with a democratic political system, and that in a crisis, and perhaps also in the long term, unbridled capitalism was likely to make democracy impossible. Inequality due to the concentration of power under capitalism constantly threatened democracy, which "is unstable as a political system, as long as it remains a political system and nothing more, instead of being . . . not only a form of government, but a type of society."[6]

Finally, Tawney from his Christian point of view saw capitalism as ungodly, both for its irreverence toward nature, and because it has "like its totalitarian rival miscalled Communism, some of the characteristics of a counter religion."[7] Instead of encouraging in man a creaturely attitude to the divine creation, capitalism puts a premium on a Promethean lust for limitless, almost blasphemous, exploitation of nature and dominion over nature. It puts productivity and associated materialist values on an altar where Tawney felt no economic or political value should be put.

Tawney viewed capitalism historically, which was rare in England when he started to write. Political economy had been considered by the classical economists almost a natural science, as if "economic man" was a cosmic fact like rocks or gravity. Even among Tawney's contemporaries, it was uncommon to view capitalism historically. When *Religion and the Rise of Capitalism* appeared, a sympathetic reviewer in a serious journal deprecated as polemical the use of the term "capitalism" in a work of academic history.[8]

There seem to have been three main streams of twentieth-century British interpretation of modern British history: A Whig stream, in which G. M. Trevelyan was a great figure, which found its central theme in the struggle for liberty; a Tory stream, in which Namier has been notable, which stressed ideas less than power; and a socialist stream, of which Tawney was the pioneer. Tawney's innovation was to analyze the sixteenth century and seventeenth century as the cradle of capitalism in England.

The other two streams of historiography give little indication of when they consider capitalism to have arisen. Tawney might have seen in such historians "the intellectual villager, who takes the fashion of his own day for the nature of mankind."[9] He set himself the task of showing Englishmen that their society was capitalist, not just English in some timeless sense. He stressed that capitalism's appearance had been relatively recent; that a rich tradition of social philosophy antedated it; that the triumph of capitalism had taken place at the expense of these prior traditions.

Tawney also stressed that the coming of capitalism was not inevitable. No immutable law made England substitute mechanism for purpose in its economic and social life. Religious thought was not a mere reflection of productive forces. It had abdicated its responsibilities in the field of social ethics, which made it easier for commercial men to charge exorbitant interest and landlords to drive peasants off the land. Machines and capitalist organization of machine processes were not inseparable. Nor was it impossible, as the case of the Soviet Union proved, for industrial civilization to exist on a noncapitalist basis.

It followed that capitalism need not be expected to last indefinitely. History had no more granted to it the blessing of permanence than to feudalism before it. Its continuance was no more inevitable than its coming. In demonstrating the historical mortality of capitalism, Tawney strengthened the resolve of those who did not like capitalism but had no conviction of the possibility of replacing it.

Tawney's advocacy of socialism gained credibility from his knowledge of capitalism's origins. Were not capitalists upstarts, innovators, iconoclasts, in their day? The institutions of capitalism (such as the share) and the social organizations serving it (such as the British public schools) were children of yesterday. In the year of Queen Victoria's accession to the throne, was it not still held that joint stock companies, with shares assignable at the will of the holder, were illegal? Were not the public schools, so traditional in the eyes of those who wished to fuse business values with aristocratic forms, less than one hundred years old?

Commanding an audience in church, as well as labor, circles, Tawney was able to exercise on Christians an influence unmatched by any other English socialist of the twentieth century. To religious people, he demonstrated that capitalism had dethroned certain Christian values from their previously acknowledged dominion over social and economic affairs. If capitalism was "absolutely irreligious" (as Keynes declared) it was because capitalism had become itself a religion.[10] Two religions cannot claim one heart, nor one purse, and the rise of the stronger one, capitalism, was accompanied by the decline of the weaker one, Christianity.

Tawney was able to bring out the similarities between the religious fanaticism of the seventeenth century, and the industrial fanaticism which replaced it as the dominant social philosophy of England and climaxed in the years between the Great Exhibition and the scramble for Africa. To give Christians a sense of capitalism as an historical phenomenon was at the same time to provide them with a partial explanation of the loss of authority of the churches. Christendom had been shattered by the manner in which the new industry and commerce had been permitted moral autonomy.

Tawney also gained credibility as an advocate of socialism by acknowledging capitalism's achievements in earlier eras. He did not deny its dynamism and inventiveness, but applying the principle of function to property he showed that the capitalist may be socially useful in one set of circumstances yet parasitic in another. Capitalism, once the vehicle of freedom, had by the twentieth century reintroduced its own kind of feudal bondage: "industrial feudalism."[11] The consumer faced monopolies. The producer faced giant companies which sometimes controlled, as in a feudal manor, the entire working and leisure conditions of a township. Thus, through an historical analysis of capitalism's development, Tawney turned an argument about freedom, and about the contribution of property to progress and happiness, into arguments for socialism.

Tawney's historical view of capitalism lent him perspective on the nonindustrialized world. He analyzed Chinese society, not in terms of unchanging "stagnant China," bound by some law of race or climate or culture to lag, but in terms of a transition from feudalism to capitalism, comparable to that of England in the sixteenth century. He saw, as few then did, that the peasant problem was crucial, that political power could not base itself elsewhere but upon the peasantry. So his focus on communism in China (and in other nonindustrialized lands) was historical rather than ideological. Communism was one possible ideology for spurring industrialization, workable in certain circumstances. Absolute moral stands about it were generally beside the point.

Tawney's study of capitalism in England gave him ground for analyzing contemporary relations between the West and the nonindustrialized world. The transition from agrarian to industrial society in England had been no less revolutionary than it promised (or threatened) to be in much of the less developed world in the twentieth century. In his discussion of confiscation of private property as a means of hastening development, Tawney neatly chose as an illustration, not bolshevism, but the seizure of ecclesiastical property by the Protestant rulers of England and Scotland.[12] Pitching his political theory historically, Tawney avoided a facile double-standard on the use of violence in premodern societies (had not England once killed a king?).

Tawney saw the capitalism of his day as a creaking system; a jungle wherein economic struggle took priority over social purpose; with persons treated as means and wealth as an end; encouraging not solidaristic instincts but acquisitive instincts; shriveling culture into a matter of personal possession and pretension, when it should be the energy of a cooperative common life; inculcating not only arrogance in the successful, but an unworthy subservience in the stragglers; prone to make war, because of its concentrations of economic power; a threat to democratic forms for the same reason; and an enemy of religion, because of its uncreaturely exploitation of nature, and because its purse was where its heart should be.

He became an historian to understand the origin and dynamics of this system he abhorred. Tawney was the first figure in Britain to take a comprehensive, critical view of capitalism. There had been other social systems, he said, there could have been other ways of carrying through the industrial revolution, and there would in the future be other ways of relating the making of a living to the common life of men. He showed what an upstart ideology capitalism was. How it was a kind of fanaticism, as puritanism had been a fanaticism. He acknowledged the achievements of economic individualism in an earlier era, but argued that the meaning of ownership had so altered, that property, once an aid to creativity was now a ticket to parasitism. Viewing capitalism historically, he took an unideological approach to problems of communism and "development" in the less industrialized countries, and did not adopt an absolutist position on violence used for political ends.

COMBATING UNBRIDLED CAPITALISM AND AUTHORITARIANISM

Some critics of unbridled capitalism made a panacea out of planning, or pinned their hopes (and yielded their minds) to inevitable laws whose logic would soon do away with capitalism. Tawney from the start thought these arguments ill-based.

> I do not share Marx's mid-Victorian conviction of the inevitability of progress; nor do I regard social development as an automatically ascending spiral with Socialism as its climax. On the contrary, I think that, in the absence of sustained and strenuous efforts, the way is as likely to lead down hill as up, and that Socialism, if achieved, will be the creation, not of any mystical historical necessities, but of the energy of human minds and wills.[13]

Planning was a means, not an end. History would accomplish nothing admirable without the constantly exerted purposes of free citizens. It was possible for unbridled capitalism to be replaced by a number of alternatives, only one of which was socialism.

When in the 1930s British socialism had to confront communism and fascism, its old arguments lost their effortless power. Was not Stalin's Russia the citadel of planning, and the offspring of those inevitable laws? Of course many socialists rejected Stalinism. But most (expecially those who rejected it in the 1940s rather than in the 1930s) did not do so for reasons that arose from the theoretical core of their socialism. More frequently it was the question-begging argument that the Comintern was against the West that served to keep the skirts of democratic socialism secure from the slush of Stalinism—or it was an assertion of an essentially anarchist objection to state power.

But Tawney met Stalinism and fascism as he had met capitalism—with beams, as it were, from his own lamp of democratic socialism, which threw into relief the evil both of tyranny of wealth and tyranny of power.

Tawney's was a socialism of principles, as distinct from a socialism of historical laws, or of an ideal vision. Those principles were grounded outside any self-contained system, in his Christian humanism (they were even outside Tawney's own socialist system, which got tested, like other systems, alongside the principles). The problem with capitalism was not low wages, but the confusion of means and ends. The problem with communism was not bureaucratic excess, but the erection of a governmental and party system into an end when it should be a means. Human beings should be the end, yet they were treated as ends neither by capitalism whose mechanism required them only as "hands," nor by Stalinism whose precarious edifice of power built them in as "cogs."

Socialism for Tawney was a matter of certain kinds of social relationships. Wealth and power were to be so arranged that people would be within reach of each other. Equipped with that principle, Tawney criticized unbridled capitalism for subordinating social relationships to economic productivity, and Stalinism for subordinating social relationships to bureaucratic equilibrium. He criticized both for subordinating social relationships to a Faustian notion of progress.

Tawney prized democracy not as a tactic but as a value. Socialism was in part an extension of democracy from the formal-legal or constitutional realm to the industrial and social realms. He did not wobble on democracy during the 1930s, as Laski did, because his democracy, rooted in a humanism, had been a deeply felt line of objection to capitalism, and was thus not incidental in his encounter with communism. Its basis was respect for and trust in the dignity, equal worth, and self-governing capacity of ordinary men.

Tawney thought capitalism made democracy almost impossible, and he thought communism was too frightened of human nature to attempt democracy. In his view, to wobble on democracy and approve Stalinism would be to toss away half the case against unbridled capitalism. How could you object to the British industrial system, which bottled up Dubb by forcing him to sell his labor to capital, declining to trust his cooperative powers and solidaristic instincts, if you winked at the Soviet system which bottled up Dubb by forcing his opinions and conscience out of politics, declining to trust his loyalty to his country and his judgment of socialism?

Tawney's socialism hinged upon his confidence that a society could, for all the difficulties, lay down social purposes, and arrange priorities and rewards by reference to their function in relation to those purposes. His criticism of unbridled capitalism was that it allowed an economic mechanism to determine ends which should be determined by social purposes arrived at through democratic processes. So long as the capitalists had enough freedom to make their economic decisions as they saw fit, it was naively believed in the City of London, social well-being would follow.

Tawney could no more accept Stalinism, which by-passed the question of social purpose by subsuming it into the question of class. So long as the government was run by the "pure in class," it was naively believed in Moscow, social purposes would take care of themselves. The power question, itself simplified to a class question, was considered inseparable from policy questions.

For Tawney the power question *was* separable from questions of purpose, just as the productivity question was separable from questions of purpose. If the proletariat comes to power, that is not the end, but only the beginning of the moral problems of socialism. The ground of this assertion is the same as when Tawney says (with capitalist worship of productivity in mind): "As long as men are men, a poor society cannot be too poor to find a right order of life, nor a rich society too rich to have need to seek it."[14] In a word, neither power nor wealth are ends in themselves, for the end is right relationships among free and equal individuals.

THE CHALLENGE OF COLLECTIVISM

Though Tawney was over seventy when the Attlee government fell in 1951, he joined the theoretical debates of the following decade—he was the only notable socialist thinker who had been active in the 1920s to do so—and his "British Socialism Today" (1952) was as influential as any political article he wrote. He found much to praise in the collectivism of the welfare state. When young socialists came to him in the fifties and demonstrated that the working class was little better off than fifty years before, he dissented and told them about the Manchester of his youth, when some families had fewer pairs of shoes than children, and each child would wait his turn to put on the shoes and go out.[15]

There was now less poverty, Tawney pointed out. The share of national income taken by wages had risen, that taken by profits, rent, and interest had fallen. Health and education were more nearly services, available as a matter of course, than before. A certain small shift of power had occurred, which decreased the autonomy of the mechanisms of capitalism and increased the possibility of social controls and social purposes. That the ordinary voters of Britain gave the Labour party a landslide victory in 1945, discerning that Churchill was better at facing the enemy than facing the future, Tawney took as a confirmation of his faith in the judgment of "Henry Dubb."

On the other hand, if the Labour government reduced poverty and advanced social services, it did not greatly diminish inequality, and when it left office half the country's wealth was owned by one percent of the population. The shape of socialism had only to a modest degree been institutionalized. The dynamics of socialism had hardly appeared at all. Tawney's criticism of the Attlee government was not that it shrank from wholesale nationalization. And he was not a maximalist who would rebel in the Garden of Eden, inevitably disappointed by anything that any government ever does. He addressed to collectivism the same questions, though more softly, that he had addressed to capitalism and totalitarianism. In 1953 he observed: "The two great apostasies, the idolatry of riches and the idolatry of power, have had a long reign. If the successor to these pretenders were merely a more widely disseminated cult of betting coupons, comforts and careers, there might be some gain; but it would hardly be worth the century of sweat which . . . has been needed to produce it."[16] Socialist values had won no hegemony. The class-ridden British way of life had little changed. "Socialism," he summed up, "ought to mean something vital and inspiring in the lives of the great majority of workers. The social and full employment policies of the Labour Government did, I think, come home to them. I doubt whether its industrial policy, which to most of them was a spectacle, rather than a personal experience, did."[17] What was wrong?

True, in the 1950s Tawney occasionally uttered moralisms which owed more to nostalgia than to his socialist principles. His experiences at Rochdale and Longton (no betting coupons there) dictated too much his image of the *type* of life working men should aspire to. He also carped a little on the style of life of Labour ministers, especially those who accepted Honours and found the House of Lords ("that grotesque anomaly")an agreeable pasture.[18]

But Tawney's general line of analysis came from the foundations of his long-established socialist position, and it seemed as apt in the fifties as it had when he scorched the paper with *The Acquisitive Society*. While Strachey, in the sadly complacent *New Fabian Essays*, was pinning his major hopes on the "extreme buoyancy of the British economy" and defining "full socialism," which he rejected, by reference to Marx and Lenin, Tawney was restating his own rather different perspective:

> The revolt of the ordinary man against Capitalism has had its source neither in its obvious deficiencies as an economic engine, nor in the conviction that it represents a stage of social evolution now outgrown, but in the straightforward hatred of a system which stunts personality and corrupts human relations by permitting the use of man by man as an instrument of pecuniary gain. The socialist society envisaged by them is not a herd of tame, well-nourished animals, with wise keepers in command. It is a community of responsible men and women working without fear in comradeship for common ends, all of whom can grow to their full stature, develop to the utmost limit the varying capacities with which nature has endowed them, and—since virtue should not be too austere—have their fling when they feel like it.[19]

Here Tawney demonstrated the power and durability of his socialism, at a time (1952) when the labor movement seemed low in theory and morale. It was a radical voice, yet realistic in its political expectations.

There was a commonsense British Labourism about Tawney, so that when he said, as he did in his last public speech, "British Socialism . . . has become dehumanised," few were inclined to take his anxiety lightly, or be unmoved by his challenge to make commonsense Labourism the vehicle of moral purpose.[20] The long statement above indicates three parts to this moral purpose: socialism as a way of life; socialism as right relationships; socialism as the hegemony of socialist values.

The Labour government had not sufficiently trusted the people. It did not throw down to them the responsibility of creating, in factory and neighborhood, patterns to make socialism "an inspiring force in daily life."[21] Tawney's idea of citizenship took on new importance in the 1950s. If Labour governments were to "create an economic system socialist all through, and not merely at the top," the energies of ordinary citizens must be enlisted to put equality into practice through local, cooperative initiatives. Tawney's insistence that "you cannot have democracy without democrats" was as apt during the civic stagnation of the 1950s, as when it formed the basis of his early efforts in workers' education.[22]

British collectivism, in theory as in practice, did not ask much from the people. It did not see that a good society cannot exist without good citizens, and this became a flaw. It was no longer as widely believed in the 1950s as during the interlude, that governments can accomplish almost anything they wish. It became evident that in democracies power is sometimes powerless to achieve positive goals, unless there is a groundswell of concern, self-education, and action from the populace. A key contribution of Tawney's was to insist that socialism is the product of a dialectic between legislation from above *and* active citizenship from below.

Tawney's idea that socialism amounted to a certain kind and quality of relationships laid out a fresh agenda for British Labour in the early fifties. Equality had been seen too much in arithmetical terms; too little in relational terms. The welfare state had brought a kind of administrative justice; but British society was still ridden by class values. Workers still expected to be treated as instruments for ends determined by class superiors (or administrative guardians). Tawneyism is the finest criticism ever made of affluent society.

"If socialism is not merely to be tolerated as a lesser evil," Tawney urged at a Fabian dinner in 1954, "but to be welcomed as an emancipating and energising force, it is to men's imaginations, as well as to their interests that its appeal must be addressed."[23] Men's imaginations were essential to the dynamics of a socialist society. Only socialism as fellowship would capture men's imaginations, and harness for the building of a good society their creative and cooperative instincts.

But did collectivism not bring fellowship? Are not the servants of the corporations and bureaucracies placed in more entangling mutual proximity than in any society since medieval days? Some who see capitalism through the eyes of managerial theory claim that social solidarity has been achieved within the corporations and bureaucracies. However—to take two leading exemplars—what Mayo has to say about community and Selznick about cohesion and participation have little in common with Tawney's fellowship.[24] In the corporations from whose practice these thinkers distill their theory, there is no equality. Organizational theory talks of masses and elites, notions incompatible with the idea of equal citizens.

Selznick lauds spontaneity, but it is induced and created "spontaneity". "The aspirations of individuals are so stimulated and controlled," he writes, "and so ordered in their mutual relations, as to produce the desired balance of forces."[25] In effect, this describes a community fabricated from the top, which is not surprising, since the goals of a corporation are not open, as the goals of Tawney's political community would be open. Corporate goals are set by the elites and by the market. Community and homogeneity among the workers denotes not a fellowship of citizens deciding their destinies, but a therapeutic ambience functional to the profit-making needs of the corporation.

Tawney's fellowship is a thoroughly political idea. Mayo and Selznick have squeezed the "political" out of their organizational theory. It is a stage-managed fellowship, designed, Tawney might have said, not for men but for tame animals. He wrote in "The New Leviathan": "The relationship between employer and wage-earner is an immoral one. That, and not merely certain incidents (low wages etc.) is the root of the evil."[26] He did not think fellowship could exist between two categories of men when one was the instrument of the purposes of the other. And it was not only within the industrial system, but up and down the whole society that fellowship was to exist. Far from draining the political off into groups pursuing private goals, he wanted to alert in people a constant sense of the political, and of the human realities behind public policies, so that fellowship would mean a cooperative commonwealth of citizens deciding their common life. That is the challenge he addressed to collectivism.

Tawney taught three generations of socialists to base their political strategy, not on outrage over this, or a scheme for that, but on an understanding of the capitalist system as a whole and a determination to transform it. "Onions can be eaten leaf by leaf", he summed up, "but you cannot skin a live tiger paw by paw".[27] If he was moderate in his political strategy, he was radical in his analysis, and because he went to the root of social problems, he could sustain his socialist case against the three successive challenges it had to confront.

Tawney offered a synthesis, an overall philosophy of democratic socialism. He pushed education, but his hopes for education were set within the context of his political efforts to curtail the power of wealthy men over public policy. He spoke of the need for a new culture, enshrining equality, eschewing deference, but he did not think it possible to have a new culture without a new politics. His impulses against the tyranny of wealth and the tyranny of power were fierce. But he disciplined his impulses into a theory of democratic socialism, because that way alone could the substance, not just the shadow, of a radical alternative to capitalism be won. He saw socialism as a way of life. But the dynamics of socialism could only be realized if the shape of socialism—dispersion of power and equality—was the law of the land. He gave a notable formulation to the socialist principles of equality and function. Yet they were not isolated absolutes; the argument for them rests finally with the high value placed on fellowship. And fellowship is a matter not of good feelings but of structures which facilitate, but do not compel, social solidarity among free and equal citizens.

CHRISTIANITY AND SOCIALISM

How did Tawney leave the religious tradition he encountered and struggled with? Following the passionate altercations of the mid-seventeenth century, the English church had slumbered before fundamental political questions, broken only by the Wesleyan revival, the Evangelical movement, and Tractarianism. Christian authorities seldom challenged the Lockean compromise of bourgeois constitutionalism. Where a concern for the lower orders did arise, it took a largely philanthropic form.

When Tawney went to Oxford, the social question was newly in the air. The idealists had put forward a theoretical basis for concern with the social question, and in the 1880s the university settlements appeared as arenas for practical service. The social effects of industrialization had provoked the conscience of a string of eminent critics (as Carlyle, Ruskin). Fringes of the church were stirred by Kingsley and Maurice; the Guild of St. Matthew was formed to go among the masses, and the Christian Social Union to galvanize the solid church folk.

There were, Charles Gore recalled of the later Victorian years, "a faithful knot of Broad Churchmen pegging away at *social amelioration.*"[28] But the impulse for social action was almost never structural. At the grass-roots level, the Charity Organisation Society was typical, with self-help as its watchword. The social and political structures of England were neither queried nor understood. When Beatrice Webb urged on the secretary of the COS the need for old age pensions, she was accused in horror of depreciating thrift.[29] Among Christian public figures, the devout paternalism of Gladstone was the pristine example in the late Victorian age of Christian concern for one's fellowman through politics.

Tawney's significance lay in the structural and political expression he gave to the radical potential of Christianity. He shunned the charitable approach. The working man was becoming too little inclined, in the early twentieth century when Tawney went to Toynbee Hall (unlike in Lord Shaftesbury's day), to remain socially quiescent in return for sugarplums of relief from virtuous superiors.

From Gladstone's paternalism Tawney differed in three ways. Intellectually, religion was crumbling; Tawney felt it was no longer acceptable or even intelligible to proffer biblical axioms as political proposals. Gladstone had seen politics fundamentally in evangelical terms. "Politics would be an utter blank to me," he confessed in a letter to Manning, "were I to make the discovery that we were mistaken in maintaining their association with religion".[30] For Tawney, it would be truer to say he saw religion fundamentally in political terms.

Gladstone thought education was mainly important as a tool for instructing children in religion. For Tawney, it needed no such sectarian justification. It was a door to political awareness and an instrument of socialist politics. For Gladstone, the political world was a jungle into which he forayed with Christian shield held firm; even social events like dinner parties and balls were morally dangerous. Tawney saw more moral peril in a church grown unconcerned with social reform, than in a political world where few honored doctrinal orthodoxy and Christian personal morality. Third, whereas Gladstone's outrage at injustice led him to try and correct particular abuses, Tawney's led him to seek changes in the overall power relations of English society. His theories of Christianity and politics were designed to spur and sanction such changes.

Tawney hovered between affection and despair for the church, and for much of the latter part of his life (except in the very last years) he had little hope that the church could serve what he thought of as a Christian social purpose.[31] These attitudes, and his achievements, have to be weighed in the context of the declining authority in English life of the churches, especially the declining credibility of Christianity among the two groups with which Tawney was primarily concerned: workers and intellectuals.

As faith and authority crumbled, the political and social message of Christianity became for many people its major appeal. In *Religion and the Rise of Capitalism*, Tawney observed that the business virtues of Puritanism remained even after the "religious reference, and the restraints which it imposed, had weakened or disappeared."[32] A parallel dissolution of religious commitment into social practice took place in the case of Victorian Christianity. This time, however, faith fertilized not business zeal but the politics of socialism. Many socialist figures of Tawney's generation, some the offspring of clergy, distilled residual religious conviction into strong political conviction. "I belong to a family of three generations of missionaries," Fenner Brockway testified: "My interest in Asian and African peoples was theirs; my expression of it became political and socialist rather than religious and paternalistic."[33] In most such cases religious conviction withered away within a generation.

A second response to the decline of faith and authority, from groups firmly within the church, was a new "Christendom" position, rejecting the secular, industrial, sociological reality behind the religious decline. A new Christian sociology of essentially medievalist character was put together. But the Christendom Group, and the influence of its publications, was short-lived.[34] As with the National Guilds, it hardly extended beyond the 1920s.

Tawney did not go either way. He remained Christian, attending church conferences and sitting on church committees concerned with the church's role on political questions. At the same time, he was against the Christendom approach. The church could not reclaim its former authority over English life. Christianity could now expect only the attention that the intrinsic merit of its ideas may command. Tawney's significance was that amidst the decay of the faith and authority of the church he formulated the most influential case from the socialist side for an expression of Christianity in political terms.

It may be true, as claimed by Reckitt, a member of the Christendom Group and much less secularist than Tawney, that Tawney "failed to regenerate Christianity"; few have done that.[35] Tawney was no theologian and never attempted a fresh statement of Christianity. He probably suspected he was fighting a rearguard action. It was as if he said to the church: "If you believe these doctrines, then apply them to politics, for politics is what affects the lives of ordinary men and women." Tawney himself believed the simple doctrines he took to be Christianity (it may have been in part the simplicity of his beliefs which kept him believing).

But belief in them grew rarer, as he realized. He did not regenerate Christianity, but simply urged Christians to be true to the doctrine they still believed, and to give it political expression. "Whatever may be right," he would remark when sketching a Christian approach to the social order, "certain things are wrong." The minimum is to oppose these things. Whether Christianity can then point the way to a better social order—on that he did not greatly dwell.

A leader of the Christendom group, V. A. Demant, said that the church should ask its own questions about politics and then answer them, rather than supply answers to questions which "the world has put."[36] By contrast, Tawney demanded that the church answer the questions which the "world" (essentially the socialist movement) had put. It ought to find in its scriptures and traditions reasons to criticize capitalism and favor socialism. Perhaps the church might renew itself in the course of such a commitment; perhaps not; Tawney was not sure.

So Tawney, pursuing socialism as fellowship, refurbished radical strands in Christianity, neglected since the Augustan calm of the eighteenth century muffled the raw-edged conscience of seventeenth-century puritanism. He stressed the prophetic traditions of the Old Testament, rather than the doctrine of grace of the New Testament (which the pre-eminence of Karl Barth in theology was bringing to the fore), with its implied pessimism as to what man could achieve within history. No one could doubt that the prophets were referring to the historical realm, or that their weight was thrown on the side of the weak and the poor. Among New Testament teachings, Tawney stressed the parables of Jesus, rather than the doctrines of redemption of Paul, and he saw in Jesus a kind of rebel, who put concern for the individual personality above concern for the rules.

His view of the political imperative of the gospel was not what Reinhold Niebuhr has called "simple moralism": the direct implementation of scriptural injunctions, such as the Sermon on the Mount, by political means.[37] But he was equally distant from the mainstream of the Church of England, which saw itself (as Hooker had seen it) as English society in its religious aspect, and which tended to act, except in extreme crisis, as a comforting chaplain to whatever elites dominated each succeeding phase of English history.

Tawney was too aware of power politics, and of the declining hold of the Bible over the mental world of Englishmen, to espouse "simple moralism." And he was too aware that under the mellow reasonableness of respectable English society lay the sovereign mechanism of a basically anti-Christian capitalism, to follow the bishops into the fold of the Hookerian compromise.

Instead, Tawney came to enunciate several middle-level axioms, distilled from Christian teaching into a form apt for modern politics. Since all men are equal in the sight of God, Christians should seek a social order which assumes them to be, not equal in capacity, but equal in value. Upon this basis Tawney challenged the church to reject the English class system. Since all are sinners and none righteous, no one man or group of men should be entrusted with absolute power. None is sufficiently superior to be set up high or permanently over others, so concentrations of power are bad, and pretensions that some are born to rule are false. Power, no less than wealth, should be evenly spread throughout the community. Upon this basis, Tawney opposed both the concentration of political power in communist dictatorships, and the concentration of economic power in unbridled capitalism.

Tawney also derived from the gospel the value of brotherhood or fellowship. In Christian terms, man achieves his fullness only in relationship with God, and his relationship with

God is expressible only through the human relations of men who are "members one of another." Thus the test of a political order was not simply the amount of well-being it affords individuals, but the quality of the social relationships it promotes. By this test, capitalist stress upon competition, which leads to a heightened scope for individual self-advancement, was less desirable than socialist stress upon cooperation, which leads to social solidarity. With these axioms and others Tawney challenged Christian opinion to reconsider the implicit approval it generally gave to capitalism.

Tawney did not try to make a synthesis of Christianity and socialism. True, he thought Christians ought to lean to the socialist side, and chided his friend William Temple when Temple, out of a desire to be impartial, resigned from the Labour party on being made bishop of Manchester.[38] True, there were kinds of societies which Christians could affirm and kinds they could not. "Granted that the Kingdom of God is something more than a Christian social system," he reasoned, "we can hardly take the view that it is something less."[39]

Yet because the Kingdom is a suprahistorical concept, to synthesize it with a merely historical philosophy was to invite, among the believers, a zealotry that comes from absolutizing one's cause. People who thought they were legislating for a genuine heaven upon earth were likely, he considered, to end up raising hell. Better that Christian values leaven the political order, rather than be equated with some particular political order.

Behind this hesitancy about setting the claims of politics too high, lay Tawney's respect for the common sense of his "Henry Dubb." Political zealotry would set a gulf between its grandiose self and Dubb. Religion could be the opiate of the people, and so too could socialism. A synthesis of Christianity and socialism might threaten Dubb's freedom to be different, to be irreverent, to be obstinate. That would be its political flaw. It might also subvert the humility of a Christianity whose victories were supposed to be won by a "still small voice" rather than by the coercive hand of secular authority. That would be its religious flaw. Though few twentieth-century Englishmen did more to cross-fertilize socialism and Christianity than Tawney, he thought it better for both not to blend the political and the religious into a single social cause.

Today when Christianity and Marxism are in "dialogue," it is interesting to recall that Tawney was called both Christian and Marxist. Does that mean he achieved some kind of synthesis between the two philosophies? Tawney found certain common ground between Christianity and Marxism, but his synthesis is Christian rather than Marxist. He fitted historical materialism together with a sacramentalist theology. If "matter" was pivotal to Marxism's analysis, it was also pivotal to Christianity's values. The incarnation sanctified matter, and made material things spiritually significant. The iconoclastic impulse which spurred Marx to his theory was also present in Christianity. As an emotional trigger, "the first shall be last" was a Christian equivalent of Marx's confidence that the oppressed class would inevitably overthrow the oppressors. This is to say no more than that Tawney was a Christian materialist, as distinct from Marx who was a dialectical materialist.

At the same time, if Tawney was not a philosophical idealist, he was an ethical idealist. Understanding the power of economic forces in history was important, precisely in order that men might dream their dreams, mobilize their most enlightened will, and in true freedom shape their society. History contained no values within itself, and the future contained nothing but open possibility. It seems that Tawney kept clear of just those aspects of Marxism which have proved least valid and least attractive: historicism; traces of Prometheanism; the vanguard theory of an all-wise elitist party (which follows in part from the first two aspects). Be that as it may, Tawney was not a Marxist. Not because he did not agree with some of Marx, but because he was something else: a democratic socialist with philosophic roots in Christian humanism. As such, Tawney not only eschewed certain Marxian errors, but provided a resource which socialist thought, especially Marxism, has sometimes lacked. He reminds us that political and social systems (and the writing of history) rest on some *view of man*, which is likely to be less unsatisfactory if it is known and made explicit than if it is considered nonexistent.

Tawney did not try to call back a world in which the church had authority, as if by right. At the same time, he did not, like many of his generation, turn the religious impulse into a merely secular political commitment. Without making a "political religion" out of Christianity and socialism, Tawney drew out the radical strands in the gospel, making Christianity lean to the side of socialism, without, however, equating a socialist social order with the Kingdom of God. He kept doctrine in the background, conscious that Christianity had a poor claim on the world's attention after so many follies and failures. He stressed the Old Testament prophets, and Jesus as an individualistic, disrespectful rebel. From biblical sources he distilled middle-level axioms, such as equality, fellowship, and a sceptical yet ultimately hopeful view of man's nature. These were the real foundations of his socialism, which, drawing also on Marxism, became a blend of ethical idealism and historical materialism.

HUMANISTIC SOCIALISM

Tawney's socialism wears well because it is humanistic, which in the first place means it eschews historicism. Though Tawney was an historian and believed a sense of history essential to socialist politics, he saw socialism as a matter not of the movement of history but of the will of men.

He complained in "The New Leviathan" that not only conservatives and individualists, but collectivists too, envisaged society as an organism or a machine. The organism or machine was thought to be directed to a certain destination by a self-propelling force. The measure of a society's health and success was the degree of perfection of the organism or mechanism, rather than the wishes and values of real-life people. This was true of Fabian collectivists and of communists, and also of utopian socialists who projected a comprehensive ideal society.

There were times when Tawney's humanism seemed to some fellow socialists an awkward piece of baggage to carry aboard the streamlined socialist locomotive. Yet in retrospect it seems a key to Tawney's achievement in sustaining an effective socialist appeal over half a century. Tawney was a *democratic* socialist because his socialism was humanistic, not because democracy seemed a good tactic, or a way of carving out a socialist position midway between communism and capitalism.

It is a commonplace that the democratic component of socialist theories which claimed to be democratic has had an uncertain career. Not only at the hand of communists but also of Fabians like Shaw and Labour party intellectuals like Laski. But today it is arguable that the democratic character of socialism has become crucial.

In Tawney's youth the natural appeal of socialism seemed to lie in its rationality, as against the irrationality of capitalism which had led Europe into World War I; and during the 1930s in its magic key of planning, to escape the disorder of capitalism which had produced the Depression. But in the 1970s, rationality is at a discount and planning is no longer the special badge of socialism. Instead, demands for participation, decentralization, the protection of diversity, preservation of humane intercourse amidst organizational and technical intricacies, all address afresh to socialist thought the democratic question it hitherto often found embarrassing or even a liability.

Socialism which is not democratic, which does not have "a human face," has little appeal in the industrialized countries. At the same time, given the current degree of disillusion with democratic forms, socialism which can achieve democracy at the basic levels of factory and neighborhood may have increased appeal among people who are not attracted by socialism as a metaphysic or as a gospel of economic planning. In a word, the appeal of socialism in industrialized countries today (unlike for many decades) may depend on whether it can prove itself *more democratic* than alternative systems. If so, Tawney's humanistic socialism offers clues.

One key to Tawney's humanism is the idea of history as an open-ended process. All three major streams of socialism in Britain, other than Tawney's own humanistic stream, seem to envisage a resting place for history when socialism is attained: Marxist, Fabian collectivist, utopian (as in William Morris's vision of the disappearance of politics).[40] At first sight it seems that Crosland has Tawney's kind of open-endedness in his view of socialism and history. Yet looking back on what Crosland wrote in the 1950s (and on what Daniel Bell and other "end of ideology" prophets wrote in that decade) it appears that Crosland and Bell, eager to revise socialism, particularly to shear off what Bell called its "apocalyptic" trimmings, foreclosed political creativity by proclaiming the arrival of Western societies at a fixed postideological destination.[41]

Viewed across the surge of political rebellion and theorizing of the late-1960s, Bell's "exhaustion of utopia" looks merely like the exhaustion of a "seduced" generation of ex-Marxists. Ironically, Bell's proclamation of the end of ideology has all the marks of a frozen utopianism. Peter Sedgwick summed up a parallel point about "Croslandism." Fifteen years later it seems notable for its "sweeping rationalism" and for its "utopian vision of a world *controlled*."[42] Bell and Crosland, deeply engaged in debating Marxism, came to seem enclosed in their own ideological straitjacket. Unlike Tawney, but like their Marxist adversaries, they discussed socialism in terms of the movement of history rather than in terms of the nature of man. It was this which enabled them to imply that the valley of politics, with its twists and turns, conflicts, moral issues, will somehow be left behind and a smooth administrative plateau attained.

George Lichtheim concluded that "Marx's humanism comes to appear utopian, while his political program is travestied by totalitarian regimes in the pre-industrial hinterland of the modern world." And if Marxism evaporates to an impossible ideal, democratic socialism is reduced "to the modest dimensions of an essay in economic planning."[43] Yet these are not the only alternatives. Tawney's socialism neither leaps out of history to a fixed utopia, nor remains a mere essay in economic planning.

His socialism of right relationships among free and equal citizens keeps history open-ended and keeps men within history. Face to face with Marxism which, to follow Lichtheim for a moment, turned utopian because of disillusionment with Stalinism, Tawney asserted that socialism is for ordinary people here and now. If it means anything, there must be concrete political steps which can be taken toward it. Against the high-priests of planning, especially "future-planning," Tawney spells out a never ending moral challenge to better social relationships, and to the creation by the people of their own patterns of social life by cooperative activity.

Tawney saw the industrial revolution as a continuing process, not an event in history. He did not think that once a communist government industrialized a country it had, by that act, created a new and finished type of society with its own values and its own solutions to the great questions of how men should arrange their common life. For the same reason he doubted that economic planning of the welfare state variety would itself deliver answers to all the problems and aspirations socialism had arisen to meet.

In terms of the varieties of socialist thought, Tawney's open-ended, humanistic emphasis can be located this way. Socialism as the rule of the proletariat may disappoint, because working men are no greater natural socialists than other men, and no matter how high they sit (to adapt Montaigne) they sit on the behind of their own human imperfection.

Socialism as the triumph of rationality may be exposed as a chimera, because it is no more rational for men to treat others as equals than to treat them as pawns, and because it is not certain that state officials will be more tightly guided by rational canons than private citizens.

Socialism as the ineluctable product of historical laws may become a casualty of twentieth-century disillusion (and of the rebellion of free spirits), and seem a piece of intellectual imperialism no more to be honored than Adam Smith's idea of an invisible hand bringing wealth and harmony from the operation of the free market.

Socialism as an ideal, spun from the imagination, defiant of history and politics alike, may evoke cynicism by the enormity of the abyss between its glistening shores and the muddy ground on which we presently stand.

But the possibility of socialism as fellowship remains, a moral option at all points of history, in scarcity or abundance, town or country, so long as men's common humanity seems a sufficiently overriding concern for the institutions and incentives of society to be ordered so that people are within social reach of each other.

Some have puzzled that Tawney was radical in analysis yet moderate in strategy.[44] But now we see that Tawney's moderation on questions of political method was not an uneasy compromise between competing extremes, but a direct result of a humanistic aspect of his socialism: respect for "Henry Dubb" as the man whom socialism is all about. Tawney was moderate because he claimed only what he knew could be delivered.

He was not one who would have liked to have been a conspiratorial revolutionary socialist, if only the need to oppose communism had not removed that option. He never became an anticommunist out of the need to be safe and respectable, because he was a noncommunist out of a conviction that the Communist party did not respect the views and wishes of ordinary people. Discussing with a colleague the work of a young Marxist historian, Tawney urged on his colleague that here was fine scholar of Tudor and Stuart England. The colleague, an anticommunist, was resistant and said several times: "But he's a communist, you know, he's a communist." Tawney eventually enquired evenly: "Now is that a good thing or a bad thing?"[45]

Yet if Tawney was not "a democrat by virtue of not being a communist," he had no time for the British Communist party because of its readiness to abandon persuasion for coercion when necessary. The root of his caution about violent methods is a clue to the character of his political moderation. Tawney discovered on the fields of France that war was an awful thing, hated by the ordinary soldier. "One's like a merry, mischievous ape tearing up the image of God," he recounted of the Great War. "When I read now the babble of journalists about 'the sporting spirit of our soldiers' it makes me almost sick."[46] Himself shot through the stomach during the advance on the Somme, Tawney was unimpressed by leftists who praised violent revolution but did not understand violence, and therefore, he felt, had no right to urge it on working men.

He got his views on war from his fellow soldiers, and his views on labor politics in large part from the people around Toynbee Hall and in Manchester, and the weavers, miners, and potters in his tutorial classes. Both sets of experiences made him the kind of moderate he was in political methods. It was the moderation of respect for the rank and file.

He was also moderate because he saw socialism as a way as well as a goal. There was no socialist destination qualitatively richer than the life of socialism which the labor movement could begin to create through concrete first steps toward socialist practices. Tawney viewed socialism as "principles" rather than "ideals," a conception probably derived from his Christianity. The man who sees an ideal state ahead asks, with St. Thomas, "We know not whither Thou goest; how can we know the way?"; but St. Thomas got from Jesus the answer: "I am the Way."[47] Tawney said that the nature of socialism had to be discovered by taking steps along the socialist way. Although England was not yet socialist, for example, socialists could bear witness to socialism by declining "Honours" offered by a capitalist Establishment.

Does humanistic socialism mean simply principles of social morality? Should we say that Tawney was more of a Christian humanist than a socialist? I prefer only to say that the basis of Tawney's socialism was moral. In some ways Tawney does not seem a moralist. Since he thought mankind a speckled breed, he did not waste his breath appealing for naked altruism. His socialism was not predicated on saintly conduct from the citizenry. The shape of socialism is structural; it does not require especially heroic types to make it work. On the other hand, the overall rationale of Tawney's socialism had to do with the quality of social relationships, and consideration of relationships brings us to morality.

Tawney thought inequality a profounder problem than poverty.[48] It was a more characteristic mark of capitalism. Poverty was no greater under capitalism than it had been before. Poverty, a matter of conditions, hinders culture. Inequality, a matter of social relationships, hinders the spirit. It would be hard to find a stronger foe of poverty in his generation than Tawney. Nevertheless he did not think that poverty (short of destitution) need be degrading unless it was cheek by jowl with affluence. Inequality, on the other hand, was always degrading because it precluded human communication. So Tawney's socialism of right relationships had a moral root.

Tawney also held that ultimately a good society could not exist without good people. That did not mean that people had to be good *before* society could be good. On the contrary, Tawney said it was unreasonable to expect people to be good when, as under capitalism, they were treated not as ends but as means. He scorned moral exhortation directed at poor people and workers caught in the web of capitalist industry.

Tawney urged advance on two fronts at the same time: the shape of socialism was to be legislated; the dynamics of socialism were to be cultivated. The problems this raises come less from Tawney's theories concerning structures and conduct than from the largeness of the assumptions he made about the degree to which his own high standards were understood and accepted in society at large.

Again, Tawney was integrating a moral factor into the overall framework of his socialism. Socialist governments will not be able to accomplish great things by flicking a legislative or administrative switch. That has been proved in China and the Soviet Union and must be truer of democratic socialist governments. During the interlude, stress was placed, by Tawney and others, on the "growth of a social mind" and the "growth of new social tissue."[49] The triumph of state power which came with the ideologies smothered this concern. Yet today the omnicompetence of political will is again severely in question. The difficulty of changing societies from the top alone is widely apparent.

In a fragmentary note about democracy Tawney wrote that "Democracy [is] a society where ordinary men exercise initiative. Dreadful respect for superiors. Mental enlargement ... Real foe to be overcome ... fact that large section of public *like* plutocratic government, and are easily gullible. How shake them!"[50] Here is the point of his notion that only with good people can society itself be good. Tawney's genuine moral concern was a factor in his political realism.

The "end of ideology" theorists aborted the cut and thrust of democratic politics by positing a frozen condition of political consensus. They foreclosed political creativity, because they did not allow for (much less call for) the dialectic that ought to take place in a democracy between fundamental moral concerns and political policies. Tawney saw that the neglect of moral factors was ultimately weakening to a polity, and that a socialist theory built on a dialectic between moral and structural factors was the best kind.

TAWNEY'S PLACE IN BRITISH SOCIALISM

Tawney's influence straddled Labour's left and right. Both *Socialist Commentary* and the *New Statesman* were able to write about him as if he were one of theirs. Crossman, when a figure on the Labour left, called Tawney's *The Acquisitive Society* his socialist Bible; Gaitskell, when a partisan of the Labour right, said, "I always think of him as *the* Democratic Socialist *par excellence.*"[51]

Tawney was not a typical Fabian. The roots of his thought were not in Benthamite utilitarianism; he possessed little evolutionary optimism; he was not attached to middle-class values; his polemical thrust as a socialist was not to dispute efficiency with capitalism. Yet he shared the Fabian stress on meticulous backroom research, education, permeation through a web of elitist contacts, and its confidence that the rational presentation of a case would bear political fruit.

If Fabianism in the manner of the Webbs was the character-istic brand of British socialism until the 1920s, as Tawney judged it was, the next decade brought the one period of Marxist dominance Britain has experienced.[52] Tawney was a radical but not a Marxist radical. During the 1930s he kept his Fabian head, as it were, when Fabians all around were losing theirs. In so far as guild socialism, until its abortive decline in the mid-1920s, formed a further substrand of Brit-ish socialism, Tawney's position was that of a participant who was nevertheless in it rather than of it.

More than any other place, Tawney belongs with the non-Marxist ethical socialism of the Labour left. With its twin origins in the concrete organizational life of the nineteenth-century British working class, and the critique of British in-dustrialism by Ruskin, Owen, and other moralists. With its Christian associations; its praise of fellowship; its lurking hos-tility to all aspects of the London Establishment.

Certainly there are differences. Tawney did not share the pacifist internationalism of this strand. He was not so dis-trustful of governments as to remain outraged even after a government had taken what action it reasonably could on an issue. He had a disconcerting habit of snapping the spell of slightly self-righteous solidarity and "good feelings" which this Labour left cast upon itself, by declining to blame all failures on the enemy or renegades, but pointing instead to the lack of courage, rigor, and honesty among the socialist believers themselves.[53]

But if Tawney differed from each major strand of British socialism, he fertilized them all. He is the one twentieth-cen-tury British socialist thinker who can be saluted from every quarter; Bevanite left, Gaitskellite right, guild socialist, Marx-ist, Fabian, Christian socialist—the philosopher who has most nearly provided an overall framework for socialism in British conditions and according to the British temper.

If he criticized the sectionalism of guild socialists, he gave high priority to their desire to "democratise the practical routine of industrial life," and he offered, in *The Acquisitive Society*, the most comprehensive application of the theory of function to appear. If his uncompromising advocacy of set-ting before the electorate the full dimensions of Labour's plan for a socialist commonwealth gave him influence on the left of the Labour party, his commitment to completely democratic means of attaining it made him seem, to Gaitskell, Durbin, Gordon Walker, and their wing, the "democratic socialist *par excellence*."

He was sharply aware of class, and gave weight to economic factors in his historiography, which satisfied Marxists. But he worked for unity in British society based on the acceptance of certain principles, rather than puffing up class analysis to a political value, and he integrated the Marxist elements of his thought into a much broader synthesis. If he built his book about religion and English history on substantially Marxist foundations, so that the largely religious audience to which he first presented it got a dose of Marxism without always knowing it, he put religious themes into his book on the acquisitive dynamics of capitalism, so that his secular readers found themselves introduced to Christian arguments for socialism.

In style, if some Fabians found his moralizing a bit patriarchal, they respected the originality of his research and the amazing detail of his grasp of educational and industrial policy issues. If the workers of Cradley Heath found his books on *Minimum Rates* too dense with facts, and his imagery oblique, they liked his debunking manner and could see he knew the mood of the factories. At the other end of the social spectrum, if cultured classes were only half persuaded by his strictures about snobbery, and his blunt references to the thieving nature of the economic activities of "Top People," his knowledge, range of allusion, and grace were sufficient (as the impact of his most militant books indicates) to convince many of them of the shaky basis of their privileges.

Tawney's catholicity was his humanism. Guarding an open-ended view of history, he withstood the tempests of totalitarianism. A pioneer of workers' education, he kept the needs and nature of "Henry Dubb" as the point of orientation for his socialism (socialists of every hue acknowledged workers' education's importance to socialism). Using as his yardstick "what is fit for men," which leant on Christianity's sobriety about human virtue yet also on its expansiveness about human possibilities and insistence on man's common humanity, Tawney was radical in an unshakable way. Not wildly zig-zagging with the accidents and disappointments of history, he was as radical at eighty as he had been at twenty.

Because his principles were forthright, and lived up to, socialists could make common cause with Tawney on particular issues, even if they surpassed him in their doctrinal subtleties or their exhilarating sense of moving inexorably upward on history's escalator. Tawney's overall socialist framework, though implicit, had its coherence. Even more important, it had the power to keep his own convictions firm, and to guarantee a clear distinction between ends and means.

His stand on the thorny issue of nationalization provides an illustration of the last point. The left claimed him as a fundamentalist. Yet the right pointed to him as the source of their view that it was wrong to make nationalization a principle, since it was but one means to an end. The latter view was in fact Tawney's (as early as 1921).[54] But he wanted to nationalize more industries than Gaitskell and the revisionists did, because his view of the end involved was more radical than theirs.

To get equality, to break the social and political power of wealth, to encourage active citizenship, to move toward a society where the basis of rights and rewards would be function, Tawney saw nationalization as one method, alongside schemes for workers' control, educational reform, drastic redistribution of capital, and others. So if he seemed to be at once left and right, it was because his overall goal was firm enough to make him open about methods, and less inclined than some to cling to one particular method as the throbbing heart of socialism.

Tawney's humanistic socialism was catholic in one further respect. J. A. G. Griffith recalled in 1970: "when I was a young man, the case for revolution was that radical changes were desirable in order that utopia might come more quickly. Now only revolution is likely to save us from a degeneration which will embrace us all."[55] This dichotomy is interesting in socialist history. There are "crisis socialists" (socialism is the way to get out of a mess), and there are "light on the hill socialists" (socialism is an ideal that beckons).

Tawney cannot without qualification be called a "light on the hill socialist." Yet he was more nearly that than a "crisis socialist." If he did not construct an ideal state, he held up a better way, argued in terms of the fundamental human condition. He was deeply influenced, like everyone else, by the chronic malfunctioning of the British economy during the 1930s, but his case for socialism was not built on the particular features of that sad decade. Tawney's power was that he challenged not only what many saw were Britain's vices, but also what many thought were Britain's virtues. To raise fresh questions, to alter the agenda, to call transitory what looks eternal, to demonstrate the moral shabbiness of the socially estimable—this was powerful social criticism.

He offered not only a solution for known problems, but an entire alternative to the acquisitive society, touching educational and social matters no less than economic and political. At the same time, he was not quite a "light on the hill socialist," because his socialist man was no bloodless abstraction or shimmering ideal, but a fully human, recognizable, believable figure. Except for his partial neglect of a power strategy for attaining socialism, there is little reason to call Tawney utopian. His view of man was down to earth, and he never dreamed, at least aloud, dreams which could not be pursued by concrete steps.

He could with confidence challenge accepted virtues, without seeming pompous, irresponsible, or a bore, because he did it from the depths of a transparent humanism. He was taking his stand, not for himself, or for a section of Britain; not for an idea, or for a theory of the universe; but for the sake of a belief in the dignity of human beings which he stated in frank and simple terms. He posited certain common attributes of all men, and then asserted that the generality of men, rather than one class or kind, or the exceptionally cultured or rational man, should be the unit in terms of which arguments about social morality were to be made. These two steps, taken together, gave Tawney his simplicity and power, and made him a socialist for all seasons.

ON SOURCES, BIBLIOGRAPHY OF TAWNEY'S
WRITINGS, NOTES, INDEX

ON SOURCES

The main sources are as follows:

1. The works listed in my Bibliography of the Published Writings of R. H. Tawney.

2. The collection of unpublished historical and political papers—and some letters—of Tawney held (in the care of Professor F. J. Fisher) at the British Library of Political and Economic Science, London School of Economics and Political Science. These are contained in twenty-one boxes labeled as follows:

Papers Re Proposed Biography of Sidney Webb
Lectures for Denmark and Sweden
Various Lectures Given in US, 1941-42
Public Lectures Given in Chicago, 1939
Notes for Speeches on Various Occasions
Speeches Given on Various Occasions
Speeches on Various Occasions
Notes and Talks on French Revolution, Longton 1910-13 (2 boxes)
LSE—Bristol—Cranfield
Nineteenth-Century Economic History, LSE
Notes for Classes or Lectures on Nineteenth-Century Economic History
Lectures on Nineteenth-Century Agriculture Given at LSE
Lectures on English Economic History in Sixteenth Century and Seventeenth Century
Lectures on Seventeenth-Century English History
Lectures on Seventeenth Century Given at Oxford (Ford) and Chicago
Fragments of Ford and Chicago Lectures
Lectures on Economic History, 1485-1800
Memoranda on Education and Educational Policy
The Labour Party and Education
Lectures on Education

These papers are no better organized than Tawney's papers ever were.

Labels of boxes seem at times arbitrary (for example, there is no clear difference in nature between the papers in "Speeches Given on Various Occasions" and those in "Speeches on Various Occasions") and the label sometimes belies the contents (for example, the outline of a book on political theory, "The New Leviathan," is found in "Notes and Talks on French Revolution, Longton 1910-1913").

However, I preferred to keep the labels as Tawney wrote them, and so refer accurately to the physical location of each paper. In many cases pagination is not given, either because it does not exist in the manuscript or because the pagination in the manuscript is so disordered that a page reference would merely mislead. However, none of the papers to which no page reference is possible are very long.

3. Tawney's diary (or "Commonplace Book"), 1912-1914; manuscript in possession of Mr. Michael Vyvyan, Trinity College, Cambridge.*

4. Additional unpublished material as follows:

Balliol College Papers (letters and papers involving Tawney, at Balliol College Library, Oxford).

Beveridge Collection, LSE (the papers of William Beveridge).

Boone Papers (letters and other papers which Professor Gladys Boone of Sweetbriar College, Virginia, has collected in the course of her long interest in Tawney).

Creech Jones Papers (the papers of Arthur Creech Jones, at the Rhodes House Library, Oxford).

Gaitskell Papers (letters between Tawney and Gaitskell, in the care of Mr. P. M. Williams, Nuffield College, Oxford).

Guardian Papers (letters between Tawney and two editors of the Manchester Guardian, William Crozier and A. P. Wadsworth, contained in the Editorial Correspondence from the Guardian Archives now in the library of Manchester University).

Nef Papers (the papers of Professor John Nef, which contain many letters of Tawney, at the Joseph Regenstein Library, University of Chicago).

Passfield Papers (papers of Sidney and Beatrice Webb, at the British Library of Political and Economic Science, LSE).

Rewley House Collection (papers and letters relating to tutorial classes and WEA, at the Department for External Studies, Rewley House, University of Oxford).

*While this book was at press, Tawney's diary was published (*R. H. Tawney's Commonplace Book*, edited and with an introduction by J. M. Winter and D. M. Joslin, Cambridge, Cambridge University Press, 1972).

Tawney's Foreign Office Reports (written from Washington, 1941-1942; at the Foreign and Commonwealth Office).

Wadsworth Papers (papers and letters about Tawney, belonging to Miss Janet Wadsworth of Manchester).

WEA Archive (letters and papers relating to tutorial classes, WEA work, and adult education in general, in the Library of Temple House, Upper Berkeley Street, London).

Yule Papers (letters of Tawney to Professor George Yule, Ormond College, Melbourne).

Also, letters of Tawney's were made available to me by Professor H. L. Beales (Tawney to Laski) and Professor S. G. Raybould (Tawney to Raybould).

5. Conversations were held with the following people who knew Tawney well or had information about him or his work:

Professor James L. Adams, Mr. David Ayerst, Lord Noel Annan, Professor H. L. Beales, Miss Pearl Buck, Lord Ritchie Calder, Professor E. Carus-Wilson, Mrs. Margaret Cole, Mr. Arthur Crook, Rt. Hon. C. A. R. Crosland, Rt. Hon. R. H. S. Crossman, Professor G. R. Elton, Mr. Lionel Elvin, Lord Fenner Brockway, Professor F. J. Fisher, Professor Joseph Fletcher, Professor J. K. Galbraith, Rt. Hon. Patrick Gordon Walker, Dr. Ernest Green, Professor William L. Holland, Dr. Gordon Huelin, the late Dr. Rita Hinden, Dr. Christopher Hill, Mrs. Hill, Mr. Frank Jessup, the late Professor David Joslin, Professor A. V. Judges, Sir Walter Moberley, Professor John Nef, Mr. Harry Nutt, Professor Talcott Parsons, Mr. Frank Pickstock, Professor M. M. Postan, Canon Ronald Preston, Professor S. G. Raybould, Mr. Scott Rankine, Mr. Maurice Reckitt, the late Sir Richard Rees, Lady Shena Simon, Lord Donald Soper, Baroness Mary Stocks, Professor Lawrence Stone, Professor Richard Titmuss, Mr. Michael Vyvyan, Miss Janet Wadsworth, Baroness Eirene White of Rhymney, Rt. Hon. Harold Wilson, Mr. Raymond Williams, Baroness Barbara Wootton, Professor George Yule.

6. Letters to the author with material about Tawney from the following persons:

Mr. Ian Angus (December 17, 1968).

Dr. John C. Bennett (January 17, 1969).

Mr. B. N. Bhattacherjee, Librarian, Presidency College, Calcutta (April 20, 1971).

Mr. Thomas S. Derr (December 28, 1968; March 19, 1971).

Professor R. M. Crawford (February 26, 1971).

Lord Morris of Grasmere (June 7, 1971).
Professor William L. Holland (March 21, 1972).
Mr. N. C. Kittermaster, Librarian, Rugby School (April 1, 1971).
Mr. Michel H. Ridgeway (March 24, 1968).
Mrs. Frances Temple (April 5, 1971).

BIBLIOGRAPHY OF THE PUBLISHED WRITINGS OF R. H. TAWNEY

The items marked with a double asterisk (**) were collected by Tawney in *The Attack and Other Papers* (1953), which also contains previously unpublished material. The items marked with a single asterisk (*) are in *The Radical Tradition: Twelve Essays on Politics, Education, and Literature* (1964). This volume was edited by Rita Hinden two years after Tawney's death, and contains material Tawney himself set aside with a view to republication, together with one previously unpublished piece.

The bibliography is divided into three sections and eleven parts. Section one contains books and pamphlets. It is divided into four parts according to the type of publication and the nature of Tawney's contribution to the publication. Section two contains articles. It is divided into seven parts according to the subject matter of the article. Within each of the eleven parts the arrangement of items is chronological. Certain articles could as easily have been placed in one part as in another (e.g. item 405 belongs as much in articles on industry as in articles on religion); however, each item has been listed once only. The place of publication of WEA items is London. Section three contains book reviews by Tawney.

I have relied for several items on the recently published "A Bibliography of the Published Writings of R. H. Tawney" by J. M. Winter, *Economic History Review*, 25 (February 1972); though extensive and generally accurate, Dr. Winter's bibliography lacks seventy-odd items contained in the present one.

I. BOOKS AND PAMPHLETS

BOOKS

1. *The Agrarian Problem in the Sixteenth Century.* London, Longmans, Green and Co., 1912.
2. *The Establishment of Minimum Rates in the Chain-Making Indus-*

try under the Trade Boards Act of 1909. London, G. Bell & Sons, Ltd., 1914.

3. *The Establishment of Minimum Rates in the Tailoring Industry under the Trade Boards Act of 1909.* London, G. Bell & Sons, Ltd., 1915.

4. *The Acquisitive Society.* New York, Harcourt, Brace and Co., 1920; London, G. Bell & Sons, Ltd., 1921; London, Collins, 1961; Chinese ed., 1928; Indian ed., 1943; Arabic ed., 1963.

5. *The British Labour Movement.* New Haven, Conn., Yale University Press, 1925.

6. *Religion and the Rise of Capitalism.* London, John Murray, 1926; New York, Harcourt, Brace and Co., 1926; Spanish ed., 1936; German ed., 1946; French ed., 1951; Japanese ed., 1956; Polish ed., 1963; Dutch ed., 1964; Italian ed., 1967.

7. *Memorandum on Agriculture and Industry in China.* Honolulu, Institute of Pacific Relations, 1931.

8. *Equality.* London, Allen & Unwin Ltd., 1931; 4th revised edition of 1952 has a new chapter; Spanish ed., 1945.

9. *Land and Labour in China.* London, G. Allen & Unwin Ltd., 1932; Japanese ed., 1935.

10. *The Attack and Other Papers.* London, Allen & Unwin Ltd., 1953; New York, Harcourt, Brace, and Co., 1953.

11. *Business and Politics under James I: Lionel Cranfield as Merchant and Minister.* Cambridge, Eng., Cambridge University Press, 1958.

12. *The Radical Tradition: Twelve Essays on Politics, Education, and Literature.* New York, Pantheon Books, 1964; edited, after Tawney's death, by Rita Hinden; Japanese ed., 1967.

13. *Commonplace Book.* Cambridge, Cambridge University Press, 1972; edited and with an introduction by J. M. Winter and D. M. Joslin.

PAMPHLETS BY TAWNEY

14. *Boy and Girl Labour.* London, 1919. With Nettie Adler.

15. *Education and Social Progress.* Manchester, 1912.

16. *Poverty as an Industrial Problem.* Inaugural lecture by Tawney as director of Ratan Tata Foundation, October 22, 1913, London; The Ratan Tata Foundation, London School of Economics, 1914.

17. *Democracy or Defeat.* London, WEA, 1917; from *The Welsh Outlook,* January 1917.

*18. *The Nationalisation of the Coal Industry.* Part of a Labour party pamphlet. London, Labour Party, 1919 and 1921.

19. *The Sickness of an Acquisitive Society.* Fabian Society, London, Allen & Unwin Ltd., 1920.

20. *The Possible Cost of Raising the School Leaving Age.* Address at

National Educational Conference, National Union of Teachers and WEA, 1927.

21. *The Case for Nursery Schools: Being the Report of a Committee.* London, 1929. Tawney the principal author.
22. *The Education of the Citizen.* WEA, 1932.
23. *The Condition of China.* Earl Grey Memorial Lecture, Newcastle, The Registrar, Armstrong College, 1933.
24. *Juvenile Employment and Education.* Oxford, Oxford University Press, 1934.
25. *Labour and Education.* London, Labour Party, 1934.
26. *The School Leaving Age and Juvenile Unemployment.* WEA, 1934.
27. *The School Leaving Age and Exemptions.* WEA, 1936.
28. *What is Beneficial Employment?* WEA, 1938.
29. *Some Thoughts on the Economics of Public Education.* L. T. Hobhouse Memorial Trust Lecture, London, H. Milford, Oxford University Press, 1938.
30. *Can Democracy Survive?* WEA, 1940.
31. *Harrington's Interpretation of His Age.* Raleigh Lecture, London, Milford, 1941. Also in *Proceedings of the British Academy,* 27 (1941).
32. *Education: The Task Before Us.* WEA Presidential Address, 1943.
33. *A Sermon For Socialists.* London, S.C.M., 1945.
**34. *The Webbs and Their Work.* Webb Memorial Lecture, London, Fabian Publications, 1945. Reprinted in H. W. Spiegel, *Development of Economic Thought,* New York, John Wiley, 1964.
35. *The Western Political Tradition.* Burge Memorial Lecture, London, SCM Press, 1949.
*36. *Social History and Literature.* Lecture to National Book League, London, Cambridge University Press, 1950; republished, with modifications, as the Goerge Arnold Wood Memorial Lecture, under same title, Sydney, 1956.
37. *The Webbs in Perspective.* Webb Memorial Lecture, 1952, London, Athlone Press, 1953.
*38. *The WEA and Adult Education.* Fiftieth Anniversary WEA Lecture, University of London, 1953.
**39. *Christian Politics.* Reprint of 1937 memorandum written for Oxford Conference on Church, Community, and State, Socialist Christian League, 1954. In *The Attack* it is entitled "A Note on Christianity and the Social Order."

BOOKS EDITED OR PARTLY WRITTEN BY TAWNEY

40. *Papers and Proceedings, Second National Conference on the Prevention of Destitution.* London, 1912. Tawney's essay "The Present Position of Opinion as to the Labour of Adolescents."

41. A. E. Bland, P. A. Brown, and R. H. Tawney, eds. *English Economic History: Select Documents.* London, G. Bell & Sons Ltd., 1914.

*42. S. J. Chapman, ed. *Labour and Capital After the War.* London, J. Murray, 1918. Contains Tawney's essay "The Conditions of Economic Liberty."

43. *Continued Education Under The New Education Act.* London, Labour Party Advisory Committee on Education, 1918. Tawney principal author.

44. *Christianity and Industrial Problems.* Report of the archbishop of Canterbury's Fifth Committee of Inquiry, London, 1918. Tawney one of twenty-eight authors.

45. H. Smith et al., eds. *The Mines for the Nation.* London, Daily Herald, 1919. Tawney's essay "The Case for Industrial Freedom."

46. P. Alden et al. *Labour and Industry.* London, Longmans, Green, and Co., 1920. Contains Tawney's essay "Recent Thoughts on the Government of Industry."

47. *Official Report of the Church Congress.* Birmingham, 1921. Tawney part-author of "Industrial Problems: Capital, Labour and Competition."

48. *Secondary Education for All.* London, Labour Party, 1922. Tawney principal author.

49. *Education: The Socialist Policy.* London, Independent Labour Party, Publication Department, 1924. Tawney principal author.

50. E. Power and R. H. Tawney, eds. *Tudor Economic Documents.* 3 vols.; London, Longmans, Green and Co., 1924.

51. T. L. Humberstone, ed. *Science and Labour.* London, Benn, 1924. Tawney's essay "Educational Organisation."

52. Thomas Wilson, *A Discourse Upon Usury.* London, G. Bell & Sons Ltd., 1925. Edited and with a long introduction by Tawney.

53. *Adult Education in the Life of the Nation.* Papers at 5th Conference of British Institute of Adult Education, 1926. Contains Tawney's essay "Adult Education in the History of the Nation."

54. League of Nations Union, *Towards Industrial Peace.* London, King, 1927. Report of Conference on Systems of Fixing Minimum Wages and Methods of Conciliation and Arbitration. Tawney's essay "The Trade Boards Systems: The Historical Aspects of the Subject."

55. *Studies in Economic History: The Collected Papers of George Unwin.* London, Published for The Royal Economic Society by Macmillan and Co., Ltd., 1927. Edited and with an introductory memoir by Tawney.

56. E. Power and R. H. Tawney, eds. *Studies in Economic and Social History.* London, Routledge and Sons, 1929 and later years. Tawney general co-editor of series of six studies.

57. C. H. Becker et al. *The Reorganisation of Education in China.* Paris, 1932, French and English editions. Tawney a co-author.

**58. C. Latham et al. *What Labour Could Do*. London, G. Routledge & Sons, Ltd., 1945. Contains Tawney's essay "We Mean Freedom;" also published in *Review of Politics*, April 1946.

*59. W. Scarlett ed., *The Christian Demand for Social Justice*. New York, New American Library, 1949. Contains Tawney's essay "Social Democracy in Britain."

PREFACES OR SHORT INTRODUCTIONS BY TAWNEY

60. A. Greenwood, *The Health and Physique of School Children*. London, P. S. King & Son, 1913. Introductory Note by Tawney.

61. M. E. Bulkley, *The Feeding of School Children*. London, G. Bell & Sons, Ltd., 1914. Introduction by Tawney.

62. ____*The Establishment of Legal Minimum Rates in the Box-Making Industry*. London, G. Bell & Sons, Ltd., 1915. Introduction by Tawney.

63. A. L. Bowley and A. R. Burnett-Hurst, *Livelihood and Poverty*. London, G. Bell & Sons, Ltd., 1915. Introduction by Tawney.

64. V. de Vesselitsky, *The Homeworker and the Outlook*. London, Bell, 1916. Introduction by Tawney.

65. M. Beer, *History of British Socialism*. 2 vols., London, G. Bell & Sons, Ltd., 1919. Introduction by Tawney.

*66. *The Life and Struggles of William Lovett*, Vol. I. London, G. Bell & Sons, 1920. Introduction by Tawney.

67. C. L. Goodrich, *The Frontier of Control*. New York, Harcourt, Brace and Howe, 1920. Foreword by Tawney.

68. R. B. Haldane, *The Problem of Nationalisation*. London, Allen & Unwin, 1921. Introduction written jointly by Tawney and Laski.

69. Susan Lawrence, *London Education*. London, WEA, 1923. Preface by Tawney.

70. T. W. Price, *The Story of the Workers' Education Association*. London, Labour Publishing Co., 1924. Introduction by Tawney.

71. B. Drake, ed. *Staffing in Public Elementary Schools*. London, 1924. Introduction by Tawney.

72. K. Lindsay, *Social Progress and Educational Waste*. London, Routledge, 1926. The introduction, though signed by Viscount Haldane, was written by Tawney.

73. Max Weber, *General Economic History*, trans. F. H. Knight. London, Allen & Unwin, 1927. Preface by Tawney.

74. R. Firth, *Primitive Economics of the New Zealand Maori*. London, Routledge, 1929. Preface by Tawney.

75. M. Weber, *The Protestant Ethic and the Spirit of Capitalism*. London, Allen & Unwin, 1930. Foreword by Tawney.

76. W. H. Warburton, *The History of Trade Union Organisation in the North Staffordshire Potteries*. London, Allen & Unwin, 1931. Introduction by Tawney.

77. W. Boyd, ed. *The Challenge of Leisure*. London, New Education Fellowship, 1936. Introduction by Tawney.
78. *Workers Education in Great Britain: A Record of Educational Service to Democracy Since 1918*. London, WEA, 1938. Preface by Tawney.
79. *Agrarian China: Selected Source Materials from Chinese Authors*. Institute of Pacific Relations, London, Allen & Unwin, 1938. Introduction by Tawney.
80. J. P. Mayer, *Political Thought: The European Tradition*. New York, Viking Press, 1939. Introduction by Tawney.
81. *The Adult Student as Citizen: A Record of Service by WEA Students Past and Present*. London, WEA, (1939?). Preface by Tawney.
82. *Education for Freedom: A Statement of Policy*. London, WEA, 1939. Preface by Tawney.
83. Charles Gore, *Christianity Applied to the Life of Man and Nations*. Essex Hall Lecture, 1920; reprinted, with Tawney's introduction, London, Lindsey Press, 1940.
84. G. C. Leybourne and K. White, *Education and the Birthrate: A Social Dilemma*. London, J. Cape, 1940. Introduction by Tawney.
85. D. M. Goodfellow, *Tyneside: The Social Facts*. Newcastle-upon-Tyne, 1941. Introduction by Tawney.
86. B. Drake, *Education for Democracy*. British Association for Labour Legislation, 1943. Introduction by Tawney.
87. *The Future in Adult Education*. WEA pamphlet, 1947. Preface by Tawney.
88. S. G. Raybould, *WEA: The Next Phase*. WEA, 1949. Introduction by Tawney.
89. St. John B. Groser, *Politics and Persons*. London, Student Christian Movement Press, Ltd., 1949. Foreword by Tawney.
90. J. Thirsk, *Fenland Farming in the Sixteenth Century*. Leicester, University College of Leicester, 1953. Introduction by Tawney.
91. *Jubilee Addresses on Adult Education*. WEA, 1953. Concluding observations by Tawney.
92. D. Brunton and D. H. Pennington, *Members of the Long Parliament*. London, Allen & Unwin, Ltd., 1954. Introduction by Tawney.

II. ARTICLES

ARTICLES ON CHINA

93. "A Visit to China: I. The Background of the Past," *Manchester Guardian*, May 18, 1931.

94. "A Visit to China: II. Monuments," *Manchester Guardian*, May 19, 1931.

95. "A Visit to China: III. Agriculture," *Manchester Guardian*, May 20, 1931.

96. "A Visit to China: IV. Industry Ancient and Modern," *Manchester Guardian*, May 21, 1931.

97. A Visit to China: V. Politics," *Manchester Guardian*, May 22, 1931.

**98. "A Visit to China: VI. The Picture as a Whole," *Manchester Guardian*, May 23, 1931. (Portions, but not all, of the above six articles are collected in *The Attack and Other Papers*).

99. "The National Government as Viewed by an English Professor," *China Weekly Review*, June 20, 1931.

100. "Impressions of China," *The Highway*, March 1932.

101. "China's Future," *Manchester Guardian*, March 1, 1933.

ARTICLES ON EDUCATION

102. "The University and the Nation: I. Introductory," *Westminster Gazette*, February 15, 1906.

103. "II. Ways and Means," *Westminster Gazette*, February 16, 1906.

104. "III. The University and the Colleges," *Westminster Gazette*, February 17, 1906.

105. "IV. The Scholarship System," *Westminster Gazette*, February 23, 1906.

106. "V. The Oxford Entrance Examination," *Westminster Gazette*, February 24, 1906.

107. "VI. The Limitations of the College System," *Westminster Gazette*, March 2, 1906.

108. "VII. Research," *Westminster Gazette*, March 3, 1906.

109. "VIII. What a New Commission Might Do," *Westminster Gazette*, March 10, 1906.

110. "Labour and Culture," *Morning Post*, August 16, 1907.

111. "Schools and Scholars: Education in 1907," *Morning Post*, January 3, 1908.

112. Editorial (Educational Controversy), *Morning Post*, February 24, 1908.

113. "Schools and Scholars: The Annual Report of the Board of Education; A Plea for more Information," *Morning Post*. [March?] 1908.

114. Editorial (on the Education Bill of Mr. McKenna, President of the Board of Education), *Morning Post*, March 11, 1908.

115. Editorial (on the Bishop of St. Alsaph's Education Bill), *Morning Post*, March 31, 1908.

116. Editorial (on Government's rejection of Education Compromise), *Morning Post*, December 3, 1908.

117. Editorial (on the case for Dissolution), *Morning Post*, December 5, 1908.
118. "The Technical School", *Rochdale Times*, September 22, 1909 (text of speech at Rochdale Technical School).
119. "Sunday Meetings," *Rochdale Times*, November 21, 1909 (letter to editor).
120. "The Report of the Consultative Committee on Attendance at Continuation Schools," *The Highway*, November 1909.
121. "Schools and Scholars: Voluntaryism V. Compulsion in Continuing Education," *Morning Post*, January 14, 1910.
122. "Schools and Scholars: The First Report of the Medical Officer," *Morning Post*, February 11, 1910.
123. "Schools and Scholars: The Labour Exchange in Relation to Boy Girl Labour," *Morning Post*, April 10, 1910.
124. "Schools and Scholars: A School Medical Officer's Report," *Morning Post*, May 6, 1910.
125. "Schools and Scholars: The Effects of Street Trading," *Morning Post*, September 23, 1910.
126. "Schools and Scholars: Medical Treatment-A Problem," *Morning Post*, November 25, 1910.
127. "Schools and Scholars: The Reform of Oxford," *Morning Post*, December 30, 1910.
128. "The Report of the Board of Education 1909-10," *The Highway*, June 1911.
129. "Schools and Scholars: Critique of Mr. Runciman's Bill," *Morning Post*, June 2, 1911.
130. "Schools and Scholars: Progressive Educational Policy," *Morning Post*, [August?] 1911.
131. "A Task for WEA Branches," *The Highway*, January 1912.
132. "School Clinics," *Manchester Guardian*, May 1, 1912.
133. "A Sheaf of Reforms," *The Highway*, October 1912.
134. "University Tutorial Classes," *Manchester Guardian*, November 17, 1913.
*135. "An Experiment in Democratic Education," *Political Quarterly*, May 1914.
**136. "A National College of All Souls," *Times Educational Supplement*, February 22, 1917.
137. "An Educational Programme," *Manchester Guardian*, March 10, 1917.
*138. "Keep the Workers' Children in their Place," *Daily News*, February 14, 1918 (original title: "Prussianism in the Schools").
139. "Works Schools," *Daily News*, April 29, 1918.
140. "The Employment of Schoolchildren," *Saturday Westminster*, May 13, 1918.
141. "The Perils of Education," *Daily News*, May 17, 1918.
142. "The WEA Education Yearbook," *The Highway*, September 1918.

143. "Comparative Education," *Manchester Guardian*, December 6, 1918.

144. "Canon Barnett and University Reform," *Canon Barnett: His Life, Work, and Friends*, by His Wife. Vol. II, Chap. xxxvii. London, 1919. Tawney contributed this one chapter to Mrs. Barnett's biography.

145. "A Pioneer in Working Class Education," *Manchester Guardian*, August 17, 1920.

146. "Adult Education," *Manchester Guardian*, October 7, 1920.

147. "A Valuable Report," *Manchester Guardian*, November 16, 1920.

148. "The Attack on the Education Act," *Manchester Guardian*, January 18, 1921.

149. "The Hold Up in Education," *Manchester Guardian*, March 7, 1921 (leader).

150. "The Geddes Report and Education I: An Examination of the Proposals and Their Aims," *Manchester Guardian*, February 21, 1922.

151. "The Geddes Report and Education II: Facts of Educational Expenditure," *Manchester Guardian*, February 22, 1922.

152. "Struggle over Educational Economy in England," *New Republic*, May 10, 1922.

153. "The Training of Teachers," *Manchester Guardian*, January 18, 1924.

154. "Next Steps in Education," *Manchester Guardian*, Feburary 16, 1924.

155. "The New Direction in Education," *Manchester Guardian*, May 6, 1924.

156. "The Next Step in Education: The Case for Raising the School Age," *Manchester Guardian*, June 24, 1924.

157. "Workers Education Association," *Manchester Guardian*, July 11, 1924.

158. "Scholarships to Universities," *Manchester Guardian*, September 19, 1924 (leader).

159. "Adult Education in England," *New Republic*, November 19, 1924.

160. "Staff Work in Education," *Manchester Guardian*, November 20, 1924.

161. "The Health of the School Child," *Manchester Guardian*, December 19, 1924.

162. "Adolescent Education," *Manchester Guardian*, January 16, 1925.

163. "The Training of Teachers," *Manchester Guardian*, May 21, 1925.

164. "A Danger to Education," *Manchester Guardian*, October 29, 1925.

165. "Circular 1, 371," *Manchester Guardian*, December 3, 1925.

166. "The Threat to Education," *Manchester Guardian*, January 6, 1926 (leader).

167. "A Circular and a Memorandum," *Manchester Guardian*, January 18, 1926 (leader).

168. "That 'Widespread Dismay,'" *Manchester Guardian*, February 9, 1926 (leader).

169. "Internationalism in Education," *Manchester Guardian*, March 5, 1926 (leader).

170. "Education and Economy," *Manchester Guardian*, March 17, 1926 (leader).

171. "Sir Michael Sadler on Elementary Education," *Manchester Guardian*, June 1, 1926 (leader).

172. "Essential Points in Education," *Manchester Guardian*, July 24, 1926 (leader).

173. "Gaps in the Ladder," *Manchester Guardian*, November 26, 1926 (leader).

174. "Youth and Education," *Manchester Guardian*, December 16, 1926 (leader).

175. "Grading English Education," *Manchester Guardian*, January 3, 1927 (leader).

176. "Lord Eustace Percy Again," *Manchester Guardian*, January 5, 1927 (leader).

177. "Education and Politics," *Manchester Guardian*, January 8, 1927 (leader).

178. "Education Issues in 1927," *Manchester Guardian*, January 27, 1927 (leader).

179. "Circular 1,388," *Manchester Guardian*, February 15, 1927 (leader).

180. "Pestalozzi," *Manchester Guardian*, February 17, 1927 (leader).

181. "Secondary Education," *Manchester Guardian*, February 17, 1927.

182. "The Outlook in Education," *Manchester Guardian*, March 25, 1927 (leader).

183. "Equality in Education," *Manchester Guardian*, April 27, 1927 (leader).

184. "Progress in Education," *Manchester Guardian*, June 9, 1927 (leader).

185. "An Ungrateful Rejoinder," *Manchester Guardian*, June 14, 1927 (leader).

186. "The Education of the Adolescent," *The Highway*, July 1927.

187. "The Next Move in Education," *Manchester Guardian*, September 28, 1927 (leader).

188. "The Outlook for Education," *Manchester Guardian*, January 11, 1928 (leader).

189. "Figures and High Spirits," *Manchester Guardian*, February 1, 1928 (leader).

190. "An Academic Romance," *Manchester Guardian*, June 23, 1928 (leader).

191. "Education in Agriculture," *Manchester Guardian*, July 23, 1928 (leader).
192. "Educating Themselves," *Manchester Guardian*, September 22, 1928 (leader).
193. "A Critical Moment in Education," *Manchester Guardian*, October 16, 1928 (leader).
194. "The Future of the WEA," *The Highway*, October 1928.
195. "Teachers in Conclave," *Manchester Guardian*, April 5, 1929 (leader).
196. "The Next Advance in Education," *Manchester Guardian*, April 26, 1929 (leader).
197. "The Future in Education," *Manchester Guardian*, June 15, 1929 (leader).
198. "The School Leaving Age," *Manchester Guardian*, July 9, 1929 (leader).
199. "The Educational Programme," *Manchester Guardian*, October 28, 1929 (leader).
200. "The Future of the WEA," *The Highway*, November 1929.
201. "The Bill this Session," *Manchester Guardian*, February 19, 1930 (leader).
202. "The Government and the School Age," *New Statesman*, February 22, 1930.
203. "The School Leaving Age Bill," *The Highway*, February 1930.
204. "The Necessity for Early Legislation," *The Schoolmaster & Woman Teachers Chronicle*, March 13, 1930.
205. "Denominational Schools," *Manchester Guardian*, April 25, 1930 (leader).
206. "The Education Bill," *Manchester Guardian*, May 30, 1930 (leader).
207. "Saving Money on Education," *Manchester Guardian*, May 10, 1932.
208. "The Government and Education," *Manchester Guardian*, September 19, 1932 (leader).
209. "New Children's Charter," *New Statesman*, October 1, 1932.
210. "Education and Economy," *Manchester Guardian*, November 28, 1932 (leader).
211. "Lord Irwin and Education," *Manchester Guardian*, January 9, 1933 (leader).
212. "Education," *Manchester Guardian*, April 21, 1933 (leader).
213. " 'Economy in Education: Panic Policy," *Manchester Guardian*, May 24, 1933.
214. " 'Economy' in Education: Admitted Needs," *Manchester Guardian*, May 25, 1933.
215. "Whither Education?" *Manchester Guardian*, July 10, 1933 (leader).

216. "Unemployment and the School Leaving Age," *New Statesman*, November 18, 1933.

217. "The 'National' Government and Education," *Manchester Guardian*, November 25, 1933 (leader).

218. "Podsnappery in Education" (WEA Presidential Address, 1933), *The Highway*, December 1933.

219. "The Educational Future," *Manchester Guardian*, June 13, 1934 (leader).

220. "The School Age," *Manchester Guardian*, July 12, 1934 (leader).

221. "Should the School-leaving Age be Raised: Is It Justifiable on Social Grounds?" *The Listener*, August 15, 1934.

222. "The Government and Education," *Manchester Guardian*, October 31, 1934 (leader).

223. "Retrospect and Renewal," *The Highway*, December 1934.

224. "A Strong Case," *Manchester Guardian*, February 21, 1935 (leader).

225. "Education Questions," *Manchester Guardian*, May 1, 1935.

226. "The Progress of Education," *Manchester Guardian*, May 2, 1935.

227. "Policy in Education," *Manchester Guardian*, June 19, 1935 (leader).

228. "Problems of Education," *Manchester Guardian*, August 17, 1935 (leader).

229. "A Question of Brass Tacks," *Manchester Guardian*, October 31, 1935 (leader).

230. "The Government and Education," *New Statesman*, December 14, 1935.

231. "The Educational Outlook," *Manchester Guardian*, December 16, 1935 (leader).

232. "Break Down the Walls," *Labour*, January 1936.

233. "Educational Reforms," *Manchester Guardian*, January 7, 1936 (leader).

234. "A Review of our Policy," *The Highway*, February 1936.

235. "The Educational Bill," *Manchester Guardian*, February 3, 1936 (leader).

236. "Raising the School Age?" *Manchester Guardian*, February 13, 1936 (leader).

237. "Education Bill Prospects," *Manchester Guardian*, March 12, 1936 (leader).

238. "The Education Bill Again," *Manchester Guardian*, May 25, 1936 (leader).

239. "The Realities of Democracy," *The Highway*, January 1937.

240. "Schools and the Child," *Manchester Guardian*, January 14, 1937 (leader).

241. "Teachers and Physical Education," *Manchester Guardian*, February 19, 1937 (leader).

242. "Secondary Education for All," *Manchester Guardian*, April 2, 1937 (leader).

243. "A Forward Policy," *Manchester Guardian*, June 19, 1937 (leader).
244. "Our Schools," *Manchester Guardian*, August 17, 1937 (leader).
245. "The Administration of the Education Act, 1936," *The Highway*, November 1937.
246. "The Maturity of the Movement," *The Highway*, January 1938.
247. "Needs in Education," *Manchester Guardian*, January 11, 1938 (leader).
248. "The Child and the School," *Manchester Guardian*, April 22, 1938 (leader).
249. "The School Age," *Manchester Guardian*, May 27, 1938 (leader).
250. "Educational Policy," *Manchester Guardian*, June 9, 1938 (leader).
251. "Educational Outlook," *Manchester Guardian*, July 11, 1938 (leader).
252. "Education and its Aim," *Manchester Guardian*, August 25, 1938 (leader).
253. "Raising the School Age," *Manchester Guardian*, October 8, 1938 (leader).
254. "The Spens Report," *Manchester Guardian*, December 30, 1938 (leader).
255. "The Work of Secondary Schools," *Manchester Guardian*, January 2, 1939 (leader).
256. "The Scope of the Subject," *The Highway*, April 1939.
257. "Education in Time of Crisis," *Manchester Guardian*, August 17, 1939 (leader).
258. "The Problem of the Children," *Manchester Guardian*, January 5, 1940 (leader).
259. "Issues in Education," *Manchester Guardian*, March 8, 1940 (leader).
260. "Educational Policy," *Manchester Guardian*, October 23, 1940 (leader).
261. "A False Expedient," *Manchester Guardian*, December 21, 1940 (leader).
262. "Ends and Means in Education," *Manchester Guardian*, April 2, 1941 (leader).
263. "A Message From Our President," *The Highway*, November 1941.
264. "Education," *Manchester Guardian*, November 11, 1942 (leader).
265. "The Schools," *Manchester Guardian*, December 8, 1942 (leader).
266. "Educational Pillars," *Manchester Guardian*, December 16, 1942 (leader).
267. "The 'Public Schools,' " *Manchester Guardian*, February 5, 1943 (leader).
268. "Fee-charging Schools," *Manchester Guardian*, February 16, 1943 (letter to editor).
269. "An Urgent Problem," *Manchester Guardian*, February 18, 1943 (leader).

270. "The Schools," *Manchester Guardian*, March 29, 1943 (leader).
271. "The Study of Education," *Manchester Guardian*, May 7, 1943 (leader).
272. "Time for Action," *Manchester Guardian*, June 11, 1943 (leader).
273. "A Great Advance," *Manchester Guardian*, July 17, 1943 (leader).
274. "Education," *Manchester Guardian*, August 11, 1943 (leader).
275. "The Norwood Report," *Manchester Guardian*, August 23, 1943 (leader).
276. "The Fleming Report," *Manchester Guardian*, August 27, 1943 (leader).
277. "The Open Door," *Manchester Guardian*, October 5, 1943 (leader).
*278. "Problem of the Public Schools," *Political Quarterly*, 14 (October 1943) (also printed as pamphlet, WEA, 1944).
279. "The Opportunity," *Manchester Guardian*, November 4, 1943 (leader).
280. "The Education Bill," *Manchester Guardian*, November 30, 1943 (leader).
281. "A Great Bill," *Manchester Guardian*, December 17, 1943 (leader).
282. "The Education Bill," *Manchester Guardian*, January 22, 1944 (leader).
283. "The Universities," *Manchester Guardian*, March 14, 1944 (leader).
284. "The Education Bill," *Manchester Guardian*, April 15, 1944 (leader).
285. "The Teachers," *Manchester Guardian*, May 4, 1944 (leader).
286. "Educational Freedom," *Manchester Guardian*, June 15, 1944 (leader).
287. "The Teachers," *Manchester Guardian*, July 21, 1944 (leader).
288. "William Temple and the W.E.A.," *Manchester Guardian*, October 31, 1944.
289. "Presidential Address" (WEA, 1944), *The Highway*, January 1945.
290. "The Universities," *Manchester Guardian*, January 9, 1945 (leader).
291. "Education," *Manchester Guardian*, March 19, 1945 (leader).
292. "Starting-Point," *Manchester Guardian*, March 31, 1945 (leader).
293. "Fees or Free?" *Manchester Guardian*, May 7, 1945 (leader).
294. "A Case for Drive," *Manchester Guardian*, September 24, 1945 (leader).
295. "Education," *Manchester Guardian*, November 13, 1945 (leader).
296. "Adult Education," *Manchester Guardian*, January 4, 1946 (leader).
297. "Adult Education," *Manchester Guardian*, April 13, 1946 (leader).

298. "The Leaving Age," *Manchester Guardian*, May 15, 1946 (leader).
299. "Transition," *Manchester Guardian*, November 20, 1946 (leader).
300. "New Order," *Manchester Guardian*, April 1, 1947 (leader).
301. "A New Service," *Manchester Guardian*, July 14, 1947 (leader).
302. "Programme for Action," *The Highway*, November 1947.
303. "The Universities," *Manchester Guardian*, December 4, 1948 (leader).
304. "Education Cuts," *Manchester Guardian*, December 12, 1951 (leader).
305. "Mansbridge," *The Highway*, November 1952.
306. "The Moral of It All," *The Highway*, April 1953.

GENERAL POLITICAL ARTICLES

307. "Municipal Enterprise in Germany," *Economic Review*, October 1910.
308. "The Philosophy of Power I," *Athenaeum*, April 1917.
309. "The Philosophy of Power II," *Athenaeum*, May 1917.
310. "The Sickness of an Acquisitive Society," *Hibbert Journal*, April 1919.
311. "The Inequality of Incomes," *The Highway*, January 1921.
312. "Two Warnings," *The Highway*, March 1923.
313. "British Labor Looks Ahead," *New Republic*, August 22, 1923.
314. "What England is Thinking," *New Republic*, November 7, 1923.
315. "What British Labor Wants," *New Republic*, November 28, 1923.
316. "In Memoriam: The Master of Balliol," *The Highway*, June 1924.
317. "The British Election and After," *New Republic*, November 5, 1924.
318. "L. T. Hobhouse: Intellectual Power and Moral Enthusiasm," *Manchester Guardian*, July 29, 1931.
319. "Stray Impressions from Moscow," *The Highway*, October 1931.
**320. "The Choice Before the Labor Party," *Political Quarterly*, 3 (July-September 1932) (reprinted as a pamphlet by the Socialist League, 1933).
321. "The Choice Before the Labour Movement: Mr. Tawney's Answer," *Political Quarterly*, October-December 1932.
322. "Labour Honours," *New Statesman*, June 22, 1935.
323. "Death of Sir Henry Hadow," *Manchester Guardian*, April 10, 1937.
324. "An Indictment of the Government's Foreign Policy," *Manchester Guardian*, March 23, 1938 (long letter to editor).
325. "Chamberlain-Hitler Negotiation: Why Was Russia Ignored and Parliament Not Consulted?" *Manchester Guardian*, October 17, 1938 (long letter to editor).
326. "The Future of Society," *New Statesman*, November 26, 1938.
327. "Englishmen, What Now?" *Living Age*, December 1938.
328. "Two Peoples," *Manchester Guardian*, October 6, 1942 (leader).

**329. "Beatrice Webb 1858-1943," *Proceedings of the British Academy*, 29 (1943).

330. "U.S.A." *The Highway*, April 1943.

331. "Harold Clay—An Appreciation," *The Highway*, January 1945.

332. "Some Thoughts on the Election," *The Highway*, October 1945.

333. "A Temple Memorial," *Manchester Guardian*, February 12, 1946 (leader).

334. "In Memory of Sidney Webb," *Economica*, N. S., 14 (November 1947).

335. "Why I am a Socialist," *Labour Forum*, April-June 1948.

336. "The Way Ahead: First Thoughts on Labour's Programme," *Socialist Commentary*, May 1949.

337. "Mr. E. S. Cartwright," *The Highway*, October 1950.

*338. "British Socialism Today," *Socialist Commentary*, June 1952.

339. "Economy," *Manchester Guardian*, February 21, 1953 (leader).

340. "Purging the Socialists?" *New Statesman*, September 19, 1953 (letter to editor).

341. "A. P. Wadsworth: A Memory of Fifty Years," *Manchester Guardian*, November 5, 1956.

342. "A. P. Wadsworth," *The Highway*, January 1957.

343. "G. D. H. Cole: A Tribute," *Quarterly Bulletin of the International Society for Socialist Studies*, March 1959.

ARTICLES ON HISTORY

344. "The Assessment of Wages in England by the Justices of the Peace" (two articles), *Vierteljahrschrift fur Sozial und Wirtschaftsgeschichte*, 1913, pp. 307-337, 533-564. Reprinted in W. E. Minchinton, ed. *Wage Regulation in Pre-industrial England*, Newton Abbot, David and Charles, 1972.

*345. "John Ruskin," *The Observer*, February 9, 1919.

346. "History and Education," *Manchester Guardian*, November 17, 1923.

347. "Obituary: George Unwin," *Economic Journal*, 35 (March 1925).

348. "The Industrial Revolution," *The Highway*, January 1929.

349. "Modern Capitalism" (Studies in Bibliography, II) *Economic History Review*, 4 (October 1933).

350. "The Study of Economic History," *Economica*, 13 (February 1933).

351. "Obituary: Vladimir J. Gelesnov," *Economic Journal*, 43 (December 1933).

352. "Obituary: J. M. Kulisher (1878-1933)," *Economic Journal*, 44 (March 1934).

353. "Obituary: Vladimir Dehn (1867-1933)," *Economic Journal*, 44 (March 1934).

354. "An Occupational Census of the Seventeenth Century (with A. J. Tawney), *Economic History Review*, 5. (October 1935).
355. "J. A. Hobson, 1858-1940," in *Dictionary of National Biography*.
356. "Eileen Postan (Power), 1889-1940," in *Dictionary of National Biography*.
357. "Obituary: Prof. W. R. Scott," *Economic History Review*, 10 (November 1940).
358. "Obituary: Dr. Eileen Power," *Economic History Review*, 10 (November 1940).
359. "The Rise of the Gentry, 1558-1640," *Economic History Review*, 11 (1941); Japanese edition, 1957.
360. "The Abolition of Economic Controls, 1918-21," *Economic History Review*, 13 (1943).
361. "Istoriia," *Britanski Soyuznik*, July 15, 1945.
362. "A History of Capitalism" (Essays in Bibliography and Criticism), *Economic History Review*, 2d ser., 2 (1950).
363. "The Rise of the Gentry: A Postscript," *Economic History Review*, 2d ser., 7 (August 1954).
364. "The Eastland Trade," *Economic History Review*, 2d ser., 12 (December 1959).
365. "J. L. Hammond, 1872-1949," *Proceedings of the British Academy*, 46 (1960).

ARTICLES ON INDUSTRY

366. "Impressions of Toynbee Hall," *Toynbee Hall Twentieth Annual Report*, 1904.
367. "Employment Exchanges," *Westminster Gazette*, November 7, 1906.
368. "Labour Exchanges and Casual Labour," *Glasgow Herald*, November 16, 1907.
369. "Unemployment and Its Remedies: The Example of Germany," *Morning Post*, October 27, 28, 29, 31, 1908.
370. "Report of the Central Unemployed Body for London," *Economic Journal*, 18 (December 1908).
371. "Report of the Fair Wages Committee," *Economic Journal*, March 1909.
372. "The Theory of Pauperism," *Sociological Review* (Manchester), October 1909.
373. "The Departmental Committee on Half-Time," *The Highway*, October 1909.
374. "Report of a Visit to Germany made by Members of the Rochdale Branch," *The Highway*, March 1910.
375. " 'Blind Alley' Occupations and the Way Out," *Women's Industrial News*, October 1910.

376. "The Halving of Boy and Girl Labour," *The Crusade*, June 1911.
377. "Economics of Boy Labour," *Economic Journal*, December 1911.
378. "Shop Stewards Movement: I. How It Arose," *Manchester Guardian*, February 7, 1919.
379. "Shop Stewards Movement: II. Its Future," *Manchester Guardian*, February 8, 1919.
380. "Reorganisation of the Building Industry," *Manchester Guardian*, August 18, 1919.
381. "The Coal Industry Commission and the Consumer," *Contemporary Review*, August 1919.
382. "Fixing Post War Wages," *Manchester Guardian*, October 1, 1919.
383. "Industry and Politics" (text of Tawney speech) *The Challenge*, December 19, 1919.
384. "The Case for the Consumer." *The Guildsman*, December 1919.
385. "The Recent Proposals for the Nationalisation of the British Coal Industry" (address at Clark College, Worcester, Mass.), *Clark College Record*, 15, (1920).
386. "The British Coal Industry and the Question of Nationalisation," *Quarterly Journal of Economics*, 25 (November 1920).
387. "The British Coal Situation," *New Republic*, November 10, 1920.
388. "The Unemployment Crisis in England," *New Republic*, February 23, 1921.
389. "The Miner's Plan: I. Not Revolutionary and Hardly Novel," *Manchester Guardian*, May 9, 1921.
390. The Miner's Plan: II. Different Kinds of Fooling," *Manchester Guardian*, May 10, 1921.
391. "Industry and the Expert," *The Guildsman*, June 1921.
392. "The Coal Problem: II," *Contemporary Review*, June 1921.
393. "End of the Struggle in the British Coal Industry," *New Republic*, August 24, 1921.
394. "The Minimum Wage in Great Britain," *New Republic*, June 28, 1922.
395. "A Study of Juvenile Unemployment," *Manchester Guardian*, April 8, 1925.
396. "Problem of the British Coal Industry," *New Republic*, April 7, 1926.
397. "Coal Industry Must Be Reorganized," *Manchester Guardian*, June 1, 1926.
398. "Reorganising the Mines," *Manchester Guardian*, June 4, 1926.
399. "How the Strike Came: A Day to Day Diary of the Negotiations," *Labour Magazine*, June 1926.
400. "The Twilight of the Consumer," *Manchester Guardian*, January 27, 1927 (leader).
401. "The Problem of the Coal Industry," *Encyclopedia of the Labour Movement*, I, 1928.

402. "Some Suggestions for Students" (on the Coal Industry), *The Highway*, January 1928.
403. "Juvenile Unemployment," *Manchester Guardian*, September 5, 1933 (leader).
404. "Education to Meet the Modern Needs of Trade Unions," *The Highway*, June 1949.

ARTICLES ON RELIGION

405. "The Daily News Religious Census of London," *Toynbee Record*, March 1904.
406. Editorial (Role of the Church in the Industrial Society), *Morning Post*, October 8, 1908.
407. "The Enabling Bill," *Manchester Guardian*, June 7, 1919.
408. "The Army and Religion," *The Challenge*, October 10, 1919 (Symposium with F. R. Barry and H. F. Houlder).
409. "Church and Industry," *New Republic*, April 27, 1921.
410. "Religion and Business," *Hibbert Journal*, October 1922.
411. "Religious Thought on Social and Economic Questions in Sixteenth and Seventeenth Centuries," *Journal of Political Economy*, 31 (August, October, December, 1923). Three articles.
412. "The Churches and Social Ethics," *New Republic*, May 21, 1924.
413. "Industry and Property," *The Pilgrim*, October 1924.
414. "Protecting Our Churches," *Manchester Guardian*, December 4, 1925 (leader).
415. "Puritanism and Capitalism," *New Republic*, May 12, 1926.
416. "Irreligion of Capitalism," *New Republic*, May 19, 1926.
417. "God and Mammon," *Manchester Guardian*, July 23, 1931.
418. "William Temple—An Appreciation," *The Highway*, January 1945.
419. "Religion and Economic Life," *Times Literary Supplement*, January 6, 1956.

ARTICLES ON WAR

420. "The *Personnel* of the New Armies," *The Nation* (London), February 27, 1915.
**421. "The Attack," *Westminster Gazette*, October 24, 25, 1916.
**422. "Some Reflections of a Soldier," *The Nation* (London), October 21, 1916. Reprinted in Guy Chapman, *Vain Glory*, London, Cassell, 1968.
423. "Sword of the Spirit," *Athenaeum*, December 1917. Reprinted as pamphlet, 1918.
424. "Make the Children Pay for the War," *The Highway*, February 1921.
425. "The WEA in Wartime," *The Highway*, November 1939.

**426. "Why Britain Fights," *New York Times*, July 21, 1940. Expanded into "Macmillan War Pamphlet," 1941. Reprinted in *International Conciliation* (Carnegie Endowment for International Peace), September 1940; also as a pamphlet *Why the British People Fight*, New York, Workers' Education Bureau Press, 1940.

427. "Labour in the War," *The Highway*, January 1941.

III. BOOK REVIEWS BY TAWNEY

(Title of the book being reviewed is given first, followed by the name of the book's author, then the journal where Tawney's review appeared)

428. *La Révolution Industrielle aux dix-huitième siècle* by Paul Mantoux, *Economic Journal*, September 1906.

429. *Railway Nationalization* by Clement Edwards, *Sociological Review*, January 1908.

430. *An Outline of English Local Government* by Edward Jenks, *Sociological Review*, January 1908.

431. *West Ham: A Study in Social and Industrial Problems* by F. G. Howarth and Mona Wilson, *Sociological Review*, July 1908.

432. *Riches and Poverty* by L. G. Chiozza Money, *Sociological Review*, January 1910.

433. *The Working Life of Shop Assistants* by J. Hallsworth and R. J. Davies, *The Highway*, October 1910.

434. *Norwich: A Social Study* by C. B. Hawkins, *The Highway*, January 1911.

435. *What Is and What Might Be* by Edmond Holmes, *Morning Post*, July 31, 1911.

436. *The Labour Exchange in Relation to Boy and Girl Labour* by F. Keeling, and *Juvenile Labour Exchanges' After Care* by A. Greenwood, *Economic Journal*, December 1911.

437. *The Liverpool Docks Problem* by R. Williams, *Economic Journal*, June 1912.

438. *University Tutorial Classes* by A. Mansbridge, *Manchester Guardian*, November 17, 1913.

439. *How the Labourer Lives* by S. Rowntree and M. Kendall, *Economic Journal*, March 1914.

440. *The Town Labourer, 1760-1832* by J. L. and Barbara Hammond, *The Times Literary Supplement*, July 19, 1917.

441. *The Town Labourer 1760-1832* by J. L. and Barbara Hammond, *The Challenge*, October 19, 1917.

442. *Comparative Education* ed. by Peter Sandeford, *Manchester Guardian*, December 6, 1918.

443. *The History of an East Anglian Soke* by M. C. Hoare, *History*, April 1919.

444. *Syndicalism and Philosophic Realism* by J. W. Scott, *Manchester Guardian*, May 12, 1919.

445. *A Pioneer in Working-Class Education* by A. Mansbridge, *Manchester Guardian*, August 17, 1920.

446. *Cambridge Essays on Adult Education* by R. St. John Parry, *Manchester Guardian*, October 7, 1920.

447. *Commerce and Industry 1815-1914* ed. by W. Page, *History*, January 1921.

448. *The War and Social Reform* by B. Worsfield, and *Economic Phenomena Before and After War* by S. Secerov, *History*, January 1921.

449. *The Inequality of Incomes* by Hugh Dalton, *The Highway*, January 1921.

450. *Christian Socialism* by Charles Raven, *Nation and Athenaeum*, March 12, 1921.

451. *The Yorkshire Woollen and Worsted Industries* by H. Heaton, and *The History of the Woollen and Worsted Industries* by E. Lipson, *History*, October 1921.

452. *The Early English Cotton Industry* by G. W. Daniels, *History*, January 1922.

453. *The Place of Rye in the History of English Food* by Sir W. Ashley, *Working Life of Women in the Eighteenth Century* by A. Clark, and *Introduction to Rural History* by G. Guest, *History*, October 1922.

454. *The Enclosure and Redistribution of Our Land* by W. H. R. Curtler, *History*, October 1922.

455. *If Britain Is To Live* by N. Angell, and *The Decay of Capitalist Civilization* by Beatrice and Sidney Webb, *The Highway*, March 1923.

456. *The English Village: The Origin and Decay of Its Community* by H. Peake, *History*, July 1923.

457. *The British Coal-mining Industry during the War* by R. A. S. Redmayne, *Economica*, November 1923.

458. *Histoire des Corporations de Métiers* by E. Martin Saint-Léon, *Economic Journal*, December 1923.

459. *Capital and Steam-Power, 1750-1800* by John Lord, *The Romance of the Law Merchant* by W. A. Brewer, and *The Historical Foundations of Modern Company Law* by R. R. Formoy, *Economica*, January 1924.

460. *Labour in the Coal-mining Industry* by G. D. H. Cole, *Economica*, June 1924.

461. *The Fall of the Monasteries and the Social Changes in England*

leading up to the Great Revolution by S. B. Liljegren, *English Historical Review*, January 1925.

462. *Samuel Oldknow and the Arkwrights* by G. Unwin, *English Historical Review*, January 1925.

463. *L'Angleterre* by André Siegfried, *New Republic*, February 18, 1925.

464. *Legal Foundations of Capitalism* by John R. Commons, *The Oil Trusts and Anglo-American Relations* by E. H. Davenport and S. R. Cooke, and *The Politics of Oil* by R. Page Arnot, *Economica*, March 1925.

465. *Iron and Steel in the Industrial Revolution* by T. S. Ashton, *English Historical Review*, October 1925.

466. *The Rise of the Irish Linen Industry* by Conrad Gill, *Economica*, November 1925.

467. *The Medieval Village* by G. G. Coulton, *Manchester Guardian*, January 12, 1926.

468. *From Nursery School to University* by J. R. McDonald, *Manchester Guardian*, May 24, 1926.

469. *H. G. Wells Educationist* by F. H. Doughty, *Manchester Guardian*, December 16, 1926.

470. *Procrustes, or the Future of English Education* by M. Alderton Pink, *Manchester Guardian*, December 28, 1926.

471. *Les Origines du capitalisme moderne* by H. Sée, and *La France économique et sociale au xviii siècle* by H. Sée, *Economic History Review*, January 1927.

472. *Wages and the State* by E. M. Burns, *Economica*, March 1927.

473. *Études sur les Colonies Merchandes Meridionales (Portugais, Espagnols, Italiens) à Anvers de 1488 à 1567* by J. A. Goris, *English Historical Review*, January 1927.

474. *The English Brass and Copper Industries to 1800* by H. Hamilton, *English Historical Review*, April 1927.

475. *The Nation's Schools: Their Task and Importance* by H. Bompas Smith, *Manchester Guardian*, May 2, 1927.

476. *L'Agriculture et les Classes Paysannes: La Transformation de la Propriété dans le Haut Poitou au xvi Siècle* by P. Raveau, *English Historical Review*, July 1927.

477. *The Foundations of Education* ed. by J. J. Findlay, *Manchester Guardian*, August 12, 1927.

478. *The British Coal Dilemma* by I. Libben and H. Everett, *New Republic*, December 14, 1927.

479. *Social Theories of the Middle Ages, 1200-1500* by Bede Jarett, *Economica*, December 1927.

480. *The Schools of England* ed. by J. Dover Wilson, *Manchester Guardian*, May 31, 1928.

481. *The Account Book of a Kentish Estate, 1616-1704* ed. by E. C. Lodge, *English Historical Review*, January 1929.

482. *Thomas Delaney: le Roman des Métiers au Temps de Shakespeare* by A. Chevally, *History*, January 1929.

483. *Calendar of the Patent Rolls preserved in the Public Record Office, Edward VI*, Vols. IV, V, and *Alderman Cockayne's Project and the Cloth Trade* by A. Friis, *Economic History Review*, January 1929.

484. *Education for Commerce and Industry* by Anonymous, *Manchester Guardian*, January 10, 1929.

485. *Imperialism and Civilization* by Leonard Woolf, *Economica*, April 1929.

486. *The English Craft Guilds: Studies in Their Progress and Decline* by S. Kramer, *History*, October 1929.

487. *Jacob Fugger der Reiche* by J. Streider, and *La Vie Économique de la France sous la Monarchie Censitaire, 1815-48* by H. Sée, *Economic History Review*, January 1930.

488. *The Coal Industry of the Eighteenth Century* by T. S. Ashton and J. Sykes, *Economic Journal*, March 1930.

489. *Wealth and Life* by J. A. Hobson, *Political Quarterly*, April 1930.

490. *The Seventeenth Century* by G. N. Clark, *History*, October 1930.

491. *Economic Causes of the Reformation in England* by O. A. Marti, *English Historical Review*, January 1931.

492. *Mémoires et Documents pour servir à l'Histoire du Commerce et de l'Industrie en France* ed. by J. Hayem, *Economic History Review*, January 1931.

493. *God and Mammon* by J. A. Hobson, *Manchester Guardian*, July 23, 1931.

494. *Les Origines Historiques des Problèmes Économiques Actuels* by H. Hauser, *Economic History Review*, April 1932.

495. *The Capital Question of China* by Lionel Curtis, *New Statesman and Nation*, July 23, 1932.

496. *Manchuria, Cradle of Conflict* by O. Lattimore, *New Statesman and Nation*, October 29, 1932.

497. *William Penn, Quaker and Pioneer* by Bonamy Dobree, *New Statesman and Nation*, November 26, 1932.

498. *The Superlative Prodigall: A Life of Thomas Bushell* by J. M. Gough, and *The Inhabitants of London in 1638* ed. by T. C. Dale, *History*, January 1933.

499. *Les Caractères Originaux de l'Histoire Rurale Française* by M. Bloch, *Economic History Review*, April 1933.

500. *The Nation at School* by F. S. Marvin, *Manchester Guardian*, October 23, 1933.

501. *American Economic Thought in the Seventeenth Century* by E. A. J. Johnson, *History*, March 1934.

502. *A Study of History*, Vols 1-3 by A. Toynbee, *International Affairs*, January-February 1935.

503. *England in the Reign of Charles II* by D. Ogg, *Economic History Review*, April 1935.

**504. *Christianity and the Social Revolution* ed. by K. Polanyi, J. Needham, C. Raven, and J. MacMurray, *New Statesman and Nation*, November 9, 1935.

505. *Répertoire critique des Cahiers de Doléances pour les États généraux de 1789, Cahiers de la Révolution Française* ed. by B. F. Hyslop, and *La Directoire du II Brumaire an IV au 18 Fructidor an V* by A. Mathiez, *Economic History Review*, April 1936.

506. *Rural Weaving and Merchant Employers in a North-China District* by H. D. Fong, and *L'industrie textile à domicile dans L'Inde moderne* by B. V. Keskar, *Economic History Review*, April 1936.

507. *Full Stature* by H. G. Stead, *Manchester Guardian*, June 5, 1936.

508. *Commons Debates 1621* ed. by W. Notestein et al., *Political Quarterly*, October-December 1936.

509. *An Historical Geography of England Before 1800* ed. by H. C. Darby, *Economica*, November 1936.

510. *History of Parliament: Biographies of the Members of the Commons House, 1439-1509* by J. C. Wedgwood, *Political Quarterly*, July-September 1937.

511. *The New Social Order in China* by T'ang Leang-li, *Politica*, September 1937.

512. *Robert Loder's Farm Accounts, 1610-1620* ed. by G. E. Fussell, *History*, December 1937.

513. *The German Universities and National Socialism* by E. Y. Hartshorne, Jr., *Political Quarterly*, January-March 1938.

514. *The Ordinance Book of the Merchants of the Staple* ed. by E. E. Rich, *Economic History*, February 1938.

515. *An Inspector's Treatment* by F. H. Spencer, *Manchester Guardian*, March 1, 1938.

516. *The Educational Needs of the 14-15 Group* by A. Greenough, *Manchester Guardian*, July 26, 1938.

517. *Civilisation: The Next Step* by C. Delisle Burns, *New Statesman and Nation*, November 26, 1938.

518. *The Charity School Movement* by M. G. Jones, *Economic History Review*, May 1939.

519. *Education in Pacific Countries* by F. M. Keesing, *International Affairs*, May-June 1939.

520. *The Diary of John Milward Esq. Member of Parliament for Derbyshire, September, 1666, to May, 1668, History of Parliament: Register of the Ministers and of the Members of Both Houses* ed. by C. Robbins, *Political Quarterly*, October-December 1939.

521. *A Study of History*, Vols. 4-6 by A. Toynbee, *International Affairs*, November-December 1939.

522. *Gladstone and the Irish Nation* by J. L. Hammond, and *The*

Pastoral Heritage of Britain by E. H. Carrier, *Economic History Review*, February 1940.

523. *The Agricultural Revolution in Norfolk* by N. Riches, *History*, March 1940.

524. *Unser Kampf: Our Struggle* by Sir Richard Acland, *Manchester Guardian*, March 5, 1940.

525. *Newcastle-under-Lyme in Tudor and Early Stuart Times* by T. Pape, *English Historical Review*, April 1940.

526. *Barbarians and Philistines: Democracy and the Public Schools* by T. C. Worsley, *Manchester Guardian*, September 3, 1940.

527. *Left-wing Democracy in the English Civil War* by D. W. Petegorsky, *Manchester Guardian*, December 31, 1940.

528. *Labour in the War* by John Price, *The Highway*, January 1941.

529. *The Judgment of the Nations* by C. Dawson, *Manchester Guardian*, March 24, 1943.

530. *Education for a World Adrift* by Sir Richard Livingstone, *Manchester Guardian*, April 7, 1943.

531. *The English People* by D. W. Brogan, *The Observer*, June 6, 1943.

532. *Policy and Progress in Secondary Education 1902-1942* by J. Graves, *Manchester Guardian*, October 8, 1943.

533. *Towards a New Aristocracy* by F. C. Happold, *Manchester Guardian*, October 27, 1943.

534. *A Student's View of the Universities* by B. Simon, *Manchester Guardian*, December 15, 1943.

535. *Freedom in Education* by E. H. Partridge, *Manchester Guardian*, December 22, 1943.

536. *Red Brick and These Vital Days* by Bruce Truscot, *Manchester Guardian*, June 27, 1945.

537. *Adult Education in New Zealand* by A. B. Thompson, *Manchester Guardian*, November 7, 1945.

538. *About Education* by C. E. M. Joad, *Manchester Guardian*, November 14, 1945.

539. *Aspects of British Economic History, 1918-1925* by A. C. Pigou, *Political Quarterly*, July-September 1947.

540. *Acres and People, The Eternal Problem of China and India* by E. S. Wilcox, *International Affairs*, January 1948.

541. *The First Europe* by C. Delisle Burns, *Observer*, January 11, 1948.

542. *The Social Structure in Caroline England* by D. Mathew, *Manchester Guardian*, March 23, 1948.

543. *Historical Manuscripts Commission 78, Report on the Manuscripts of the late Reginald Rowden Hastings, Esq.*, Vol. IV, ed. by F. Bickley, *Economic History Review*, 1, 2, and 3, 1949.

544. *Earth-Bound China: A Study of Rural Economy in Yunnan* by Fei Hsiao-tung and Chang Chih-i, *Manchester Guardian*, April 5, 1949.

545. *Secondary Education for All* by H. C. Dent, *Manchester Guardian*, June 24, 1949.

546. *Foundations of Tudor Policy* by W. Gordon Zeeveld, *Manchester Guardian*, July 26, 1949.

547. *Patriarcha and Other Political Works of Sir Robert Filmer* ed. by P. Laslett, *Manchester Guardian*, August 5, 1949.

548. *Michael Ernest Sadler* by Sir Michael Sadler, *Manchester Guardian*, January 10, 1950.

**549. *Problems of Social Policy* by R. M. Titmuss, *New Statesman and Nation*, April 22, 1950. In *The Attack* the essay is entitled "The War and Social Policy."

550. *Tudor England* by S. T. Bindoff, *Manchester Guardian*, May 2, 1950.

551. *The State and School Education in England And Wales 1640-60* by W. A. L. Vincent, *Manchester Guardian*, September 19, 1950.

552. *Citizenship and Social Class and Other Essays* by T. H. Marshall, *Manchester Guardian*, September 26, 1950.

553. *The Educational Thought of Matthew Arnold* by W. F. Connell, *Manchester Guardian*, January 16, 1951.

554. *The England of Elizabeth* by A. L. Rowse, *Manchester Guardian*, March 6, 1951.

555. *Landmarks in the History of Education* by T. L. Jarman, *Manchester Guardian*, October 12, 1951.

556. *Principles of Social and Political Theory* by E. Barker, *Times Literary Supplement*, February 15, 1952.

557. *Welsh Brother* by Thomas Jones, *Manchester Guardian*, March 18, 1952.

558. *The Life and Times of Sir Edwin Chadwick* by S. E. Finer, *Times Literary Supplement*, December 12, 1952.

559. *Achievement in Education* by Lynda Grier, *Manchester Guardian*, June 23, 1953.

560. *The Dilemma of Democratic Socialism: Eduard Bernstein's Challenge to Marx* by P. Gay, *Times Literary Supplement*, August 28, 1953.

561. *La Formation du Capitalisme Moderne dans la Principauté de Liège au XVIe siècle* by J. Lejeune, *Economic History Review*, V, 3, 1953.

562. *Godfrey Goodman, Bishop of Gloucester* by Geoffrey Inge Soden, *Manchester Guardian*, December 1, 1953.

*563. *Robert Owen of New Lanark* by M. I. Cole (written in 1953 for *Manchester Guardian*, but first published in *The Radical Tradition*, 1964).

564. *The Wars of Truth* by H. Baker, *Manchester Guardian*, April 2, 1954.

565. *The English People on the Eve of Colonisation, 1603-1630* by W. Notestein, *Manchester Guardian*, February 11, 1955.

566. *The Long Parliament* by M. F. Keeler, *Parliamentary Affairs*, Spring 1955.
567. *Economic Growth and Human Welfare* by E. H. Phelps Brown, *Economica*, May 1955.
568. *The Cambridge Economic History of Europe* and *Trade and Industry in the Middle Ages* ed. by E. E. Rich and M. M. Postan, *Economic Journal*, June 1955.
569. *Twentieth Century Socialism* by a study group of Socialist Union, *Socialist Commentary*, July 1956.
570. *Economic Problems of the Church* by C. Hill, *Times Literary Supplement*, February 1, 1957.
571. *War and Society in the Seventeenth Century* by G. N. Clark, *Times Literary Supplement*, August 1, 1958.
572. *The Chartist Challenge, A Portrait of George Julian Harney* by A. R. Schoyen, *Times Literary Supplement*, January 16, 1959.

NOTES

The date and place of publication of a work, and the publisher's name, are given only at its first mention. In the case of Tawney's writings, these details may be found in the Bibliography. Where an article or pamphlet by Tawney has been gathered into a book, the page reference given—to ease accessibility—is to the book version, though at first mention the original location of the article is also given.

INTRODUCTION: AN APPROACH TO TAWNEY

1. Cited in *Yorkshire Post*, November 28, 1960.

2. T. Parsons, "Richard Henry Tawney (1880-1962): In Memoriam," *American Sociological Review*, 27 (December 1962), 890.

3. Hugh Gaitskell, "An Appreciation," in Tawney, *The Radical Tradition*, ed. Rita Hinden (London, Allen and Unwin, 1964); R. H. S. Crossman, *The Charm of Politics* (London, Hamilton, 1958), p. 140; *Tribune* (London), January 26, 1962.

4. *Letters of Queen Victoria*, ed. G. E. Buckle, 2d ser., III (London, John Murray, 1928), 166; Friedrich Engels in the *Labour Standard*, July 23, 1881; cited in H. Pelling, *The Origins of the Labour Party, 1880-1900* (London, Macmillan, 1954), p. 7. Rosebery cited in J. A. Hobson, *Imperialism: A Study* (London, Allen & Unwin, 1938), p. 160; and Lord Wolseley, "Is a Soldier's Life Worth Living," *Fortnightly Review*, May 1889, p. 597.

5. Cited in E. T. Raymond, *The Man of Promise: Lord Rosebery* (London, T. F. Unwin Ltd., 1923), p. 228.

6. Alfred North Whitehead, *Adventures of Ideas* (New York, Macmillan, 1933), p. 241.

7. R. G. Collingwood, *An Autobiography* (London, Oxford University Press, 1939), p. 167.

8. Gaitskell, "An Appreciation," in *The Radical Tradition*, p. 214; Mansbridge to Tawney, August 8 [1913?], WEA Archive, London; Diary of Beatrice Webb, vol. 49, December 8, 1935 (Passfield Papers). See also Kingsley Martin, *Father Figures* (London, Hutchinson, 1966), p. 155: "He was one of the very best men alive, as well as one of the finest minds."

9. Correspondence from some of Tawney's early students exists at the WEA Archive, London. I cite from it in Chapters 1 and 2.

10. *Evening Standard* (London), January 18, 1962. Of the several varying accounts of Tawney's reply to MacDonald, Green's is probably the most accurate.

11. Crossman, *The Charm of Politics*, p. 140.

12. Cited in W. K. Hancock, *Country and Calling* (London, Faber, 1954), p. 95.

13. Lecture 1, p. 2 (Lectures on Seventeenth-Century English History; LSE).

14. A bibliography of Tawney's published writing begins on p. 287; indications of additional writings are given in the section "On Sources."

15. Sir Richard Rees, conversation with the author, London, February 14, 1970.

16. Before his eightieth-birthday dinner he wrote to William Beveridge: "Of course don't dream of coming to this ridiculous celebration. [I told] Creech Jones that I hoped that he would make the dinner a small gathering of old acquaintances. Doubtless with the best of intentions, he seems to have done the opposite; with results that I personally dislike, yet am now powerless to alter." Tawney to Beveridge, December 12, 1960 (Beveridge Collection, L.1.211 [C]; LSE).
The colleagues who sketched out his life for a birthday tribute felt it necessary at the end to "ask his pardon that we wound him with our homage and embarrass him with our praise." *R. H. Tawney: A Portrait by Several Hands* (private publication, London, 1960), p. 33.

17. See "The Webbs and Their Work," in *The Attack and Other Papers* (London, Allen & Unwin, 1953), p. 130.

18. "Sources of Tudor Economic History" (LSE-Bristol-Cranfield; LSE).

19. E.g. Lecture 1, p. 1 (Lectures on Seventeenth-Century English History; LSE).

20. Introduction to M. Beer, *History of British Socialism* (2 vols.; London, G. Bell and Sons, 1919), I, xvi.

21. The notion of "conscious responses to situations" as the substance of intellectual biography owes something to Benjamin I. Schwartz. See his "The Intellectual History of China: Preliminary Reflections," in John K. Fairbank, ed., *Chinese Thought and Institutions* (Chicago, University of Chicago Press, 1957), pp. 16ff.

22. See, e.g., the penultimate page both of *The Acquisitive Society* (Latin) and *Land and Labour in China* (German). Even Laski complained that Tawney "refers in an offhand way, and without explanation, to facts that I for one don't know—so that I don't get his point." M. Howe, ed., *Holmes-Laski Letters* (2 vols.; Cambridge, Mass., Harvard University Press, 1953), I, 738.

23. *The Attack*, p. 67.

24. *Religion and the Rise of Capitalism* (New York, Harcourt, Brace, 1926), p. 287.

25. George Orwell, *A Collection of Essays* (New York, Doubleday, 1954), pp. 175, 165.

26. *The Radical Tradition*, p. 212.

27. "Sources of Tudor Economic History" (LSE-Bristol-Cranfield; LSE).

28. Lecture VI (Lectures on Nineteenth-Century Agriculture Given at LSE; LSE).

29. "Presidential Address to L.S.E. Students Union" (Speeches on Various Occasions; LSE), pp. 23-24.

30. Professor F. J. Fisher, conversation with author, London, October 29, 1969.

31. Isaiah Berlin, "Does Political Theory Still Exist?" in Peter Laslett, ed., *Philosophy, Politics, and Society* (Oxford, Blackwell, 1962), *II, 8.*

32. Judith N. Shklar, *After Utopia* (Princeton, Princeton University Press, 1957); "Facing up to Intellectual Pluralism," in D. Spitz, ed., *Political Theory and Social Change* (New York, Atherton Press, 1967).

33. Isaiah Berlin, "Political Ideas in the Twentieth Century," *Foreign Affairs*, April 1950, pp. 359, 360.

34. Samuel H. Beer, *British Politics in the Collectivist Age* (New York, Alfred A. Knopf, 1965), p. 390.

35. *The Acquisitive Society* (New York, Harcourt, Brace, 1920), p. 2.

36. *The Acquisitive Society* (London, Collins, 1961), p. 13. This passage does not appear in the American edition.

---

1 MORAL QUEST, 1880-1914

1. Cited in *Manchester Guardian*, January 17, 1962; see too "Portrait Speech" (Speeches Given on Various Occasions; LSE), p. 2.

2. Frank Fletcher, *After Many Days* (London, R. Hale and Co., 1937), pp. 59, 90.

3. Mention of these ancestors may be found in L. S. Pressnell, *Country Banking in the Industrial Revolution* (Oxford, Oxford University Press, 1956), pp. 34-36, 56, 232, 243, 390, 399.

4. T. S. Ashton, "Richard Henry Tawney, 1880-1962," *Proceedings of the British Academy*, 1962, p. 461.

5. Tawney's studied lack of interest in India is recalled by Sir Richard Rees (conversation with author, London, February 14, 1970) and Professor M. M. Postan (conversation with author, Cambridge, Eng., February 11, 1970.) See, too, the memories of W. H. B. Court, *Scarcity and Choice in History* (London, Edward Arnold, 1970), p. 56; also see William Beveridge, *India Called Them* (London, Macmillan, 1947).

6. H. Hartley, *Balliol Men* (Oxford, Blackwell, 1963), p. 1; and Fletcher, *After Many Days*, p. 79.

7. Fletcher, *After Many Days*, p. 91. See also *Toynbee Hall Record*, March 1904, pp. 87ff, where Tawney's abhorrence of religious formalism is made clear.

8. *The Radical Tradition*, p. 168.

9. H. L. Elvin, conversation with author, London, January 28, 1971.

10. M. Richter, *The Politics of Conscience: T. H. Green and His Age* (Cambridge, Mass., Harvard University Press, 1964), p. 52.

11. M. Holroyd, *Lytton Strachey* (2 vols.; London, Heinemann, 1967), I, 161.

12. H. W. C. Davis, *A History of Balliol College* (Oxford, Blackwell, 1963), p. 222.

13. W. Beveridge, in *Balliol College Record*, 1962, p. 39; also *Beveridge Collection*, L.1.211 additional; LSE ("Notes for BBC Recording, March 13, 1962"); and H. Jones and J. H. Muirhead, *The Life and Philosophy of Edward Caird* (Glasgow, Maclehose, Jackson, and Co., 1921), p. 376.

14. "Presidential Address to LSE Students Union," undated (Speeches on Various Occasions; LSE), pp. 13-14. Information on Tawney at Balliol is contained in *Balliol College Record*, for Tawney's years there, 1899-1903, and for 1962.

15. Darwin to Marx, October 1, 1873, cited in J. Clunie, *Labour Is My Faith* (Fife, Scotland; published by author, 1954), p. 23; and Acton, cited in R. Dawson, *The Chinese Chameleon* (London, Oxford University Press, 1967), p. 77.

16. "Speech to Dervoiguilla Society, Balliol," undated (Notes for Speeches on Various Occasions; LSE).

17. Fletcher, *After Many Days*, p. 71.

18. Davis, *Balliol College*, pp. 241, 245.

19. Tawney to Beveridge, August 1903 (Beveridge Collection, L.1.211); Ashton, *British Academy*, pp. 461-462; Fletcher, *After Many Days*, p. 69; and H. L. Beales, conversation with author, London, January 25, 1971.

20. *Times*, April 30, 1918.

21. C. Booth, *Life and Labour of the People in London* (London, 1902), I, 122.

22. Lady Mary Stocks, conversation with author, London, January 23, 1971.

23. Ashton, *British Academy*, p. 462; and Tawney to Beveridge, September 8, 1903 (Beveridge Collection, L.1.211).

24. See exchange of letters between Tawney and others, *Times*, September 12, 28, 1905.

25. J. M. K. Vyvyan, conversation with author, Cambridge, Eng., February 11, 1970.

26. "Speech to Jubilee Weekend Conference of LSE, Students Union, Beatrice Webb House, February 17-19, 1956" (Notes for Speeches on Various Occasions; LSE).

27. Tawney to Beveridge, August 1903; November 7, 1903; December 15, 1903; December 28, 1903 (Bereridge Collection, L.1.211).

28. Tawney to Beveridge, September 8, 1903; August 1903 (Beveridge Collection, L.1.211).

29. *Toynbee Record*, November 1904, Calendar; *ibid.*, March 1905; and William Beveridge, *Power and Influence* (London, Hodder and Stoughton, 1953), p. 31.

30. *Toynbee Record*, March 1904; July-September 1904; March 1905. Among the memoranda on university reform, see "The Expense of Education at Oxford" (Memoranda on Education and Educational Policy; LSE); "Workpeople Demand the Appointment of a Royal Commission Upon University Education in England" (WEA). On this second item, Tawney wrote "This was drawn up sometime between 1908 and 1911 for the use of a small committee in London." Lord Morris of Grasmere, who saw much of Tawney at Balliol after World War I, recalls Tawney's hostility at that time to the elitism of Oxford students: "I used to think then that he was rather severe about the Oxford undergraduate, not being able to believe that with all his advantages he could be a serious student" (letter of Lord Morris to the author, June 7, 1971).

31. Beveridge, *Power and Influence*, pp. 23-24.

32. *Ibid.*, p. 25; and Tawney to Beveridge, November 7, 1903 (Beveridge Collection, L.1.211). On the social atmosphere of Barnett's parish of St. Jude's, with which Toynbee Hall was closely associated, see the amusing glimpses in M. T. Hodgen, *Workers Education in England and the US* (London, K. Paul, Trench, Trubner & Co., 1925), p. 106.

33. Canon Barnett, in *Toynbee Hall Twenty-Second Annual Report* (1906), p. ix.

34. Tawney, "The Daily News Religious Census of London," *Toynbee Record*, March 1904, pp. 87-88, 90-91.

35. Canon Barnett, "The Outlook," *Toynbee Record*, October 1905.

36. Recorded in *Toynbee Hall Twentieth Annual Report* (1904), p. 24.

37. "Christianity and the Social Order" (Notes for Speeches on Various Occasions; LSE).

38. *Toynbee Record*, March 1904, p. 90; *Toynbee Hall Twentieth Annual Report* (1904), p. 22.

39. Tawney to Beveridge, September 20, 1903 (Beveridge Collection, L.1.211).

40. Lady Eirene White (daughter of Tom Jones), conversation with author, London, January 28, 1971.

41. Ashton, and others, say Tawney got £50 per year, but Tawney's letter to Beveridge of October 22, 1903, says £50 for five months work (Beveridge Collection, L.1.211).

42. Tawney to Beveridge, April 29, 1907 (Beveridge Collection, L.1.211).

43. *Glasgow Herald*, November 16, 18, 19, 1907.

44. Tawney to Beveridge, April 13, 1907 (Beveridge Collection, L.1.211).

45. "Presidential Address to LSE Students Union" (Speeches on Various Occasions; LSE), p. 22.

46. A. Mansbridge, *The Trodden Road* (London, J. M. Dent & Sons, Ltd., 1940), p. 64; see also F. A. Iremonger, *William Temple* (London, Oxford University Press, 1948), p. 74 and passim.

47. "A. P. Wadsworth: A Memory of Fifty Years," written for the *Guardian*, published also in part in the *Highway*, January 1957. Much of what Tawney says about A. P. Wadsworth as an historian ("not by the beaten track of academic curricula but with the passion of an explorer") applies also to himself.

48. Sidney Ball to Barnett, March 21, 1907; Tawney's notations were added in 1914 (at WEA Archive).

49. Mary Stocks, *The Workers Educational Association* (London, Allen & Unwin, 1953), pp. 37, 43; and (for Mansbridge's words) *R. H. Tawney: A Portrait by Several Hands* (private publication; London, 1960), p. 5. Stocks calls the report "a supremely important landmark in the history of adult education."

50. Beveridge, *Power and Influence*, p. 34.

51. These exchanges are recounted in a memo from the editor of the *Guardian* to Professor Gladys Boone, October 8, 1963 (Boone Papers), which Professor Boone kindly let me see. Also, Temple to Tawney, January 27, 1908 (WEA).

52. A list of Tawney's published work, arranged chronologically and by subject, appears in the Bibliography.

53. *The Radical Tradition*, p. 82.

54. "The Outlook," *Toynbee Hall Record*, October 1905.

55. H. P. Smith, "R. H. Tawney," *Rewley House Papers*, 1962, p. 38.

56. Mansbridge to Tawney, November 26, 1907 (WEA Archive).

57. This figure is made up of 105 essays at Littleborough, 190 at Longton, 116 at Rochdale, 112 at Wrexham (Central Joint Advisory Committee on Tutorial Classes, *Second Annual Report*, 1910-1911). In 1909, Tawney remarked to Mansbridge that he was handling 150 papers a fortnight; Tawney to Mansbridge, March 30, 1909 (Rewley House Collection).

58. J. E. Henighan to Mansbridge, February 2, 1908 (WEA Archive).

59. Cited in H. P. Smith, *Rewley House Papers*, p. 40.

60. H. L. Beales, conversation with author, London, January 25, 1971.

61. These essays, with Tawney's comments, are contained in a file, "Essays 1910-1914" (WEA Archive).

62. "Rochdale No. 1 Tutorial Class:Report, 1909-1910" (Rewley House Collection), p. 2.

63. Smith, *Rewley House Papers*, p. 41.

64. J. Warburton to Tawney, October 31, 1913 (WEA Archive).

65. Tawney to Mansbridge, March 30, 1909 (Rewley House Collection).

66. Mansbridge to Tawney, January 29, 1908; March 27, 1908 (WEA Archive).

67. Stocks, *Workers Educational Association*, p. 40; the wording is slightly different in Mansbridge, *University Tutorial Classes* (London, 1913), p. 194.

68. F. Jessup, conversation with author, Oxford, February 13, 1970.

69. Tawney to Mansbridge, March 19, 1909 (Rewley House Collection).

70. Tawney to Mansbridge, February 23, 1909 (Rewley House Collection). Further instances exist of disagreements between Tawney and Mansbridge. Tawney, for example, criticized Mansbridge for what he considered Mansbridge's careless methods of financial administration. When, in 1915, Mansbridge was weighing, following an illness, whether or not he should resign as general secretary of the WEA, Tawney took the view that the WEA needed a change and that Mansbridge should go. (Mr. B. Jennings, of Leeds University, letter to the author, March 28, 1972.)

71. H. P. Smith, *Rewley House Papers*, p. 39.

72. See M. Stocks, *Ernest Simon of Manchester* (Manchester, Manchester University Press, 1963), p. 32 and passim.; also, Lady Simon, conversation with author, Manchester, January 29, 1971.

73. "Manchester WEA Speech" (Speeches on Various Occasions; LSE).

74. I have called it a diary but in fact Tawney gave it no name. Its title page merely reads: "If found, please return to R. H. Tawney, 24 Shakespeare St., C-on-M, Manchester. PRIVATE." The diary lacks pagination: therefore entries are referred to by date.

75. Diary, October 6, 1912; June 30, 1913.

76. Diary, June 3, 1912; October 16, 1912.

77. Richard Rees, conversation with author, London, February 14, 1970.

---

2 SOCIALIST POLITICS, 1915-1931

1. Diary, December 23, 1914.

2. Sir Walter Moberley, conversation with author, Oxford, January 26, 1971.

3. *Democracy or Defeat*, pp. 3-4, 5.

4. *Ibid.*, p. 8.

5. Tawney to Beveridge, December 22, 1915 (Beveridge Collection, L.1.211, Additional [A]); see also A. Toynbee, *Acquaintances* (London, Oxford University Press, 1967).

6. Lady Stocks, conversation with author, London, January 28, 1971; and Tawney to Beveridge, December 22, 1915 (Beveridge Collection L.1.211, Additional [A]).

7. Tawney to Beveridge, December 22, 1915 (Beveridge Collection, L.1.211, Additional [A]).

8. H. L. Elvin, conversation with author, London, January 28, 1971; and Lawrence Stone, conversation with author, Princeton, January 17, 1971.

9. This account based chiefly upon *The Attack*, pp. 14-20.

10. Jeannette Tawney to Beveridge (telegram), July 8, 1916 (Beveridge Collection, L.1.211, Additional [A]); and Beveridge, *Power and Influence*, p. 137.

11. "Presidential Address to LSE Students Union" (Speeches on Various Occasions; LSE).

12. Among various accounts of this incident, see the *Times*, January 25, 1962.

13. Thomas Jones, *Whitehall Diary* (London, Oxford University Press, 1969), I, 16.

14. *The Attack*, p. 20.

15. Information on Tawney's wartime meetings with Attlee comes from M. M. Postan, conversation with author, Cambridge, Eng., February 11, 1970.

16. *The Attack*, pp. 21-22, 28.

17. H. A. L. Fisher, *An Unfinished Autobiography* (London, Oxford University Press, 1940), p. 110. Important wartime advisory work by Tawney is recounted in Jones, *Whitehall Diary*, I, pp. 2-8.

18. M. Cole, *The Story of Fabian Socialism* (New York, Wiley, 1964), p. 187.

19. Coal Industry Commission, *Reports and Minutes of Evidence on the First Stage of the Inquiry*, CMD 359, 1919. The *Reports and Minutes* of the second stage, CMD 360, are paginated consecutively with those of the first stage.

20. Beatrice Webb, *Diaries, 1912-1924*, ed. M. Cole (London, Longmans, 1952), p. 161. Also see M. Cole, *Beatrice Webb* (New York, Harcourt, Brace, 1946), p. 156.

21. *Reports and Minutes*, pp. 431, 1038.

22. *Reports and Minutes*, pp. 685, 1022, 447.

23. Some of these letters are at the WEA; see, e.g., Meadowcroft to Tawney, April 1, 1912; Cryer to Tawney, October 6, 1912, June 10, 1914.

24. *Reports and Minutes*, pp. 103, 740, 163.

25. *Reports and Minutes*, p. 140.

26. *Reports and Minutes*, p. 252.

27. *Reports and Minutes*, pp. 314, 575.

28. *Reports and Minutes*, pp. 685, 1131.

29. "Presidential Address to LSE Students Union" (Speeches on Various Occasions; LSE), p. 33.

30. Tawney cited this remark when on a visit to the United States (*Amherst Student*, April 19, 1920).

31. See Ashton, *British Academy*, p. 466.

32. This and subsequent statements of Meiklejohn in the present paragraph are from a letter of Meiklejohn to Professor Boone, February 25, 1964, which Professor Boone has kindly shown me (Boone Papers).

33. Tawney's visit to Amherst is reported in some detail in the following numbers of the *Amherst Student:* April 19, 1920; April 29, 1920; May 3, 1920; May 6, 1920; May 13, 1920.

34. No. 385 in Bibliography.

35. These are the memories of John Comer, member of the faculty at Williams College when Tawney visited, in a letter to Professor Boone, September 24, 1964, which Professor Boone has kindly shown me (Boone Papers).

36. *Past and Present*, book II, chap. vi.

37. See R. C. D. Jasper, *George Bell* (London, Oxford University Press, 1967), p. 24. Also W. Temple, "The Life and Liberty Movement," *Contemporary Review*, February 1918.

38. Arnold Toynbee, *Acquaintances* (London, Oxford University Press, 1967), pp. 89-90.

39. M. B. Reckitt, conversation with author, London, September 6, 1968.

40. "A Christian World Order" (Speeches on Various Occasions; LSE).

41. G. R. Elton, *Reformation Europe, 1517-1559* (New York, Harper & Row, 1966), p. 315.

42. Iremonger, *Temple*, p. 396.

43. The Memorandum, first draft January 1937, second draft May 1937, was entitled "Church, Community, and State in relation to the Economic Order," and was done for the Research Department of the Universal Christian Council for Life and Work. An altered version, entitled "A Note on Christianity and the Social Order," appeared in *The Attack*, pp. 167-192.

44. Canon Ronald Preston, conversation with author, Manchester and London, January 27, 1971.

45. "Christianity and the Social Revolution," in *The Attack*, p. 160.

46. Canon Ronald Preston, in a conversation with the author, January 27, 1971, testified that he had studied economic history under Tawney at LSE, as a non-Christian, and as a result of the experience became a Christian and got ordained.

47. Joseph Fletcher, conversation with author, Cambridge, Mass., May 1, 1968.

48. Diary of Beatrice Webb, vol. 49, p. 210, December 8, 1935 (Passfield Papers); and M. Cole, conversation with author, London, September 9, 1966.

49. Diary of Beatrice Webb, vol. 51, p. 25, March 11, 1937; and vol. 52, p. 9, January 21, 1939 (Passfield Papers).

50. John Nef, conversation with author, Washington, D.C., January 16, 1971.

51. Laski to Holmes, September 26, 1922, in M. Dewolfe Howe, ed., *Holmes-Laski Letters*, p. 450.

52. Election Speech, February 13, 1950 (Speeches Given on Various Occasions; LSE); and letter of Tawney to Arthur Creech Jones's representative, May 12, 1929 (Creech Jones Papers). Tawney seems to be in error in recalling that he fought three elections; he apparently fought four.

53. This is the view of Patrick Gordon Walker, conversation with author, London, February 12, 1970.

54. *Diaries of Beatrice Webb 1924-1932*, ed. M. Cole, (London, Longmans, 1956), p. 2.

55. *Times*, April 24, 1922.

56. *Times*, January 14, 1924; January 2, 1926; January 9, 1925.

57. See the testimony of Ernest Barker, *Age and Youth* (London, Oxford University Press, 1953), p. 146.

58. "The Study of Economic History," *Economica*, February 1933, p. 9.

59. "Presidential Address to LSE Students Union" (Speeches on Various Occasions; LSE), p. 16. Tawney gives slightly different figures in his "Portrait Speech" (Speeches Given on Various Occasions; LSE).

60. "The Study of Economic History," p. 2; Lecture I (Lectures on Seventeenth-Century English History; LSE).

61. According to Miss Carus-Wilson, conversation with author, London, February 15, 1970.

62. Joseph Fletcher, conversation with author, Cambridge, Mass., May 1, 1968.

63. "The Study of Economic History," pp. 7-8.

64. Beales, conversation with author, London, January 25, 1971; see also Tawney to Nef, September 26, 1938 (Nef Papers).

65. *Holmes-Laski Letters*, p. 890.

66. Elvin, conversation with author, London, January 28, 1971.

67. Tawney to Laski, undated but evidently 1930; this letter is in the possession of Beales, who kindly allowed me to see and cite it.

68. *Times*, December 22, 1921.

69. Carus-Wilson, conversation with author, London, February 15, 1970; Joslin, conversation with author, Cambridge, Eng., February 11, 1970; Stone, conversation with author, Princeton, January 17, 1971.

70. *Religion and the Rise of Capitalism*, p. 278.

71. Hammond wrote of the book to Tawney in December 1932: "As for the composition of the book . . . it makes all other writers look awkward & bald, to themselves and to others"; Ashton, *British Academy*, p. 469; and W. K. Hancock, *Economic History at Oxford* (Oxford, Oxford University Press, 1946), p. 16.

72. Franklin L. Ho, in a letter dated December 8, 1961, to Dr. James C. Thomson of Harvard, who kindly allowed me to see and cite it.

73. *Land and Labour in China*, pp. 74, 194.

74. According to Postan, conversation with author, Cambridge, Eng., February 11, 1970. The League's education mission to China is examined in Ernst Neugebauer, *Anfange Paedagogischer Entwicklungshilfe Unter Dem Volkerbund In China* (Hamburg, Institut fur Asienkunde, 1971).

75. Miss Pearl Buck, conversation with author, Danby, Vermont, December 26-27, 1971; Rees, conversation with author, London, February 14, 1970; and William L. Holland, conversation with author, New York, March 29, 1972.

76. Postan, conversation with author, Cambridge, Eng., February 11, 1970; and Pearl Buck, conversation with author, Danby, Vt., December 26-27, 1971.

---

3 SQUIRE OF HOUGHTON STREET, 1932-1942

1. Thomas Jones, *A Diary With Letters, 1931-1950* (London, Oxford University Press, 1954), pp. 102-103.

2. According to Beales, conversation with author, London, January 25, 1971.

3. S. E. Koss, *Lord Haldane: Scapegoat for Liberalism* (New York, Columbia University Press, 1969), p. 231.

4. "Labour Honours," *New Statesman*, June 22, 1935.

5. *The Attack*, p. 129.

6. Diary, November (no day given), 1914.

7. "Jubilee Weekend Speech" (Notes For Speeches on Various Occasions; LSE).

8. *The Attack*, p. 127.

9. *Ibid.*, pp. 125, 130; *The Webbs in Perspective*, p. 4; *The Attack*, p. 130.

10. Diary of Beatrice Webb, vol. 52, January 21, 1938; vol. 49, December 8, 1935; vol. 51, March 11, 1937; vol. 54, July 11, 1940 (Passfield Papers); and *Diaries of Beatrice Webb, 1924-1932*, p. 127.

11. Diary of Beatrice Webb, vol. 52, January 21, 1938, p. 9 (Passfield Papers).

12. *Ibid.*, vol. 54, July 11, 1940, p. 126; and Postan, conversation with author, Cambridge, Eng., February 11, 1970.

13. Tawney to Beatrice Webb, December 6, 1942 (Passfield Papers, item II, 4, m, 141); for this passage, see below at n. 60.

14. Rees, conversation with author, London, February 14, 1970. For a tracing of the indebtedness of the use of the term "totalitarianism" to political fashion, see Ross Terrill: "Problems in Applying the Concept of Totalitarianism to the USSR," *Politics* (Sydney, Australia), May 1968.

15. Laski to Tawney, May 24, 1949 (Papers Re Proposed Biography of Sidney Webb; LSE).

16. Tawney to M. Cole, June 7, 1949; Tawney to Mrs. Barbara Drake, June 21, 1949 (Papers Re Proposed Biography of Sidney Webb; LSE); and Tawney to Wadsworth, April 4, 12, 15, 1949; Wadsworth to Tawney, April 26, May 17, August 21, 1949 (Guardian Papers).

17. Laski to Tawney, May 24, 1949 (Papers Re Proposed Biography of Sidney Webb; LSE).

18. Tawney did not continue to harbor bad feelings about Mrs. Cole. Just before the dinner marking his eightieth birthday he wrote to Creech Jones: "Has Mrs. G. D. H. Cole been asked to the dinner? If not, may I suggest that she should be? I once had a minor [bout?] with her and should not like her to think that I bore her any grudge" (Tawney to Creech Jones, November 23, 1960; Creech Jones Papers). Mrs. Cole attended the dinner.

19. H. Dalton, *The Fateful Years* (London, Muller, 1957), p. 53.

20. Rees, conversation with author, London, February 14, 1970; cf. Ashton, *British Academy*, p. 466.

21. Diary of Beatrice Webb, vol. 49, December 8, 1935, p. 208 (Passfield Papers); Tawney to Creech Jones, October 23, 1935 (Creech Jones Papers).

22. W. T. Rodgers, ed., *Hugh Gaitskell, 1906-1963* (London, Thames and Hudson, 1964), pp. 37, 51.

23. Tawney to Nef, September 26, 1938 (Nef Papers).

24. *The Radical Tradition*, pp. 212-214.

25. Rees, conversation with author, London, February 14, 1970.

26. Lady Barbara Wootton, conversation with author, London, January 27, 1971.

27. Carus-Wilson, conversation with author, London, February 15, 1970.

28. *International Affairs*, 1939, p. 804.

29. Miss Janet Wadsworth, conversation with author, Manchester, January 28, 1971.

30. This paragraph is based chiefly upon the following letters: Tawney to Nef, January 2, 1936; March 17, 1942; Nef to Tawney, March 19, 1942; Tawney to Nef, March 22, 1942; April 3, 1942 (Nef Papers).

31. See Chapter 4, note 8.

32. See, for example, Tawney to Creech Jones, August 2, 1943 (Creech Jones Papers).

33. Mr. David Ayerst, conversation with author, near Oxford, January 26, 1971.

34. "Retrospect and Renewal," *The Highway*, December 1934, p. 70.

35. "The Realities of Democracy," *The Highway*, January 1937, p. 72.

36. This and the following paragraph are based chiefly upon the memories of Dr. Ernest Green, conversation with author, near Harrowgate, January 30, 1971.

37. Nef, conversation with author, Washington, D.C., January 16, 1971.

38. As Barbara Wootton recalls, conversation with author, London, January 27, 1971.

39. On foreign policy issues, which now predominated, we find Tawney writing letters to the press (e.g., *New Statesman*, August 22, 1936). It was not a method the earlier Tawney needed to resort to.

40. Diary of Beatrice Webb, vol. 53, January 21, 1939, p. 11 (Passfield Papers).

41. A record of negotiations between Tawney and Chicago University is contained in the Nef Papers.

42. Tawney to Nef, August 22, 1940, June 8, 1940 (Nef Papers).

43. Tawney to Nef, August 22, 1940 (Nef Papers).

44. See, for example, Creech Jones to Tawney, July 23, 1940 (Creech Jones Papers).

45. Thomas Jones, *A Diary with Letters*, p. 463.

46. The exact title of Tawney's position at Washington was "Advisor on Social and Politico-Economic Affairs"; he was not given the position at the direct wish of Ernest Bevin, as is often said (Tawney to Creech Jones, August 16, 1941; Creech Jones Papers).

47. Tawney to Nef, August 18, 1941 (Nef Papers); Tawney to Crozier, September 7, 1941 (Guardian Papers); and Diary of Beatrice Webb, vol. 54, July 11, 1940, p. 127 ("Like many other elderly intellectuals he is hurt that the government does not want his services.") (Passfield Papers); and Tawney to Creech Jones, July 4, 1940, July 15, 1940 (Creech Jones Papers).

48. Present paragraph based on information from Nef, conversation with author, Washington, D.C., January 16, 1971.

49. Toynbee, *Acquaintances*, pp. 90-91.

50. Tawney to Beatrice Webb, December 6, 1942 (Passfield Papers, item II, 4, m, 141).

51. These three reports, held by the Foreign and Commonwealth Office, are, at time of writing, officially inaccessible; copies have, however, filtered out.

52. Tawney to Nef, January 25, 1942 (Nef Papers); see also Tawney to Creech Jones, May 1, 1942 (Creech Jones Papers).

53. Tawney to Creech Jones, September 25, 1942 (Creech Jones Papers).

54. Tawney to Creech Jones, December 15, 1943 (Creech Jones Papers).

55. Nef, conversation with author, Washington, D.C., January 16, 1971.

56. Tawney to Beatrice Webb, December 6, 1942 (Passfield Papers).

57. Tawney to Wadsworth, [March?] 15, 1950 (Guardian Papers).

58. Tawney to Nef, November 11, 1940 (Nef Papers).

59. Tawney to Professor George Yule, September 30, 1951 (Yule Papers).

60. Tawney to Beatrice Webb, July 5, 1942 (Passfield Papers, item II, 4, m, 123).

61. Tawney to Wadsworth, [March?] 15, 1950 (Guardian Papers).

4 SAGE, 1943-1962

1. Jones, *A Diary with Letters, 1931-1950*, p. 518.

2. Carus-Wilson, conversation with author, London, February 15, 1970.

3. *Oxford University Gazette*, June 22, 1950; see also the *Times*, June 22, 1950.

4. Declined invitations reflected the toll. In 1945, UNRRA asked Tawney to go again to China as an advisor. But he did not feel up to it, and was unsure he had any advice to give. Tawney to Nef, April 27, 1945 (Nef Papers).

5. *The Attack*, p. 153.

6. Crozier to Tawney (telegram), September 22, 1942 (Guardian Papers).

7. Kingsley Martin, *Editor* (London, Hutchinson, 1968), p. 313.

8. See his "Speech to Students Union," Melbourne, 1955 (Notes for Speeches on Various Occasions; LSE). His efforts to secure the release of Dragoliab Jovanovic, a Yugoslav scholar put into prison under Soviet pressure, are interestingly revealed in letters exchanged with Hugh Gaitskell (Tawney to Gaitskell, March 8, 1953, March 11, 1953; Gaitskell to Tawney, March 8, 1953; Tawney to Morgan Phillips, December 7, 1952). These letters are in the Gaitskell Papers, shown to me by the kind courtesy of Mr. P. M. Williams of Nuffield College, Oxford.

9. Tawney to Wadsworth, [March?] 15, 1950 (Guardian Papers).

10. According to Postan, the sounding out of Tawney on this question was done by Ashton, presumably on behalf of Attlee, and Gaitskell did not know of the approach.

11. Tawney to Wadsworth, October 6, 1951 (Guardian Papers).

12. Tawney to Creech Jones, September 11, 1954 (Creech Jones Papers).

13. L. Jeger, "Ideas and the Man," *Tribune*, January 26, 1962.

14. "Presidential Address to LSE Students Union" (Speeches on Various Occasions; LSE), p. 9. The figures are Tawney's.

15. Elvin, conversation with author, London, January 28, 1971.

16. Tawney to Creech Jones, undated but evidently mid-1942 (Creech Jones Papers).

17. Tawney to Creech Jones, September 25, 1942 (Creech Jones Papers).

18. Tawney to S. G. Raybould, September 29, 1948.

19. R. H. S. Crossman, conversation with author, London, January 25, 1971.

20. *The Schoolmaster*, January 26, 1962.

21. "Portrait Speech" (Speeches Given on Various Occasions; LSE).

22. For the basic works see note 23, below, and Bibliography, items 31, 359, 363.

23. H. R. Trevor-Roper, "The Gentry, 1540-1640," *Economic History Review*, 2d ser., 6, supplement 1 (1953), and "The Elizabethan Aristocracy: An Anatomy Anatomised," *Economic History Review*, 2nd ser., 3 (1951); Lawrence Stone, "The Anatomy of the Elizabethan Aristocracy," *Economic History Review*, 18 (1948); Tawney, "Rise of the Gentry: A Postscript," *Economic History Review*, 2d ser., 7 (1954); J. P. Cooper, "The Counting of Manors," *Economic History Review*, 2d ser., 8 (1956); J. H. Hexter's pieces collected in *Reappraisals in History* (New York, Harper & Row, 1963); and Nef, conversation with author, Washington, D.C., January 16, 1971.

24. Nef, conversation with author, Washington, D.C., January 16, 1971.

25. "Rise of the Gentry: A Postscript," p. 97.

26. Tawney to Nef, April 7, 1960 (Nef Papers).

27. *The Agrarian Problem in the Sixteenth Century*, p. 409.

28. Hexter complains of those who "resolve research problems by reference to current ideological conflicts" (*Reappraisals in History*, p. 8). If this has Tawney as one of its targets, it misses its mark.

29. Tawney to Beveridge, January 27, 1961 (Beveridge Collection, L.1.211 [C]).

30. Hexter, *Reappraisals in History*, pp. 12, 13.

31. Tawney to Nef, March 8, 1958 (Nef Papers).

32. Mrs. Lucy Rice to Ashton, undated [1962] (Boone Papers). See also, Tawney to Beveridge, January 27, 1961 (Beveridge Collection, L.1.211 [C]). Tawney says of the book that "it is a dull, though informative work, which only a dislike of throwing up a job one had started induced me to complete."

33. *Business and Politics Under James I*, p. 83.

34. Janet Wadsworth, conversation with author, Manchester, January 28, 1971.

35. "J. L. Hammond, 1872-1949," *Proceedings of the British Academy*, 1960, p. 293.

36. These impressions of Tawney's Australian visit are based in part upon Professor R. M. Crawford's letter to the author, February 26, 1971, and Crawford's memo to Ashton, cited in Ashton, *British Academy*, p. 476.

37. Tawney to George Yule, December 31, 1949; see also letter to Yule of December 18, 1961 (Yule Papers).

38. Beales, conversation with author, London, January 25, 1971; Tawney to Nef, August 22, 1940 (Nef Papers).

39. E.g., his lectures for Bristol, April 1952 (LSE-Bristol-Cranfield; LSE).

40. E.g., Tawney to Nef, January 13, 1952 (Nef Papers); Tawney to Janet Wadsworth, July 10, 1957 (Janet Wadsworth Papers).

41. E.g., Tawney to Nef, July 31, 1953; June 7, 1955 (Nef Papers); Tawney to Janet Wadsworth, July 9, 1958 (Janet Wadsworth Papers).

42. Nef, conversation with author, Washington, D.C., January 16, 1971; William Beveridge, *India Called Them*, p. 377.

43. Jeannette to Beveridge, April 19, 1937; September 13, 1937; October 4, 1937; January 14, 1938 (Beveridge Collection, L.1.211).

44. Jeannette to Beveridge, October 24, 1938; February 14, 1939; October 1, 1939; December 11, 1939 (Beveridge Collection, L.1.211). Curiously, William Beveridge mentions Jeannette only twice in his autobiography, and then not by name but as "my sister" (*Power and Influence*, pp. 16, 69).

45. Nef, conversation with author, Washington, D.C., January 16, 1971; diary of Beatrice Webb, vol. 49, December 8, 1935, p. 208 (Passfield Papers).

46. Dr. Gordon Huelin, conversation with author, London, February 16, 1970; Rees, conversation with author, London, February 14, 1970.

47. Janet Wadsworth, conversation with author, Manchester, January 28, 1971. Jeannette's prose style can be glimpsed in the first lines of this letter to Mrs. Nef's mother, written from Chicago, March 31, 1939: "From the warmth and comfort of your daughter's lovely home I must send you a few lines to tell you first how happy and grateful we are to your daughter and John for the beautiful welcome that they have given us. I am occupying your lovely room and enjoying its atmosphere which radiates kindliness and peace of mind. We arrived harassed and weary and are now calmed and our minds reposed. I had occasion to visit your very good chiropodist Miss Warren as I have a very troublesome corn to which she has applied soothing balm" (Nef Papers).

48. Tawney to Janet Wadsworth, January 27, 1958 (Janet Wadsworth Papers).

49. The planning group was by now broader; the letter of invitation to the dinner was signed by the following: A. Briggs, Clay, Gaitskell, T. Williamson, Titmuss, J. R. Williams, Woodcock, R. Gould, H. Nutt, Shearman, Cousins, Green, H. Douglass. Preparations for the honoring of Tawney on his eightieth birthday can be traced in the correspondence in section ACJ 6/2 of the Creech Jones Papers.

50. Tawney to Beveridge, December 7, 1960 (Beveridge Collection, L.1.211 (C)).

51. See *Times*, December 12, 1960; Dr. Green kindly allowed me to see the text of his speech.

52. *Times*, December 12, 1960.

53. Tawney to Creech Jones, December 13, 1960 (Creech Jones Papers).

54. *Times*, November 28, 1960; *Guardian*, November 26, 1960; *Daily Herald*, November 30, 1960; *New Statesman*, November 26, 1960; Nef and Shils to Tawney (telegram), November 30, 1960 (Nef Papers).

55. Notes for a speech to a Christian Socialist meeting, January 22, 1960 (Notes For Speeches on Various Occasions; LSE); Rees, February 14,1970; Tawney to Creech Jones, December 1959 (Creech Jones Papers).

56. L. Jeger, "Ideas and The Man," *Tribune*, January 26, 1962; "R. H. Tawney," *New Statesman*, January 19, 1962.

57. *The Attack*, p. 18; Mrs. Rice to Ashton, undated (January 1962) (Boone Papers).

58. Diary, June 30, 1912.

59. *Times*, February 9, 1962; *Daily Telegraph*, February 9, 1962. A partial list of organizations represented at the Memorial Service evokes Tawney's range: Royal Economic Society, Swedish Embassy, L.S.E., London University, Institute of Historical Research, L.C.C., American Economic History Association, National Institute of Adult Education, Economic History Society, Peterhouse College, Parliamentary Labour Party, *Times Literary Supplement*, University of Keele, University of Leicester, King's College (London), Christian Socialist Movement, National Union of General and Municipal Workers, Nottingham University, 22nd Manchester Old Comrades Association, Eileen Power Memorial Trust, Rhodes Trust, W.E.A., *Political Quarterly*, G. Bell & Sons, *The Guardian*, Printing and Kindred Trades Federation, Oxford University Delegacy for Extra-Mural Studies, Fabian Society, Balliol College, Ruskin College, George Allen & Unwin.

60. *The Attack*, p. 14; *The Radical Tradition*, p. 214; the *Times*, April 14, 1962.

---

5 EQUALITY

1. Diary, April 21, 1912; *Equality*, pp. 89-90.

2. Jean-Jacques Rousseau, *Discourse on the Origins and Foundations of Inequality*, R. D. Masters, ed. and trans., (New York, St. Martins, 1964), p. 151. Cf. Tawney, Diary, February 26, 1913.

3. Cf. Rousseau (of the state of nature) "Those barbarous ages were the golden age, not because men were united but because they were isolated"; cited in Robert Derathé, *Jean-Jacques Rousseau et la Science Politique de son temps* (Paris, Presses Universitaires de France, 1950), p. 146.

4. *Equality*, pp. 150, 113; see also pp. 43, 56, 71-72, 164.

5. Isaiah Berlin, "Equality," *Proceedings of the Aristotelian Society*, new ser., 56 (London, 1956), 325.

6. *Equality*, p. 49.

7. Richard Wollheim, "Equality," *Proceedings of the Aristotelian Society*, new ser., 56 (London, 1956), 281; Berlin, *ibid.*, p. 326.

8. *Equality*, pp. 103, 110.

9. See, for example, *ibid.*, p. 80; *The British Labour Movement*, p. 173.

10. *Equality*, p. 105.

11. Diary, March 6, 1913.

12. Berlin, "Equality," pp. 302-303; italics added.

13. Tawney, *Addresses* (private edition, WEA), p. 25.

14. *Equality*, p. 48.

15. Diary, March 6, 1913.

16. Tawney to Beveridge, December 22, 1915 (Beveridge Collection, L.1.210, Additional [A]).

17. *The Highway*, January 1945, p. 45.

18. "The W.E.A. and Adult Education," in *The Radical Tradition*, p. 82. Tawney said of his first tutorial class at Rochdale that the work done by the best of the students "was on a level with that in the honour schools of the only Universities with which he is acquainted" ("Mr. Tawney's Report on the First Session," Rochdale File, WEA).

19. Sartre cited in Thomas Molnar, *The Decline of the Intellectual* (Cleveland, World Publishing Co., 1961), pp. 148-149.

20. George Orwell, *The Road to Wigan Pier* (New York, Berkeley Publishing Corp., 1961), p. 103.

21. Cited in David Marquand, "Prophet of Equality," *Manchester Guardian*, November 26, 1960.

22. J. M. Keynes, "A Short View of Russia" (1925), in *Essays in Persuasion* (New York, W. W. Norton, 1963), p. 300. Keynes's full remark is: "How can I adopt a creed which, preferring the mud to the fish, exalts the boorish proletariat above the bourgeois and the intelligentsia who, with whatever faults, are the quality in life and surely carry the seeds of all human advancement?"

23. "Christianity and the Social Revolution," in *The Attack*, p. 163.

24. *Equality*, pp. 46-47.

25. Speech to WEA (Speeches on Various Occasions; LSE). See also *Equality*, pp. 225-226; *The Attack*, pp. 93-96; diary, April 21, 1913.

26. H. A. Bedau, "Egalitarianism and the Idea of Equality," in *Nomos IX* (American Society for Political and Legal Philosophy, New York, 1967), p. 9.

27. *Equality*, p. 136.

28. C. J. Friedrich, "A Brief Discourse on the Origin of Political Equality," *Nomos IX*, p. 217; S. I. Benn and R. S. Peters, *Political Thought*, pp. 128, 131.

29. *Equality*, p. 112.

30. See, e.g., *The Acquisitive Society*, p. 37.

31. *Ibid.*, p. 175.

32. J. P. Plamenatz, "Diversity of Rights and Kinds of Equality," *Nomos IX*, p. 97. Later quote, p. 86.

33. *Equality*, p. 28.

34. See, for example, *The Radical Tradition*, pp. 173ff.

35. S. I. Benn and R. S. Peters, *Political Thought*, pp. 132, 153.

36. *The Acquisitive Society*, (London, Collins, 1961), p. 179. This passage does not appear in the American edition.

37. C. J. Friedrich, "Political Equality," *Nomos IX*, p. 227.

38. *Equality*, pp. 51-52.

39. *Equality*, p. 26.

40. *Equality*, pp. 43, 90. Quotations in the following two paragraphs, pp. 57, 164.

41. André Malraux, *Antimémoires* (Paris, Gallimard, 1957), p. 549 (citation translated by R.T.)

42. "Portrait Speech" (Speeches Given on Various Occasions; LSE), p. 8.

43. "The Choice Before the Labour Party," *Political Quarterly*, July-September, 1932 (reprinted in *The Attack*, p. 68).

44. *Equality*, p. 43.

45. *The Great Learning*, chap. 10, para. 9. Legge's translation reads: "the accumulation of wealth is the way to scatter the people; and the letting it be scattered among them is the way to collect the people" (*The Chinese Classics*, trans. James Legge, 5 vols.; Hong Kong, Hong Kong University Press, 1960, I, 376).

46. "Notes on Education" (Speeches on Various Occasions; LSE).

47. John Dewey, *The Public and Its Problems* (New York, H. Holt and Co., 1927), p. 150; J. P. Plamenatz, "Diversity of Rights and Kinds of Equality," in *Nomos IX*, p. 83.

---

6 DISPERSION OF POWER

1. *The Western Political Tradition*, pp. 18-19.

2. "The New Leviathan" (Notes and Talks on French Revolution; LSE). This document is oddly located; it has nothing to do with 1789.

3. J. P. Mayer, *Political Thought: The European Tradition* (London, Viking Press, 1939), Introduction by Tawney, p. vi; following quotations, pp. 20-21 (all are Tawney's words).

4. H. R. Trevor-Roper, *The Gentry, 1540-1640* (London, Cambridge University Press, 1953), p. 1. See also F. J. Fisher, *Essays in the Economic and Social History of Tudor and Stuart England, in Honour of R. H. Tawney* (Cambridge, Cambridge University Press, 1961), pp. 1ff.

5. Sheldon S. Wolin, *Politics and Vision* (Boston, Little, Brown, 1960), p. 214; italics added.

6. *The Western Political Tradition*, p. 16.

7. Introduction to Mayer, *Political Thought*, p. xvii.

8. See Wolin, *Politics and Vision*, pp. 402, 422.

9. Introduction to Mayer, *Political Thought*, p. xvi.

10. *Religion and the Rise of Capitalism*, p. 117; *Equality*, p. 25; *The Western Political Tradition*, p. 15.

11. *The Agrarian Problem in the Sixteenth Century* (1912).

12. *The Acquisitive Society*, pp. 18-19.

13. Diary, August 9, 1914.

14. L. Woolf, *Growing: An Autobiography of the Years 1904-1911* (London, Hogarth Press, 1961), p. 11; Kingsley Martin, *Father Figures* (London, Hutchinson, 1966), p. 110; J. M. Keynes, *Two Memoirs* (London, R. Hart-Davis, 1949), p. 103.

15. L. T. Hobhouse, *Liberalism* (New York, Oxford University Press, 1964; first published 1911), pp. 66, 70.

16. *Equality*, pp. 159-160. Next four quotations from the same pages.

17. *The Acquisitive Society* (London, Collins, 1961), p. 77. This passage does not appear in the American edition.

18. *Equality*, p. 161.

19. Reinhold Niebuhr, *The Children of Light and the Children of Darkness* (London, Nisbet and Co., 1945), pp. 126ff. and passim.

20. See Jean Bodin, *Six Books of the Commonwealth*, trans. M. J. Tooley (Oxford, Blackwell, 1955), book I, chaps. viii, x.

21. *Equality*, p. 30.

22. See "Fragment on Democracy" (Public Lectures Given in Chicago, 1939; LSE); "Democracy and Socialism, Psychology, and Sociology" (Speeches Given on Various Occasions; LSE).

23. J. S. Mill, *Representative Government*, chap. iv (Everyman Edition, London, 1957), p. 225. Later reference is to p. 207.

24. Introduction to Mayer, *Political Thought*, pp. xxi-xxii.

25. Diary, December 23, 1914.

26. L. Woolf, *Beginning Again: An Autobiography of the Years 1911-1918* (London, Hogarth Press, 1964), p. 184; and Maurice B. Reckitt, *As It Happened: An Autobiography* (London, J. M. Dent and Sons, 1941), p. 125.

27. It is instructive in this regard to compare Laski's *The State in Theory and Practice* (1935) with his *Where Do We Go From Here?* (1940).

28. *The Acquisitive Society*, p. 42.

29. Diary, December 23, 1914.

30. *Equality*, p. 112.

31. One of Tawney's earliest writings is an interesting, unpublished series of lectures on the French Revolution, "Notes and Talks on the French Revolution, Longton, 1910-1913" (Notes and Talks on French Revolution; LSE).

32. *Equality*, p. 29 (italics added); see also "Democracy and Socialism, Psychology, and Sociology" (Speeches Given on Various Occasions; LSE).

33. Tawney to Creech Jones, March 25, 1938 (Creech Jones Papers).

34. Diary, June 16, 1914.

35. Kingsley Martin, *Father Figures*, p. 111.

36. C. B. Macpherson, *The Real World of Democracy* (Oxford, Clarendon Press, 1966), pp. 12ff., 23ff.

37. *The Attack*, pp. 165-166.

38. Franz Neumann, "Approaches to the Study of Political Power," in *The Democratic and the Authoritarian State*, (New York, Free Press of Glencoe, 1964), p. 8.

39. John Locke, *Two Treatises of Government* (London, Mentor, 1965), p. 308.

40. Wolin, *Politics and Vision*, pp. 433-434.

41. See Max Weber, "The Social Psychology of the World Religions," in H. Gerth and C. W. Mills, eds., *From Max Weber* (New York, Oxford University Press, 1958), pp. 295ff.

42. Introduction to Mayer, *Political Thought*, pp. x, xi, xii, xiii.

43. *The Attack*, p. 164.

7 SOCIAL FUNCTION

1. "Speech to University of London Fabian Society" (Speeches Given on Various Occasions; LSE).

2. In so far as metaphor provides a clue, we are first struck by a similarity to the social thought of the sixteenth century. Then the image of the "body politic" began to be replaced by an image of movement: "ship of state." As William Prynne used the ship-at-sea analogy, Tawney spoke of "path," "way," "road," and frequently borrowed "journeying" images from Bunyan.

Yet the imagery is different from Calvinism's. A conception of politics as *construction* in Calvinism is foreign to Tawney. Indeed Tawney is in some respects happier with the "body politic" image than with that of the ship of state. The notion of constructing the political order belonged to the utilitarian socialist position, not to Tawney's.

Moreover, whereas the ship of state tended to have a divinely appointed destination, for Tawney history was not teleological. The socialist pilgrims were on their own, without guaranteed haven, without chart or compass other than their own reason, will, and sense of common humanity. Unable to share the sharp clear certainties of the Calvinist "Saints," Tawney's socialist wayfarers huddle together all the closer for their metaphysical nakedness. And striving may be just as important as the goal and its reward. "What matters to the health of society is the objective towards which its face is set" (*Equality*, p. 56). Both freedom and doubt are suggested by Tawney's imagery, as they are not by Calvinist imagery.

In sum, Tawney uses organic analogies as well as the "movement" imagery. He does not use imagery of construction (as Calvinism and Hobbes); imagery of the artist with his clay (employed by Machiavelli to depict statecraft); or imagery which suggests a closed view of history (as in Calvinism). The metaphors suggest that Tawney saw socialism as an open-ended way of life, to be achieved by cooperative, ongoing efforts of citizens, against difficulties which were endemic in human nature.

3. Robert K. Merton, *On Theoretical Sociology: Five Essays, Old and New* (Glencoe, Ill., The Free Press), p. 107.

4. C. Kluckhohn, *Navaho Witchcraft* (Papers of Peabody Museum, Harvard University, Cambridge, Mass., 1944), vol. XXII, no. 2, p. 47.

5. L. T. Hobhouse, *The Elements of Social Justice* (London, Allen and Unwin, 1922), p. 163.

6. See J. N. Figgis, *Churches in the Modern State* (London, Longmans, Green and Co., 1913), passim.; G. D. H. Cole, *Self-Government in Industry* (London, G. Bell and Sons, 1917), passim.; *Guild Socialism Restated* (London, L. Parsons, 1920), passim.

7. See H. J. Laski, *Introduction to Politics* (London, Barnes and Noble, 1962), pp. 24ff.; Bertrand Russell, *Roads to Freedom* (London, Allen and Unwin, 1918), passim.

8. Cited in *Religion and the Rise of Capitalism*, p. 148.

9. Contrary to common belief, Tawney did not find the *cause* of this development in the social thought of Protestantism. He found it in certain social and economic factors, especially population, prices, and land use and land ownership. Important seventeenth-century versions of Protestantism—not the Reformers' own teachings—lent weight and sanctity to the new economic doctrines, *inter alia* by jettisoning the doctrine of a just price and dismantling the prohibition of usury. But Tawney considered Weber's thesis concerning the relation of Protestantism to capitalism too "idealist" in its assumptions about social causation. His own views were closer to historical materialism. See *Religion and the Rise of Capitalism*, pp. 84ff., 316-317; also foreword by Tawney to Max Weber, *The Protestant Ethic and the Spirit of Capitalism* (London, Allen and Unwin, 1930).

10. *The Acquisitive Society*, pp. 183-184.

11. *Ibid.*, p. 181. There is no trace of Luddism in Tawney. Nor did he think socialism could be built in some "model colony" aside from the structures of the modern industrial state. Interestingly, his treatment of William Lovett, the early nineteenth century radical political organizer, is more sympathetic than his treatment of Robert Owen, the

communitarian experimenter of the same era. Cf. *The Radical Tradition*, pp. 15ff and pp. 32ff.

12. *The Acquisitive Society*, pp. 44, 46.

13. *Equality*, p. 144.

14. *The Acquisitive Society*, pp. 44-45.

15. *Ibid.*, p. 60.

16. *The Radical Tradition*, p. 104.

17. *The Acquisitive Society*, p. 99.

18. *Ibid.*, p. 152.

19. Cf. "Memories of the 1880s" in J. Clayton, *The Rise and Decline of Socialism in Great Britain 1884-1924* (London, Faber and Gwyer, 1926), p. 231.

20. *The Radical Tradition*, pp. 100-101.

21. *Ibid.*, p. 48.

22. Hobbes, *Leviathan*, pp. 132, 127.

23. *The Radical Tradition*, p. 100.

24. "Fragment on poverty and the industrial system" (Speeches Given on Various Occasions; LSE).

25. *Religion and the Rise of Capitalism*, p. 230.

26. *Ibid.*, p. 260.

27. *The Agrarian Problem*, p. xxiii.

28. *Religion and the Rise of Capitalism*, p. 36.

29. John Ruskin, *Unto This Last*, in W. D. P. Bliss, ed., *The Communism of Ruskin* (New York, 1891), p. 92.

30. *The Acquisitive Society*, p. 54.

31. *Religion and the Rise of Capitalism*, p. 33.

32. *The Acquisitive Society*, pp. 70, 87.

33. John Ruskin, *Unto This Last*, in Bliss, *Communism of Ruskin*, p. 64.

34. *Equality*, p. 72.

35. *The Acquisitive Society*, p. 88. Following two quotations, pp. 69, 90.

36. *Ibid.*, p. 84.

37. Proverbs, 30:8, cited in *Religion and the Rise of Capitalism*, p. 55.

38. *The British Labour Movement*, p. 158.

39. *Ibid.*, pp. 89, 91.

40. See quotation at note 43.

41. Jeremy Bentham, *Theory of Legislation: Principles of the Civil Code* (Boston, 1840), p. 194.

42. *The British Labour Movement*, pp. 146, 33.

43. "The New Leviathan" (Notes and Talks on French Revolution; LSE), p. 16; italics added.

44. *The Radical Tradition*, p. 99.

45. *The Acquisitive Society*, p. 149.

46. *The Radical Tradition*, p. 99.

1. *Equality*, pp. 206, 197.

2. See E. P. Thompson, *The Making of the English Working Class* (London, Penguin Books, 1968).

3. J. Bruce Glasier, *William Morris and the Early Days of the Socialist Movement* (London, Longmans, Green, 1921), pp. 27-28.

4. Cited in the *Times*, March 8, 1924.

5. E. P. Thompson, *English Working Class*, p. 915.

6. Adam B. Ulam, *The Philosophical Foundations of English Socialism* (Cambridge, Mass., Harvard University Press, 1951), p. 68.

7. See T. H. Marshall, *Citizenship and Social Class and Other Essays* (Cambridge, Eng., Cambridge University Press, 1950), pp. 27ff.

8. Beatrice Webb, *My Apprenticeship* (London, Longmans, 1926), p. 143.

9. "The Expense of Education in Oxford" (Memoranda on Education and Educational Policy; LSE).

10. *The Attack*, p. 184.

11. "Christianity and the Social Order" (Notes For Speeches on Various Occasions; LSE). I parenthesize "reasonable" because Tawney's handwriting makes it less than certain that this is the word he wrote. A similar statement is found in *The Attack*, p. 174.

12. G. M. Young, *Victorian England: Portrait of an Age* (2d ed.; London, Oxford University Press, 1960), p. 13.

13. M. Richter, *The Politics of Conscience: T. H. Green and his Age* (Cambridge, Mass., Harvard University Press, 1964), pp. 31, 109.

14. *The British Labour Movement*, p. 20.

15. See T. H. Green, *Lectures on the Principles of Political Obligation*, in *Works*, 3 vols. (London, 1889-1890), II, 345; "Liberal Legislation and Freedom of Contract," in *Works*, III, 372-82.

16. *The Attack*, p. 170.

17. Speech at Melbourne, Australia, January 1959.

18. Lloyd George said to a Labour deputation in 1917: "The whole state of society is more or less molten"; and he added, "you can stamp upon that molten mass almost anything, so long as you do so with firmness and determination" (*Labour Party Annual Conference Report*, 1917, p. 163).

19. "WEA at Manchester" (Speeches on Various Occasions; LSE).

20. "The WEA and Adult Education," Lecture, May 8, 1953, reprinted in *The Radical Tradition*, p. 83.

21. "WEA Notes" (Speeches on Various Occasions; LSE); the word interpreted as "perspectives" is not clear in Tawney's handwriting. See also "Fragment on Secondary Education" (Speeches on Various Occasions; LSE).

22. *The British Labour Movement*, p. 171.

23. See Paul Henri Thiry, Baron d'Holbach, *La Morale Universelle: ou les Devoirs de l'Homme Fondés sur sa Nature*, 3 vols. (Tours, 1793), I, sec. 1, chap. xii; and III, sec. 5, chap. iii.

24. Kingsley Martin, *Editor* (London, Hutchinson 1968), p. 325.

25. "Fragment on Democracy" (Public Lectures Given in Chicago, 1939; LSE).

26. "Labour Honours," *New Statesman*, June 22, 1935.

27. Walter Bagehot, *The English Constitution* (London, Collins, 1963), pp. 266, 85.

28. *Equality*, p. 54.

29. "Labour Honours," *New Statesman*, June 22, 1935.

30. *Ibid.*, p. 214.

31. Tawney's preface to R. Firth, *Primitive Economics of the New Zealand Maori* (London, Routledge, 1929).

32. Cited in "An Anthology of Tawney," *New Statesman*, November 26, 1960.

33. *New Statesman*, June 22, 1935.

34. J. R. Clynes, *Memoirs* (London, Hutchinson, 1937), I, 343.

35. *New Statesman*, February 4, 1966.

36. See Hodge's staggering memoir, *Workman's Cottage to Windsor Castle* (London, Sampson Low, Marston & Co., 1931), which fulfills its title.

37. *Equality*, p. 56.

38. *The Acquisitive Society* (London, Collins, 1961), p. 156. This passage does not appear in the American edition.

39. In a postmortem on the debacle of 1931 Tawney wrote: "The seed sown by the pioneers began to bear fruit. The movement became a political power. Whole battalions were shepherded into it, much as the troops of Feng Yu-hsiang, "the Christian general," were baptised with a hose. Thanks to the judges, the unions were the first wave. The war brought another; the election of 1923 a third; the events of 1926 a fourth. By that time a generation had grown up to which it seemed as easy to be a Socialist—as easy, if you please!—as it had seemed difficult in 1900." ("The Choice Before the Labour Party," in *The Attack*, p. 59).

40. Statement of Evidence before London Advisory Council for Juvenile Employment, undated (Memoranda on Education and Educational Policy; LSE), p. 1.

41. Cited in David Marquand, "R. H. Tawney: Prophet of Equality," *Manchester Guardian*, November 26, 1960.

42. *The Acquisitive Society*, p. 178.

43. *The Acquisitive Society* (London, Collins, 1961). This passage does not appear in the American edition.

44. *The Attack*, p. 32.

45. *Equality*, pp. 40, 87.

46. Letter from Tawney to the *Cotton Factory Times*, October 23, 1927 (Memoranda on Education and Educational Policy; LSE), in reply to *Cotton Factory Times*, October 21, 1927.

47. *The Acquisitive Society*, p. 179. (London, Collins, 1961). This passage does not appear in the American edition.

48. *Equality*, p. 204.

49. *Equality*, p. 207. Tawney did not view citizenship only as a means to an end, but also as an end in itself. British idealist liberalism has frequently been ambivalent as to whether it is a philosophy of methods or a philosophy of ends. Is the starting point for political reflection the individual (and his nature) or is it the state (and its requirements)? The Chinese philosopher, Yen Fu (1853-1921), who drank deep at the fountains of British liberalism and introduced much of it to China, holds up a mirror to British thought on this question in an interesting manner. His desire was to gather from Western thought whatever could serve to make the Chinese nation powerful and wealthy. Because he admired the "public spirit" of Britain, his interpretation tended to wrench liberal thought far towards a Machiavelli-like concern for corporate ends. It is a distortion but an illuminating one. There is implicit in British liberalism a strong concern for "public spirit" (though much less than in Machiavelli). But it rests upon an assumed harmony between the values of the capitalist system and the values and interests of the entire community. Yen Fu does not focus on the enormity of the assumption because it posed no problem for him; his idea was that in China "public spirit" would be directly marshalled to enhance state power. The interesting thing is that Tawney's public spirit differs both from public spirit as construed by Victorian liberals and from public spirit as construed by Yen Fu. Yen Fu gleaned the truth that public spirit *was* operative in England; Tawney saw, however, that it was not buttressing the common good so much as Bagehot's (middle class) version of the English constitution. "Public spirit" came close to being one of the myths of Mumbo-Jumbo. It was no less justifiable to put public spirit to the service of the Leviathan of state power in underdeveloped China, than to put it to the service of industrialism in Britain; yet Tawney distrusted also this idea. The kernel of his position is that public spirit—or citizenship—should not principally be a means to anything preordained but the open-ended way of life of a free and equal people. (See Benjamin I. Schwartz, *In Search of Wealth and Power: Yen Fu and the West* [Cambridge, Mass., Harvard University Press, 1964].)

50. *The Attack*, pp. 160, 162.

51. Fabian Society Dinner, May 15, 1954 (Speeches Given on Various Occasions; LSE). See also "The New Leviathan" (Notes and Talks on French Revolution; LSE), p. 1 and passim.

52. George Orwell, *Nineteen Eighty Four* (New York, New American Library, 1961), p. 178.

53. *Ibid.*, pp. 205, 218, 211.

54. *Ibid.*, p. 167.

55. Karl Mannheim, "The Problem of the Intelligentsia," in *Essays on the Sociology of Culture* (London, Routledge & Paul, 1956).

56. On this see Jean Duvignaud, *Pour Entrer Dans le Vingtième Siècle* (Paris, Grasset 1960), p. 73; also *Equality*, p. 201.

57. Tawney delivered a swashbuckling condemnation of leftwing "paladins of paper revolution" as early as 1938, remarkably prescient for its time:

> After the collapse of 1931, an epidemic of the "infantile disease of Left-wingism" was obviously overdue. It raged for some years like measles in Polynesia, and set thousands gibbering. Private socialisms flourished. There were absurd exhibitions of self-righteous sectarianism by cliques thanking God—or the latest improvement on Him—that they were not as their benighted neighbours, in particular, of course, the besotted mandarins who conspire against the revolution from their den in Transport House. The great game of overtrumping the Left of today, for fear of not being in the swim of tomorrow, went merrily forward among the *intelligentsia*. Bloomsbury—not the geographical area, but the mental disease—discovered the recondite truth of the existence of a class struggle, and announced its conversion to it with blood curdling bleats. Invitations to hunt tigers were issued by sportsmen with whom a brave man might well hesitate to shoot rabbits.

Yet, Tawney points out, despite its huffing and puffing this ideological zeal seemed to have no firm foundation in a view of politics and of man. As international pressures increased, hey presto, "the Hot fit passed into a cold:"

> No compromise with capitalism had been the motto of yesterday; compromise at any cost became the watch-word of today.... Long reproached with an anaemic liberalism, the Labour party was denounced for its sectarian reluctance to take the Liberals to its bosom. The stalwarts who had fumed at the mildness of its socialism protested at its intransigence. (*Equality*, pp. 198-199.)

Tawney is pointing to the lack of a humanistic basis for the ideology of the 1930s, and its consequent brittleness. The steadiness of his own views over five decades is due in large part to his insistence on making ordinary human beings the raison d'étre of his socialism, and their opinions and energies the foundation of socialist citizenship.

58. U.S. Wartime Talk (Various Lectures Given in US, 1941-42; LSE). See also *Equality*, p. 223.

59. *Equality*, p. 207.

60. Norman McKenzie, ed., *Conviction* (London, MacGibbon & Kee, 1958); E. P. Thompson, ed., *Out of Apathy* (London, Stevens, 1960); P. Anderson and R. Blackburn, eds., *Towards Socialism* (London, Collins, 1965).

61. *Equality*, p. 89.

62. Tawney, *The Education of the Citizen* (1932), p. 6.

63. *The Attack*, p. 163.

64. Fabian Society Dinner, May 15, 1954 (Speeches Given on Various Occasions; LSE).

---

9 FELLOWSHIP

1. *Equality*, p. 164.

2. W. D. P. Bliss, ed., *The Communism of Ruskin* (New York, 1891), p. vii.

3. W. Bagehot, *Physics and Politics* (New York, 1901), pp. 11-12.

4. *The Acquisitive Society*, (London, Collins, 1961), p. 182. This passage does not appear in the U.S. edition.

5. *The Amberley Papers* (London, Hogarth Press, 1937), I, 462.

6. B. Seebohm Rowntree, *Poverty: A Study of Town Life* (London, 1901); Charles Booth, *Life and Labour of the People in London* (collected ed. London, 1904).

7. "Some Reflections of a Soldier," *The Nation* (London) October 21, 1916, in *The Attack*, p. 27.

8. See, e.g., Tawney to Beveridge, December 22, 1915 (Beveridge Collection L.1.210, Additional (A), LSE); Tawney, "Democracy or Defeat," *Welsh Outlook*, January 1917, pp. 11-12.

9. See Fritz Stern, *The Politics of Cultural Despair: A Study in the Rise of Germanic Ideology* (Berkeley, University of California Press, 1961), passim.

10. Lord Hugh Cecil, *Conservatism* (London, 1912).

11. J. B. Bury, *A History of Freedom of Thought* (London, 1913), p. 247.

12. See J. A. Hobson, *The Social Problem* (New York, 1901), p. v; and William Morris, review of Bellamy's *Looking Backward* in *Commonweal* (London), January 22, 1889.

13. Ernest Barker, *Father of the Man: Memories of Cheshire, Lancashire, and Oxford, 1874-1898*, National Council of Social Service, (London, 1948), p. 73.

14. "The New Leviathan" (Notes and Talks on French Revolution; LSE), pp. 1, 5, 6. This is the outline for a book which Tawney never wrote. It is undated but was evidently written during World War I. See also Tawney's diary, December 2, 1912, August 13, 1913.

15. "The New Leviathan" (Notes and Talks on French Revolution; LSE), p. 1; diary, June 16, 1914. Also see Karl Mannheim, *Ideology and Utopia* (London, K. Paul, Trench, Trubner & Co., 1936), pt. 1.

16. The chronological Bibliography, Section II, nos. 366-404 makes plain Tawney's declining concern, after the 1920's, with industrial problems as such.

17. Robert Michels, *Political Parties* (New York, Dover Publications, 1959), p. 408.

18. H. J. Laski, *A Grammar of Politics* (London, Allen & Unwin, 1925), p. 15.

19. See Chapter 8, note 18.

20. Winston Churchill, speech in House of Commons, April 23, 1936.

21. Arthur M. Schlesinger Jr., *The Politics of Freedom* (London, Heinemann, 1950), p. 36.

22. Laski, *A Grammar of Politics*, p. 24.

23. Samuel H. Beer, *British Politics in the Collectivist Age*, chaps. 5, 6.

24. Laski, *A Grammer of Politics*, pp. 17, 16.

25. J. A. Hobson, *The Social Problem* (New York, 1901), p. 264; italics added.

26. *The Radical Tradition*, p. 97.

27. *The Attack*, p. 165; *The Radical Tradition*, p. 170.

28. See *The Acquisitive Society* (London, Collins, 1961), p. 179. This passage does not appear in the American edition.

29. Matthew Arnold, *Culture and Anarchy*, ed. Lionel Trilling (New York, Viking Press, 1949), pp. 523, 504.

30. *Ibid.*, pp. 572-573, 477.

31. See William Morris, *News From Nowhere*, ed. A. L. Morton (London, Panther Books, 1968), pp. 224, 278-279.

32. Tawney, *Social History and Literature* (1949); reprinted in *The Radical Tradition*, pp. 193, 194, 195, 199, 198.

33. *Ibid.*, pp. 197, 204, 208, 198, 196. On Tawney's view of the relation between socialism and preindustrial society, see also his diary, October 22, 1912, October 14, 1912.

34. W. Kornhauser, *The Politics of Mass Society* (Glencoe, Ill., The Free Press, 1959), p. 223.

35. The first quotation from Rousseau is cited in R. Derathé, *J. J. Rousseau et la Science Politique de son temps* (Paris, Presses Universitaires de France, 1950), p. 146; the second is from *Du Contrat Social*, in *Political Writings*, trans. F. Watkins (Edinburgh, Thomas Nelson & Sons, 1953), II, 234.

36. Wolin, *Politics and Vision*, p. 371.

37. William Morris, *A Dream of John Ball*, ed. by A. L. Morton (London, Panther Books, 1968), p. 51.

38. See *Why Britain Fights*, pamphlet version only, p. 27.

39. Diary, March 6, 1913. Tawney has more in common with Calvin on the topic of community than with Luther. He is far from agreeing with Luther that "if all the world were composed of real Christians . . . no prince, king, lord, sword, law, would be needed" ("Secular Author-

ity: To What Extent it Should be Obeyed"); and the radical separation of realms that Luther proposed seemed to open the door to authoritarian possibilities in the secular realm. Tawney stands nearer to Calvin's insistence on providing political "bones" for the organization of community. Calvin sculpted a Christian way of life for the secular here and now, and likewise Tawney sculpted a concrete socialist pattern of life.

40. "The Challenge of Our Time" (1946), in E. M. Forster, *Two Cheers for Democracy* (London, Arnold, 1951), p. 57.

41. Leonard Woolf, *Downhill All the Way: An Autobiography of the Years 1919-1939* (London, Hogarth Press, 1967), p. 26.

42. Leonard Woolf, *Beginning Again: An Autobiography of the Years 1911-1918*, p. 173.

43. See *The Attack*, pp. 33-34; *Equality*, p. 85.

44. Diary, July 29, 1913.

45. Eduard Bernstein, *Voraussetzungen*; cited in Peter Gay, *The Dilemma of Democratic Socialism* (New York, Collier, 1962), p. 247.

46. "Speech to Jubilee Weekend Conference of the LSE, February, 1956" (Notes For Speeches on Various Occasions; LSE).

47. Ulam, *Philosophical Foundations of English Socialism*, p. 9.

48. H. J. Laski, *Faith, Reason, and Civilisation* (London, Gollancz, 1944), p. 32.

49. Noel Annan, Book Review in *New York Review of Books*, November 21, 1968.

50. Samuel H. Beer, *British Politics*, p. 130; see also p. 238.

51. William Morris, *A Dream of John Ball*, p. 37.

---

10 VULNERABILITIES

1. *The Acquisitive Society* (London, Collins, 1961), p. 180. This passage does not appear in the American edition.

2. Tawney used the Latin "privata opulentia et publica egestas" ("The Conditions of Economic Liberty," in *The Radical Tradition*, p. 111). He may have got the phrase from Matthew Arnold, who wrote in *Culture and Anarchy:* "London, with its unutterable external hideousness, and with its internal canker of *publice egestas, privatim opulentia*—to use the words which Sallust puts into Cato's mouth about Rome—unequalled in the world."

3. *Religion and the Rise of Capitalism*, pp. 19-20.

4. *The Acquisitive Society*, p. 99.

5. V. I. Lenin, *State and Revolution*, in *Selected Works*, 2 vols., in English (Moscow, Foreign Languages Publishing House, 1951), II, part 1, p. 305.

6. *Religion and the Rise of Capitalism*, p. 56.

7. *The Radical Tradition*, pp. 197, 194.

8. *Religion and the Rise of Capitalism*, p. 219; and E. Halévy, *L'ère des Tyrannies* (Paris, Lib. Gallimard, 1938), p. 266.

9. "Why Britain Fights," *New York Times*, July 21, 1940; reprinted in *The Attack*, pp. 72, 78.

10. Introduction to *The Life and Struggles of William Lovett*, I (London, 1920); reprinted in *The Radical Tradition*, p. 25; italics added.

11. Cited in Maurice Shock, "The Intellectuals and the Labour Movement: R. H. Tawney," *The Listener*, November 3, 1960, p. 778.

12. Harold Macmillan, *Winds of Change* (New York, Macmillan, 1966), p. 3; also pp. 4, 20.

13. "Speech to St. Pancras Labour Party" (Speeches Given on Various Occasions; LSE).

14. Cited by Tawney in *Equality*, p. 127.

15. "Speech for Evan Durbin" (Speeches Given on Various Occasions; LSE). See also "Why Britain Fights," pamphlet version only, p. 46.

16. See *The Condition of China* (1933), pp. 6ff.

17. For a revealing anecdote on Tawney's impatience with Chinese nationalism, see Joseph Fletcher, *William Temple: Twentieth Century Christian* (New York, Seabury Press, 1963), p. 135.

18. *Religion and the Rise of Capitalism*, p. 58 (italics added).

19. The slightly equivocal character of his approach to questions of colonialism, at least during World War II, came out in speeches made in the United States. Once, after urging Indian independence, and also mounting a limited defense of British rule in India, he went on: "As far as other parts of the world are concerned, some will be ready, it may be hoped, to go the same way as India. Others, for example large parts of Africa, obviously are not. There is little reason to think that the steel rods and concentration camps of Nazis and Japanese would be a change for the better for the people of the latter, nor as far as can be judged do the people think so either. It is arguable, however, that all people not yet ready for self-government should be protected against exploitation by becoming wards of an international trustee" ("US Speech, 1942," Various Lectures Given in US, 1941-42; LSE).

20. J. M. Keynes, "Democracy and Efficiency," *New Statesman*, January 28, 1939.

21. George Orwell, *A Collection of Essays* (New York, Doubleday, 1954), p. 239.

22. Kingsley Martin, *Editor*, p. 323.

23. J. M. Keynes, "Shaw on Wells on Stalin," *New Statesman*, November 10, 1934; see also John Lehmann, *The Whispering Gallery* (London, Longmans, 1955), pp. 218ff.

24. Cited in Francis Hope, "My Country Right or Left," *New Statesman*, December 19, 1969.

25. John Strachey, *The Theory and Practice of Socialism* (New York, Random House, 1936), p. 459.

26. The phrase is from George Lichtheim, *Marxism*, revised ed. (London, 1964), p. 358.

27. George Orwell, *Essays*, p. 242.

28. "Speech in US: The War and Contemporary and Postwar Political Issues" (Various Lectures Given in US, 1941-42; LSE).

29. Guido de Ruggiero, *The History of European Liberalism*, trans. R. G. Collingwood (Boston, Beacon Press, 1959), pp. 393, 443.

30. See, e.g., *The Attack*, pp. 174ff.

31. Orwell, *Essays*, p. 242. See, too, Tawney's delicate but pointed discussion of F. A. Hayek in *The Radical Tradition*, pp. 164-165.

32. "Poverty as an Industrial Problem," Inaugural Lecture by Tawney as director of the Ratan Tata Foundation, October 22, 1913, p. 9; see also "The New Leviathan."

33. See also *The British Labour Movement*, p. 137.

34. "Fragment on Democracy" (Public Lectures Given in Chicago, 1939; LSE).

35. Joseph Schumpeter, *Capitalism, Socialism, and Democracy*, revised ed. (New York, Harper & Bros., 1950), p. 263 and passim.

36. "Speech to WEA, 1945" (Speeches on Various Occasions; LSE).

37. See Thomas B. Macauley, *Critical and Historical Essays*, I (London, 1843), pp. 83-84.

38. "Speech to WEA, 1945" (Speeches on Various Occasions; LSE).

39. Tawney employed this "house" image in his presidential address to the WEA of 1944 (*The Highway*, January 1945).

40. H. G. Wells, *Experiment in Autobiography* (New York, Macmillan, 1934) pp. 198-199.

41. *Renewal of British Government*, Political and Economic Planning, Broadsheet 513, July 1969, p. v.

42. Cited in *New Statesman*, December 20, 1968.

43. *The British Labour Movement*, p. 147. On Tawney's attitude to the civil service, see "Piece on WEA" (Speeches on Various Occasions; LSE).

44. Hugh Gaitskell, "An Appreciation," in *The Radical Tradition*, pp. 213-214.

45. See "Is the Party Over?" *New Statesman*, September 19, 1969.

46. Anthony Sampson, *Anatomy of Britain* (London, Hodder & Stoughton, 1962), p. 638.

47. "A Christian World Order" (Speeches on Various Occasions; LSE), p. 1.

48. See *The Attack*, pp. 177, 183-184; and Bishop H. Henson, *Retrospect of an Unimportant Life*, 3 vols.; (London, Oxford University Press, 1942-1950) I, 317-318; "The New Leviathan," p. 4.

49. "A Christian World Order," p. 8 (Speeches on Various Occasions; LSE).

50. *Religion and the Rise of Capitalism*, pp. 192, 50.

51. "Christianity and the Social Order" (Notes for Speeches on Various Occasions; LSE); and *The Acquisitive Society* (London, Collins, 1961), p. 13. This passage does not appear in the American edition.

52. Though Tawney did not begin his chapters with a biblical text, as Headlam, Widdrington, or A. J. Penty often did, his prose drips with biblical allusions and a new generation may boggle at these phrases: "the spectacle of Lazarus in the House of Lords"; "hewn in pieces before the Lord"; "If the Kingdom of Heaven is not eating and drinking"; "as though the miners alone were the children of sin." Discussing Pareto, Tawney suddenly observed: "There are other ways than that of the eagle in the air and the serpent on the rock, which baffles the author of the Book of Proverbs." Britons of the 1970s, not to mention readers from countries without a Judao-Christian tradition, might be as baffled at the image as the writer of Proverbs was at the eagle and the serpent. (*Equality*, pp. 168, 104, 55, 82; *The Acquisitive Society*, p. 145.)

53. "Speech to C.S.M." (Notes for Speeches on Various Occasions; LSE); and "Christianity and the Social Order," in *The Attack*, p. 175.

54. *Ibid.*, p. 172.

55. Tawney's introduction to Charles Gore, *Christianity Applied to the Life of Men and Nations* (Essex Hall Lecture 1920, reprinted 1940), p. 7.

56. See Tawney, "The Daily News Religious Census of London," in *Toynbee Record* (March 1904), pp. 90-91.

---

11 TAWNEY'S IMPORTANCE

1. *The Acquisitive Society*, p. 140. By 1931 he was prepared to say that the liberal capitalist order "work[s] no longer" (*Equality*, p. 210).

2. *The Acquisitive Society*, p. 146.

3. *Equality*, p. 83.

4. *The Acquisitive Society*, (London, Collins, 1961), p. 179. This passage does not appear in the American edition.

5. Cf. Tawney's remark: "I do not believe that capitalism is the sole cause of wars . . . I do not believe that national fears and ambitions are unimportant as compared with economic interests." ("Speech to University of London Fabian Society," Speeches Given on Various Occasions; LSE). See also *The Acquisitive Society*, pp. 47ff, and compare with Tawney's statement: "There are many causes of international friction; but the rivalry of nations struggling for markets, fields of investment, and privileged access to [favored?] areas is not the least among them" ("Speech for Evan Durbin"; Speeches Given on Various Occasions; LSE).

6. *Equality*, pp. 29-31.

7. *The Attack*, p. 170.

8. "After more than half a century of work on the subject by scholars of half a dozen nationalities and of every variety of political opinion," Tawney responded, "to deny that the phenomenon exists; or to suggest that, if it does exist, it is unique among human institutions, in having, like Melchizidek, existed from eternity; or to imply that, if it has a history, propriety forbids that history to be disinterred, is to run wilfully in blinkers." (*Religion and the Rise of Capitalism* [London, Penguin, 1938], p. viii. This passage does not appear in the American edition.) For Tawney's explanation of why capitalism, as a word and a theory, was so long excluded from English historiography, see Tawney, "A History of Capitalism," *Economic History Review*, 2d ser., 2 (1950), 307.

9. Lecture 1, p. 3 (Lectures on Seventeenth-Century English History; LSE).

10. J. M. Keynes, *Essays in Persuasion*, p. 306.

11. See "The New Leviathan" (Notes and Talks on French Revolution; LSE), pp. 7-8.

12. *The Acquisitive Society*, p. 103.

13. *The Radical Tradition*, p. 170.

14. *The Acquisitive Society*, p. 13 (London, Collins, 1961). This passage does not appear in the American edition.

15. Reminiscence of Professor M. M. Postan, conversation with the author, Cambridge, Eng., February 11, 1970.

16. *The Attack*, p. 191.

17. *The Radical Tradition*, p. 174.

18. "Why Britain Fights," pamphlet version, p. 43.

19. *The Radical Tradition*, p. 168. Compare John Strachey, "Tasks and Achievement of British Labour," in R. H. S. Crossman, ed., *New Fabian Essays* (London, Turnstile Press, 1952), pp. 187, 199.

20. "Speech to Central London Fabians" (Speeches Given on Various Occasions; LSE).

21. *The Radical Tradition*, pp. 176, 177.

22. See "Podsnappery in Education" (WEA Presidential Address, 1933), *The Highway*, December 1933.

23. "Fabian Society Dinner, May 15, 1954" (Speeches Given on Various Occasions; LSE), p. 8.

24. See Elton Mayo, *The Political Problem* (Cambridge, Mass., Harvard University Press, 1947), p. 23, and passim; and *The Human Problems of an Industrial Civilisation* (New York, Macmillan, 1933), pp. 152, 182. See Philip Selznick, *Leadership in Administration* (Evanston, Ill., Row & Peterson, 1957), chaps. i, ii.

25. Selznick, *Leadership*, p. 100.

26. "The New Leviathan" (Notes and Talks on French Revolution; LSE), p. 8.

27. *The Attack*, p. 63.

28. Charles Gore, ed., *Property: Its Duties and Rights, Historically, Philosophically, and Religiously Regarded* (London, 1913), Introduction, p. viii.

29. Kitty Muggeridge and Ruth Adam, *Beatrice Webb: A Life, 1858-1943* (London, Secker & Warburg, 1967), p. 110.

30. Philip Magnus, *Gladstone: A Biography* (New York, Dutton, 1964), pp. 35, 203, 29.

31. This is the recollection of Professor Joseph Fletcher; conversation with the author, Cambridge, Mass., May 1, 1968. After the death of his wife in 1959, Tawney was more regular in church attendance and more concerned with religious issues than he had been for decades (Dr. Gordon Huelin, vicar of the church Tawney attended in these last years, conversation with author, London, February 16, 1970).

32. *Religion and the Rise of Capitalism*, p. 273.

33. Fenner Brockway, "Eighty Years On," *New Statesman*, November 15, 1968.

34. See *The Return of Christendom*, by a Group of Churchmen (London, Allen & Unwin, 1922); A. J. Penty, *Towards a Christian Sociology* (London, Macmillian, 1923).

35. Maurice B. Reckitt, conversation with author, London, September 6, 1968.

36. As recalled by Reckitt, conversation with author, London, September 6, 1968.

37. See Reinhold Niebuhr, *An Interpretation of Christian Ethics* (New York, Harper & Brothers, 1935), pp. 9, 169ff. Simple moralism means an insistence on "the direct application of the principles of the Sermon on the Mount to politics and economics" (p. 169).

38. According to Professor Joseph Fletcher, conversation with the author, Cambridge, Mass., May 1, 1968.

39. "Christianity and the Social Order" (Notes for Speeches on Various Occasions; LSE).

40. The following dialogue occurs in *News From Nowhere:*
Said I: "How do you manage with politics?" Said Hammond, smiling: "I am glad that it is of *me* that you ask the question . . . I believe I am the only man in England who would know what you mean; and since I know, I will answer your question briefly by saying that we are very well off as to politics—because we have none." (*Three Works by William Morris*, Introduction by A. L. Morton; London, Panther Books, 1968, p. 267).

41. Daniel Bell, *The End of Ideology* (New York, Collier, 1962), pp. 312, 273ff.

42. Peter Sedgwick, "Varieties of Socialist Thought," *Political Quarterly*, 84 (October-December, 1969), 397; italics added.

43. Lichtheim, *Marxism*, p. 403.

44. See, e.g., Norman Fruchter, "Echoes of an Evolutionary," *The Nation* (New York), September 28, 1964.

45. The colleague was a Cambridge economic historian; the young Marxist an Oxford historian.

46. *The Attack*, p. 16.

47. St. John 14: 5-6.

48. See *Equality*, p. 197.

49. The first phrase is from L. T. Hobhouse, *The Elements of Social Justice*, p. 118; the second is Tawney, "Presidential Address," *The Highway*, January 1945, p. 47.

50. "Fragment on Democracy" (Public Lectures Given in Chicago, 1939; LSE).

51. "In Debt to Tawney," *Socialist Commentary*, February 1962; "A Man For All Seasons," *New Statesman*, January 19, 1962; Crossman, *The Charm of Politics*, p. 140; Hugh Gaitskell in *The Radical Tradition*, p. 212.

52. *The Attack*, p. 141.

53. See, e.g., his analysis of the debacle of 1931, "The Choice Before the Labour Party," in *The Attack*, pp. 52ff.

54. See *The Acquisitive Society*, p. 104.

55. J. A. G. Griffith, "Why We Need a Revolution," *Political Quarterly*, 84 (October-December 1969), 392.

INDEX

Academic committees, 99
Acquisitiveness, 49, 158, 200, 251, 255
Acquisitive society, 95, 149, 160-161, 171, 247, 249
Acquisitive Society, The, 10, 260; and Christianity, 278; and conquest of nature, 216; Crossman on, 7; and definition of society, 223-224; and function, 277; and functionless property, 55; importance of, 53; published, 73; on rights, 155; and socialist industry, 217; and Tawney's other writings, 204-205; and Jeannette Tawney, 108
Acton, Lord John, 26, 203
Affluent Society, The, 224
Agrarian Problem in the Sixteenth Century, The, 39, 103
Altruism, 275
Amberley, Lady, 200
Amherst College, 56-57
Anarchism, 142-143, 146, 243
Anderson, Perry, 195
Angell, Norman, 5, 207
Annan, Noel, 216-217
Anthropology, 184
Anticommunism, 92, 238, 273-274
Anti-Sweating League, 98
Appropriate differentiation, 130
Aristotle, 124, 128
Arnold, Matthew, 10, 211, 227, 228
Arrogance, 158
"Art and Labour," 174
Ashton, T. S., 110, 115; illustration of, 102; and Tawney, 46, 66, 80-82; on Tawney and COS, 29-

30; on Tawney's family, 22; and Tawney's eightieth birthday, 113
Asia, 206, 232
Asquith, Herbert Henry, 25, 240
"Assessment of Wages in England by the Justice of the Peace, The," 39
Association of Assistant Masters in Secondary Schools, 64
Athenaeum, 52
Atomic bomb, 209
Atomization, 158, 213
Attack and Other Papers, The, 105, 197
Attlee, Clement, 6, 52, 113
Attlee governments, 196; fall of, 258; and nationalization, 56; Tawney's evaluations of, 75, 91, 97-98, 134, 231, 259-261
Austin, John, 144
Australia, 22, 106
Authoritarianism, 256-258. *See also* Dictatorship; Era of tyrannies; Ideologies; Totalitarianism
Authority, 150, 153, 168, 191-193, 202, 226

Bagehot, Walter, 13, 183, 184, 198, 200, 246
Baldwin, Stanley, 72
Balfour, Arthur J., 244
Ball, John, 213
Ball, Sidney, 37-38, 84
Balliol College, 21, 22, 23, 42, 177, 244; ambience of, 25-28; appoints Tawney Fellow, 53; influence on Tawney, 24; liberalism at, 203; and WEA, 37, 43. *See also* Oxford

351

demystification of, 183; destruction of, 150; and economic expediency, 228; effects of, 251, 255, 260; and efficiency, 276; and equality, 123, 125-126; fanatacism of, 254, 255; history of, 252-255; and inequality, 275; and morality, 251, 255, 275; mortality of, 253; myths of, 183-185; and nature, 252; origins of, 13, 140; as a religion, 253-254; rise of, 228; and social cohesion, 199-201; and socialism, 209; social relations of, 176; Tawney's view of, 250-255, 256-258; view of man, 191; and war, 148-149, 251, 255; waste of, 133
Cardiff University, 35
Carlyle, Thomas, 58, 200, 264
Carlyle Club, 114-115
Cartwright, E. S., 41, 42, 45-46, 107, 117
Carus-Wilson, Elaine, 82, 113
Cecil, Lord Hugh, 202
Chain Trades Board, 53
Chamberlain, Joseph, 4, 72
Character, and circumstance, 178
Charity, 178, 179, 264. *See also* Philanthropy
Charity Organisation Society, 24, 29-30, 249, 264
Chartism, 146, 174, 175-176, 198
Chesterfield, 40
Chesterton, G. K., 5
Chicago, University of, 79, 83; confers honorary degree on Tawney, 87, 101; Tawney's visits to, 86-88, 91, 106
Chicago Tribune, 87
Chichester, Sir Francis, 130
Child labor, 32, 68
Children of Light and the Children of Darkness, The, 145
Children's Country Holiday Fund, 29-30, 35-36
China, 13, 22, 231, 232, 275; communism in, 254; education in, 70; mystification in, 186; nationalism in, 69; peasant problem in,

254; revolution of 1911, 69; Tawney's trips to and writings on, 10, 67-71; transition to capitalism, 254; unity of, 153
China Weekly Review, 71
Chinese revolution, 233
"Choice Before the Labour Party, The," 72
Christ Child Opportunity Store, 88, 90
Christ Church, 46
Christendom Group, 265-266
Christian Demand for Social Justice, The, 98
Christian Directory, 110
Christianity: and capitalism, 32, 268; and citizenship, 177; and class, 267; decline of, 254, 264-265, 267; defined, 246; and equal worth, 137; and fellowship, 218; and Marxism, 269, 270; and order, 213-214; radical potential of, 264-270; and property, 164, 165, 166; and social change, 34; and socialism, 175, 238, 246-247, 248-249, 265-270; and status quo, 164; Tawney's influence on, 253; Victorian, 263-265; and workers, 32. *See also* Church of England; Religion; Tawney, R. H.
"Christianity and Industrial Problems," 58
"Christianity and the Social Order," 197, 247
Christian Social Union, 24
"Christian World Order, A," 246
Churchill, Winston, 72, 87, 92, 207, 226, 259
Church of England, 57, 60-62; and capitalism, 246; decline of, 248-249, 254; and evangelism, 249; historical role of, 267; and social action, 265-267; and socialism, 246; and social problems, 246-249; and state management, 143; Tawney's attitude to, 246-249; Tawney's influence on, 246, 253

Economic equalizing, 97
Economic fundamentalism, 184-185
Economic history, 83; goal of, 165; Tawney's development of, 39-40, 41-42; Tawney's doubt about, 65-66; Tawney's justification of, 12-13; Tawney's motivations toward, 103; Tawney's path to, 204; Tawney's research in at Oxford, 25; and Unwin, 46. *See also* History
Economic History Review, 83, 95, 105
Economic History Society, 7, 67, 136
Economic Journal, 39, 105
Economic man, 199, 252
Economic mechanism, 199, 224
Economic Review, 39
Economics: autonomy of, 141, 184-185, 199-200; and politics, 141, 144, 151, 154, 218; Tawney's dislike of, 66; theory of, 36; and values, 159
"Economics of Boy Labour," 39
Ede, Chuter, 113
Edinburgh University, 67
Education: in China, 70; defined, 136; goals of, 101, 264; importance of, 241-242; and politics, 183, 263; and power, 183; reforms in sought by Tawney, 100; and self-fulfillment, 136-137; and socialism, 10, 47, 100, 182; and social policy, 182; and social purpose, 162; Tawney's ideals of, 23, 32; Tawney's influence on, 63-64, 84; Tawney's writing on, 63-64, 84-85, 99; theories of, 182; today, 242; at WEA, 41; and will, 241; and workers, 32, 37. *See also* Workers Educational Association; Workers education
Education Act of 1918, 53
Education Act of 1944, 64, 84
Education Committee of London County Council, 64

"Education of the Adolescent, The," 64
Education: The Socialist Policy, 63
Egalitarianism, 123, 132, 135-136
Election campaigns, 62, 63, 78, 97; and private wealth, 146
Eliot, T. S., 61, 82, 217
Elites, 228, 241, 262, 269
Elizabethan age, 212, 226
Elton, G. R., 59-60
Elvin, Lionel, 24, 50, 67, 98, 99, 113
Emery, A. E., 113
Emigrés, 239-240
Empiricism, 209
"Enabling Bill: What It Seeks to Do and Why, The," 59
Enclosure, 164
Engels, Friedrich, 3
English Constitution, The, 183, 246
Enlightenment, 197
Ensor, R. C. K., 26, 38
Equality, 7, 10, 53, 73-75, 174, 204-205, 261, 263; Aristotelian, 124, 128; Bacon on, 138-139; Bentham on, 139; and capacity, 125, 133; and capitalism, 123; and Christianity, 124-128, 129-130; and citizenship, 176; and class, 198; and common ends, 227; and democracy, 173; economic and social, 123, 133; English version of, 121; as "equal consideration," 124-125; as fairness, 122-123; and fellowship, 136-137, 210, 217; and freedom, 134-135, 217, 227; fruits of, 133-137; and function, 167; and governmental forms, 138-139; Hobbes on, 139; and human nature, 123, 246; and income, 122; and individuality, 134; legal and political, 123, 133; and liberalism, 137; and liberty, 197; and need, 129-130; of opportunity, 123; and order, 213-214; and personality, 134; three

pillars of, 133, 134; and power, 134-135, 146; and privilege, 121; proportional, 122-123, 125, 128; quantitative, 122-123, 128, 130; as relationship, 135; and right relationships, 133; of rights, 125, 128; Rousseau on, 121-122; Ruskin on, 166; and socialism, 139, 217; and social obligation, 214; sponsors of, 198; Tawney's vision of, 121-137, 139; and World War II, 134. *See also* Inequality

Equal worth, 133-134, 136. *See also* Common humanity

Era of tyrannies, 193, 232

Eschatology, 191

Essays in Honour of R. H. Tawney, 114

Eurocentrism, 92, 93, 232

Europe, decline of, 15, 232

Evangelism, 33-34, 249, 263

"Expense of Education in Oxford, The," 177

Fabian Essays, 230

Fabianism, 157, 191, 202, 206, 209, 245; and Church of England, 246; and end of history, 271; and fixed world, 243; and knowledge, 240; and Marxism, 235; mechanism of, 270; and power, 142-143; Tawney's divergence from, 276-277; and Webbs, 277

Fabian Society, 35, 62, 78, 148

Faith, Reason and Civilisation, 216

Falski, M., 69

Fascism, 5, 73, 87, 202; and British socialism, 256; and capitalism, 148; cure for, 148; and democracy, 147; and economics, 141; and fraternity, 198; and interlude of possibility, 205; and Labour party, 231; and nation, 197; in 1930s, 235; and romantic-conservatism, 141; and social democracy, 147-148; and vitalism, 202-203

Federation of British Industries, 162

Fellowship, 277; and acquisitiveness, 49, 149; centrality of, 136-137, 210-216, 217, 223, 263; and Christianity, 218, 267-268, 270; and citizenship, 210-211; and collectivism, 261-262; and common ends, 227; and communalism, 213; and conservatism, 217; in Elizabethan age, 212; and e-quality, 210, 217, 218; in *Equality*, 205; and fraternity, 199; and function, 210; and human nature, 162, 246; and individualism, 214-215; and labor movement, 211; Morris on, 197, 213; and organizationalism, 217; and personality, 219; and politics, 218; and power, 154, 210; and purpose, 171; and right relationships, 199, 217; and sentiment, 214; and socialism, 176; and socialist economics, 217; and Tawney's life and thought, 9-10; today, 243; and totalitarianism, 213, 217; and vitalism, 217; and war, 171; in WEA classes, 42-43; and working class, 34-35, 211. *See also* Fraternity

Feudalism, 123

Field, Marshall, 88

Figgis, J. N., 157

Fisher, F. J., 67, 104, 113, 114

Fisher, H. A. L., 52

Fisher Education Act (1918), 84, 162

Fishing, 83

Fitzroy Square, 115

Fletcher, Frank, 23

Fletcher, Joseph, 60

Ford Lectures, 83

Foreign Office, 90-91, 245

Foreign service, 91

"For Socialism and Peace," 78

Forster, E. M., 214-215

Fourier, Charles, 216

"Fragment on Education," 173

France, 50-51, 106, 200

Impartiality, 130
Imperial Education Conference, 64
Imperialism, 4, 24
Imperialism, 4, 16, 24, 93, 179, 200. *See also* British Empire; Colonialism
Importance of Being Earnest, The, 36
Income, 122, 132, 167, 172
In Darkest England and the Way Out, 24
Independent Labour Party, 35, 46
India, 25, 126, 180
India Called Them, 22
Indian Education Service, 22
Individualism: capitalist, 182; and competition, 131; economic, 143, 200, 255; liberal, 244; of nineteenth century, 208; and socialism, 214-215
Individuality, and equality, 134
Indolence, 180
Industrial feudalism, 254
Industrialism, 144, 172, 179, 200; consequences of, 160; defined, 159-160; and international relations, 200-201; and militarism, 159-160; moralist critique of, 277; and social justice, 200-201; and Stalinism, 191; triumph of, 200; Victorian, 185; virtues of, 180; and war, 149
Industrialization, 13, 141, 158, 159, 254, 263-264
Industrial militancy, 245
Industrial revolution, 22, 272
Industry, 243; control of, 155; defined, 163; and function, 167-168; and international corporations, 231-232; and professionalism, 168, 171; and purpose, 159, 160-161, 172; and service, 172; and socialism, 173-174; western obsession with, 156
Inequality: in Britain, 132, 259; and capitalism, 275; and decline of religion, 124; and demystification, 186; effects of, 275; justifi-

cation of, 129; and poverty, 275; and power, 146; and self-fulfillment, 128-129; and social function, 130-131; source of, 121-122, 125
Institute of Pacific Relations, 67-68, 71
Interlude of possibility, 205-210, 228, 230, 251, 261, 276
International Institute of Intellectual Co-operation, 69
International Missionary Council, 60
International relations, 97, 148
Irrationality, 178-179. *See also* Human nature; Rationalism

James, H. A., 23
Jeffersonianism, 142
Jeger, Lena, 97
Jones, Arthur Creech, 87, 88, 90-91, 99, 115; on Tawney's eightieth birthday, 111, 113, 114
Jones, Tom, 35-36, 72, 87, 94
Journalism, 38-39
Journal of Political Economy, 59
Jowett, Benjamin, 25, 200
"Juvenile Employment and Education," 84

Keynes, J. M., 127, 143, 148, 235, 236
Kluckhohn, C., 156-157
Knight, Frank, 91
Knowledge, 240, 242
Korean War, 233
Kornhauser, William, 213

Labor, 160, 251
Labor movement: American, Tawney's writings on, 90; disunity in, 113-114; and education, 37; and fellowship, 211; and fraternity, 198; and Labour party, 97; in 1950s, 260; and political power, 56; and social-

Purpose (continued)
ship, 171; and function, 156; and industry, 172; and mechanism, 141, 253; and power, 149, 154, 258; and productivity, 258; religious, 224-225; and rights, 163, 171-172; and Stalinism, 258; today, 242; and unity, 163; and utility, 169; and war, 170-171, 172; and World War I, 172. *See also* Common purpose

Radical Tradition, The, 105, 111
Ratan Tata Foundation, 48, 240
Rationalism: and class and nation, 197; decline of, 202, 240-246; and education, 183; in Green, 178-179; and Marxism and Fabianism, 235, 276; and rights, 198; and socialism, 207, 271; Victorian, 245. *See also* Human nature; Irrationality
Raybould, S. G., 100
"Realities of Democracy, The," 173
Reckitt, Maurice, 59, 148, 266
Rees, Richard, 8, 71, 77, 86; and Tawney, 80-82; and sea cruise for Tawney, 115; and Tawney's eightieth birthday, 113; and *The Attack*, 105
Reform Act of 1867, 183-184
Reform Act of 1884, 198
Reform Club, 115
Refugees, 83-84. *See also* Émigrés
Reijchman, Ludwig, 69-70
Religion: alternatives to, 138, 140; and capitalism, 253-254; and common ends, 224-225; decline of, 33, 124, 138; and politics, 140, 263-264; and poverty, 33-34; and social change, 23; Tawney's attitudes to, 57-62, 66, 192, 234; Tawney's writing on, 58, 59-60. *See also* Christianity; Church of England; Socialism; Tawney, R. H.
"Religion and Business," 59
Religion and the Rise of Capitalism,

59-60, 68, 73, 199-200, 204, 232, 252; and business virtues, 265; and common ends, 224; importance of, 59-60; and Marxism, 278
Religiosity, 31
"Religious Thought on Social and Economic Questions in the Sixteenth and Seventeenth Centuries," 59
Rentiers, 160
Rents, 167
Reorganization of Education in China, The, 70
Republic, The, 182, 183
Resentment, ideology of, 202
Respectability, 179, 212
Reward: and common humanity, 176; and function, 130-131, 137, 167-168; and functionless property, 172; and need, 130-131; and service, 166
Ricardo, David, 199
Rice, Lucy, 110, 113, 115
Right relationships, 193, 223, 258; and equality, 133; and fellowship, 199, 217; and morality, 228; and politics, 218; and socialism, 145, 156
Rights: basis of, 158, 168-169, 223; conditionality of, 155, 172; economic, 177; in eighteenth century, 169, 177; and liberalism, 198; natural, 165, 169, 172; and property, 169, 172; and purpose, 163, 171-172; and service, 168-169; and social function, 168-169, 171
"Rise of the Gentry, The," 67,101-103
Robbins, Lionel, 79
Robertson, D. H., 79
Rochdale, 38, 57, 64; influence on Tawney, 127, 259; Tawney's image of workers at, 56; Tawney's 1918 campaign in, 53; Tawney's nostalgia for, 98; Tawney's WEA class at, 40-43, 49
Rogers, Claude, 100
Roosevelt, Franklin Delano, 92

and self-fulfillment, 162; test of, 162. *See also* Purpose
Society, 140, 196, 223, 270
Society for Research in Education, 100
Sociology, 205, 206, 208
"Some Thoughts on the Economics of Public Education," 84
Somme River, 26, 49, 51, 87, 115, 117, 274
Sorel, Georges, 173, 189, 203
South Africa, 124-125
Soviet Communism: A New Civilisation?, 76
Spain, 237
Spencer, Herbert, 157, 161, 208
Spender, Stephen, 236
Spengler, Oswald, 206, 208, 209
Stalinism, 202, 237; and British socialism, 256; and bureaucratism, 257; and liberal capitalism, 239-240; and fascism, 139; and industrialism, 191; and interlude of possibility, 205; and Marxism, 272; and socialism, 239; and social purpose, 258; Tawney's disagreement with Webbs on, 75; and Western civilization, 236
State, the, 140, 151-152, 173-174
State and Revolution, 225
Stevenson, Sir Daniel, 55
Stocks, Mary, 29, 50, 113
Stone, Lawrence, 101
Strachey, John, 5, 10, 191, 192, 236, 260
Strauss, Leo, 83-84
Stroud, 136
Student Christian Movement, 59
Study of History, The, 83
Sudan, 4
Syndicalism, 142-143, 168, 172, 202
Swindon, 63
Sweden, 106

Ta Kung Pao, 69
Talbot, Bishop C. S., 58
Tawney, C. H., 22, 23

Tawney, Jeannette, 22, 30, 40, 51, 72, 117; in Australia, 106; character of, 108-111; in China, 71, 110-111; class feelings of, 108-109, 110; death of, 108, 111, 113, 114; effect on Tawney, 110-111; finances of, 108-109; illnesses of, 94-95, 106; illustrations of, 70, 81, 96; intelligence of, 110; at Mecklenburgh Square, 48; and prostitution, 106; religious attitudes of, 61-62; at Rose Cottage, 82; and sex, 110-111; and social causes, 109-110; in USA, 57, 86-87, 89-90
Tawney, R. H.: and Balliol, 23, 53; and Bethnal Green Workman's Club, 33; birth of, 3, 22; and British Academy, 83; and British socialism, 276-280; burial of, 117; Christianity of, 8, 75, 124-128, 175, 178, 191, 203, 213-214, 216, 227, 231, 246-249, 251, 257, 264-270, 274, 277, 278; class feelings of, 109; on Coal Commission, 53-56; consistency of, 5, 8-9, 21, 278; convalescence of, 51, 52; death of, 4, 6, 115-117; egalitarianism of, 136; eightieth birthday party, 3, 111-114, 136; election campaigns of, 53, 62-63, 76, 78, 97, 98; Euro-centrism of, 92, 93, 232; and Fabian Society, 35, 62, 78; family history of, 22-23; finances of, 40, 46, 70, 72, 85, 86-87; and fishing, 83; love of France, 106; friendships of, 80-82, 83-84, 107; Gaitskell on, 6, 12; visits to Germany, 31, 33; at Glasgow University, 35-36; goals of, 162, 203-205, 223; and Home Guard, 87, 88; honorary degrees of, 101; Honours offered to, 6, 73, 97; idealism of, 223, 228; illness of (1943), 94-95; illustrations of, ii, 27, 62, 70, 74, 81, 89, 96, 102, 107, 112, 116; influence of, 3, 5, 6,